Familienunternehmen und KMU

Reihe herausgegeben von

Sowohl Familienunternehmen als auch kleine und mittlere Unternehmen (KMU) zeichnen sich durch eine Reihe spezifischer Besonderheiten aus, die ihnen im Marktumfeld einen klaren Wettbewerbsvorteil bieten aber auch zu besonderen Risiken führen können. Die vorliegende Schriftenreihe präsentiert wissenschaftliche Arbeiten, die einen empirischen und theoretischen Beitrag zur Erkundung dieser Besonderheiten und deren Auswirkungen auf die betriebswirtschaftliche Praxis leisten. Übergeordnetes Ziel ist es, die Theorieentwicklung des Managements von Familienunternehmen und KMU voranzutreiben. Both Family Firms and Small and Medium Sized Enterprises (SME) feature a number of distinct behaviors and characteristics which could provide them with a competitive advantage in the market but could also lead to certain risks. The scientific series at hand presents research which provides an empirical and theoretical contribution to the investigation on these specific characteristics and their impact on business practice. The overall aim of this series is to advance the development of theory in the areas of family firm and SME management.

Maximilian Lantelme

The Continuity and Discontinuity of the 250 Largest Enterprises in Germany

A History-Based Analysis of Family Influence, Corporate Development and Ownership Transactions

Springer Gabler

Maximilian Lantelme
München, Germany

Dissertation Zeppelin University, 2023
Supervisors: Prof. Dr. Hermut Kormann, Prof. Dr. Torsten M. Pieper,
Prof. Dr. Andreas Hack
Date of the disputation: 19th April 2023

ISSN 2520-1174 ISSN 2520-1182 (electronic)
Familienunternehmen und KMU
ISBN 978-3-658-42374-2 ISBN 978-3-658-42375-9 (eBook)
https://doi.org/10.1007/978-3-658-42375-9

This Springer Gabler imprint is published by the registered company Springer Fachmedien Wiesbaden GmbH, part of Springer Nature.
The registered company address is: Abraham-Lincoln-Str. 46, 65189 Wiesbaden, Germany

Paper in this product is recyclable.

To my parents Ulrike and Dieter

Foreword

What is special about family businesses and in which aspects carry these enterprises the general burden of business risks? And if they are special in their long-term orientation, does it matter—do they excel in longevity? Or is the popular statistic by John Ward still relevant today, in that only 13 percent of family businesses reach the third generation 60 years after their foundation?

Maximilian Lantelme explores in his dissertation this fundamental question which lies at the core of strategic management and business policy research; namely, what causes the survival or demise of organizations over the long run? Specifically, to what extent do ownership structure, operations, and solvency affect organizational development over time?

Given the relevance of the question, prior studies in mainstream management as well as family business have explored the phenomenon from various angles, methodologies, and settings. Maximilian Lantelme goes one step further than any of the earlier research on the subject, and this is one of the many strengths of his dissertation, employing a longitudinal approach, he creatively combines methods from history as well as social science to systematically analyze the 250 largest family and non-family enterprises in Germany between 1958 and 2018 to distill the key drivers of their long-term development. Thereby, he is able to identify consistent patterns predictive of their survival or demise.

By investigating not only the survival, but also the demise of the enterprises, he effectively overcomes a shortcoming that many prior studies in the area suffered, namely the issue of survivorship bias and erroneous conclusions drawn from studying successful (living) cases only. Following a painstaking process of sorting and sifting through volumes of corporate data, analyzing and arranging historical information, Maximilian Lantelme created a comprehensive dataset that captures the development and downfall of these organizations at a level of detail and granularity like no other effort has achieved before. There are many comparisons and often surprising insights which show on the one hand the survival requirements for any type of business, and on the other hand the comparative performance of family enterprises.

Maximilian Lantelme leverages this unique dataset to identify consistent patterns that can help predict the survival (or demise) of organizations. Researchers can use these findings to further theorize and design future studies to explore how certain variables affect one another and what antecedents and contextual factors need to be in place and how to align them to maximize synergies and improve organizational outcomes. Practitioners and decision-makers in business can leverage the insights to devise strategies to enhance the chances of survival (and reduce the likelihood of decline) in their organizations. Policy makers can employ the results to stimulate debate about how best to help organizations achieve long-term survival and sustainability for the benefit of all stakeholders.

This dissertation marks an important achievement in the fields of family business and strategic management, and it shall become a go-to resource for those interested in the topics of firm performance, longevity, and family influence. It offers valuable perspectives for family business owners and managers, and provides promising directions for future research that shall motivate further exploration of this critical subject. It has been a pleasure and a privilege to interact with Maximilian Lantelme and to follow his impressive academic and personal development over the years. We are eager to see where his next steps will lead him, and we are proud to call Dr. Lantelme a fine colleague and dear friend!

1 August 2023

Prof. Dr. Hermut Kormann
Zeppelin University
Friedrichshafen, Germany

Prof. Dr. Torsten M. Pieper
The University of North Carolina at Charlotte
Charlotte, USA

Acknowledgements

This dissertation would not have been possible without the support of my family, friends and companions. Looking back, the journey has unconsciously started many years before the decision to apply for the PhD program at Zeppelin University.

The starting point is the long-lasting cooperation with my first supervisor Apl. Prof. Dr. Hermut Kormann which began more than twelve years ago with the scanning and printing of scientific literature. Since then, we have jointly published books and visited several conferences across the globe. Your dedication to research on family businesses and business families as well as your support of bachelor's, master's and doctoral students is the foundation of my academic development. It is an honor and pleasure for me to have walked this path together—with all the other steps that are still to come.

The discussions with my second supervisor Prof. Dr. Torsten Pieper were critical and challenging but also always encouraging and motivating. You are a role model for researchers and your support has significantly influenced my academic development since we first met at Lake Constance in 2019.

A big thank you goes to Prof. Dr. Andreas Hack who took over the role as third supervisor.

Prof. Dr. Johannes Bähr gave me valuable insights into the historical research on family businesses. Our discussions in Ningbo and Berlin never ended before midnight. I am looking forward to the pending meeting in Munich.

A heartfelt thank you goes to the EQUA Foundation. Their scholarship has given me the opportunity to focus entirely on the doctoral thesis. Furthermore, the discussions with you, Dr. Rena Haftlmeier-Seiffert, and all the other *EQUAtorianer* were valuable input. As an alumnus, I also enjoy coming to the upcoming colloquia.

The pioneer award goes to Dr. Laura Seibold! You have mastered your PhD as the first candidate in this unique setting. Thank you very much for your continuous support and yes, we will celebrate this with a great bottle of wine.

Simone von Bischopinck has provided outstanding university support. Thank you very much for making the PhD program at Zeppelin University an unforgettable experience.

Dr. Veronika Caspers is an outstanding lecturer and already appointed "the guardian of grammar and spelling". Your reviews make the life of readers much easier.

My wife, Kerstin Weinheimer-Lantelme, was with me when I took the decision to start the PhD and has always supported me on this journey—when I was enthusiastic but also when the motivation waned. Thank you very much for being by my side during this period and I look forward to all our other small and big adventures.

I would not have met all the people I have mentioned so far if my parents, Ulrike and Dieter Lantelme, had not given me the confidence, the opportunities and the freedom to do what I wanted. You have strengthened my curiosity and my belief to achieve my goals. I want to pass this support on to the next generation.

Abstract

This dissertation studies the long-term development of the 250 largest family and non-family enterprises in Germany between 1958 and 2018. In particular, the continuities and discontinuities of the companies' ownership structure, operations and solvency are examined. Historical methods are used to advance the understanding of the attributed long-term orientation of family firms in family business research. The collected data of the 250 largest enterprises of 1958 provide the most comprehensive historical overview of the industrial landscape of this period. The long-term analyses show that more than half of the companies fail and less than a quarter keeps their ownership structure in the observation period of 60 years. In this timeframe, family-owned businesses have relatively stable ownership structures and superior survival rates compared to public companies although the latter experience higher growth rates. A listing of a family firm leads to the discontinuity of the family's majority ownership in the mid-to long-term. Furthermore, company types like foundation-owned enterprises and foreign subsidiaries show even higher survival rates. The dissertation closes with practical implications based on the identified development patterns of the surviving and failed enterprises.

Contents

Abbreviations

CAGR	Compound Annual Growth Rate
DM	Deutsche Mark
EUR	Euro
e.g.	For Example
GDP	Gross Domestic Product
HdG	*Handbuch der Großunternehmen*
HSS	Humanities and Social Sciences
IF	Impact Factor
IPO	Initial Public Offering
LTO	Long-Term Orientation
MRQ	Main Research Question
ROE	Return On Equity
ROI	Return On Investment
R&D	Research and Development
SAf	*Saling Aktienführer*
SBU	Single Business Unit
SEW	Socio-Emotional Wealth
SME	Small and Medium-Sized Enterprises
SRQ	Sub-Research Question
TSR	Total Shareholder Return
Wgzw	*Wer gehört zu wem*

List of Figures

List of Tables

1 Introduction

"I'm sure you understand these things much better than my generation. And who knows, maybe we'll learn something new, such as: taking a step always helps; […] that the simple explanations are often wrong and that one's own point of view is always incomplete; that the future is more important than the past; […]. You have to take a risk for things that are worth it, and any day during which you discovered something new – one where you gazed beyond your horizon – is a good day." (As Commander of ISS-Expedition 57, Alexander Gerst recorded his message "Letter to my grandchildren" in the International Space Station (ISS) around 400 km above the Earth's surface; see Gerst (2018).)

Alexander Gerst

European Space Agency Astronaut

For centuries, generations of entrepreneurs have founded new companies to improve their own and their customers' future and conditions. In some cases, the entrepreneurs landed a moonshot and in other cases they built their company gradually over decades until they had to pass them on. But not all entrepreneurs have seen their firms[1] thriving. Many—and maybe even the majority—have seen their companies fail over time. Some companies were successfully handed over

[1] In this thesis the terms firm, enterprise, business, company, etc., are used as synonyms also in combination with the term family and family-owned.

M. Lantelme, *The Continuity and Discontinuity of the 250 Largest Enterprises in Germany*, Familienunternehmen und KMU,
https://doi.org/10.1007/978-3-658-42375-9_1

to the next generation of the founder's family, others were sold or acquired and again others became successful on the stock exchange. The development of a company and its influential individuals can be manifold and results in a unique history of each firm. Often, the development of a firm is strongly tied to the history of a family. Moreover, family-owned enterprises are considered to be of great economic and social importance not only in Germany but also in many other countries around the world. Despite this relevance their histories are often unknown and their visibility in public is often limited—partly intentional. Large listed enterprises—of which only a very limited number is family-owned in Germany—and their recent developments as well as their daily stock performances are more present in the media.[2] Also, the long-term development of companies is rarely studied scientifically.[3] But precisely because *the simple explanations are often wrong* a firm's development should be captured, investigated and understood over the longest possible period especially if science is intended to provide an explanatory framework which should help to improve decisions for future generations. Therefore, this doctoral thesis takes a step to further investigate and helps to better understand the long-term developments of private as well as of listed family and non-family enterprises. A company's history shows the development up to the present day or to the day the company ceases to exist. Therefore, this thesis applies historical analyses to the field of family and non-family business research to investigate the successful entrepreneurial moonshots as well as the entrepreneurial expeditions which have failed on their way.

1.1 Starting Observations: Developments of Family and Non-Family Enterprises

Despite the overall rare attention paid to and rare research on the long-term development of enterprises, long-term orientation is a characteristic which is attributed by customers, employees and scientists to family-owned enterprises. The basic idea is to pass the company on to the next family generation which requires the firm's survival. The ranking "Germany's 50 oldest family businesses"

[2] Referencing the daily media coverage of the development of the 40 companies included in the German Stock Index DAX, e.g., "*Börse vor acht*" on the television channel *ARD* in prime time.

[3] See Section 2.2 for a critical overview of current research.

[*"Deutschlands 50 älteste Familienunternehmen"*] published by *Stiftung Familienunternehmen*[4] provides an idea of this characteristic by listing the oldest family-owned enterprises in Germany. The oldest firm of the list is *The Coatinc Company Holding GmbH* which was founded in 1502 and is currently in the 17th family generation operating in galvanizing. It is followed by *William Prym Holding GmbH* founded in 1530 and today in the 19th generation. The company operates in metalworking and in textile accessories. On third position is the glass manufacturer *Von Poschinger Glass Projects e.K.* founded in 1568 and in 15th generation. These three companies are more than 450 years old and were already operating in the Holy Roman Empire and before the Thirty Years' War. The *youngest* firm on the list on position 50 is the metal construction company *Stadler Anlagenbau GmbH* founded in 1791 and in seventh generation. In the same year, the first written constitution in France was created in the course of the French Revolution. The key attribute of the ranking "Germany's 50 oldest family businesses" is that each enterprise is continuously owned by one or more interrelated families. This requires that the company still exists and continues its operations over the decades and centuries since its foundation.[5] Furthermore, the enterprise has not gone into insolvency which would lead to the cessation of the company. The ranking also includes more well-known and larger enterprises like the pharmaceutical, science and technology company *Merck KGaA* founded in 1668 (13th generation) with revenues of EUR 14.8bn in 2018 on position 16 as well as the diversified investment holding *Franz Haniel & Cie. GmbH* founded in 1756 (eighth generation) with EUR 4.7bn in revenues as 36th oldest family business. Today they are not only among the oldest but also among the largest companies in Germany.[6] Old family-owned enterprises do not only exist in Germany. In Italy as well as in Switzerland the oldest enterprises are also family owned and in Japan family businesses exist which are more than 1,300 years old.[7]

Other types of companies that reach a similar age as family businesses are foundation-owned enterprises as well as state-owned enterprises. *DHS—Dillinger*

---

[4] See Stiftung Familienunternehmen (2021a, 2021b).

[5] Also, the (proclaimed) oldest company in Germany the winery *Staffelter Hof* presumably founded in 862 is family-owned today by the Schneiders / Klein family in seventh generation. It is told that they bought the winery in 1805 from the French State (see Goldrichs UG (2022)).

[6] See Section 5.7.2 for their position among the largest enterprises of 2018.

[7] See Goto (2006, 2014). The oldest company in Japan *Kongo-gumi* which was founded in 578 went into liquidation and was sold in 2006 after 40 generations owned by the same family. Today, it operates as a subsidiary of *Takamatsu Construction Group*.

Hütte Saarstahl AG was founded in 1685 and is ultimately majority-owned by *Montan-Stiftung-Saar* in 2018. The company with revenues of EUR 2.2bn in 2018, which is the oldest *Aktiengesellschaft* in Germany (the legal form was changed in 1809 and approved by imperial decree), has experienced several changes of ownership since its foundation and thus does not have one continuous owner.[8] Another company with no continuous owner but a high age is the brewery *Bayerische Staatsbrauerei Weihenstephan.* Since 1803 in the course of secularization, it is owned by the Bavarian state but has a much longer history as part of the Weihenstephan Abbey—at least back to 1675.[9] Since its foundation in 1158, the *Bavarian State Mint* is state-owned and the oldest company in Munich. Due to several political changes and different occupiers the history of the mint is manifold but remains state-owned for more than 860 years.[10]

The attributed characteristic of long-term orientation is seen as a distinguishing feature of family businesses from, for example, listed enterprises which are in free float. In addition, they are assigned other characteristics like the vulnerability due to family disputes.[11] Besides these specific characteristics, family businesses are highlighted as a key player in economies and societies worldwide. They account for the largest share of all enterprises in nearly all economies. In Germany, family companies account for around 90% of all firms. Moreover, they generate around 45% of the total revenue and employ around 54% of all employees in Germany.[12] A similar significance of family firms can be observed for other countries as well.[13]

Despite this importance, representing the majority of firms, business research is mainly focused on companies without considering the specific ownership structure of families. And even within family business research there are only few studies which empirically investigate the attributed long-term orientation and which include a long-term perspective in their methodology. Therefore, the development of family firms over a long period of time and across multiple generations is often assumed but rarely investigated in family business research. Such a long

[8] See the commemorative publication for the 325th anniversary of *Dillinger Hütte* by Fuchs, Munninger, and Schu (2010, pp. 32–33). Interestingly, the foundation of the *Aktiengesellschaft* in 1809 is not specifically mentioned in the commemorative publication for the 250th anniversary by Ham (1935).

[9] See Uhl (1979, p. 36).

[10] See Greger (1986, pp. 13–14).

[11] See Section 2.2.2.1 for a more detailed overview of the attributed characteristics.

[12] See Gottschalk, Lubczyk, Hauer, and Keese (2019, p. 6). Public / state-owned companies are considered in the figures.

[13] See La Porta, Lopez-De-Silanes, and Shleifer (1999).

study period can almost exclusively be found in the historical sciences and in connection with enterprises in business and economic history. Moreover, rankings like the above-mentioned list of the oldest German family firms only include surviving enterprises without considering the companies which failed over the last centuries or decades. This leads to an incomplete picture of company developments and hides the dangers of entrepreneurial activity in general. As shown, companies owned by foundations or states can also become hundreds of years old. There might be additional ownership structures which can reach similar ages.

1.2 Overarching Research Project: Growth and Downfall of Family Businesses

The research on family businesses is diverse and the range of topics which still need to be studied is broad. Overall, the research field is relatively young—especially compared to the classical business administration. This doctoral thesis is part of a larger research project to examine some of the open topics. It focuses on the development, growth, and longevity of listed and private family enterprises in Germany. Researchers mainly from Zeppelin University in Friedrichshafen and University of Leipzig are jointly working on this overarching project to better understand the most common type of companies in modern economies.[14] This project has been initiated by the publication by Kormann in 2005 with the comparison of growth rates between large family and public enterprises. He shows that the former have higher rates during the observation period.[15] Since then, several other studies have been conducted, among others, by Seibold, Frericks and Lantelme to investigate the long-term development, downfall and growth of family firms.[16] The most recent publication by Seibold provides one of the most comprehensive growth models for family businesses based on a grounded theory

[14] See Seibold (2020, pp. 12–13) for an overview of the research project as well as related bachelor and master theses. More recent theses include the work of Kuchenbaur (2020) about the consolidation of the German paper producing industry in which family businesses play a significant role.

[15] See Kormann (2012), with the first edition in 2005, for the starting point. For an overview of governance-related topics see Kormann and Suberg (2021).

[16] See Lantelme, Seibold, and Kormann (2021, 19–44) for a growth model of family enterprises since their foundation. Seibold (2017) identifies growth drivers in family firms and Frericks (2019) investigates the downfall of large German listed companies.

approach.[17] At the same time as this thesis Stotmeister is working on her dissertation focusing on the ownership development of family businesses after their IPO.[18] The compilation of the project's findings also includes an analysis of the structure and age of this company type in Germany based on a dataset covering around 10,000 firms.[19] Despite this comprehensive work and some groundbreaking results like the identified underlying growth corridor as well as growth spurts in later generations, there are still lots of open questions around the development of family enterprises. Therefore, this thesis builds on the previous work and helps to advance the relevant findings especially in the area of the family firms' long-term developments in comparison to non-family companies as well as their failures. Methods from historical science are combined with family business research for this purpose. This used methodology can also be applied to future research which focuses on the company's long-term development.

1.3 Research Objectives: Long-Term Analysis of German Enterprises

Based on the previously discussed observations this doctoral thesis has three main research objectives:

1. Explain the long-term development of German enterprises including failures
2. Preserve historical corporate data
3. Provide practical implications for owners and employees

These objectives should support the identification of research questions and the analyses of the datasets. The first objective should provide explanations of the long-term development of German enterprises with a special consideration of family-owned businesses. Therefore, the thesis contributes to family business research but is not limited to this research area. It is assumed that the ownership structure has an impact on the strategic decision-making process which results in different corporate developments. Therefore, the ownership structure acts as a distinguishing factor among companies. This thesis is not limited to success factors only but also considers the decline and downfall of enterprises in the observation period. Hence, survival and failure rates can be calculated which

[17] See Seibold (2020).

[18] See Stotmeister (in press).

[19] See Chapter 2 in Lantelme et al. (2021) for the structure analysis.

ensures a comprehensive picture of the companies' corporate developments and corporate histories, respectively.

In addition to the contributions to family business research this thesis also has the objective to collect and preserve historical corporate data. This should lead to a more comprehensive understanding of the past existence and development of the largest enterprises in Germany from a business and economic history perspective. As companies can perish over time it is necessary to provide an overview at a certain point in time otherwise some companies and their data might get lost. The datasets of this thesis provide such an overview for the years 1958 and 2018 and could act as the basis for further historical research because the datasets are more accurate and detailed than existing rankings.

The last objective is related to the definition of practical implications based on this thesis. They should provide guidance to business families as well as to managers of family and non-family firms to better understand the development of their company in the historical context and in comparison to the other enterprise types examined. Because a single person cannot experience the long-term development of a company which exists over generations this thesis should raise awareness *that one's own point of view is always incomplete* and that history can teach lessons for the more important future.

1.4 Structure of the Dissertation: From Concept to Results

In the following, the structure of the dissertation is presented to provide an overview of the research from the motivation of the dissertation to the end results (see Figure 1.1).

Chapter 1 introduces the topic and the motivation of this dissertation. It highlights that family-owned businesses can become hundreds of years old. Nevertheless, it is shown that also other company types can achieve such an age although with ownership changes. The question comes up if these long developments are exceptions or characteristic of family firms. Furthermore, the overarching research project is presented of which this dissertation is a part of. In the last sub-chapter, the research objectives are presented before this overview of the structure.

In the second chapter (Chapter 2), the relevant scientific literature is summarized to identify the research gaps. Starting with the broader picture, the concepts of survival and failure are presented to identify the characteristics which influence the development of enterprises. Furthermore, the concept of growth is outlined because it is seen as a key driver for survival. To sharpen the focus, the relevant historical and family business research literature is summarized. The former discipline is interested in the long-term development of enterprises including the historical context but hardly investigates changes of ownership structures or a larger number of enterprises in the same study. Family business research deals with these gaps of historical sciences but only considers an observation period of a couple of years which contradicts the long-term orientation of the research object. Therefore, the research gaps are identified which are related to quantitative long-term studies with a focus on the ownership structure. Furthermore, the definitions of family firms as well as all other required company types are derived based on different concepts.

Chapter 3 presents the used methodologies which leads to the research questions as well as to the creation of the dataset. Business and economic history provide the necessary tools to investigate the long-term development of companies. In combination with family business research topics and theories the quantitative analysis is presented which is used to investigate the long-term development of family and non-family enterprises. Based on data availability as well as the considerations of various limitations the dataset creation is introduced. Data of the 250 largest enterprises of 1958 and 2018 are collected. Furthermore, their ownership, operations and solvency continuities and discontinuities are tracked over 60 years. The research questions are presented in the penultimate sub-chapter before the dataset collection is outlined in detail.

As part of historical research, the context in which the research objects operate needs to be understood. Chapter 4 presents the economic, political and legal developments between 1958 and 2018. It further outlines earlier developments which are required to understand the situation in 1958. These developments include the overall economic progress in Germany as well as the structural changes. Furthermore, the European integration leads to a large single market with huge export opportunities. Stricter competition laws restrict cooperation between companies and promote competition.

Chapter 5 starts with the first analysis of the two datasets. The quantitative insights for both years are presented, and data is compared on a company type level between 1958 and 2018. Various characteristics like the company's age, size and industry are highlighted to provide an overview of the status for the beginning and the end of the observation period. On company level the 25 largest and smallest as well as the 25 oldest and youngest enterprises are presented to show the companies behind the aggregated numbers. Single companies are used to emphasize specific developments.

In Chapter 6 the first long-term analysis is conducted which investigates the development of the 250 largest enterprises of 1958 until 2018. Again, the companies are investigated based on their characteristics. Furthermore, the survival and downfall rates per company type are calculated. The ownership continuity and discontinuity rates follow which identify companies which remain in the same ownership or not. The chapter closes with patterns which can be derived based on the long-term observations.

Chapter 7 presents the findings of the second long-term analysis which deals with the development of the 250 largest enterprises of 2018 back to 1958. The new joiners and reappearers are investigated in detail to understand their differences although both groups are within the 250 largest enterprises. Again, the ownership continuities and discontinuities are tracked and highlighted. In the last sub-chapter, characteristic patterns are identified using the previous findings.

Based on the previous three analyses Chapter 8 summarizes overarching patterns of the long-term developments of the largest enterprises in Germany. These patterns lead to practical implications which are one research objective of this dissertation.

In Chapter 9, the research questions are answered based on the findings from the previous chapters. Furthermore, three avenues for future research are presented based on new questions which have come up in the research process of this dissertation. The chapter and this dissertation closes with a concluding summary.

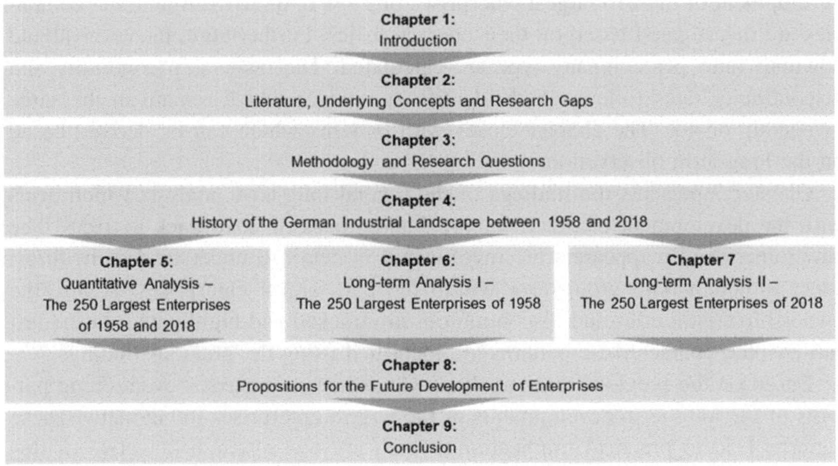

Figure 1.1 Structure Overview of Dissertation. (Source: Author's own figure)

2 Literature, Underlying Concepts and Research Gaps

The key focus area of this dissertation is the long-term development of German enterprises—including family businesses—and their ownership structure. To analyze the companies' continuities and discontinuities as well as their growth, stagnation and decline Section 2.1 presents an overview of relevant research literature on the underlying concepts of survival and failure as well as of growth. Next, the perspectives of historical sciences and of family business research on the long-term development of family-owned enterprises are presented in Section 2.2. This also includes the definitions of the research objects of this thesis. Based on the literature and the relevant observations the research gap is highlighted in Section 2.3.

2.1 Theoretical Perspectives: The Development of Enterprises

In management research as well as in economics and in history, several streams have been investigating the development of enterprises, and all from different perspectives. Studies on the survival of enterprises as well as on their growth are key

Supplementary Information The online version contains supplementary material available at https://doi.org/10.1007/978-3-658-42375-9_2.

M. Lantelme, *The Continuity and Discontinuity of the 250 Largest Enterprises in Germany*, Familienunternehmen und KMU,
https://doi.org/10.1007/978-3-658-42375-9_2

research areas in these disciplines, though with different focuses.[1] Nevertheless, their focus is highly concentrated on success factors based on performance analyses with limited attention to failed or declining enterprises.[2] The aforementioned topics are also studied to a limited extent in family business research, although all mentioned disciplines except the historical sciences often only consider an observation period of a few years.[3] Long-term observations are rare.[4] Key questions of the mentioned research areas include how many companies survive and fail over a certain period of time, and what are the conditions for a company's survival or failure. Several factors are investigated which are expected to enable a long-term survival and the continuity of an enterprise or to trigger the opposite development. The following sub-chapters describe the conditions relevant for this thesis which include, among others, age, size, ownership, industry and growth. These sub-chapters do not provide a comprehensive literature review of the topics. Instead, they summarize the relevant findings which are required to develop the research questions and will help identify the required variables for a dataset to analyze the long-term development of German enterprises.

2.1.1 Conditions of Survival and Failure: Company and Industry Characteristics

"[It] usually takes longer to walk down a mountain than to roll off a hillock—but both large and small firms commonly die."[5] With this statement the business historian Hannah describes the overall survival chances of companies. Nevertheless, he investigates the long-term development of large, listed enterprises in the 20th century to determine their survival rates and growth trajectories from 1912 to

[1] In management and economics, the topics are often referred to as *firm survival*, *firm failure*, *mortality*, *hazard rate* and *firm demography*. For the development of scientific articles about the topic over the last decades see Josefy, Harrison, Sirmon, and Carnes (2017, pp. 771–773). This paper will be further discussed in Section 3.4.

[2] See Kieser and Nicolai (2005).

[3] As an example of a family business research publication related to survival see Wilson, Wright, and Scholes (2013) who, however, only investigate a period of four years.

[4] See, for example, the analysis of ownership changes and firm survival in Germany by Heiss and Köke (2004) with an observation period of only ten years covering listed and non-listed enterprises. As one of the exceptions, see Hannah (1999) for a historical analysis of the survival and failure of large enterprises over 83 years which will be further described in the following.

[5] Hannah (1999, pp. 260–261).

1995. Although the majority fails, there are firms which are still alive after 83 years. Hannah sees the same outcome for small and large companies over time, yet there are conditions which are expected to have an impact on the continuity of enterprises and size is one of them. Following Woywode, two levels of impact can be identified: on the one hand characteristics of the company and on the other hand characteristics of the industry.[6] In the following, the key concepts are briefly described to identify the ones relevant for this thesis.

In organizational theory, structural characteristics of companies such as size but also age are seen as determinants of an enterprise's survival or failure. The *liability of newness* (age)[7] as well as the *liability of smallness* (size)[8] are two of the key related concepts which have been (empirically) tested quite extensively over the last decades.[9] The former concept describes the tendency of young companies to exit a market more frequently than old ones due to, for example, the required new establishment of internal and external relations with customers and suppliers. Established firms can rely on already existing relations. As Woywode highlights, it is noteworthy in this context that age is often correlated with size. This leads to the second concept. The liability of smallness refers to the relationship between the size of the company at the time of its foundation and its probability of failure. Small enterprises are expected to have a lower probability of survival than large ones mainly due to a limited number of resources and capabilities compared to larger companies. This also implies that smaller companies are more vulnerable to environmental changes. Prior research shows that size and age are important characteristics which need to be taken into account when studying the survival and failure of enterprises, either by controlling for them or by selecting a sample of companies with similar characteristics.[10]

---

[6] For an overview of theoretical approaches explaining the probability of survival of firms see Woywode (2018). For a business management perspective on a company's survival see also the publication by Arie de Geus who focuses on *personality traits* of the firms to explain their longevity (see Geus (1997)).

[7] See Stinchcombe (1965) for the origins of the liability of newness and Freeman, Carroll, and Hannan (1983) as well as Dunne and Hughes (1994) for its further application. For a study of West German companies and their mortality see Brüderl and Schüssler (1990) who also define the liability of adolescence (a decrease in the probability of survival in the first 15 months followed by an increase).

[8] See again Freeman et al. (1983) as well as Aldrich and Auster (1986).

[9] See Woywode (2018, pp. 49–52) for an overview of empirical studies some of which also find contradicting results.

[10] Researchers have identified additional liabilities besides the two highlighted ones like the *liability of foreignness* and the *liability of outsidership* (for both see Johanson and Vahlne (2009)). They are not further elaborated to focus on the relevant key topics of this thesis.

Ownership has been identified as an additional company characteristic which can impact the survival and failure.[11] This is especially relevant for family business research which sees ownership as a key component of a family firm's set of characteristics. As an example, Wilson et al. find that family firms in the United Kingdom have a significantly lower failure rate than non-family firms. They also identify the previously described components of size and age but also those of industry as well as of board composition as factors for the firms' survival.[12] Furthermore, growth is another characteristic impacting the survival and failure probability and is associated with the size and age of companies.[13] Larger companies have higher survival rates than smaller ones. To become bigger, a (small) company needs to grow—which can then lead to a higher probability of survival. Furthermore, the mentioned high correlation between age and size shows that older companies have grown over time, thereby achieving a larger size than they had as young companies. Growth is therefore another key aspect of survival and will be further elaborated on in the following sub-chapter.

Besides the above-mentioned company characteristics of size, age, ownership, and growth, the characteristics of industries are also relevant factors for the survival and failure of companies.[14] They include, among others, the level of barriers to entry of the respective industry, the research intensity, or the intensity of new foundations in an industry as well as the prevailing level of competition. Additionally, the importance of *economies of scale* for an efficient production as well as the level of a *minimum efficient scale* in an industry can significantly influence the survival probability of a company.[15] For example, high barriers to entry can increase the probability of survival because the companies operating in the industry do not face an increased threat of new competitors. Similarly, a high minimum efficient scale also protects established companies against new entrants. They either need to grow fast to achieve this minimum efficient scale or have a vast number of resources available.[16] Depending on the industry studied, research can show different results for relevant survival and failure conditions. But again,

[11] See Woywode (2018, p. 53).

[12] See Wilson et al. (2013) as well as the critical comment from Le Breton–Miller and Miller (2013).

[13] For a study which identifies growth as a critical survival factor see Dunne and Hughes (1994).

[14] See Jovanovic (1982) for a learning-theoretical approach as well as Sharma and Kesner (1996). Further, see Woywode (2018, pp. 69–78) for an overview of industry-specific factors.

[15] See Oster (1999) for a comprehensive analysis and again Woywode (2018, pp. 74–78) for an overview.

[16] See Almus and Nerlinger (1999).

the conducted studies often only cover a short period of time and therefore miss major changes taking place in the mid- and long-term. The results are of limited help in understanding a company's long-term development.[17]

Following the different research streams dealing with the survival and failure of companies, it becomes evident that there is a vast amount of literature, both across different research disciplines but also within each discipline. A first-of-its-kind management literature review of survival and failure is conducted by Josefy et al. in 2017. They structure the applied concepts of 222 articles and develop a framework which can be used by researchers to focus on the specific aspects of their survival and failure-related research question.[18] They also consider the company's stage of development. The framework covers the three dimensions of ownership, operations and solvency which can represent the survival or failure of a company by their continuity or discontinuity. Although Josefy et al. propose this multi-dimensional conceptualization of survival—including ownership as one dimension—their literature analysis shows that ownership is used as the underlying concept of survival in only 2% of the articles. In combination with one or two of the other dimensions, operations and solvency, ownership is used in some of the 27% of the articles which use multiple concepts. However, as will be shown in Section 2.2.2.3, ownership is a key variable for the definition of family firms. Thus it is not surprising that only a very small amount of Josefy et al.'s reviewed articles specifically deals with family firms. The majority of publications use operations and solvency as their major concepts.[19] In summary, the existing organizational literature on survival and failure only provides little insights into the development of family-owned enterprises despite their huge economic relevance. In family business research, the survival of the company is often highlighted as a key objective which can be achieved through stability, profit, and growth.[20]

Looking at the historical sciences Hannah's study of the survival and failure of large enterprises is also an exception. In their work, historians Plumpe as well as Köhler and Rossfeld highlight that research on the downfall of companies is rare especially for the case of Germany.[21]

---

[17] See, exemplary, Brown (2018) with a period of six years.

[18] See Josefy et al. (2017) and Section 3.4 for a detailed overview of the framework as well as the version applied in this thesis.

[19] See Josefy et al. (2017, pp. 772–773). For the exceptions see also Section 2.2.2.2

[20] See Section 2.2 for the comprehensive overview and Seibold (2020, pp. 29–30) for an overview of the goal cascade of family enterprises.

[21] See Plumpe (2018, pp. 17–18) as well as Köhler and Rossfeld (2012, pp. 9–14).

Overall, it becomes clear that age, size, growth and industry are key characteristics for the survival and failure of companies.[22] Moreover, ownership is also among the relevant factors though it is not often studied in detail over a longer period of time. Instead, only a snapshot is often taken at one specific point in time. A longer period would be necessary to better understand family-owned enterprises due to their attributed long-term orientation as well as enterprises in general to better understand development patterns over the companies' entire lifespan. Therefore, research on the survival and failure in relation to the ownership structure of a company is one of the identified research gaps. In addition, these insights are applied in Section 3.6 to identify the relevant variables which are included in a dataset to study the long-term development of German enterprises.

2.1.2 Growth, Stagnation and Decline: Research Focuses on Success Developments

Besides the survival and failure of enterprises, growth is a key topic in management research as well as in the advisory literature.[23] The mentioned topics are closely linked to each other. Among others, Seibold concludes in her comprehensive analysis of growth that "[...] growth is a prerequisite condition for survival [...]"[24]. Therefore, the concept is further analyzed to apply it in this dissertation and to understand its relevance for the research objectives—especially the long-term development. Seibold also provides an overview of the theoretical concepts of growth in her dissertation including neoclassical business theory, evolutionary approaches, organically oriented growth models, the growth theory by Penrose as well as behavioral approaches. She clusters the literature according to the input-process-output framework.[25] This shows the broad range and extensive coverage of growth in business studies as well as the complexity of the topic. Because of Seibold's comprehensive work an additional description of the growth theories is

---

[22] As a side note, Daniel Kahneman states that luck is of high relevance for the success of a company while other factors are often overstated (see Kahneman (2011, pp. 199–208)).

[23] See for example the influential practitioner book "Good to Great" by Collins (2001) who identifies seven characteristics which should lead to a superior growth of financial performance beating competitors and the market average. Additional advisor examples and scientific work are named in this and the following chapters.

[24] Seibold (2020, p. 6). Additionally, see Haberlandt (1970) and Ward (2011) for the necessity of growth.

[25] See Seibold (2020, pp. 34–42).

not included in this dissertation. Instead, this dissertation builds on her summary as part of the overarching research project and uses her findings as the basis for the research questions. Seibold describes the previously identified conditions of survival age, size and ownership as well as macroeconomic determinants which also include the industry characteristics as "enablers" of growth.[26] This reaffirms the close connection between growth and survival. In a last step Seibold outlines the theories which are used in family business research related to growth and shows again the complexity of the growth process.[27] Based on a grounded theory approach she develops a multi-dimensional general theoretical model of growth with the four dimensions "Options", "Need", "Capabilities" and "Willingness" which provide insights into family firms' growth and shows that the family influence based on ownership can have a major impact on the growth and development of the firm. Therefore, growth is also seen as an enabler and as a goal (like profit, stability and survival) for family businesses and the family influence can make a difference compared to non-family firms like public or state-owned companies. But what does growth stand for?

Overall, growth measures a relative or an absolute change between two points in time. Although growth can also be negative, i.e., a decrease, the term is mainly associated with an increase of a certain amount. Such an increase can indicate a successful development and a positive outlook for the future.[28] Growth can be measured based on various operating figures of a company. Revenue and number of employees are the most frequently used ones.[29] Growth is also used as a performance indicator similar to figures like return on equity (ROE), return on investment (ROI), operating margin, profit margin as well as liquidity ratio.[30] These indicators are often used for a short- or mid-term evaluation. This can be seen, for example, in the annual reports of enterprises. Only the last two to five years are included in these publications to provide an overview of the company's development. Longer periods which would cover full business cycles including an economic upturn and downturn are rare.[31] However, also in business

---

[26] See Seibold (2020, pp. 51–55).

[27] See Seibold (2020, pp. 88–99).

[28] Among others, positive growth can lead to an increased market share and economies of scale which provide an advantage compared to competitors.

[29] See Delmar (1997), Daunfeldt, Elert, and Johansson (2014) as well as Seibold (2020, pp. 70–72).

[30] See Stadler (2011, pp. 210–211).

[31] For example, see the 2018 annual reports of *Bayer AG* and *Volkswagen AG*. Bayer offers an overview of the last five years and Volkswagen only shows the key figures for the last year. After all, BASF SE offers m mid-term view of ten years.

research corporate developments are mainly studied over a short period of time and company declines or downfalls are rarely considered.[32] Furthermore, growth is a key factor of the concepts of liability of newness and liability of smallness. It is assumed that small and young enterprises are required to grow faster to achieve a minimum efficient size which increases the probability to survive in the mid- to long-term.[33]

For research purposes, the choice of the growth or performance indicator—which shows change—should be dependent on the research goal. Unfortunately, this choice is often limited by the availability and accessibility of corporate data especially for long-term studies.[34] Thus, the limitations of the selected growth indicator of a company need to be understood and set in the context of the research period to interpret the calculated growth rates. For example, an enterprise's revenue growth needs to be analyzed by also showing the overall growth rate of the economy the enterprise operates in. Such a comparison enables the researcher to evaluate if the company's development is superior or in line with the overall economic development.

Similar to the research on failed companies, corporate stagnation (the absence of growth) and decline (negative growth) are studied only to a very limited extent compared to growth—the increase of, for example, revenue. This trend is supported by the criticism of success factor research and the focus of strategic management on success. Using quantitative management studies researchers often link growth or other performance indicators to independent variables (success factors) which should explain the success of a company and provide practitioners guidance based on rigor analyses.[35] Yet, these analyses often show contradictory findings.[36] Therefore, their relevance and meaningfulness is limited. In one of their latest critique, Joe Astrachan and Claudia Binz Astrachan highlight the shortcomings of data collection, operationalization and interpretation of statistical significance also in family business research which often lead to less relevant outcomes—for researchers, family businesses, business families and practitioners.[37] Therefore, other approaches need to be considered to understand the growth but

[32] See Section 2.2.2.2 for more details.

[33] See Almus and Nerlinger (1999).

[34] See Section 3.1 for the limitations of historical data.

[35] See Kieser and Nicolai (2005) and Kormann (2011, pp. 39–40).

[36] See, among others, the meta-analyses related to financial performance of family firms by Wagner, Block, Miller, Schwens, and Xi (2015) as well as O'Boyle, Pollack, and Rutherford (2012). Both studies try to explain the contradictory findings of performance studies whether being a family firm has a positive or negative impact on the performance.

[37] See Astrachan and Binz Astrachan (2021).

also stagnation and decline of companies. An exception of success factor research and the strategic focus on success is the idea developed by Kormann to strengthen the competences to avoid critical mistakes.[38] Instead of trying to explain how to achieve success Kormann proposes to understand how to reduce the risk of insolvency. It is obvious that insolvencies occur and that enterprises cease to exist.[39] Therefore, additional research is required to understand the decline and downfall of enterprises as well as research which provides empirical insights into growth without focusing only on success factors.

Overall, because growth is seen as a prerequisite for survival as well as a goal on its own and hence a key indicator for the development of a company, it is included in the analyses of this thesis. In this context, not only the positive growth developments are studied, but also the stagnating and declining corporate developments—up to the downfall of companies.[40] After studying survival and failure as well as growth literature the perspective switches from the relevant functional topics towards a company type perspective. In a next step, research on family businesses including the historical sciences is reviewed to understand the underlying concepts of this discipline to further develop the research questions.

2.2 Current State: Historical Sciences and Family Business Research

The overview of the historical sciences in Section 2.2.1 show that family businesses are not a new phenomenon as a research topic. Nevertheless, their own research discipline has just evolved over the last decades, with an increasing number of articles published since the 1980s as well as specific research centers and professorships being founded around the world. The development of family business research is summarized in Section 2.2.2 followed by the description of their specific characteristics which are essential for the development of the research gaps and questions of this thesis. Furthermore, the various definitions of this specific company type are analyzed to select the relevant approach which is used in this thesis.

---

[38] See Kormann (2011, p. 44) and the concept of *„Nicht zulässige Fehler"*.

[39] See, for example, the insolvency data by the German Federal Statistical Office (German Federal Statistical Office (2022b)). For 2018, 19,302 business insolvencies are reported. The number continuously decreases from 32,687 in 2009.

[40] For the operationalization of growth see Section 3.7.1.3.

2.2.1 Historical Perspective: The Long-Term Development of (Family) Enterprises

The rise of the modern company in the western world started at the beginning of the 19th century.[41] The scientific historic discussion, on the other hand, began only towards the end of the same century although first anniversary publications of companies appeared already earlier.[42] Especially in Germany such anniversary publications have been an essential part of business history over a long period of time. The single company and its individual development until the firm's anniversary are the focus of these publications.[43] Because the work is usually commissioned, critical aspects are often omitted, and the focus is on success. Additionally, those publications are written only for living companies and hardly any of these are scientific. On the other hand, Schmoller, Weber and Sombart, among others, have further developed and analyzed the concepts of entrepreneurs as well as of companies as organizations. Their works are scientifically motivated and the basis for lots of following researchers. In this way, they make a significant contribution to the development of the subject of business history.[44] In the 1980s, the reappraisal of the National Socialism era leads to profound and scientific analyses of corporate histories. They shed light on the role of individual companies in the Third Reich.[45] Studies on single family businesses are also covered by business history although the family influence is not explicitly addressed.[46] Additionally, autobiographical histories exist which should provide personal insights into the company's and the family's development.[47]

In the USA, business history was an essential part of the emerging business schools in the first half of the 20th century.[48] It is therefore not surprising that some of the most influential and heavily discussed historical studies related to companies are published by an American, namely Alfred D. Chandler Jr. His

---

[41] See Berghoff (2016b, pp. 2–3).

[42] See Plumpe (2018, pp. 92–94).

[43] For a recent example see Deckers (2021). He describes the development of the winery *St. Antony* which was founded by *Gutehoffnungshütte* in 1920 and celebrated its 100th anniversary in 2020.

[44] See Schmoller (1890a, 1890b), Sombart (1929a, 1929b) and M. Weber and Winckelmann (2002).

[45] As an example, see Gall, Feldman, James, Holtfrerich, and Buschen (1995) for a study on *Deutsche Bank* between 1870 and 1995.

[46] See Lubinski (2010, p. 10).

[47] See Spitz, Roth, Bosecker, and Kambartel (2016).

[48] See Plumpe (2018, p. 95).

studies combine business as well as economic history and build on quantitative and empirical analyses over several decades. In his work "The Visible Hand" Chandler describes the increasing separation of ownership and management, thus the development from family firms towards entrepreneurial and managerial enterprises. Other governance structures replace the family and due to an increased investment need additional shareholders are required which leads to a listing of the firm.[49] Chandler sees family firms as a development stage towards other forms. Regarding the research objectives of this thesis, it should be emphasized that Chandler sees the managerial enterprise as more long-term oriented than other types—including family firms:

> "[...] in making administrative decisions, career managers preferred policies that favored the long-term stability and growth of their enterprises to those that maximized current profits.
>
> For salaried managers the continuing existence of their enterprises was essential to their lifetime careers. Their primary goal was to assure continuing use of and therefore continuing flow of material to their facilities. They were far more willing than were the owners (the stockholders) to reduce or even forego current dividends in order to maintain the long-term viability of their organizations. [...]".[50]

Overall, Chandler proposes that the success of a company is based on the right managerial decisions which require specific capabilities. Current research still follows this idea. Based on Chandlers work some few studies have further examined the long-term development of family and non-family firms. The historian Hartmut Kaelble, for example, investigates the discussed development towards a managerial enterprise in his study "From the Family Enterprise to the Professional Manager: the German Case". From a data perspective he mentions that "[a]ccording to a conservative estimation even in the 1960's every sixth large-scale German enterprise was controled by a business family (Hartmann)."[51] This number corresponds to a share of 16.7% of family-owned enterprises. Nevertheless, despite Chandlers research and some additional studies, family enterprises

---

[49] See A. D. Chandler (1977).

[50] See A. D. Chandler (1977, p. 10). It is noteworthy that in a later publication Chandler mentions that German family firms can survive and will not necessarily be replaced by managerial enterprises if they invest in necessary management structures (see A. D. Chandler (1990), Kocka and Siegrist (1979), Siegrist (1980) and Lubinski (2010, p. 13)).

[51] Kaelble (1982, p. 52). Unfortunately, his source, Hartmann, cannot be verified because his literature data in the publication is incomplete.

were an undeveloped area from a historical perspective still in the 1980s.[52] With the emergence of family business research interdisciplinary approaches including the historical sciences have been getting more interest.[53] The specific literature of family business research is presented in the next sub-chapter.

The study "Enduring Success" by Stadler in 2011 is another historical analysis which investigates the long-term development of enterprises but with a focus on the company level.[54] Conducting historical empirical analyses Stadler selects nine *gold medalists* and investigates the companies' histories to identify five principles for *enduring success*.[55] He further uses comparative analyses by comparing the *gold medalist* enterprises with *silver medal* companies which have not been as successful as the former ones. In Stadler's study success is defined as the total shareholder return (TSR) over 55 years (from 1953 to 2008).[56] He and his team use a broad range of archival corporate data to diligently analyze the companies' long-term developments. Nevertheless, the choice of the success definition shows the limitations of the study. It only focuses on listed enterprises—specifically on companies which were on the stock market in 1953 and still were in 2008. Hence, only surviving companies are included. The advantage of historical business sources is that they contain data of companies which have not survived. Such data cannot be available using only recent data. Nevertheless, science rarely takes into account this valuable treasure of data—which only (business) history can dig up.

Business history as part of the historical sciences started with unscientific anniversary publications but developed into a science which helps to understand the role of companies in the economy and society. It uses empirical methods from other research areas to provide more insights into the historical developments of companies. In addition, business history can analyze a company's long-term development considering the historical context the firm operates in.

---

52 See Brockstedt (1984, p. 238).

53 See, for example, the historical analysis of family businesses until the mid-20th century by Sachse (1991), the phase model by Joly (1998), the comparative studies by Colli and Rose (2003) and Urban (2018) as well as the long-term study by Nowak, Ehrhardt, and Weber (2006).

54 See Stadler (2011).

55 The five principles are 1) Exploit Before You Explore, 2) Be Conservative in and beyond Your Finances, 3) Remember and Share both Mistakes and Triumphs, 4) Diversify into Related Businesses and 5) Change in Culturally Sensitive Ways.

56 The *gold medalists* are *Allianz*, *Glaxo*, *HSBC*, *Lafarge*, *Legal & General*, *Munich Re*, *Nokia*, *Shell* and *Siemens*.

2.2.2 Family Business Research: An Emerging Research Area

The field of family business research has been growing steadily and gaining in importance over the last decades. The number of published articles and books as well as citations is increasing annually and the content is becoming more rigorous.[57] Following Hernández-Linares, Sarkar, and Cobo, the starting point of family business research can be dated back to two publications in the USA from 1953, one book written by Carl R. Christensen with the title "Management succession in small and growing enterprises" and a doctoral dissertation by Grant H. Calder with the title "Some management problems of the small family controlled manufacturing business".[58] For Germany, Kormann and Wimmer name the juridical dissertation of W. Hengstmann from 1935 which elaborates the characteristics of a family company (*Familiengesellschaft*) as one of the earliest publications related to family businesses.[59] Since then, lots of research and consulting work has been done to better understand and support family businesses, which provided a solid basis for subsequent research and facilitated its development. Today, (endowed) professorships as well as institutes have been created all around the world to drive the subject forward, and there are three dedicated journals on family business research.[60] In 1988 the first issue of *Family Business Review (FBR)* was published followed by the *Journal of Family Business Strategy (JFBS)* in 2010. FBR is published by *Sage*, JFBS by *Elsevier*, and both journals have 2020 Impact Factors (IF) between five to ten, which is quite outstanding in humanities and social sciences (HSS) and speaks for the impact of that research area.[61] The *Journal of Family Business Management (JFBM)*, published by *Emerald*, appeared for the first time in 2011. The main area of research sits within management and social sciences, with thousands of articles published in the last

[57] See Xi, Kraus, Filser, and Kellermanns (2015) for a recent overview and Bird, Welsch, Astrachan, and Pistrui (2002) for an early analysis.

[58] See Hernández-Linares et al. (2018, p. 931) as well as Christensen (1953) and Calder (1953) for the initial publications.

[59] See Kormann and Wimmer (2018) as well as Seibold (2020, p. 81) for a brief overview of the development of the research field. For the juridical dissertation see Hengstmann (1935).

[60] In the German speaking countries see, among others, "Witten Institute for Family Business" and "Friedrichshafen Institute for Family Entrepreneurship" as well as the "Global Center for Family Enterprise" and the "EQUA Endowed Chair for the Study of Family Companies, Their Culture and Ownership" at Technical University of Munich.

[61] See SAGE Publishing (2022) and Elsevier (2022).

three decades. Other research disciplines contribute to the literature to a much smaller extent.[62]

One reason for the growing interest in and the research output on family businesses is their ongoing macroeconomic contribution not only in Germany but worldwide.[63] Furthermore, unique characteristics are attributed to family enterprises which classical studies of business administration do not consider in their theories and research. Therefore, family business research has become an important discipline in the research community.

The following sub-chapters present selected characteristics of family businesses, the current state of research on their long-term development as well as their different definition approaches. This ensures that the research object is clearly identified to formulate the research questions.

2.2.2.1 Family Business Characteristics: Long-Term Orientation as Key Objective

In research, specific characteristics are attributed to family enterprises which have been investigated in several studies over the last decades. In the following, a selection of characteristics and research findings relevant to the topic of this thesis are presented.

The interplay between and the combination of the two social systems of the family and the business are key differences to other company types.[64] These two systems are connected by the ownership and / or management subsystem.[65] But they can also have different and conflicting goals.[66] The overlaps of the systems are the challenging and key differentiators of family businesses which can lead to a positive or negative impact on the development of each individual system. The family can therefore be a unique resource for the enterprise based on its ownership.[67] From a legal perspective, ownership refers to voting rights, share or

---

[62] See among others the bibliometric overview by Rovelli, Ferasso, Massis, and Kraus (2021) and the analysis by Hernández-Linares et al. (2018).

[63] See La Porta et al. (1999) for a global, Pieper, Kellermanns, and Astrachan (2021) for a US as well as Lantelme et al. (2021) for a German perspective.

[64] See the overview by Seibold (2020, p. 79) and the cited reference of Schlippe (2010).

[65] See Pieper and Klein (2007, pp. 306–307) as well as Schlippe and Frank (2013, p. 387) who distinguish between the three systems of family, business and ownership / management. Earlier contributions include the pioneering work of the "Three-Circle Model" by Tagiuri and Davis (1996).

[66] See Williams, Pieper, Kellermanns, and Astrachan (2018).

[67] See Habbershon and Williams (1999) for a resource-based perspective.

company capital.[68] The involvement of family members in the board of directors or in the supervisory board can be additional resources among others. It is, however, not necessary that a family member is part of a corporate body to include the family as a resource for the company.[69] Nevertheless, the uniqueness of the different systems within family businesses requires for their management "[...] an additional set of competencies when compared to managing other businesses."[70]. Also, Pieper sees a key to ensure the survival of family firms over generations in the effective management of the family and not only of the business. An effective governance system implemented in the company is not sufficient.[71] Based on cohesion, its four basic dimensions, (1) the emotional attachment to the family, (2) the emotional attachment to the business, (3) the financial attachment to the business and, (4) the financial attachment to the family, as well as their combination, a family and its members can get orientation and see the survival of the group as the overarching goal. This requires training of the family members already in early years.[72]

Long-term orientation is an additional characteristic of family businesses often referred to in the research community and by the businesses themselves. In his dissertation of 1969, which is most likely one of the first business management studies about family firms in Germany, Arend Oetker already highlights the intention of the entrepreneur to keep the equity in a small group of people which allows the preservation of the company as a family business. This requires not only planning for the next years but beyond one generation—for the long-term.[73] More recent research also focuses on this characteristic and covers a broad range of concepts of "long-term orientation" (LTO). A concept similar to long-term orientation is the characteristic of "the will for longevity"[74]. Furthermore, a way

---

[68] As an additional perspective, Pieper and Klein (2007) also refer to psychological ownership as "a source of competitive advantage" following Pierce, Kostova, and Dirks (2001).

[69] See Section 2.2.2.3.

[70] Lantelme et al. (2021, p. 87).

[71] See Pieper (2021, p. 157).

[72] See also Pieper (2007, 2010) for the concept of cohesion as "mechanisms to assure long-term family business survival".

[73] See Oetker (1969, pp. 11–12). It is also one of the first studies which investigates the structure of the largest family enterprises in Germany including listed and private companies like *Horten AG, Axel Springer Verlag GmbH, Haniel & Cie, Quelle/Versand KG* and *Wilhelm Werhahn oHG*.

[74] See Lantelme et al. (2021, p. 50) as well as the entire chapter for an overview of longevity because there is a broad stream of research focusing on the topic not only in the context of family businesses.

to implement a long-term orientation and perpetuate the ownership of a company can be seen in setting up a foundation.[75] In general, following Lumpkin and Brigham long-term orientation can be defined as "the tendency to prioritize the long-range implications and impact of decisions and actions that come to fruition after an extended time period"[76]. This definition can be operationalized in different ways as J. A. Chandler, Zachary, Brigham, and Payne show in their review of LTO concepts in family business research.[77] For example, based on long-term investments Miller and Le Breton-Miller conclude that family firms are heavily oriented towards long-term initiatives and "the only way to sustain good performance is to act in the long-run interests of the company and all its stakeholders"[78]. How the owner families perceive time is an underlying factor. In another study, the two researchers find that the family's stewardship attitude in family businesses is a critical requirement for the long-term orientation and a singular advantage of successful family firms.[79] Looking at other long-term measurements, Block uses R&D investments, employment downsizing and executive pay concepts to provide evidence that companies with a family ownership have a more long-term oriented corporate strategy.[80] His study investigates listed and surviving companies between 1992 and 2003 in the USA. Apart from that, studies show that the (strategic) decision-making in family firms is influenced by their long-term orientation to create, among others, "patient capital".[81] Chua, Chrisman, and Sharma see the intended goal of transgenerational survival as a reason for the focus on the long-term orientation in family firms. Therefore, they also include the long-term orientation in their proposed theoretical definition although it is not a necessary condition.[82] Other researchers see long-term orientation as

[75] See Block, Jarchow, Kammerlander, Hosseini, and Achleitner (2020) and Thomsen, Poulsen, Børsting, and Kuhn (2018) with references to family business research and Werner, Saenger, Fischer, and Andrick (2019, pp. 30–31) as well as Richter (2019, pp. 37–57) for the development of foundations in Germany especially from a legal perspective.

[76] Lumpkin and Brigham (2011, p. 1152). Further, see Block (2009, pp. 42–53) for a discussion of LTO within family business research.

[77] See J. A. Chandler et al. (2016, p. 76).

[78] Miller and Le Breton-Miller (2005, p. 232).

[79] See Le Breton-Miller and Miller (2015).

[80] See Block (2009). His findings are related to a family ownership of more than 30%. In companies with a lower family ownership the correlation cannot be found.

[81] See Sirmon and Hitt (2003).

[82] See Chua et al. (1999, p. 25).

a critical element of their definition of a family firm.[83] Furthermore, the objective of transgenerational survival is also supported by Kotlar and Massis, who, in their study on goal setting in family firms, identify that "family members [are] committed to keeping company control in the hands of the family and to generate various forms of wealth for the family"[84]. This should lead to stability which can be seen as a key strategic objective of family firms.[85] The attributed long-term orientation has also a signaling effect. Job applicants chose family businesses as their new employee based on this orientation.[86]

In contrast, researchers applying a socioemotional wealth (SEW) approach propose that family firms are more likely to make a strategic decision by evaluating a potential loss of socioemotional wealth or its increased risk rather than by a long-term orientation.[87] This shows the diverse concepts and root causes of decision-making in family firms.

Overall and despite some opposing findings, LTO is seen as an important characteristic for family firms to continue as such in family business research.[88] The very existence of multi-generational family enterprises supports this concept, but it requires more data and research to have a solid basis to better understand the LTO concept as well as its underlying motives.

It is noteworthy that a (family) company which is long-term oriented can still discontinue or fail in the short- or mid-term as well as in the long-term, of course. The possibility of the downfall of a family business after generations can also be found in the expression of the "Law of Three Generations". It states that typically the third family generation does not maintain the entrepreneurial orientation of the first and second generation and therefore the company as well as the family's wealth diminish. This "law" might be more an anecdote without much empirical evidence but reflects the existing vulnerability of family firms.[89]

---

[83] See, among others, the FIFS scale by Frank, Kessler, Rusch, Suess–Reyes, and Weismeier–Sammer (2017) which includes transgenerational orientation as a key element.

[84] Kotlar and Massis (2013, p. 1272).

[85] See Kormann (2017) and Seibold (2020, p. 26).

[86] See Mohnen (2020, p. 64).

[87] See Diaz-Moriana, Clinton, Kammerlander, Lumpkin, and Craig (2020, p. 261) and Gómez-Mejía, Haynes, Núñez-Nickel, Jacobson, and Moyano-Fuentes (2007) for the underlying SEW concept.

[88] See Zellweger, Nason, and Nordqvist (2012) and F. W. Kellermanns, Eddleston, Barnett, and Pearson (2008).

[89] See, among others, the example of the Morton family in Great Britain (Morton (1971)) as well as the Buddenbrook family in Thomas Mann's famous novel of the same name (Mann (1901a, 1901b)).

Seibold concludes "[…] that the Law of Three Generations is not an unavoidable fate"[90]. There are several examples of family enterprises which are in the fourth, fifth or older generation.

The long-term orientation of family firms is also acknowledged from a historical science perspective.[91] Nevertheless, earlier research especially in economic history proposes that family firms are only a temporary appearance and will disappear in the long-term. Moreover, family firms have been described to prefer "short-term income to the long-run growth in assets"[92] which is similar to Chandler's view that managers are long-term oriented compared to the company's owners.[93] Over the last decades, the majority of this view has changed, however, and family firms are seen as an essential part of modern institutions within a market economy.[94]

Besides such a dichotomous distinction, for example, between the characteristic of long-term oriented and short-term oriented or between the definition of family firms and non-family firms an increasing stream in family business research highlights and considers the heterogeneity of family firms.[95] Research is more and more focusing on the differences within the group of family businesses because the definitions of family firms include a broad range of companies and because previous research has provided contrary findings when comparing family and non-family business research.[96] This research should help to facilitate the insights into sources of heterogeneity and into the root causes of surviving and diminishing family companies. Conducting such research requires in-depth data on the companies studied, which becomes more difficult the longer the study period is.

---

[90] Seibold (2020, p. 4).

[91] See Berghoff (2016a, p. 19). He provides an example of Richard Hengstenberg's ethos who proposes to constitute one's own work already for the next generations. Further, see Colli (2013, p. 88).

[92] Church (1993, p. 21).

[93] See Chandler A. D. Chandler (1977, p. 10) and see Section 2.2.1 for a more comprehensive description of the historical perspective on the long-term development of (family) companies.

[94] See Casson (2000, pp. 220–221).

[95] See Rovelli et al. (2021, p. 12) and Jaskiewicz and Dyer (2017) for examples of future research related to heterogeneity within family firms.

[96] See Massis, Kotlar, Campopiano, and Cassia (2013) for a study considering the heterogeneity of family firms based on a continuous ownership variable.

There are more specific attributes of family firms besides the ones described above. Some of them have also more positive connotations such as low transaction costs or participative decision-making.[97] Others have more negative connotations and are seen as a disadvantage of family firms like destructive family feuds, financial constraints and lower levels of professionalization.[98] The latter one is often the reason why family firms are then considered an attractive target for private equity funds.[99] Moreover, an additional characteristic (which researchers might not like because it makes their research much more difficult) is the family businesses' secrecy. The companies are said to be reluctant to publish data, e.g., financial data, or provide detailed information about the company, e.g., organizational structure. If the company is a private one the legal requirements to publish corporate data are limited. This secrecy might also be a competitive advantage.[100]

The provided overview of studies also shows that the specific characteristic of long-term orientation can be attributed to family businesses. Nevertheless, the majority of the presented research in family business research only considers companies which still exist at the time of the study. Except a few historical investigations, the attributed characteristic of long-term orientation is often based on empirical studies of family firms which only look at a small part of their time of incorporation. Furthermore, they do not consider the downfall of them at all. There are just a few studies empirically investigating the long-term development of family and / or non-family firms. In the next chapter they are presented to provide a more complete overview of the current state of research.

2.2.2.2 Long-Term Development: Mismatch between Characteristics and Analyses

Despite the long-term orientation as a key characteristic of family enterprises there is little research in the social sciences which empirically investigates the long-term development of family firms. Research on the discontinuity, downfall, or failure of family businesses is even rarer.[101] Researchers have focused more on the successful companies and entrepreneurs in family business research but also

---

[97] See, among others, Gedajlovic and Carney (2010) and F. W. Kellermanns and Eddleston (2006).

[98] See, among others, Kets de Vries (1993) and.

[99] See Zeisberger, Prahl, and White (2017, pp. 52–53).

[100] See Rau (2010, p. V).

[101] See Stamm and Lubinski (2011, p. 117). Recent publications from the overarching research project of this thesis provide some insights into the downfall of companies; see Lantelme (2017), Frericks (2019) and Lantelme et al. (2021) especially chapter 3 and 7.

in the historical sciences, as highlighted in Section 2.1.2. Therefore, several calls for more long-term analyses have been issued proposing longitudinal case studies or historical methods including the contextualization of corporate development in family business research.[102] In the following, selected studies on the long-term development of family businesses are presented that reflect the current state of research as well as its historical path. Additionally, an outlook is given how the mismatch can be fixed.

In 1987, John Ward published his influential book "Keeping the Family Business Healthy: How to Plan for Continuing Growth, Profitability, and Family Leadership".[103] Ward offers the readers insights into a strategic thinking approach which should help to plan for the future. The planning should prepare the family and the company to ensure ongoing growth and profitability. Additionally, future business directions should be identified and the transition to new leadership should be initiated. All relevant family members, independent if they work in the firm or not, should be involved and future generations prepared for the tasks ahead. Although the book is addressed to "family businessmen and women"[104] it has received a lot of attention in the family business research community over the last decades.[105] One of the reasons is his study right in the first chapter which is often cited by researchers. Ward presents a study of 200 family-owned manufacturing companies from Illinois (USA). The companies were established in the market with more than 20 employees and were at least five years old. After identifying the key parameters for the starting year in 1924 he tracks the number of employees and the date the company ceases to exist until 1984. Overall, he follows their development over a period of 60 years. Furthermore, Ward calculates the growth rates based on employees. He also notes the reason for the firms' downfall. The results are not particularly promising. Over the entire study period, 80% of the family firms fail. Additionally, Ward states that only 13% of the family companies remain in the ownership of the initial family.[106] Less than a quarter of this share (3% of the total sample) show a significant growth over 60 years, similar to the companies which did not grow. Nearly twice the share (7% of the total sample) even declined. Ward further investigates the age at which the

[102] See, among others, Rovelli et al. (2021, p. 15), Suddaby, Silverman, Massis, Jaskiewicz, and Micelotta (2020) and Amato, Basco, and Lattanzi (2021).

[103] See Ward (2011) for the latest available edition which has hardly been changed compared to the first edition published in 1987.

[104] Ward (2011, p. XIV).

[105] With currently more than 2,400 citations captured in Google Scholar.

[106] Additional 2% of the companies are not controlled by the founding family anymore and 5% were sold to outsiders, see Ward (2011, p. 2).

family-owned companies ceased. From the 160 failed firms 33% ceased between the age of 0 and 29 years, 35% between 35 and 59, 16% between 60 and 89 and 16% with 90 years or more. Following the idea of a multi-generational family firm, Ward states that "[o]nly 13 percent of successful family businesses last through the third generation"[107]. These statistics appear frightening and need to be explained further.

Despite the high failure rate, 26 (13%) of the 200 companies survived the entire study period of 60 years and were at least 65 years old. Additional 14 (7%) of the initial family firms still existed in 1984 although with different owners. Ward's comparison with the *Fortune 500* companies since 1955 also indicates that not only family firms face the challenge of decline and failure in the long-term. He reports that "only 188 companies have kept their status on this list as independent concerns"[108]. Similar studies related to the *S&P 500* companies show that the average life span "has decreased from sixty-plus years in the 1950s to around seventeen years now"[109] and the list can be extended. Coming back to Ward's study with the focus on family firms he himself mentions several limitations that have to be taken into account when interpreting the data and for future research.[110] The 200 studied companies were selected randomly from a publication which only included manufacturing firms in Illinois. The choice of this source is justified by the fact that Ward was not able to identify better historic records for his starting year 1924 and the subsequent tracking over 60 years. The access to data especially of private companies remains a challenge for current research as well. Although disclosure requirements have become more stringent in recent decades and more and more companies are providing corporate data on a voluntary basis a lot of historical data is still not structured or accessible. But this data is required for long-term analyses and the investigation of failure and survival. Especially data of companies which ceased to exist needs to

---

[107] Ward (2011, p. 1). One generation lasts 30 years, see chapter 0 for a similar definition in this thesis.

[108] Ward (2011, p. 2). The *Fortune 500* list reports America's largest companies on an annual basis since 1955 and is published by the business magazine *Fortune*. It includes private and public companies (with only small exceptions). See Fortune Media IP Ltd. (2020a) for an overview of the latest list (67th edition in 2021) as well as the methodology.

[109] Ashkenas and Manville (2019, p. 148). The *S&P 500* is a stock market index of the 500 largest enterprises in the USA. Accordingly, all these companies are listed on a US stock exchange. See S&P Dow Jones Indices LLC (2021) for the historical development as well as the underlying methodology.

[110] See Ward (2011, pp. 266–274) for his mentioned limitations which are analyzed in the following paragraphs.

be recovered to have the possibility to understand the reasons for their decline and failure. Therefore, a tremendous effort is required to identify, structure, and validate historical corporate data of private but also listed companies. This also concerns the comparability of the data over the entire period. In Section 3.6 the multi-step process of historical data collection is described which is the basis for the datasets used in this thesis. An additional limitation Ward highlights is the missing generally applied definition of family businesses. This has not changed until now in the field of family business research, but researchers are dealing with this challenge by adapting the definition depending on the research focus (e.g., ownership, culture, number of family members).[111] For this thesis a definition of family firms and of eight other types of companies based on the ownership structure is introduced in Section 2.2.2. Like the fundamental criticism of works of historical science Ward mentions that "what has happened over the last 60 years is not necessarily indicative of what will happen to family businesses into the future"[112]. Moreover, it is not known how many family firms failed before the beginning of the study period in 1924. Nevertheless, investigating the past and considering the historical context of the observed developments can lead to a better understanding of the underlying processes. It is unlikely that these processes will be repeated in the same way in the future due to changing conditions, but patterns might come up which allow the description of a space of different development opportunities. Such patterns shall be identified in this thesis to prepare for the future of family enterprises.

The above mentioned and discussed limitations and shortcomings of Ward's analysis continue to pose a challenge for current and future research despite being raised more than 30 years ago. Of course, progress has been made in the research methodologies and the knowledge of family firms. But the long-term development including the failure of family and non-family firms remains a discipline which needs more attention and research. Since family firms are characterized as long-term oriented which is also stated as a basic assumption in family business research this shows the further need. Overall, Ward's study is so popular because it is one of the few which presents numbers to one of the key characteristics of family firms.

---

[111] See Steiger, Duller, and Hiebl (2015) for a most recent empirical overview of applied family firm definitions which will discussed in more detail in Section 2.2.2.

[112] Ward (2011, p. 269) and for the fundamental discussion of the importance of historical sciences see among others Koselleck (1979).

Isabell Stamm and Christina Lubinski provide additional research on this topic and have also taken Ward as a starting point for their critical analysis of survival rates in family business research. Furthermore, they provide some more insights into the long-term development of companies in two German cities as well as into the methodological framework how long-term analyses could be set up using demographic research methods.[113] Stamm and Lubinski trace the often quoted survival rates that "only 30% of family businesses survive into the second generation, and even less than 10–15% make it to the third" to their origins and conclude that their "statements coincide in the observation that many scholars have repeated these numbers, without quoting their origins, the research methodology and limitations"[114]. The numbers have often been used because they fit into a particular story line, also of family business consultants, without mentioning the limitations which Ward provides or without an additional firm empirical basis.[115] Therefore, Stamm and Lubinski present their own study on 161 German family businesses between 1960 and 2009 to analyze their survival rate and its drivers. They find a much higher survival rate compared to Ward. 25.5% of the firms (41 of 161) remain independent family companies until the end of the study period with an average age of 130 years.[116] Besides mentioning the limitations of a study and describing its sample, Stamm and Lubinski further highlights that it is necessary to understand the historical context in which the enterprises have developed. This also allows a more precise interpretation of the results of the analyses. Again, taking Ward as an example, his sample of 200 manufacturing companies in Illinois had different economic conditions in 1924 compared to their sample of German enterprises in a post-World War II era marked by high GDP growth rates. Moreover, political frameworks which have an impact on law and foreign trade, to mention just two examples, are relevant, as well. The different conditions between Illinois from 1924 to 1984 and Germany from 1960 to 2009 show that figures, especially survival rates which predominantly describe a long-term development, cannot generally be applied to (family) businesses worldwide and they always require a contextualization. This equally concerns the company characteristics in the used sample. Differences in size and industry can heavily affect the outcome of studies. In their study, Stamm and Lubinski investigate

[113] See Stamm and Lubinski (2011).

[114] Stamm and Lubinski (2011, p. 119).

[115] Besides Ward, two articles by Beckhard and Dyer from 1983 (Beckhard and Dyer (1983a, 1983b)) are often quoted as sources for the survival figures but Stamm and Lubinski find no empirical data in the articles and quoted studies which support this claim. Also Aronoff (1999) highlights the misleading figures pointing to missing comparative data.

[116] See Stamm and Lubinski (2011, pp. 120–121).

companies with at least 250 employees independent of their industry compared to Ward's sample of companies with only 20 employees or more which exclusively operate in the manufacturing industry. The two key results are that first, survival rates are not common sense and are applicable to a specific region, industry, and sample. Second, the survival of a company is dependent on the size and governance as well as on the economic and political conditions of the time and space the companies operate in.[117]

Empirical studies in family business research often do not consider these external conditions. If an empirical analysis uses an observation period of a few years these conditions might change only within a very limited scope. But as soon as the time frame becomes longer, the conditions should be considered as highlighted above.

Stamm and Lubinski's investigated survival rates are based on a larger study by Lubinski from 2010 in which she analyzes the corporate governance and shareholder culture of family enterprises in Germany from 1960 to 2009.[118] In her long-term study, Lubinski finds evidence of massive changes within family businesses in the second half of the 20th century. They have adapted and professionalized their corporate governance structures but kept their family influence over decades. In the first part, her quantitative empirical analysis focuses on the sample of the 165 family enterprises mentioned above. Besides the survival rate Lubinski also investigates the change of the legal form. Nearly half of the companies in the sample changed their legal form and often from an unlimited to a limited liability type to allowed non-family managers (and new investors) to join the management team. In the second and main part of her work, Lubinski focuses on three case studies to analyze their corporate governance structures and cultures (of the company and the shareholders). For this thesis her research design and methodology from the first part which combine quantitative empirical analyses and their historical contextualization is of importance. This thesis follows a similar approach which is described in more detail in Section 3.2.

Historical analyses as used by Ward as well as by Stamm and Lubinski seem to be a workable solution to bridge the gap between the key characteristic of family firms—their long-term orientation—and the applied methodologies in family business research—mainly with a short investigation period of a couple of years. However, before such analyses can be applied the research object needs to be defined.

---

[117] See Stamm and Lubinski (2011, pp. 120–121).

[118] See Lubinski (2010).

2.2.2.3 Family Business Definition: Choosing a Suitable Approach

Already in 1987, Ward highlights that there is not one generally applied definition of a family business in research and that even the members of a family need to be defined.[119]. This has not changed until today. The variety of definitions increased even more with the greater relevance of the research field as well as with the extensions and improvements of the scientific methods and theories in the last decades.[120] Because the used definition has an impact on the results of a scientific study the different approaches are discussed in the following. Exemplary for the differences in the outcome based on the definition is the macroeconomic relevance of family businesses around the world. Overall, the relevant contribution of family businesses to economies is acknowledged but the degree can vary significantly depending on the used criteria. In 2003, Astrachan and Shanker provide an overview of the number of family firms in the United States as well as their contribution to the GDP and employment in the country.[121] To consider the inconsistent definitions of "family businesses" they distinguish three categories within their "Family Business Bull's-Eye": the (1) broad, (2) middle, and (3) narrow definition. The broad definition only requires family participation and the family's control of the company's strategic direction. The middle definition includes the intention to pass on the business to another family member and that the founder or a descendant of the founder runs the firm. The narrow definition requires multiple generations to be involved in the company and at least one member of the owner's family needs to be active in the management. Based on these categories the results vary significantly. The first definition includes 24.2 million family businesses, the second one 10.8 million and the third one three million. Furthermore, the family businesses' contribution to GDP varies between 64%, 59% and 29% and their contribution to employment varies between 62%, 58% and 27%.[122] Similar differences in the number of family firms as well as

---

[119] See Ward (2011, p. 273).

[120] See among others Hernández-Linares et al. (2018) who identify 258 family business definitions between 1964 and 2013. Steiger et al. (2015) investigate the various definitions of 238 articles published between 2002 and 2011. Further, Xi et al. (2015) provide an overview of the most influential family business research publications until 2012 and their different definition approaches (see Xi et al. (2015, pp. 118–120)).

[121] See Astrachan and Shanker (2003). This study is currently being updated to map the latest family businesses' contribution to the U.S. economy. The authors use the same three categories for the definition of family businesses as in 2003 (see Pieper et al. (2021)). Further, for another advanced "Bulleye" model of family business see Pieper and Klein (2007).

[122] See Astrachan and Shanker (2003, p. 218).

significant changes of the regression coefficients are found by Villalonga and Amit depending on the used definition of family firms in the US.[123] For Germany, the economic contribution of family firms varies between 52% and 47% of total revenue or between 58% and 53% of total employment depending on the applied definition. The study by *Stiftung Familienunternehmen* distinguishes for example family-controlled companies and owner-managed family businesses. The latter is a subset of the first definition with a tighter set of criteria.[124]

Besides the variation of definitions within one study researchers in the field of family business research use even more diverse definitions. These different definitions make it difficult to compare the vast number of studies although all researchers investigate phenomena of "family businesses". Reasons for the variety of definitions are, for example, the availability of data as well as country-specific regulations.[125] Additionally, depending on the research question the family business definition needs to be adapted to investigate the characteristics or relationships of the research objects in the best possible way.

Despite the described differences several categories of family business definitions can be identified. Seibold provides a recent overview of the existing definitions building on the distinction between the components-of-involvement approach and the essence approach provided by Chrisman, Chua, and Sharma.[126] She further explains the definitions of family businesses based on Organizational

---

[123] See Villalonga and Amit (2006, p. 413).

[124] See Gottschalk et al. (2019, p. 6). The German names of the two definitions are *familienkontrolliertes Unternehmen* and *eigentümergeführtes Familienunternehmen.* See also Berghoff and Köhler (2019, pp. 1–5) for comparative data of several countries based on different definitions.

[125] Exemplary, identifying family members in the board of directors or the supervisory board is often difficult especially in later generations because descendants of the founder do not necessarily have the same last name. Therefore, the criterion if a family member is part of the leadership team is often neglected. Further, due to special classes of shares a minority owner can still maintain control of a company due to multiple voting rights, for example. The possibilities of such shares vary significantly depending on the country in which the company is based. In the USA (at least in several states) the laws allow a broad range of stock class configurations while, for example, in Germany the possibilities are much more limited and regulated (therefore several US studies use a share threshold of only 5% to identify family businesses, e.g., see Anderson and Reeb (2003)). See also Colli (2003, p. 19) for the impact of the economic, legal and institutional frameworks on the definition.

[126] See Seibold (2020, pp. 82–86) for the recent overview including relevant and exemplary studies. See Chrisman et al. (2005) for the underlying approaches.

Identity introduced by Zellweger, Eddleston, and Kellermanns.[127] In the following, Seibold's insights are summarized and enriched with additional research to adapt them to the research topic of this thesis. In general, all definitions have in common that the critical condition for family businesses is the family involvement. Nevertheless, this condition has multiple interpretations.[128]

The components-of-involvement approach summarizes definitions "focusing on some combination of the components of a family's involvement in the business: ownership, governance, management, and transgenerational succession"[129]. Researchers use different minimum or limit values to operationalize these components and to define a company as a family business or a non-family business. Thresholds for the equity ownership component are often used ranging from 5% to 70%, whereby the 50% threshold is "very common"[130] and can refer to voting rights or purely stocks. This component is often combined with a second one like managerial presence. Such definitions require, for example, that family members need to be part of the board of directors which equates family-owned enterprises with owner-operated businesses.[131] Following such definition combinations, Casson introduces the two categories of "family owned" and "family controlled" firms in his comprehensive study of economic institutions:

> "A firm is said to be family owned when family members own sufficient voting shares, or occupy sufficient places on the board of directors, to determine the appointment of the general manager or chief executive. A firm is said to be family controlled when the general manager is a member of this family."[132]

Casson also provides a definition of ownership which "must be large enough to block any rival coalition of shareholders that could be readily formed in order to influence the management of the firm."[133] There are no specific thresholds given but they need to be set depending on the legal framework in the investigated country, the available data and / or the research question to operationalize the definition. Also, historians like Johannes Bähr as well as Andrea

---

[127] See Zellweger et al. (2010).

[128] See Seibold (2020, p. 82).

[129] Chrisman et al. (2005, p. 556).

[130] Seibold (2020, p. 83).

[131] For Germany, see, among others, the family business definition of the *Institut für Mittelstandsforschung (IfM) Bonn* (Institut für Mittelstandsforschung Bonn (2021)) which requires that the owners belong to the management.

[132] Casson (2000, p. 198).

[133] Casson (2000, p. 198).

Colli adopt Casson's definition and use it in their own studies.[134] Furthermore, the above-mentioned study by *Stiftung Familienunternehmen* uses such an approach for Germany and has specific thresholds depending on the legal form of the investigated companies.[135]

A point of criticism of the components-of-involvement approach is that "the elements of the COI approach only measure the potential of a family to influence a company, but not their actual influence"[136]. Therefore, researchers have introduced additional measures to identify the family influence.

In the essence approach, the relevant difference between family and non-family businesses is "[..] the behavior of the family which is directed to cause distinctiveness, which indeed leads to the specific behavior of the family firm. This constitutes the familiness (Habbershon & Williams, 1999)), which defines the essence of the family firm (Pearson, Carr, & Shaw, 2008)."[137]. Furthermore, the involvement (e.g., via ownership) of the family remains a necessary condition. Several of the previously highlighted specific characteristics of family businesses are applied in the essence approach and contribute to familiness. Both the family's long-term orientation and the intention to pass on the company to the next generation are the most frequently used conditions.[138] Taken together, this means

---

[134] Bähr investigates the developments of Thyssen in the 1960s and describes the transition from a family-controlled to a public company (Bähr (2015, p. 92)). Furthermore, Colli argues that he applies a similar definition like Casson proposes because "[i]t is a sufficiently broad and appropriate notion to describe a non-homogeneous concept like that of 'family business'." (Colli (2003, p. 20)).

[135] See Gottschalk et al. (2019, 3–4). A company is defined as family-controlled if it is majority-owned by a manageable number of natural individuals. But these criteria vary depending on the legal form. For example, every sole proprietorship is defined as family-controlled while for corporations (as well as the *GmbH & Co. KG*) a maximum of three natural persons need to hold at least 50% of the voting capital of the company (or the general partner company). The second category of owner-managed family businesses needs to fulfill the family-controlled definition and requires at least one owner to be in the management of the company.

[136] Steiger et al. (2015, p. 29). A family with a majority ownership in a company can but does not need to exert their influence, e.g., by not exercising their voting rights or not sending a family member / representative to the board of directors or the supervisory board.

[137] Seibold (2020, p. 84).

[138] See, among others, J. A. Chandler et al. (2016) for an overview of the long-term orientation which also covers the succession planning.

that "[…] the firm is shaped by a dynastic motive […]"[139]. The concept of familiness thereby bundles the resources which are specific for family businesses.[140] This concept allows not only to make a dichotomous distinction between family and non-family businesses, but also a gradual and continuous definition of this company type. The heterogeneity of family businesses can hereby be reflected.[141] However, the difficulty lies in the measurement of such a comprehensive concept. In 2002, Astrachan, Klein, and Smyrnios introduced the F-PEC scale to operationalize familiness and which has become one of the key measurements of "the extent and manner of family involvement in and influence on the enterprise"[142]. This sophisticated approach covers the three subscales power, experience, and culture. It combines aspects of the components-of-involvement approach (like power as involvement of a family in the ownership, management, and / or governance) as well as of the essence approach (like culture). As Seibold outlines, this F-PEC scale has been applied extensively and researchers have built additional scales to further improve the measurement of familiness (e.g., collective psychological ownership of family over business (F-CPO)).[143] For quantitative studies with hundreds or thousands of companies the collection of all relevant data for scales like F-PEC is difficult to achieve due to a lack of data availability and accessibility. Especially when investigating companies over a long period the data collection becomes nearly impossible.[144]

Next to the component-of-involvement and the essence approaches Zellweger et al. add "organizational identity as a third dimension of familiness"[145]. Seibold explains that "[t]his theory, in the context of family businesses, focuses on how a family views and defines their business"[146]. This concept of self-perception has also been added to another more comprehensive scale, the "Family Influence Familiness Scale" (FIFS), which also measures the degree of familiness based on even more items including the transgenerational orientation.[147] With additional

---

[139] Colli (2003, p. 9) and in the German literature see May (2012, p. 29).

[140] See Habbershon and Williams (1999) for the origins of familiness.

[141] See Astrachan and Binz Astrachan (2021, pp. 24–25) for the "tremendous level of heterogeneity among both family businesses and business families" as well as their call for additional required research.

[142] Astrachan et al. (2002, p. 47) for the initial approach.

[143] See Seibold (2020, p. 85) and Rantanen and Jussila (2011) for the F-CPO scale.

[144] See Steiger et al. (2015, pp. 42–43).

[145] Zellweger et al. (2010, p. 54).

[146] Seibold (2020, p. 85).

[147] See Frank et al. (2017).

characteristics and concepts being added to the definition of family businesses or the degree of familiness, respectively, new insights can be generated. Nevertheless, the more comprehensive and detailed these concepts become the more general similarities and dissimilarities might be overlooked.

In historical sciences family businesses are already a long-established research object although the specific family characteristics are not always the research focus.[148] The used definitions in this research discipline do not differ much from the already presented ones.[149] Yet, historians note that the definitions do not account for the long-term development of companies because such a long process can hardly be described in a universally valid typology.[150] Therefore, especially corporate historians often investigate one specific case over a long period, and they collect detailed information about this specific company including their ownership, leadership and informal structures. This allows them a more nuanced description, for example, how a family influences the company based on several components and not only ownership. A general definition what a family business is is then not required.[151]

For this thesis a family business definition needs to be applied which can be used for a larger sample of enterprises and which allows an investigation over decades. Additionally, it needs to distinguish different company types based on ownership.

2.2.2.4 Company Type Definitions: Comparing Family and Non-Family Enterprises

The definition of the research object needs to consider the research objective as well as the available and observable data.[152] To approach the objective of this thesis the definition of a family business is based on the ownership structure of the company following the components-of-involvement approach used by many other family business researchers and historians as elaborated above. The two main reasons are the following: First, the ownership structure of each enterprise in the sample can be observed over the study period of 60 years compared to factors from the essence approach (like culture) or organizational identity which are not available for each company over such a long period of time. Furthermore,

---

[148] See Colli (2003, p. 2) for an overview of the historical perspective on family businesses.

[149] See Bähr (2015, p. 91) and Colli (2003, p. 20).

[150] See Bähr (2015, p. 93) and his reference to the phase model of Joly (1998).

[151] See exemplary for studies of single companies in Germany Kocka (1971), Bähr and Erker (2013), Plumpe (2014), and Bähr, Banken, and Flemming (2019).

[152] See Steiger et al. (2015, pp. 42–43).

this data cannot be queried retrospectively, either, whereas ownership structures can be identified using historical methods based on corporate and industry publications as well as on secondary sources like newspaper articles. Second, based on the ownership structure and the owners' shares of the company's stock or capital (more precisely of their voting rights) they can exert their influence on the company's development by either their active involvement in the operations (e.g., in the board of directors) or by using the control or supervisory function (e.g., in the supervisory board or in councils).[153] As outlined in the previous chapter and as the weakness of the components-of-involvement approach, this parameter might not reflect the heterogeneity of family firms and further might act only as a proxy to measure the potential family influence because it is not necessary that the owners / family members use their voting rights. This is also reflected in the study by Chrisman, Chua, Pearson, and Barnett and their proposed hierarchical order of the involvement and essence approach. They conclude that "[…] family involvement is a necessary condition for the existence of a family firm but is not sufficient to ensure that a family firm will behave in a fashion that differs from that of nonfamily firms. On the other hand, family essence suggests the likelihood of distinctive behaviors but cannot exist without family involvement. Thus, family involvement is an invariant characteristic of family firms while family essence occurs only in some family firms."[154]. Therefore, an additional measure like the presence of a family member in the board of directors or the supervisory board might help to understand the actual family influence. Nevertheless, such additional requirements can also have disadvantages. The historian Johannes Bähr considers the presence of a family member in the board of directors to be unsuitable for large enterprises. He provides several examples of the 19th and 20th century in Germany in which the owner families withdraw from the board of directors but keep the ownership majority and exert their influence based on their seats in the supervisory board. These examples include *Gutehoffnungshütte Aktienverein, Fried. Krupp, Essen* and *Hoesch AG.*[155] Also the family presence in the supervisory board is not a necessary condition because as Bähr shows for the cases of *August Thyssen-Hütte AG* and *Phoenix-Rheinrohr AG* even in the supervisory board loyal deputies of the family can exert the family's influence effectively.[156] No family member needs to be part of any corporate body and

[153] See Oetker (1969, pp. 11–12) and Chua et al. (1999, p. 25).

[154] Chrisman et al. (2012, p. 286).

[155] See Bähr (2015, p. 91).

[156] Further, Bähr describes in detail the removal of the CEO of *Phoenix-Rheinrohr AG*, Fritz-Aurel Goergen, in 1957 based on the decision of the majority owner, Amélie Thyssen, after

yet the family can have a major impact. This thesis follows Bähr's objection that a company can be defined as family business without having a family member in the board of directors or the supervisory board. This corresponds to Casson's definition of a "family owned firm". Several examples of the dataset of this thesis support Bähr's and Casson's proposal which will be presented in the results section.

After clarifying the key element of the proposed family business definition, thresholds need to be set to operationalize the definition. The simple majority of voting rights (larger than 50%) ensures that the owner (not necessarily a family) has a decisive influence on the company. Following Casson a majority fulfills his sufficiency requirement which makes it possible "to block any rival coalition of shareholders that could be readily formed in order to influence the management of the firm."[157] Exemplary, in *AGs* with a simple majority the resolutions by the general meeting can be adopted unless the law or the by-laws stipulate a greater majority ratio or impose further requirements.[158] The possible decisions based on a simple majority are extensive including the appointment of the members to the supervisory board which then supervise the management board.[159] This allows the owner to define how the enterprise should be positioned strategically because certain types of business transactions can only be implemented with the supervisory board's consent.[160] Exceptions which require a majority of at least three quarters include the amendment of the by-laws or the dissolution of the company.[161] Because a simple majority holder can block these resolutions a higher share is not required to define a company as family business. On the other hand, a simple majority holder cannot amend the by-laws or dissolve the company on their own because all other owners with a blocking minority of a least 25% can ensure that a three-fourths majority will not be achieved. Therefore, a threshold of less than 50% but more than 25% might be sufficient to ensure a significant influence on the company. Such a threshold could lead to a double classification

---

he fell from grace due to, among other things, idiosyncratic behavior in public. Thyssen was not part of the board of directors but exerted her influence via her deputy in the supervisory board based on her majority ownership (see Bähr (2015, pp. 93–99)).

[157] Casson (2000, p. 198).

[158] See § 133 (1) AktG.

[159] See § 101 and § 111 AktG. However, the removal from office of supervisory board members prior to expiry of their term requires a majority of at least three quarters of the general meeting according to § 103 AktG. This threshold can be lowered in the by-laws.

[160] See § 111 (4) AktG.

[161] See § 179 (2) AktG and § 262 (1) AktG.

with multiple strong owners because the enterprise could have another blocking minority or simple majority owner. Exemplary, in 1958 the largest owner of *Osram GmbH* is *Siemens & Halske AG* (part of the family-owned *Siemens Group* at that time) with 42.77%. Additional owners are *AEG Allgemeine Electricitäts-Gesellschaft AG* with 35.78% and *International General Electric Company* with 21.45%. Although *Siemens* has the biggest share and a blocking minority but not the simple majority, they require the support of one of the other two owners to take a decision by a majority. Therefore, *Osram GmbH* cannot be classified either as a *Siemens* subsidiary or as a family-owned company. The company is owned by multiple enterprises.[162]

The relevance of the majority threshold can also be seen in the case of companies subject to consolidation. A German enterprise which is the majority owner of another (German) company needs to include this subsidiary in its consolidated financial statement due to a controlling influence. The legal basis is § 290 (2) HGB which defines a controlling influence as the enterprise's majority ownership of the company's voting rights (sentence 1). A controlling influence, on the other hand, is not given even if an owner with a share below 50% has a recurring simple majority at the annual general meetings of an *AG* because not all shareholders with voting rights attend the meetings. Such a majority lacks legal protection.[163]

The extensive entrepreneurial possibilities based on a simple majority allow the exercise of a significant influence. Therefore, this threshold is used to define a company as a family-owned business or as other company types which will be

[162] See Commerzbank AG (1959) for the 1958 ownership structure. Over the next decade the ownership structure remains stable but also leads to uncertainty because there is no majority owner. This complicates the long-term planning. Then in 1975, *Siemens* buys the share of *AEG* to become the majority owner (simple as well as three quarters) and Osram becomes a *Siemens* subsidiary (Götz (1975)). Three years later, *Siemens* acquires the outstanding share from *GE* to become the sole owner (Frankfurter Allgemeine Zeitung (1978)). In 2013, *Siemens* takes its subsidiary public and keeps only a share of 19.5% (Köhn (2013)). *Osram Licht AG* becomes a public company due to a free float larger than 50%. *Osram* remains this type of company until 2018 when the free float is 100% (Osram Licht AG (2019)).

[163] The majority of voting rights is only one of four criteria based on which a controlling influence can result according to § 290 (2). The other three criteria are outlined in sentences 2, 3, and 4. Because they can also occur without a majority of voting rights sentence 1 is the strictest criterion related to voting rights which is the proposed operationalization of the applied definition. It is noteworthy that these four criteria are not exhaustive in the possibilities that a controlling influence exists (see Grottel and Kreher (2020, pp. 1594–1598) also for the lack of legal protection of a present voting rights majority at annual general meetings).

explained later on in this chapter. For other legal forms than the *AG* (e.g., *GmbH*) the simple majority allows similar or even more wide-ranging decisions.[164]

By using the ownership majority or voting rights majority, respectively, as threshold for the definition of a family business several limitations need to be considered. Such a definition excludes companies as family firms, for example, which are strongly influenced by families despite an ownership stake below 50%. To cover these cases additional variables and data would be required. Because this thesis investigates the development over decades and includes companies which ceased to exist within the last 60 years this information does not exist for the majority of companies. Moreover, in previous historical research evidence can be found that in Germany at the end of the 1950s most companies were majority-owned by a family.[165] The approach to use the majority threshold is in line with the historical context. Companies in 2018 which have a family owner just under 50% are highlighted in the results section and investigated separately to better understand their rationale. Besides families a similar aspect can be found with other investors. Until the mid-1960s, despite none or a very low ownership stake in a listed enterprise banks could exercise the voting rights attached to the shares they held for depositors (*Depotstimmrecht*). The depositors could provide voting instructions to their bank, but banks were not required to ask for such instructions. Because many private individual shareholders did not provide this information banks were able to vote in their favor using the shares of their depositors—in some cases achieving the simple majority and more. Therefore, the banks' influences could be higher than their actual share ownership (even if owning no shares at all banks could vote using their depositors' shares). Because this procedure was regulated over the last decades, starting in 1965, which led to a decreasing influence of banks at shareholders' meetings and because it only affects listed companies with no majority shareholder a detailed analysis of this effect is not conducted in this thesis.[166]

A second limitation of the voting rights majority as decisive criterion lies in the company perspective taken. The enterprises are investigated according to

---

[164] For the GmbH see the two main exceptions similar to the AG which require a majority of at least three quarters: (a) the amendment to articles of association ($53 (2) GmbHG) and (b) winding up the company (§ 60 (1) sentence 2 GmbHG). In partnerships the thresholds for resolutions can be agreed in the partnership agreement.

[165] See Lubinski (2010, pp. 46–47).

[166] See Edwards and Fischer (1994, p. 112) for a brief overview as well as Denton, Forsyth, and MacLennan (2017, pp. 62–72) for the impact of *Depotstimmrechte* at shareholders' meetings prior to the regulation in 1965.

how they develop and if the (family) ownership changes over time. This perspective does not cover any other investments of or decisions taken by the family or the majority owner except the continuity or discontinuity of ownership in this one specific company.[167] An alternative perspective with a focus on the family or a specific investor could, for example, provide insights in their decision-making behavior and their specific continuity or discontinuity of investments. The objective of this thesis is the long-term development of the large enterprises in Germany as well as the continuity and discontinuity of their ownership structures including family influence. Therefore, the company perspective is chosen consciously to track the enterprises and not a specific family or investor. Furthermore, this company perspective focuses on the entire enterprise and not on business units. It is the corporate development which is investigated and not the business development. Therefore, the company, if it is diversified, can change its portfolio of business units over time and remains the same entity which is investigated. It is part of the corporate strategy in which businesses the company invests and divests.[168]

Following this reasoning, the enterprises are examined for their ownership structure and the corresponding voting rights. The simple majority operationalizes the underlying criteria. Additionally, the corporate perspective is the focus of this thesis.

Despite following a components-of-involvement approach, one additional variable which is linked to the essence approach is also tracked. In the essence approach, succession is used as an indicator for the intention to pass on the company to the next generation.[169] In this thesis, if a company is identified as a family-owned enterprise the information about the family generation is collected (i.e., generation of the founder, second generation, third generation and so on) in 1958, 2018 as well as in the year of a majority ownership change. This information is retrospective and can provide insights if a family business develops into a multi-generational company or in which generation the business stops to be

---

[167] Different enterprises can be owned by the same family. *August Thyssen-Hütte AG* and *Phoenix-Rheinrohr AG* are both majority-owned by the Thyssen family in 1958. Similar cases can be found for the Flick family and Haniel family.

[168] See Porter (1989) for the general differences between corporate and business strategy. Further, see Section 3.4 for the continuity and discontinuity of operations and their application in this thesis.

[169] See, among others, Diaz-Moriana et al. (2020, p. 261) which require the criteria that "[...] Generational involvement in ownership and / or management must span at least two generations [...]".

owned by the family. It can also help to better understand in which generation growth or decline started or accelerated.[170]

Overall, a company in this thesis is defined as a family business based on its ownership structure and the associated voting rights. One or more German owner families need to hold more than 50% of the company's stock or capital. When the percentage of voting rights is different from the percentage of ownership the voting rights are decisive.[171] This requirement is independent of the legal type of the company. Shares or capital held by family foundations established by the former owner family are also attributed to the family.[172] Family members can but do not need to be in the management team or in the supervisory board.

Based on the logic of the family business definition and the underlying ownership approach eight addition types of companies are introduced. Table 2.1 provides a quick overview of all nine types and a more detailed description of the additional seven types follows afterwards.

A foreign family-owned business is defined by the same criteria as the (German) family-owned business except that the owners are foreigners. They also need to hold more than 50% of the company's stock or capital (or voting rights, respectively) and foreign family foundations are attributed to the family as well. Companies whose majority owner is a foundation are defined as foundation-owned enterprise. If a company has not a single majority owner but two or more other companies are block holders and own more than 50%, this enterprise is a multiple companies-owned enterprise. A listed company with a free float larger than 50% is defined as public company. Cooperatives themselves or enterprises which are majority-owned by one or more cooperatives are defined as such. If a country, federal state, municipality, or city is the majority owner of a company it is defined as state-owned enterprise. An enterprise which is majority-owned by at least one foreign (non-German) company is defined as foreign subsidiary. A special case is the definition of a subsidiary company. Although the lists of the largest 250 enterprises in 1958 as well as in 2018 only include independent companies this might not be the case when identifying the 2018 status of a company

---

[170] For an overview of growth patterns in and a dedicated growth model of German family firms see Seibold (2020) who also refers them to different family generations.

[171] For a detailed description of voting rights as well as multiple voting rights see Sections 3.7.1.1 and 4.3 the historical context.

[172] Legally, the family foundation is a foundation and could also be added to this category. But because the family can exert more influence through a family foundation than through a foundation it is categorized as part of the family businesses. See Block, May, Betzer, and Au (2020) for an overview of the concept.

Table 2.1 Definition of Types of Companies

#	**Type of Company**[173]	**Definition** [share of company's stock / capital / voting rights]
1	Family-owned business	>50% held by one or more German owner families
2	Foreign family-owned business	>50% held by one or more foreign (non-German) owner families
3	Foundation-owned enterprise	>50% held by a foundation
4	Multiple companies-owned enterprise	>50% held by two or more companies
5	Public company	>50% is in free float
6	Cooperative	>50% held by a cooperative or a cooperative itself
7	State-owned enterprise	>50% held by a country, federal state, municipality, or city
8	Foreign subsidiary	>50% held by one or more foreign (non-German) companies
9	Subsidiary company	>50% held by one German company (only applicable for the 2018 status of the 250 largest enterprises of 1958)

Source: Author's own table.

from the 1958 list. If a firm was acquired between 1958 and 2018, it can become a subsidiary company of another German enterprise.[174]

2.3 Research Gap: Quantitative Long-Term Analysis of Family and Non-Family Enterprises

The previous discussions of current relevant research and definitions shows that despite the vast amount of survival and research literature in various disciplines, the relevant condition of ownership and in particular family firms are not yet studied to provide a comprehensive understanding of their long-term development. This is necessary because long-term orientation is a key characteristic

[173] In the following chapters, the company types are abbreviated where necessary, e.g., in several tables, to present the findings and ensure the readability. See Appendix 10.2 in the electronic supplementary material for the list of abbreviations.

[174] The terms business, enterprise and company are used interchangeably in the definitions.

of family firms. Therefore, research also needs to consider long-term analyses when studying this particular company type. Furthermore, the comparison with other company types like public companies or state-owned enterprises ensures that observed developments are linked to the ownership structure. One reason of missing long-term analyses is the availability of data especially in the case of family firms which often do not publish detailed corporate information. This is also the reason why researchers often use listed enterprises which are obliged to publish certain data, in their samples although the total amount of listed companies is much lower than that of non-listed enterprises.[175] For Germany, research on the downfall of enterprises as well as stagnating and declining businesses is also rare.[176] Success factor research with a focus on successful and growing businesses dominates current analyses.

A discipline which uses long-term analyses and deals with limited sources to study developments over decades or even centuries are the historical sciences and in particular business history in the context of companies. But business historians mainly focus on a specific company and describe its development without providing an overview of general patterns of certain company types which can be used as guidelines for other companies or future developments.

Overall, a research gap is identified in the analysis of the long-term development of family and non-family enterprises in Germany. A second gap is research on the survival and failure in relation to the ownership structure of a company. To approach these gaps, the thesis at hand uses historical as well as social science methods from family business research but also from other management studies to investigate the long-term development of family and non-family enterprises in Germany including companies which cease to exist in the observation period. A quantitative approach is used to exceed the often-used single cases in business history and approaches large sample sizes which are used in quantitative studies of family business research to allow for generalizations of the observed developments. Moreover, not only listed companies are considered but also private ones which are often family-owned to better map the German economy. Therefore, the listing status is included in the variables of the datasets used in this thesis. To ensure that data is available for such a comprehensive sample over decades the focus is on large enterprises across all industries except the financial sector.

---

[175] As an additional example see Block (2009) who investigates only listed companies and also removes companies from his dataset which are not listed for the entire period from 1992 to 2003.

[176] For a long-term analysis of 100 years see Nowak et al. (2006) but the authors only cover surviving companies.

Overall, this thesis provides a next step towards longitudinal research with an overview of the long-term development of a large sample of family and non-family enterprises in Germany including surviving and failing companies.

The next chapter outlines the used methodologies and timeframe of the analyses. In combination with the research objectives and gaps the research questions are formulated.

3 Methodology and Research Questions

In the description of the characteristics of family enterprises their long-term orientation is highlighted. Despite this attribute family business research hardly investigates this type of company over decades or generations. This research discipline has a more short-term focus and present-oriented perspective, like business administration in general, and often does not consider methods which would enable researchers to conduct long-term studies.[1] Because of this methodological lack the present thesis takes a closer look at the historical sciences and especially business as well as economic history whose core task is the study of the past of different research objects—over longer periods than management studies do in general. The goal of this chapter is to identify useful methods and combine them with business studies to generate new insights into the long-term development of family and non-family enterprises.

[1] See, among others, Berghoff (2016b, pp. 3–5) as well as his mentioned critics of very specialized economics which should consider other disciplines in their analyses to provide a more comprehensive understanding of the observations (e.g., Allais (1988)).

Supplementary Information The online version contains supplementary material available at https://doi.org/10.1007/978-3-658-42375-9_3.

M. Lantelme, *The Continuity and Discontinuity of the 250 Largest Enterprises in Germany*, Familienunternehmen und KMU,
https://doi.org/10.1007/978-3-658-42375-9_3

3.1 Business, Economy and History: The Historical Method

Business and economic history are both research disciplines which focus on the past development and change of companies, of institutions and of processes in the business and economic context—individually or at different aggregated levels.[2] Berghoff further outlines that these developments and changes of companies, institutions and processes, like all historical phenomena, are determined by five dimensions: (1) economic, (2) social, (3) cultural, (4) legal, and (5) political factors. To fully describe and explain a historic phenomenon as well as capture the multi-dimensionality of historical processes these factors should be included. Depending on the research object and the research question, single dimensions can also be accentuated more strongly or investigated individually.[3] In this context, the science of history is not limited to the mere description of events. It can rather use theories from other disciplines like management studies and economics to strengthen its explanatory power and test these theories with historical data.[4] Exemplary theories which are considered in business and economic history are the concepts of new institutional economics, of evolutionary economics and of neoclassical economics but also systems theory.[5]

The connection between business studies as well as economics and their related historical disciplines is traditionally closely linked.[6] Although these connections have been softened and, in some areas (geographically and within sub-disciplines), have come loose over the past decades there are still several connectable concepts and research agendas as Fridenson and Köster describe in their histories of both research disciplines. This common history of the disciplines can also be seen in the work of business and economic historians across their respective discipline boundaries which is a strength of these research fields. Historians often use interdisciplinary approaches which have huge potential to better investigate research questions and to identify underlying processes. This enables historian not only to describe historical events but also to derive models

[2] For an introduction see Berghoff (2016b, pp. 6–14) for business history and Köster (2020, pp. 7–19) for economic history.

[3] See Berghoff (2016b, pp. 15–25) including a more detailed description of each dimension.

[4] See, among others, Lamoreaux, Raff, and Temin (2008) for the use of economic theories in business history.

[5] See Berghoff (2016b, pp. 27–60).

[6] See Fridenson (2008) for the development of business history in the US and its origins at Harvard Business School in 1927 as well as Köster (2020, pp. 11–19) for the development of economic history.

and implications for action.[7] Cliometrics can be seen as an example of the close collaboration in parts of the different disciplines.[8] Researchers of this discipline use quantitative approaches and methods from economics to investigate the historical development of economic processes.[9] Early examples of famous research topics are the economics of slavery or the importance of transportation on the economic development.[10]

Similar to Cliometrics, researchers in business history also consider theories and methods from management studies or contribute to this research field.[11] One of the most-well known business historians who changed the methodologies, the understanding and the impact of business history is Alfred D. Chandler in the second half of the twentieth century. With his publication "Strategy and Structure" in 1962 and his main work "The Visible Hand" in 1977 Chandler provided two novel historical analyses.[12] The first book investigates how the largest corporations in the US try to build an effective administration of their expanding businesses and establish the multidivisional structure as an advanced solution for their organizations. In the latter, he claims to explain why the companies he investigates became successful and to derive more universally valid explanations of success. Based on a *managerial revolution* the emergence of large corporations was made possible. The managerial hierarchy provides administrative coordination more efficiently than any market transaction could do (the *invisible hand*). As shown in Section 2.2.1, Chandler also provides explanations why family-owned and family-run businesses turn into manager-run corporations with separated ownership and control. These findings based on historical analyses of the long-term corporate developments including historical performance figures also provided new impetus to business sciences. Nevertheless, Chandler's work was not as influential in the historical sciences as in other disciplines.[13] Business historians predominantly stuck to the analysis of individual cases as in previous decades. Among them were family-owned enterprises as well.[14] Overall

---

[7] See Kipping and Üsdiken (2008) for an interdisciplinary approach of business history and management studies as well as Robert M. Solow's criticism of economics and his call for a link to historical and socio-cultural contexts (see Solow (1985)).

[8] Cliometrics is sometimes called New Economic History or Econometric History as well.

[9] See Köster (2020, pp. 174–189) for an overview of Cliometrics.

[10] See the early and conflictual research by Conrad and Meyer (1958) on slavery and the summary of the discussions by Fogel (2003).

[11] See Kipping and Üsdiken (2008).

[12] See A. D. Chandler (1962, 1977) and the brief summary in Section 2.2.1.

[13] See McCraw (2008).

[14] See, among others, Lorandini (2015).

and independent of Chandler's work, it should be noted that "[f]rom the historian's standpoint, the issue of family business is anything but new."[15] But as Lubinski states the family influence is hardly considered and the family firm not recognized as a separate company type.[16]

Besides the relatively new analyses in business and economic history using methods from other disciplines there is a basic set of ways of working in the science of history which can be summarized as the *historical method(s)*. There are three key aspects which have been the guideline for historians for decades and even centuries. These are the heuristic, the source criticism, and the interpretation / synthesis. First, the heuristic includes the development of the research question including its reasoning as well as including the definition and the specification of the relevant sources. The second aspect is the special handling of the used sources. Historical analyses are based on primary or secondary sources (in the case of business and economic history mainly in written form) which require a critical approach. This source criticism raises the questions of authenticity and correctness to determine reliability. The third aspect covers the interpretation of the used sources and their contents. This synthesis requires the establishment of causal relationships and the inclusion of the conditions like space and time. Furthermore, the interpretation needs to consider the psychological aspects of the observed behaviors or the written down information in the sources based on, e.g., a person's characteristics. The third aspect also requires the interpretation of the single event in the larger context of its appearance.[17] The historical context includes, for example, the development of the industry a company operates in as well as the overall economic, social, cultural, legal, and political factors as highlighted at the beginning of this chapter.

A key part of the first highlighted aspect, the heuristic, is the source itself. Limited availability and accessibility of specific sources make it more difficult to find the right sources to close the research gap. It can be assumed that the closer the period of investigation is to today, the more sources are available.[18] For example, not only the companies themselves publish and store their corporate data in the last centuries but also other institutions like associations, banks, newspapers as well as states can be useful sources. Such a variety of sources is rare for the

[15] Colli (2003, p. 2).

[16] See Lubinski (2010, p. 10).

[17] See Jordan (2018, pp. 43–45). The applied historical method in this thesis is further explained in the data collection process in Section 3.6.

[18] See Opgenoorth and Schulz (2010, pp. 49–55) for an overview of different sources.

Middle Ages or antiquity. Nevertheless, not all sources are available or accessible even in modern times. Thus, it often requires the combination of several sources to work on the heuristic. By combining various sources data series can be created if, for example, one account book does not provide all required data to show the performance development. This requires additional verifications that the different sources measure the same scope (e.g., revenue of the entire company vs. revenue of one business unit / revenue of the company group vs. revenue of one company of the group) or the duration of the period (e.g., full business years vs. nine months of a business year).[19]

An example for a combination of business studies and history is the long-term analysis of the development of the world's 100 largest enterprises from 1912 to 1995 by Hannah in 1999. He uses methods from the historical sciences to build his datasets including data series and then applies methods from management studies to calculate the companies' survival rates. The interpretation of the sources and their contents shows national differences and provides insights which companies survive and which fail. He also puts the sources and the results into the historical context to provide a better understanding of the observed national developments.

Overall, the historical sciences offer approaches and methodologies to study the long-term developments of companies. Nevertheless, they are rarely used to investigate the development of ownership structures in combination with the companies' performances. Family firms—in particular—are hardly ever considered as a specific company type in history. But how are the historical methods viewed by the family business research community? Which approaches are used and what is the outlook for interdisciplinary research?

3.2 History-Informed Approach: Family Business Research and Historical Sciences

In family business research history is not a topic which has been used frequently so far although "[h]istory is pervasive in family business settings, where values, beliefs, narratives, and artefacts of the founding family are handed down from generation to generation".[20] Family business researchers have investigated family firms for several decades but with different methods and research questions than those of historians. However, more recently the interest in the historical sciences

[19] See Opgenoorth and Schulz (2010, pp. 192–206) for the description of data series.

[20] Suddaby et al. (2020, p. 331) citing Colli (2003).

is growing in family business research. Three different underlying streams can be distinguished within this development. First, after several decades of family business research its history itself has been studied. Reflecting on and outlining its past development help to find gaps and formulate future research agendas for the field. Those identified approaches also highlight the methods of historical sciences as an additional area in family business research.[21] Second, similar to business history the history of one family firm is studied in detail or a set of companies is used for a comparative study. The specific development of one or a few family firms should provide insights how family businesses in general act or work. Furthermore, the company's development should show the connection between the family (business) history and the firm's strategy. These studies can also include the identification of success factors like the family's history itself as a lever for a competitive advantage.[22] Third, family businesses are recognized as a distinct type of company and their role in a broader economic setting (e.g., in the national economy or in a region) is studied in the long-term.[23] This type of study is rarer compared to the previous stream.[24] Furthermore, it is mainly driven by historians rather than by social scientists because the methodologies are mainly adopted from the science of history which includes quantitative long-term data series as well as comparative analyses.[25] Colli and Fernández Pérez highlight the advantages of historical methods for family business research, especially those of source criticism and longitudinal analysis. The essence of the latter one "is the use of history in order to focus on two issues, that is, the change from a status quo into another, and the dynamics introducing and governing the change"[26] which fits quite well to the understanding of the development of companies which are expected to be handed over from generation to generation and their underlying dynamics.

---

[21] See Colli (2003, pp. 6–26).

[22] See, among other, Sasaki, Kotlar, Ravasi, and Vaara (2020) and Ge, Massis, and Kotlar (2022). Furthermore, see Groote, Conrad, and Hack (2020) for success factors how family businesses can survive disruptive industry changes.

[23] See Berghoff and Köhler (2019) for a comparative approach between Germany and the USA, Hannah (1982) and Jones and Rose (1993) as well as the already introduced studies by Lubinski (2010) and Stamm and Lubinski (2011).

[24] See Casson (2000, p. 197).

[25] See also Colli and Larsson (2014) for a comparative approach between family firms in Sweden and Italy.

[26] Colli and Fernández Pérez (2020, p. 108) quoting Tosh (2015). For source criticism see Section 3.1.

As a consequence of these developments Argyres et al. introduce "history-informed strategy research" in the context of family businesses and the journal *Family Business Review* issues a call for their special issue on "history-informed family business research" in 2023.[27] The objective is in both cases "new, interdisciplinary research on family firms that extends our understanding of how and why history and historical research methods can enrich theoretical explanations of family business behavior and of temporal phenomena happening in family business settings"[28].

The dissertation at hand follows these calls as well as the third identified stream. For the analysis of family and non-family enterprises in the long-term, historical data as well as historical methods are used to generate a database which provides unique insights into the ownership structures of the largest enterprises in Germany. Moreover, it provides evidence how these enterprises have developed over time including ownership changes, their performances, and their failures. Empirical studies in family business research are mainly limited to listed companies due to the availability of and access to data at a certain point in time. In addition, the investigated time frame often covers only a couple of years or several decades.[29] With this doctoral thesis at hand the time frame of the investigation of family and non-family enterprises is extended to several decades and uses longitudinal data. It further includes listed as well as non-listed enterprises based on the search and use of archival data and the analysis of hundreds of historical sources. The existing understanding of family enterprises with their theoretically attributed long-term orientation is tested using the historical methods and data. As part of the historical analysis, this thesis also provides insights into the economic and political developments of Germany over the entire study period.[30] This contextualization includes key macroeconomic indicators like the development of the GDP and the export quota as well as political and legal events like the territorial extensions of the Federal Republic of Germany due to the reunification with the German Democratic Republic as well as the introduction of new legal forms. This historical context basis is then used for the interpretation of the results.

To further add to the historical context, not only family enterprises and public companies are investigated in this thesis, but also other types of companies. Among others, state-owned firms, cooperatives and subsidiaries of foreign enterprises are identified based on their ownership structure and included in the

[27] See Argyres et al. (2020) and Suddaby et al. (2020).

[28] Suddaby et al. (2020, p. 332).

[29] For the existing limitation see among others Astrachan and Binz Astrachan (2021).

[30] See Chapter 4.

analyses. Although public companies whose majority ownership is in free float are most suitable to be compared to family firms because of the similar independence of their entrepreneurial activities, a more comprehensive overview of the economic and corporate development in Germany over the last decades can be achieved based on the investigation of the additional economic players. Furthermore, this allows a comparison between the different company types as well, which helps to identify specific patterns in the development of family and non-family firms as well as of specific characteristics of the different company types. Adding to the consideration of state-owned enterprises, Fiedler argues that there is no plausible reason to exclude them from a list of the largest companies because these economic players often employ the most people over long periods in the German economy.[31] Additionally, enterprises which are state-owned, for example by a city, a municipality, a federal state or the federal republic are included in the analyses because they either compete with other non-state-owned enterprises on the same markets or get privatized in the long-term (e.g., *Volkswagenwerk GmbH* or *Deutsche Bundespost*). Also, public utilities compete with private providers for customers despite their special objective to act on behalf of services of general interest and universal basic services.[32]

This dissertation proposes a modified approach including historical methods to better understand the long-term development of enterprises and test and add to theoretical models in family business research. The next sub-chapters outline how this approach is operationalized in detail.

3.3 Quantitative Analysis, Sample and Contextualization: Considering the Broader Picture

This dissertation at hand uses methods from the historical sciences as well as from the social sciences to study the long-term development of German enterprises. Other disciplines like the social sciences frequently like Cliometrics. Based on historical methods sources are identified and verified, data are collected and interpreted. Empirical and statistical methods from the social sciences are used for the

[31] See Fiedler (1999, pp. 35–36). He also briefly describes the discussion about the definition of a “company”.

[32] As an example, see *Stadtwerke München* which compete in the telecommunications business with among others *Vodafone* or *Deutsche Telekom* or act as an electricity provider all over Germany as well.

processing of the data and calculations. Opgenoorth and Schulz describe empirical methods as useful and as an addition to historical research. These methods can support the traditional source criticism and reinforce its statements.[33] Therefore, this thesis uses empirical and quantitative analyses as well as longitudinal data to study the long-term development of large German enterprises.

The sample focuses on the 250 largest enterprises in Germany to ensure that the size of the companies is relatively similar. This is preferable because of three main reasons. First, a sample of large firms ensures that the effect of the liability of smallness is minimized.[34] Because companies are expected to have different survival rates depending on their size the sample should focus on a certain size range to ensure comparability. Furthermore, the enterprises in the sample have already proven that their business model works and survived their foundation phase. Otherwise, they would not have grown to become one of the largest enterprises in Germany. On the other hand, the companies in the sample are of various ages.[35] This could lead to a bias due to the liability of newness which states that with age the survival rate increases and therefore younger companies have a higher probability of failure. As highlighted in Section 2.1.1, a study should either include companies with similar characteristics in the sample or control for the expected impact. Because the main characteristic of the studied enterprises in this thesis is size[36] age is controlled for when analyzing the survival and failure rates. Other different age clusters are used in Section 6.1 to see whether younger or older companies have higher or lower rates.

Second, this thesis investigates how the largest family and non-family companies have developed rather than what happened to the new businesses founded in the observation period. This makes it possible to study enterprises which survived multiple generations instead of only one or two generations or even only one or two years. The long-term perspective is key because this is a research gap in current research. Despite this view the analysis is not able to explain and

---

[33] See Opgenoorth and Schulz (2010, pp. 192–206).

[34] See Section 2.1.1 for a description of the liability of newness and the liability of smallness. Further, see Seibold (2020, p. 32) for a similar approach regarding size.

[35] The overview of the size and age structure of both datasets, 1958 and 2018, can be found in Sections 5.1 and 5.5.

[36] Other attributes of the companies can also be used to prepare the sample. For example, Hermann Simon introduces the concept of "Hidden Champions" of which the majority, roughly two thirds, are family-owned businesses. The underlying attribute is leadership in a certain niche market (see Simon (2009, p. 285)). This type of company is not part of the largest enterprises. Therefore, the concept cannot be used to explain the development patterns of large enterprises.

understand what Pieper calls the "fallacy of the complete causal chain"[37]. This thesis provides an overview of the developments in the historical context and identifies patterns based on the companies' ownership structures. The underlying causal chains for each enterprise require additional research.

Third, the required historical information is more likely to be available for large enterprises compared to small and medium-sized enterprises (SME). The corporate reporting as well as the media coverage of large companies is more detailed and more extensive which ensures that the data is more reliable. At the same time, this choice is also a limitation to the study. The analyses provide insights into the development of the 250 largest enterprises only. Some of the observed developments may also be transferable to smaller companies but this requires further investigations.

The sample includes the 250 largest enterprises to ensure that the sample size is big enough to identify patterns in the development. For the analyses, the companies are categorized based on various variables like ownership structure or industry. Therefore, the sample is further broken down which lowers the number of companies for each category but still ensures a reasonable number of companies for the majority of categories.[38] Extending the sample beyond the 250th largest enterprise would further increase the variance within the sample which would lower the meaningfulness of the observed patterns. Furthermore, the identification of the list of the largest enterprises at a certain point in the past becomes less precise the larger the sample size from a historical perspective is. The number of unknown companies increases the smaller the companies to be identified become. Therefore, the sample is limited to 250 companies. Only industrial, trading and service companies are considered excluding financial institutions (e.g., banks, insurances, and investment companies) because of their fundamentally different business model.[39]

Besides the focus on the 250 largest enterprises this dissertation also focuses on Germany only mainly due to two reasons. First, research on the long-term development and especially the downfall of enterprises in Germany is rare as highlighted in Section 2.1.1. Second, the regional focus ensures that the (economic, social, cultural, legal and political) conditions as well as their changes

---

[37] Astrachan and Binz Astrachan (2021, p. 25).

[38] See Chapter 5 for an overview of the different categories.

[39] The indicators which are used to identify the size of the companies (e.g., revenue) cannot be compared due to the different business models (see, among others, Lantelme (2017, p. 32)).

over time are quite similar for all companies in the sample. In this dissertation, the reference to "Germany" covers the territory of the Federal Republic of Germany at the mentioned year.[40]

Furthermore, this thesis focuses on the business and economic perspective of the companies' development in the interpretation of the data and results but includes aspects of the other relevant dimensions like political and legal developments to provide a more in-depth analysis of the multi-dimensional historical processes (see Section 3.1). From recent publications of economic history the context in which the investigated enterprises operate over the last decades is included. This additional contextualization should help to better understand the observed developments in the observation period.

Based on the combination of historical and social science methods as well as the integration of quantitative analyses, the results of John Ward's famous study can be tested for another country and period. Moreover, the analyses will provide more details and insights into the long-term development of German enterprises. Overall, despite the previously described boundary conditions the research setup, the methodology and the data collection process address several of Ward's limitations as well as Stamm and Lubinski's proposals for the research on family business survival. In the next chapter the historical contextualization of the firms' developments is outlined before the results of the main analyses follow.

3.4 Applied Framework: Tracking Ownership, Operations and Solvency

In order to systematically analyze the enterprises' developments over 60 years and structure the historical events this thesis builds on the survival framework proposed by Josefy et al. This approach follows the interdisciplinary work which is often used by historians. A management study framework is applied on a historic research question to better understand the underlying processes and changes which are then further investigated.[41] Josefy et al.'s framework is based on the

[40] For example, the GDP for Germany includes the data of the former German Democratic Republic only from 1991 on. Companies headquartered in the state of Saarland are already considered in the sample after Saarland officially joins the Federal Republic of Germany as a state on 1st January 1957.

[41] See Section 3.1 for more details of the interdisciplinary ways of working.

review of 222 survival and failure studies.[42] The authors analyze firm survival and failure literature in the organizational research field which they claim is disjoint and needs to be organized as well as extended.[43] They identify three main reasons for this disjoint status. First, a firm's survival is often considered the ultimate goal of owners and managers which might not be valid for new ventures and their founders, for example, or from the perspective of other stakeholders. In line with this assumption failure is then considered the worst outcome. Second, survival and failure are often treated as a discrete outcome which undermines more specific developments like mergers and acquisitions or bankruptcy. Third, due to different theoretical approaches and their application to various samples the outcomes vary significantly and are hardly comparable.[44] Following these reasons and the literature review, Josefy et al. propose a multi-dimensional conceptualization of survival. In a first step, they contrast continuity and discontinuity of the three dimensions (1) operations, (2) ownership, and (3) solvency.[45] These dimensions are used both individually and in combination in the studies reviewed. In a second step, they distinguish survival across "firms' stage of development"[46] of which they identify the following three: (1) new ventures, (2) single-business unit (SBU) firms, and (3) diversified firms. The development stage of the firm has an impact if, for example, only parts of the company like a business unit continue or discontinue or ultimately the entire firm. In the following, these development stages as well as the multi-dimensional approach are described in more detail and are further developed to apply them to the research question of this thesis. At the same time, the framework is tested if it covers all cases observed in the dataset at hand.

Because the research object are the largest enterprises in Germany either in 1958 or 2018 the relevant development stages of companies of Josefy et al.'s framework are single business unit firms and diversified firms. Due to their size (revenue and / or number of employees) and due to their age[47] these companies

[42] See Josefy et al. (2017) and their first-of-its-kind review and framework development. For a general overview of the survival and failure literature and its evolvement to the framework see Sec. 2.1.1.

[43] See Josefy et al. (2017, pp. 770–771).

[44] See Josefy et al. (2017, p. 771).

[45] See Josefy et al. (2017, p. 775).

[46] Josefy et al. (2017, p. 777).

[47] Only two companies in the 1958 dataset and nine companies in the 2018 dataset are less than ten years old. Most of these companies are either carved out entities (e.g., *Ceconomy AG* or *Covestro AG*) or new foundations of already existing assets (e.g., *Hüttenwerke Siegerland AG* or *Handelsunion AG*). See Section Age5.5 for a more detailed analysis based on the age

are already mature firms. In both stages the companies are growing more stable with certain patterns and their structures are more formalized. Furthermore, diversified firms offer several products and / or operate in several geographic markets.[48] New ventures which are characterized as "[...] firms within a few years of inception that have more informal structures and generally are pursuing higher rates of growth than more mature organizations [...]"[49] are not part of the datasets of this thesis. Therefore, the datasets provide a relatively homogeneous sample of companies related to their development stage.

As a preliminary note regarding the three dimensions of the survival approach, Josefy et al. highlight the differences between their concept of continuation (as well as discontinuation) and performance which will become visible in several cases of the sample of this thesis as well:

> "Importantly, while we present outcomes across each dimension as opposite ends of a spectrum, we do not suggest that one represents success (or positive performance), while the other represents failure (or negative performance). Instead, we disentangle survival and failure from performance and simply identify a firm's continuation along a single dimension of survival relative to its inverse. Conceptualizing survival this way allows for a more nuanced understanding of survival and its implications that depends on the firm's stage of development and the goals of those running it."[50]

As an example from the dataset of this thesis, the continuation of ownership does not necessarily lead to a superior financial performance. Despite the same owner family from 1958 to 2018 which was also the founding family the revenue (as well as the number of employees) of *Christian Dierig AG* (later *Dierig Holding AG*) decreased during the observation period. Nevertheless, the ownership dimension continues over 60 years and the family keeps the business in the long-term.[51] A different example is the case of *August Thyssen-Hütte AG* (later *thyssenkrupp AG*). Between 1958 and 2018 the financial performance increased significantly with a revenue CAGR of 6.6%. Moreover, the number of employees

of the enterprises.

[48] See Josefy et al. (2017, p. 777).

[49] Josefy et al. (2017, p. 777).

[50] Josefy et al. (2017, p. 776).

[51] The relevant sources are *HdG*, *SAf*, Dierig (1993), Pöllmann (2005) and Dierig Holding AG (2019).

grew by 2.7% annually.[52] In the same period, the ownership dimension discontinued which led to a change of the company type from a family-owned business to a public company. The Thyssen family sold their shares over decades and did not participate in several capital increases. Therefore, their ownership decreased significantly and thus they also gave up their formative influence on the company. *August Thyssen-Hütte AG* became a public company.[53] Nevertheless, the operations continue and the company still exists today. Despite the discontinuation as a family-owned business the company has not failed. For such a case Wennberg, Wiklund, Hellerstedt, and Nordqvist state: "It should be stressed that exit by merger or acquisition need not be a sign of organizational failure. To the contrary, divesting their equity can, instead, be seen as the pinnacle of success for many firm owner-managers."[54]

Following these examples and focusing on the research questions, the key dimension of Josefy et al.'s framework for this thesis is the second one "ownership". Therefore, their multi-dimensional conceptualization is slightly adapted (see Figure 3.1). As explained in Sec. 2.2.2.1 based on ownership and the corresponding voting rights the owners (e.g., a family or anonymous shareholders as free float in an *AG*) can exert their influence on the corporate strategy, on personnel decisions as well as on operations and the use of funds. This means that the share measures the influence of the owners. The continuation of the ownership dimension means that the current owners remain in this position over the research period. Its discontinuation indicates a change of the owners due to a sale of the equity or due to an acquisition of the company (e.g., through a hostile takeover). The threshold if the ownership continues or discontinues is set at 50% which also indicates the type of company.[55] The example for the ownership discontinuation of a family-owned business is explained in the following. If a family owns more

---

[52] The data is based on the following sources: *HdG*, *SAf*, August Thyssen-Hütte AG (1959), Treue (1966), Bähr (2015) and thyssenkrupp AG (2018).

[53] The two family members Amélie Thyssen and her daughter Anita Countess Zichy-Thyssen owned around 50.74% of *August Thyssen-Hütte AG* in 1958 through two investment companies. Due to multiple required capital increases, the sale of shares as well as the donation of shares to the *Fritz Thyssen Foundation* the Thyssen family ultimately lost their ownership majority in 1964. By this time, further companies owned by the Thyssen family had been sold to *August Thyssen-Hütte AG* in exchange for shares to increase the family's stake and secure their influence (see Bähr (2015, p. 152)).

[54] Wennberg et al. (2011, p. 360). In the case of the Thyssen family one can probably not speak of a success because Amélie Thyssen tried to secure the family enterprise until her death in 1965 (see Bähr (2015, p. 157)). Nevertheless, the family secured its wealth, and the company is still operating.

[55] See Section 2.2.2 for the definitions.

than 50% of a German enterprise the company is classified as a family-owned business. As soon as the share of the family drops below the majority threshold of 50% within the observation period the ownership dimension discontinues as well as the categorization of the company as a family-owned business.[56] Because the ownership continuation is the basis for a multi-generational enterprise the long-term orientation of this family company vanishes. Nevertheless, the operations of the firm might continue under the new owner.

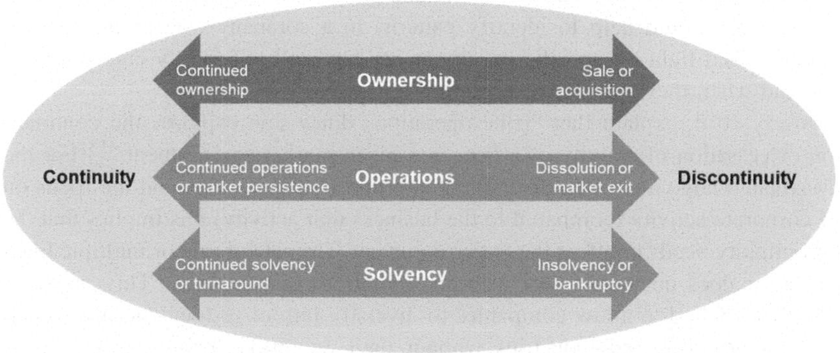

Figure 3.1 Multi-Dimensional Conceptualization of Survival. (Source: Author's own figure based on Josefy et al., 2017, p. 775)

To measure the continuity or discontinuity of the ownership variable the ownership structure of each company on the list of the 250 largest enterprises in 1958 is identified for the year 1958. Then, the ownership structures' developments until 2018 are tracked. Every change of the majority owner indicates a discontinuity while no change of the majority owner over the entire study period of 60 years indicates continuity. This definition also includes the case that a company does not have a majority owner in 1958, 2018 or in both years, e.g., a public company with their majority of shares in free float. Multiple discontinuities of the majority ownership can occur for one single company. The tracking of the developments is described in more detail in Section 3.7.1.2.

---

[56] Depending on the new majority owner the company is re-categorized as one of the eight types of companies. If the new majority owner is another family the company type is again set to "family-owned business". But because the ownership dimension discontinues the initial family business motive vanishes. Such changes are marked and reported separately in the results.

As mentioned above, the discontinuity of the ownership does not necessarily imply that the company discontinues its operations or its solvency. The disappearance of the firm is not automatically the case. Therefore, and although Josefy et al. state that "[...] each dimension need not be included in every article [...]"[57] the additional two dimensions from the framework "operations" and "solvency" are included in this thesis as well to provide a comprehensive overview of the development of the largest enterprises in Germany. Furthermore, this approach allows to track the evolution of a company and its different ownership stages over time (e.g., from a family-owned company to a public company or vice versa). This should help to identify patterns in a company's development process and shed light on specific developments especially of family enterprises if, how and when they get sold or acquired.

Josefy et al. explain that "[t]he operations dimension captures the continuation or cessation of activity of a firm in a given market environment."[58] For the investigated large and often diversified enterprises of this thesis and the focus on the corporate activity (compared to the business unit activity) this implies that the discontinuity needs to affect the entire company. The sale of one or multiple business units does not qualify for a firm's operations discontinuity. This approach is further applied to allow companies to diversify into or re-focus on other business opportunities and industries without their operations being recognized as discontinued (e.g., see the transformation of *Preußische Bergwerks- und Hütten AG (Preussag)* to *TUI AG* and their shift from ore mining to a travel agency and tour operator). If the company has relevant operations running and is acting at least on one market the dimension continues. If the company dissolves its entire operations or exits all markets in which it operates the dimension discontinues. This can also be the case if a company gets acquired by a strategic investor (ownership discontinuity) and gets integrated into the acquirer's organization or consolidated. Then, the acquired company does not act on a market by itself. The firm exits the market. On the contrary, if a company gets acquired by a strategic or financial investor (ownership discontinuity) but further acts on a market on its own the operations dimension continues (e.g., as a subsidiary company). A discontinuity of operations can also occur without an ownership discontinuity when a company ceases all its operations but remains as a legal entity with its existing owners. These cases are rare and often have special causes.[59] An indicator for

---

[57] Josefy et al. (2017, pp. 776–777).

[58] Josefy et al. (2017, p. 776).

[59] In the analysis of the dataset these cases occur for example after the foundation of *Ruhrkohle AG* in 1968 and the intended consolidation of several coalmining companies.

the operations dimension is also the company's revenue growth rate which shows the expansion or decline of the operational activities. Therefore, this rate is used to compare the enterprises from the datasets.

The last dimension introduced by Josefy et al. is "solvency". The continuity of this dimension is the continued solvency or a successful turnaround. The latter is less relevant for German enterprises because the German insolvency law focuses on the satisfaction of the creditors and not on the turnaround of the company.[60] Therefore, if a company in the sample of this thesis files for insolvency this third dimension discontinues. This incident is often followed by the discontinuity of one or even both of the other two dimensions because the insolvent company then stops to operate or even exist. In other cases, the company gets acquired and integrated or consolidated. If no insolvency is reported over the observation period, the dimension continues.

Overall, the continuity and discontinuity of the three dimensions ownership, operations and solvency are analyzed for each single enterprise between 1958 and 2018. Furthermore, because every company is categorized as one of the eight company types in 1958, in 2018 and after a majority ownership change the ownership continuity or discontinuity can also be aggregated on a company type level. This categorization helps to identify patterns in the development of each company type and allows a comparison of the different types over the study period of 60 years. Especially the development of family-owned businesses will be analyzed in detail to approach the research questions.

In the following, based on the three dimensions the criteria for the identification of the failure of a company are set. So far, only the discontinuity of ownership, operations and solvency are defined. A failed company is marked as *downfall* in the datasets. All other companies are referred to as *survivors*. Two downfall categories are distinguished. First, in the narrow definition a downfall occurs either (a) if a company's solvency discontinues, (b) if the owners decide to cease the company's operations or (c) if the firm's operations discontinue after the firm gets integrated or consolidated following a merger or acquisition (ownership discontinuity). Second and in a broader definition, downfalls include the three cases just described as well as (d) an ownership discontinuity due to an acquisition or merger but with continuing operations as a subsidiary company.

These companies transferred their operations and assets but remained as legal entities to receive dividends. Some of them started new operations in other markets (e.g., *Heinrich Bergbau AG*, see footnote 297) or were liquidated after the dividend payments stopped (see Abelshauser (1984)).

[60] See Paulus (2015) for a brief overview of the German insolvency law also in comparison to other countries.

As a subsidiary company the firm is in a dependent relationship with its parent company and further, the firm's financial results are generally consolidated in the financial statement of the parent company. An overview of the definitions can be found in Table 3.1 and both definitions are shown separately in the analyses.

Table 3.1 Definitions of Company Failures

Company downfall			**Discontinuity**		
			Ownership	**Operations**	**Solvency**
Broader definition	Narrow definition	(a)			X
		(b)		X	
		(c)	X	X	
		(d)	X	(X)	

Source: Author's own table.

The research and framework provided by Josefy et al. structures the observations of the developments of the largest enterprises by investigating three main dimensions. Based on these dimensions as well as their further development the firms' survival and failure but also their majority ownership changes can be observed. This helps to better understand development patterns of family and non-family companies.

Moreover, based on the number of downfalls and survivors the *downfall rates / failure rates* as well as the *survival rates* are calculated:

$$Downfall\ rate = \frac{Number\ of\ downfalls}{Sample\ size}$$

$$Survival\ rate = \frac{Nuber\ of\ survivors}{Sample\ size}$$

The sample size is defined by the total number of enterprises which are investigated in the calculation. If the failure rate of the entire sample of 250 enterprises is calculated the sample size is 250. If a sub-sample is used the sample size is smaller and the number of downfalls or survivors also refers only to this sub-sample (e.g., when investigating a specific company type or industry).

3.5 Applied Timeframe: 60 Years and Two Generations

As highlighted in Section 2.1 and Section 2.2.2.2, the timeframe used in the majority of current management and economics as well as family business studies is quite short despite the proclaimed long-term orientation and planning of the research object of family enterprises. To close this gap, the study period of this thesis ranges from 1958 to 2018 and covers 60 years of family and non-family ownership as well as of corporate development. This timeframe corresponds to the interval of around two family generations.[61] Furthermore, by choosing a 60 year period, this thesis is also in the tradition of John Ward's influential study of the life expectancy of 200 successful Illinois manufacturing companies between 1924 and 1984 published in 1987.[62] His research was and is still cited quite often (despite the shortcomings mentioned in Section 2.2.2.2) and is used as a reference for "the law of three generations".

The year 1958 as starting point of the research period is chosen because of three main reasons. First, from a historical perspective the firm as a type of a hierarchical organization for business transactions based on economic reasoning is rather new. In Germany it started to become the dominant type only in the second half of the 19th century favored by political, institutional and market changes. Especially due to the "Founders' Crash" (*Gründerkrach*) in 1873 and the subsequent depression, professional corporate structures often with functional departments as well as a corporate governance with a stronger separation of ownership and management were developed and implemented. Large firms became more and more bureaucratic corporations to deal with the increasing complexity due to their growing size as well as the growing need for debt capital. Smaller companies remained predominantly family-oriented (e.g., job vacancies were filled with family members instead of professional managers) with stronger patriarchal structures which also reflect the structure in the first stage of the development of the firm. Management was in the hand of the owner.[63] Because

[61] For a statistical reference of 44 countries see OECD (2019) with a mean age of mothers at birth at around 30 years. Further, for an anthropological analysis see Fenner (2005, p. 421), with a developed nations generation interval of 29.1 years (of male and female). For a sociological perspective of generations with a focus on entrepreneurship and family businesses see Lubinski (2016) who investigates the ambiguity of the term "generation"; on the one hand the break between two generations is highlighted while on the other hand and at the same time several generations refer to a continuous succession within a family.

[62] See Ward (2011) with the first publication date in 1987.

[63] See Plumpe (2018, pp. 22–26) and Brockstedt (1984) as well as Kocka (1980) for an international comparison.

this thesis focuses on the development of large enterprises, the beginning of the study period is set after the rise of the modern organization in the middle and at the end of the 19th century. It should be emphasized that with the emergence of the more bureaucratic corporation the influence of families on the development of enterprises has not stopped despite the mentioned changes. Large enterprises majority-owned and (partly) managed by families were and are still a dominant part of the corporate landscape. Several of the largest enterprises in the 20th century—not only in Germany—are family-owned and can be found in the dataset of this thesis which will be explained in more detail at a later stage (e.g., *Fried. Krupp, Robert Bosch GmbH* and *Neckermann Versand KG*). Nevertheless, the organizational structure and bureaucratic orientation including division and systematization of labor has changed and become more professional over the last 150 years—in family and non-family enterprises.[64]

Second, with the rise of the modern organization at the end of the 19th century and a subsequent economic upswing there were no stable conditions for corporations over the next decades. Only in the late 1950s the German economy and especially the economic framework conditions for enterprises became stable after devastating World War II which was marked by a strictly regulated war economy in Germany but also in nearly all other countries. This stabilization includes, as a basis, the establishment of the Federal Republic of Germany in 1949 comprising three of the four occupation zones as well as of subsequent economic reforms towards a more liberal economic system. Additionally, on an enterprise level, the disentanglement of syndicates and conglomerates like *I.G. Farben* and *Vereinigte Stahlwerke* had been executed in 1952 and in 1951/1954, respectively. After this the single enterprises started to develop (more or less) independently. The institutional factors became much more predictable, and owners and managers could operate under relatively stable conditions until today compared to the first decade after 1945. This can also be seen in the establishment of the *Bundeskartelamt* in 1958.[65] Also, before World War II since 1914 and the beginning of World War I there were only isolated normal years of economic activity.[66] Therefore, to have

---

[64] See Kocka (2004) for the historical development of organizational structures in the 19th and 20th century. He argues that larger enterprises had to find a way to deal with the increasing complexity due to their growing size. This happened by either introducing more bureaucratic structures or by a higher involvement of the owner's family but often by doing both. Further, see Sonfield and Lussier (2008) for a comparison of small and large US family firms and the differences in management activities (e.g. large family firms are more likely to use non-family members within the top management).

[65] See Section 4.3 for a more detailed overview.

[66] For an overview see Plumpe (2018, p. 27).

(relatively) stable conditions to make a comparison of the different developments of the enterprises investigated more reliable the starting point is set at the end of the 1950s.

Third, German enterprises and especially companies listed on the stock exchange with the legal form of an *Aktiengesellschaft* (*AG*)—stock corporation—started to publish more detailed and reliable business figures at the end of the 1950s. *Allgemeine Elektricitäts-Gesellschaft* (*AEG*) and *Brown, Boveri & Cie. AG* (*BBC*) are two examples which published their consolidated revenue in 1958 for the first time although they had been listed for decades.[67] Discussions of a revised version of the German *Aktiengesetz* (*AktG*)—Stock Corporation Act—with stricter disclosure requirements were ongoing and companies already implemented associated changes in their reporting (see Section 4.3 for an overview of the development of the *AktG* and the impact on the disclosure requirements). Based on these business figures available, newspapers began to create rankings listing the largest enterprises in Germany in the late 1950s. The business journalist Max Kruk published a first list of the 100 largest enterprises of 1958 based on revenue in the *Frankfurter Allgemeine Zeitung* (*FAZ*) in 1959.[68] At that time, he was aware that he did not capture all relevant enterprises because of non-disclosed revenue data (e.g., *Adam Opel AG*, *Christian Dierig AG* and *Dr. August Oetker*) but it was a starting point for an annual ranking which is still being published in the *FAZ* and is approaching completeness.[69]

Starting the study of the development of large enterprises in Germany in 1958 ensures stable political and institutional conditions as well as a maturity of corporate structures which also allow a more accurate and publicly available reporting of business figures.

2018 is chosen as the end date of the study period to cover 60 years of corporate development. Such a long observation period has several advantages. First, it ensures that the impact of short-term effects on the observed results is minimized. These short-term effects can be internal (e.g., the tenure of one CEO or one chairman of the supervisory board) or external (e.g., the current economic situation). Over six decades a (surviving) company experiences multiple leadership changes and navigates its business activities through several economic cycles including

[67] See Kruk (1959a) for a first comparison of *AEG*, *BBC* and *Siemens AG* after the first two firms published their consolidated revenue for the first time.

[68] See Kruk (1959b). Previous rankings often refer to share capital or number of employees as relevant variables—see Fiedler (1999, pp. 33–34) for an overview of existing rankings.

[69] For the latest edition using 2019 company data see Fehr and F.A.Z.-Archiv (2021) which includes multiple rankings covering among others family businesses as well as a list of the largest enterprises in Europe.

crises and upswings. The observed period from 1958 to 2018 represents an average of the corporate development and not only a snapshot of a certain point in time.

For family enterprises this implies that at least one succession process has taken place between 1958 and 2018—successfully or not. Family-owned businesses had the chance to execute their proclaimed long-term orientation and plan their intergenerational survival. In addition, during this study period the German economy developed from the reconstruction after World War II to the fourth largest economy in the world including all its upswings and downswings.[70] The enterprises had to adapt to the evolving economic developments and prove that their business models can last. It also ensures that the thesis uses the latest available data from the enterprises investigated with its start at the beginning of 2020.

Overall, the study period of 60 years is a major extension of the currently and predominantly used timeframes in family business research. This historical perspective allows studying the long-term development of the enterprises within a relatively stable political and institutional framework compared to previous decades. Furthermore, the period between 1958 and 2018 provides insights into the changes of a company's ownership, operations, and solvency.

3.6 Research Questions: Development of the Largest Enterprises in Germany

Based on the previously identified research gaps, the research objectives as well as the chosen methodology, the research questions are formulated. The main research question (MRQ) which guides through this dissertation is:

MRQ: How did the 250 largest enterprises of Germany develop between 1958 and 2018?

Additionally, sub-research questions (SRQ) are formulated to further investigate the relevant aspects of the various corporate developments or—on the level of the single enterprise—various corporate histories:

SRQ1: Which of the enterprises survive or fail between 1958 and 2018 and what underlying patterns can be identified?

[70] See Section 4.1 for the current economic status of Germany.

SRQ2: How do the enterprises' ownership structures change between 1958 and 2018 and which characteristic pattern can be identified?

SRQ3: How do the enterprises grow, stagnate or decline between 1958 and 2018 and which characteristic pattern can be identified?

This dissertation investigates all types of enterprises based on their ownership structure with a special focus on family businesses and their comparison especially with public companies. To answer some of the research questions various performance indicators are used, such as survival and downfall rates as well as growth rates.

The main research question is strongly influenced by the underlying historical sciences methodology. While addressing the research questions new propositions are coming up which will be further outlined in the result section.

In the next steps the research questions will be operationalized including the chosen timeframe and the data collection process.

3.7 Data Collection and Categorization: Comprehensive 7-Step Approach

Based on the research question the objective is to investigate the development of the 250 largest enterprises in Germany of 1958 and of 2018. To do so, two main datasets are created in a seven-step process illustrated in Figure 3.2. The variables in the datasets are chosen based on the underlying concepts of survival, failure and growth as well as the applied framework of ownership, operations and solvency discussed in Sections 2.1 and 3.4. For the data collection primary and secondary sources are used following the methodological standards of the historical and social sciences as outlined in Sections 3.1 and 3.2. It needs to be considered that because of the long study period of 60 years the available and reliable data especially for the enterprises in 1958 and the development tracking is widely scattered. Recent databases only cover a fraction of the study period and can only be used for the status collection in 2018.[71] Therefore, a comprehensive process needs to be implemented to collect all relevant data and to structure it. Moreover, all collected information for the datasets was tested against and supplemented by additional sources. This should ensure a high validity and the correct

[71] Exemplary, the *dafne* database of *Bureau van Dyk* provides financial and ownership data only from 2009 until today.

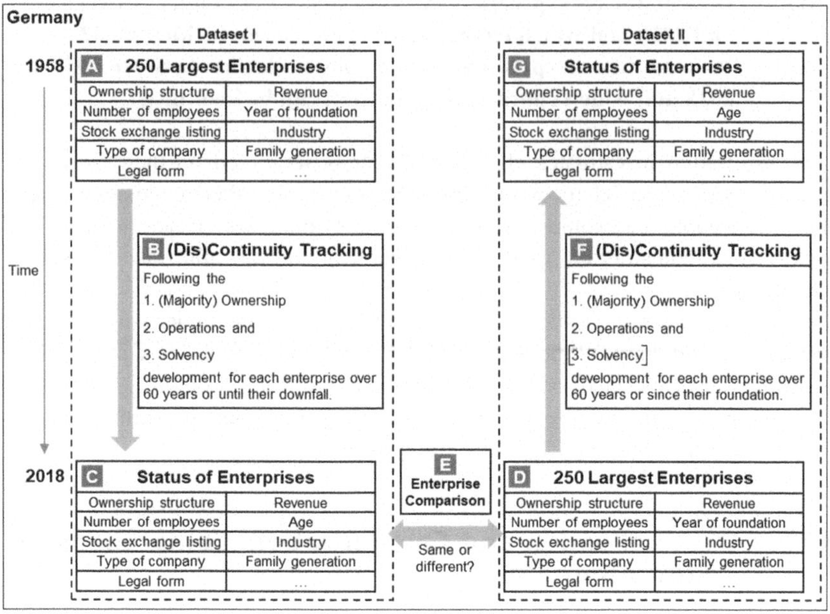

Figure 3.2 7-Step Datasets Creation. (Source: Author's own figure)

recording of the past events to also contribute to the business and economic history by preserving the historical data and providing a more accurate ranking than currently exists. This contribution to historical sciences is an objective of this thesis as mentioned in Section 1.3.

For Dataset I, in **Step A**, a list of the 250 largest enterprises of 1958 based on revenue is created and key variables collected for each company. In **Step B** the development of the enterprises is tracked until 2018 or until the downfall of the company, respectively. All changes of the (majority) ownership structure, the operations and solvency for each firm are captured. **Step C** analyses the status of each of the 250 firms of 1958 which survived until 2018 by collecting the data for the key variables.

Dataset II is set up by creating a list of the 250 largest enterprises of 2018 based on revenue in **Step D**. Again, the data for the key variables of each company is collected. In **Step E**, the 2018 list is compared with the 2018 status of the 250 largest enterprises of 1958. For all duplicates, their status in 1958 (from Step A) and their developments from (Step C) are copied to Dataset II. For all other companies the developments of their (majority) ownership, their operations, and in a limited manner of solvency back to 1958 are investigated in **Step F. Step G** closes with the collection of the status of the 250 firms of 2018 in 1958.

To provide more insights into the creation of the datasets and its validity the various steps are described in more detail in the following subchapters including their sources and initial outcomes.

3.7.1 Dataset I: The (Dis)Continuity of the 250 Largest Enterprises of 1958

Dataset I provides an overview of the 250 largest enterprises of 1958 including extended company information and key performance indicators. Moreover, it tracks the enterprises' developments by capturing the (majority) ownership, operations and solvency changes over 60 years. Thus, not only the successful and surviving companies are considered in the analyses, but also companies which declined, were acquired or even went into insolvency. For all surviving companies their status in 2018 is captured.

3.7.1.1 Step A: Identifying the 250 Largest Enterprises of 1958

As highlighted in Section 3.5, in 1959 the journalist Max Kruk published his first list of the 100 largest enterprises in Germany in the newspaper *FAZ*. The list includes the company names and their revenue figures for 1958. Where data was available at the time, revenue figures from 1957 and employee numbers from 1957 and 1958 are also added.[72] This ranking is the starting point for **Step A** of the Dataset I creation—the list of the 250 largest enterprises of 1958.

First, the data of the newspaper article is triangulated using primary sources where available and secondary sources where necessary. For this purpose, the annual reports for the financial year 1958[73] are checked. Many of them are physically available in various German libraries, among others in the library of the

[72] See Kruk (1959b). In addition, large subsidiaries and legal entities of ranked companies are part of the list but they do not have their own ranking number because they are not independent, and their revenue is already included in the revenue of their parent enterprise (e.g., *Siemens AG's* subsidiary *Siemens-Schuckertwerke AG* is listed behind #19 without being on #20 because its revenue is already attributed to *Siemens AG* on #2).

[73] If the financial year does not match with the calendar year 1958 the financial year 1957 / 1958 is used. Many of the mining and steel companies but also industrial manufacturing companies (e.g., *August Thyssen-Hütte AG* and *Siemens & Halske AG*) started their financial year in October and still do.

Deutsches Museum (Munich), in the Bavarian State Library (Munich) and in the library of the Leibniz Information Centre for Economics (Kiel), or in archives like the *Bayerische Wirtschaftsarchiv* (Munich). Nevertheless, the annual reports are predominantly available only for listed companies. Therefore, and if the figures between Kruk's list and the primary sources do not match, additional sources are consulted including newspaper articles from e.g., *Die ZEIT*, articles from news magazines like *DER SPIEGEL* or corporate publications like anniversary publications to validate the numbers. If discrepancies persist and no additional sources can be found or exist figures from primary sources are used for the dataset creation instead of figures from secondary sources. However, the sources must be critically evaluated especially anniversary publications and other corporate publications which often also have a promotional intent.[74]

The publication series "*Handbuch der Großunternehmen*" [*Handbook of Large Enterprises*] (*HdG*) as well as "*Saling Aktienführer*" [*Saling Share Guide*] (*SAf*) are two additional key secondary sources to validate the company figures and add the information for other company variables relevant for this thesis. Both publications are among the most comprehensive data collections of the time and have been published on a regular basis by *Verlag Hoppenstedt & Co* for years. The *HdG* edition published in 1959 as well as the *SAf* editions published in 1958 and 1959 cover most of the relevant data for 1958.[75] In some cases later editions are used to extract the relevant information for the companies. The *HdG* can also be found as a key data source in the study already mentioned by Lubinski on the long-term development of German companies and their corporate governance structures in Düsseldorf and Munich.[76]

Besides validating the revenue and the number of employees, all the above-mentioned primary and secondary sources are used to collect the following variables for every enterprise in 1958. Each variable is described in the section below.

In Dataset I, the official company name in 1958 is added instead of an abbreviation often found in Kruk's list; for example, *Rudolph Karstadt AG* is used instead of *Karstadt*. Furthermore, the city of the company's headquarters is extracted to validate if the company was part of the federal territory at that time. The year of foundation refers to the initial setup of the company regardless of whether

[74] See Section 3.1 for a description of source criticism.

[75] For the *HdG* 1959 edition see Verlag Hoppenstedt & Co. (1959a) and Verlag Hoppenstedt & Co. (1959b); for the *SAf* 1958 and 1959 editions see Verlag Hoppenstedt & Co. (1958) and Verlag Hoppenstedt & Co. (1959c).

[76] See Lubinski (2010, pp. 50–55). Further, *HdG* is also used by F.-M. Weber (2005) in his long-term study.

Table 3.2 250 Largest Enterprises of 1958: List of 1958 Variables

#	Dataset I 1958 variable	Description
D1-58-01	Official company name	Firm name including legal form (if applicable)
D1-58-02	Headquarters	City of the headquarters in Germany
D1-58-03	Year of foundation / Age	Initial year when the company was founded and calculation of age
D1-58-04	Revenue	In million DM and converted to million EUR
D1-58-05	Number of employees	In thousand
D1-58-06	Ownership structure	Identification of shareholders / partners and their voting rights
D1-58-07	Type of company	Based on ownership structure classification of company type
D1-58-08	Family generation	Number of family generation by which a family business is owned
D1-58-09	Stock exchange listing	Identification if company is listed on a stock exchange
D1-58-10	Industry	Main industry affiliation
D1-58-11	Legal form	Identification of legal form (e.g., *AG*, *KGaA*, *GmbH*)

Source: Author's own table.

the legal form has been changed in the meantime.[77] Moreover, several companies were re-established after World War II due to their disentanglement from conglomerates or corporate groups like *Farbenfabriken Bayer AG*, *BASF Badische Anilin- & Soda-Fabrik AG*, *Farbwerke Hoechst AG vormals Meister Lucius & Brüning* and *Chemische Werke Hüls AG* from *I.G. Farben* AG. Exemplary, *Bayer* was initially founded in 1863 but re-established in 1951 based on the decision of the Allied High Commission. A similar decision by the Allied High Commission to deconcentrate the ownership structures after World War II was the liquidation and re-establishment of *August Thyssen-Hütte AG* in 1953 although

[77] This is necessary to mention because especially in *SAf* the year of foundation often refers to the foundation of the *AG* instead of the initial foundation of the company, e.g., *Siemens* was initially founded in 1847 while the change to / the foundation of *Siemens AG* was in 1897.

the initial year of foundation is 1891.[78] For the datasets of this thesis the initial year of foundation—for *Bayer* 1863 and for *Thyssen* 1891—is used to capture the entire period in which the organizations have developed.[79] Using the data of the reestablishment would wipe out the entire previous development phases. Based on this initial year the age of the company in 1958 is calculated. The reported revenue in 1958 represents the total revenue which the company generated globally and is not limited to Germany. The figure is stated in millions and converted from *Deutsche Mark* (*DM*) to euros (EUR) using the official and irrevocable conversion rate of $EUR1 = DM\ 1.95583$ which is provided by *Deutsche Bundesbank*.[80] This allows the comparison of the 1958 and 2018 figures and the calculation of growth rates as explained later. Several sources from the 1950s (e.g., *HdG*) show two or even three separate figures for a company's number of employees. The data is often divided into blue-collar and white-collar workers as well as apprentices. For all datasets used in this thesis the numbers of employees include all employee types to ensure comparability between companies and years. In 2018 this separation of the complement of staff is rather the exemption than the standard. Furthermore, the numbers refer to reported figures for the end of the financial year instead of the average of the financial year because the latter one is less commonly reported. As a last step, the employee figures are converted into thousands to shorten them for a streamlined overview.

Ownership structure is one of the key variables whose development is tracked between 1958 and 2018. First, it is identified for the year 1958. For this specific variable the additional secondary source *"Wer gehört zu wem"* (*Wgzw*) published by *Commerzbank AG* provides valuable insights besides the *HdG* and *SAf*. Several of the larger enterprises are covered by this publication including their entire shareholder structure or at least an indication of the majority owner. The ownership structure is analyzed as detailed as possible by trying to identify all owners and their corresponding shares. The decisive factor for determining the owner of a company are the associated voting rights. Exemplary for this is the possible distinction in the *AG* or *KGaA* between common stocks (*Stammaktien*) and preferential stocks (*Vorzugsaktien*). In general, common stocks carry voting rights while the voting right can be precluded for a preferential stock. This is contrasted by the preferential right in the distribution of profits for a preferential

[78] See Treue (1966, 1969) for the history of *August Thyssen-Hütte AG*.

[79] In the 19th century, Thyssen was a leader in implementing new management systems like vertical integration, a multidivisional structure and control systems (see Fear (2005)).

[80] See Deutsche Bundesbank (2014).

stock.[81] This type of share can be seen as a tool to safeguard the control of a company.[82] A current example is *Henkel AG & Co. KGaA* which is listed on the stock exchange and has issued both types of stocks. The Henkel family remains the majority owner of the common stocks with the corresponding voting rights and can therefore have a decisive influence on the development of the company. On the other hand, due to the issued preferential stocks which are all in free float the family participates to a lesser extent in the financial success of the company in proportion to their share of voting rights.[83] Overall, by exercising their voting rights owners of common stocks can impact corporate decisions while owners of preferential shares only participate in the financial success of the company. Therefore, voting rights are the key indicator of the ownership structure of an enterprise in this thesis. This definition also follows the power subscale of the F-PEC model in which the proportion of share ownership held by the family is measured by their voting rights "[w]hen the percentage of voting rights differs from percentage of ownership […]"[84].

In addition, linked to the distinction between common and preferential stocks is the impact of multiple voting rights on the ownership structure. Despite their general prohibition since the 1937 reform of the *AktG* a limited extent of multiple voting rights has been newly granted to organizations through the exemption of the responsible authority. Moreover, existing multiple voting rights did not have to be abolished and therefore still existed in Germany in 1958. The standard approach "one share, one vote", which was part of the German Corporation Law at that time and still is, was thus partially undermined by certain shares carrying multiple voting rights.[85] These special cases must be considered when investigating the ownership structure especially of an *AG* to fully capture the actual voting rights ratios. *Siemens AG* is such an example and will be discussed in Section 3.7.3 in more detail.

Besides the three main sources, *HdG*, *SAf* and *Wgzw* mentioned above, hundreds of newspaper articles from the 1950s and 1960s are analyzed to identify

[81] For the current law see §§139–141 AktG. Preferential stocks have a long tradition in the German Corporation Law and already existed in 1958 and before. For the development of preferential stocks in Germany see Daske (2019, pp. 9–50).

[82] See Ehrhardt and Nowak (2002).

[83] See Henkel AG & Co. KGaA (2019) for the distribution of stocks in 2018 and Figure 3.3 for its development.

[84] Astrachan et al. (2002, p. 55). Furthermore, see the definition of the Family Business Index of the University of St. Gallen which also defines family businesses based on the voting rights (see Center for Family Business at the University of St.Gallen (2021)).

[85] See Kropff (2007, p. 707).

the ownership structures and voting rights of the enterprises Kruk lists in his article in 1959. The online archives of *FAZ*, *DIE ZEIT*, *Handelsblatt*, and *Der Spiegel* with articles since the mid and late1940s, as well as the printed journal volumes of the dedicated business publication "*Blick durch die Wirtschaft*"[86] since 1958 are used for this purpose. For all 100 enterprises the ownership structures can be identified.[87] Based on these structures and the definitions of the company types elaborated in Section 2.2.2 each of the enterprises is categorized into one of the eight company types to allow a comparison within and between different categories.

Following the company type structure, two enterprises from Kruk's initial list need to be removed from the dataset because in 1958 they had been subsidiary companies of other German enterprises mentioned in the list. Therefore, they are not considered as independent companies. The two companies are (1) *Union Rheinische Braunkohlen Kraftstoff AG* which was ranked on position 75 (#75) in Kruk's list and majority owned by *Rheinisch-Westfälisches Elektrizitätswerk AG* (#22) via two subsidiary companies as well as (2) *Orenstein-Koppel und Lübecker Maschinenbau AG* (#90) which was part of *Hoesch AG* (#19).[88] On the other hand, one company which Kruk identifies as a subsidiary needs to be considered as independent. *Bochumer Verein für Gußstahlfabrikation AG* was acquired by *Hütten- und Bergwerke Rheinhausen AG* (part of *Krupp*) only in 1959 after the confirmation by the *High Authority of the European Coal and Steel Community* in January of the same year. Prior and especially at the end of 1958, *Bochumer Verein* was a public company with a large portion of their shares owned by several banks.[89] Overall, 99 companies from Kruk's list are used for the next steps in Dataset I.

Based on the company type definitions, if a company has been categorized as a family-owned business the current family generation in 1958 which owns the company is identified. A founder-owned enterprise is labeled as first generation. If the company already experienced a succession the business is in the second generation, with two experienced successions in the third generation and so on. For this purpose, publicly available family trees, newspaper articles as well as

[86] See Frankfurter Allgemeine Zeitung (1959a) as well as the later editions.

[87] The data sources for each figure or company information including the ownership structure can be requested from the author of this thesis.

[88] The sources for the ownership structures in 1958 are *SAf* for the first mentioned and *SAf* as well as *Wgzw* for the second mentioned company.

[89] See FAZ (1959).

company chronicles are used.[90] In few cases where no information about the current family generation can be found the generation is estimated based on its average length of 30 years as presented in Section 3.5. However, this procedure is only the exception. Stamm & Lubinski highlight that a generation in the context of corporate ownership "may vary tremendously, depending not only on the—rather arbitrarily set—starting and end points, but also on the age of the family entrepreneurs, the age-difference between parents and children, unforeseen life events, or personal interpretations"[91]. Despite this criticism, the family generation provides insights into the number of successions within a family business and this information enables a comparison of the companies especially when these enterprises do not survive until 2018. Then, the generation in which they go down can be captured. Furthermore, if the company survives until 2018 the current family generation is also captured. If more generations own the company at the same time the number of the younger generation is used.[92]

The stock exchange listing of an enterprise is primarily identified using the 1958 edition of *SAf* which covers 803 companies listed on a German stock exchange with a cut-off date of end of October 1958. If a company is not covered by this publication it is re-checked with the 1959 edition of *SAf* as well as the business publication "*Blick durch die Wirtschaft*". If they do not indicate that a company is listed, it is labeled as non-listed. This variable makes a comparison between listed and non-listed enterprise across all company types and within a company type possible. Moreover, it allows to check for the postulated development of companies introduced by Alfred D. Chandler from a family-owned firm towards other governance structures like a public company.[93]

The industry affiliation of a company in 1958 is extracted from *HdG*. Twelve different industries (e.g., mining, trade, and transport) and in total 55 sub-industries (e.g., lignite mining, wholesale and foreign trade, and air transport) are distinguished. A company can have more than one industry affiliation in *HdG* based on their business activities. For the upcoming analyses the key industry of each company is identified and used as main industry affiliation. Furthermore, each of the industry and sub-industry categories from 1958 is translated into a *WZ 2008* code which is the official Classification of Economic Activities of the

[90] See as an example James (2006, pp. 387–392) for the family tree of the Haniel family and the company chronicle of *Franz Bruch* the predecessor company of *Globus Holding GmbH & Co. KG.*

[91] Stamm and Lubinski (2011, p. 122).

[92] Similar to Lubinski (2010, p. 63); as an example, if the founder and his son are the joint owners, the company is in the second generation.

[93] See A. D. Chandler (1977) as well as Section 2.2.1.

Federal Statistical Office of Germany based on the Statistical Classification of Economic Activities in the European Community.[94] This classification is much more detailed than the 1958 classification of *HdG.* The *WZ* codes are categorized in 21 broad industry groups and additional four sub-levels of each group. The most refined level, level 5, has 839 different codes. To ensure a comparability between 1958 and 2018 the 1958 industry classifications including the sub-industries are translated into the matching 2018 code. Afterwards, from the 2018 code the first level classification is used for the final industry of a company. This first level ranges from A for "agriculture, forestry and fishing" to U for "activities of extraterritorial organizations and bodies". Exemplary, the 1958 industry category of *Deutsche Lufthansa AG* is "air transport" [*Luftverkehr*]. In *WZ 2008* this category has the code "51". This code is part of the first level category "transportation and storage" [*Verkehr und Lagerei*] which is abbreviated with the letter "H". Therefore, the industry category for *Deutsche Lufthansa AG* in 1958 is "transportation and storage".[95]

As an additional variable the legal form of each enterprise is identified. The dataset is not limited to specific legal forms. While the information for *AGs* or *GmbHs* is often evident based on the firm's name the legal form of partnerships is not. *HdG* provides the required information for several companies but not for all. Therefore, newspaper articles and business registers from 1958 are used to collect the missing data. The legal form is of importance because it is the basis for the structure of the corporate governance.

After having validated the 99 enterprises from Kruk's initial article as independent and collected the required information for all the eleven variables the list of the largest enterprises needs to be expanded to 250 companies for a more comprehensive and insightful analysis. For this purpose, the two publications *HdG* and *SAf* are entirely examined for large enterprises. Overall, *HdG* covers 11,504 German enterprises while *SAf* provides information on 803 (1958) and 788 (1959) companies respectively listed on German stock exchanges.

From *HdG* all enterprises with more than 1,000 employees and / or more than DM 70 million in revenue are extracted to ensure that all potential candidates of the largest 250 enterprises are included. It needs to be noted that in *HdG*

---

[94] For the entire economic activity classification see German Federal Statistical Office (2008).

[95] The classifications D "electricity, gas, steam and air conditioning supply" and E "water supply; sewerage, waste management and remediation activities" are combined to "energy and water". Further, the categories M "professional, scientific and technical activities", N "administrative and support service activities" and S "other service activities" are combined to "service activities" to ensure a better comparability with the 1958 categories.

revenue and employee information are not available for all 11,504 companies. For some enterprises only one of the two or even none of the figures are available. Therefore, additional sources are used to identify the largest enterprises as explained later. Applying the thresholds to *HdG* around 1,000 large companies can be identified. Conducting the same method to *SAf* no additional enterprise can be added because all the 803 and 788 listed companies are already included in *HdG*. Nevertheless, *SAf*, provides the relevant information of a company's listing. For all identified enterprises with more than 1,000 employees for which no revenue data is provided in *HdG* more research is required. Again, based on newspaper articles and company publications the missing data is collected. Not for all the extracted enterprises the revenue figure can be identified but for the majority. After checking all companies, a list of 453 enterprises with more than DM 70 million in revenue can be compiled which is then sorted by revenue. This ranking is merged with Kruk's initial list and duplicates are removed. Because the focus is on the largest 250 enterprises the new list is shortened to 250 companies.[96]

To evaluate the impact of the previously described research, Kruk's initial list of the 100 largest enterprises in 1958 is compared with the 100 largest enterprises of the newly created list. Only 79 companies (already including *Bochumer Verein* which was marked as a subsidiary company by Kruk) from the initial list are included in the new top 100 list. This shows that 21 additional companies could be identified. Furthermore, the 100th largest company on Kruk's list, *Didier-Werke AG* with a revenue of DM 176 million, is now at position 143. 44 additional companies with a revenue larger than DM 176 million could be identified. Most likely, Kruk did not include them in his list because he was not aware of their company sizes or able to identify their revenue figures. In the accompanying text of his list, he already indicates this lack of transparency. This shows the advantages of the historical method with its access to data of decades which is outlined in the next paragraph. Overall, the list of the 250 largest enterprises in 1958 includes 151 new firms compared to Kruk's initial list.

Some of the required company variables can only be identified based on the historical approach used in this thesis. For example, some revenue figures for 1958 were not published until years later due to stricter disclosure requirements and the legal need to publish figures for previous years. In other cases, some companies published their historical revenue figures for their anniversaries

---

[96] Besides the reasons mentioned in Section 3.3, investigating all the 453 identified enterprises would require many more resources because with decreasing size of the company most likely less information is available or accessible.

only decades later.[97] Furthermore, at the end of the 1950s and at the beginning of the 1960s several enterprises only provided the percentage changes in their revenue to the public. No absolute figures had been made available in annual reports and newspaper articles or provided even at annual meetings (e.g., *Schering AG, Accumulatoren-Fabrik AG* and *Allgemeine Deutsche Philips Industrie GmbH (Alldephi)*). Only years later, these companies started to provide the absolute figures (e.g., *Schering AG* and *Accumulatoren-Fabrik AG* in 1961 and *Alldephi* in 1964) based on which the revenue of 1958 can be calculated using the percentage changes of the previous years.

The data for the variables of Table 3.2 needs to get collected for the additional 151 enterprises, as well. The process follows the previously described collection activities for each variable using primary as well as secondary sources. Again, the data points are triangulated with additional independent sources if available. At the end of the process all required data for the 250 largest enterprises in 1958 are available except some missing employee figures (e.g., for *Metallgesellschaft AG* and *Rewe Zentrale Deutscher Lebensmittel-Großhandels-Genossenschaften eGmbH*). Most importantly, the ownership structures for all 250 companies could be identified.

The descriptive statistics of the 250 largest enterprises in 1958 can be found in Chapter 5.

3.7.1.2 Step B: Tracking the (Dis)Continuity of the 250 Largest Enterprises of 1958 until 2018

In Step B, the developments of the 250 largest enterprises of 1958 are tracked. All changes of their (majority) ownership, operations, and solvency are captured until 2018. If a change occurs in one of the three dimensions the dimension discontinues. If no change occurs the dimension continues. Depending on the discontinuity the tracking is stopped (e.g., for insolvencies) or continued (e.g., for majority ownership changes).

As outlined in Section 3.4, the focus of this thesis is the continuity or discontinuity of the ownership dimension with a view to examine the long-term orientation of family-owned businesses. The operations and solvency dimensions are further tracked to identify if a company fails, either by dissolution (discontinuity of operations) or by insolvency / bankruptcy (discontinuity of solvency). If this is the case ownership discontinues in most cases as well. On the other hand,

[97] Exemplary, the company history of *Franz Bruch*, the predecessor company of *Globus Holding GmbH & Co. KG*, published in 1995 by a family member, provides the revenue data for 1958 which had not been disclosed until then.

if only the ownership dimension discontinues by a change of the majority owner, this does not imply that the enterprise fails. It can further operate as usual and be solvent only under a new owner. Nevertheless, for a family firm it implies that the company does not continue as family firm anymore but as a different company type. For the objective of this thesis, the discontinuity of a family firm based on the ownership dimension implies the end of the of multi-generational concept of the family company. In the empirical results the changes from one company type in 1958 to another in 2018 are presented. However, if only the owner changes and the company continues its operations, the company can also be included in the list of 2018 (Step D).

The starting point to track the development of the 250 enterprises are the collected ownership structures from Step A. Then, again, company publications, stock exchange documents as well as online and offline archives from *FAZ*, *DIE ZEIT*, *Handelsblatt*, *Der Spiegel*, *WirtschaftsWoche* and *manager magazin* are used to identify any change in one of the three dimensions. Moreover, corporate archives are visited or contacted to collect the necessary information (among others the corporate archives of *Bahlsen GmbH & Co. KG*, *Bertelsmann SE & Co. KGaA* and *Villeroy & Boch AG*). If a majority ownership change is identified, it is also analyzed if the operations or solvency dimension discontinues, and the company fails. The same applies vice versa. If an operations or solvency change is identified it needs to be confirmed if the ownership discontinues as well, although it is very likely. During the analysis of the change all relevant information is extracted including (1) which dimensions are affected, (2) the year in which the change happens, (3) the new ownership structure after the change (if applicable) as well as (4) the reason for the change.

For family-owned companies the year in which the change occurs is important to identify the family generation which was in charge of the discontinuity. Furthermore, for all company types the year is important to place the change in its historical context (e.g., from a state-owned enterprise to a public company during a wave of privatization or the downfall of many coal mines due to the consolidation process in the Ruhr area).

Based on the ownership structure after the discontinuity of the ownership dimension the new company type is defined if operations and solvency are continued, for example, the development from a family-owned enterprise to a public company via an initial public offering (IPO) and the sale of the majority of shares of the family. If the operations and solvency discontinue then the company fails.

For the reasons of change the following categories are identified based on the observed discontinuations of one of the three dimensions in the sample:

1. Acquisition
2. Merger
3. Consolidation
4. IPO
5. Insolvency
6. Liquidation
7. Foundation
8. Privatization
9. Other

Reason 1 and 2, acquisition and merger, can be further divided by adding the company type of the acquirer or the merger partner. An acquisition always leads to the discontinuity of ownership but not necessarily to the discontinuity of operations. A discontinuity of solvency is not observed after an acquisition. Nevertheless, due to an insolvency the ownership dimension can change because the company is taken over from insolvency. These special cases are highlighted in the presented results of the sample.

It needs to be mentioned that for one enterprise multiple changes can be tracked, for example if different majority owners discontinue their involvement in the same company one after the other between 1958 and 2018. If a company does not fail further changes can occur. This is the case for *Helmut Horten AG*. In 1969, the owner, Helmut Horten (founder and first generation), floats 50% of the company's shares on the stock exchange. The family loses their majority and decreases their share even further over the next years. 15 years later, in 1984, *British American Tobacco* (*B.A.T.*) acquires the majority in listed *Horten* which they sell to the German bank *WestLB AG* six years later in 1990. An additional change and discontinuation of ownership occurs in 1994 when *Kaufhof Warenhaus AG* (part of the *Metro Group* at that time) buys the majority. The new parent enterprise integrates and consolidates the *Horten* department stores in the subsequent years. This last ownership transfer also leads to the discontinuity of operations and the failure of the company. For the analysis of family-owned companies, the initial discontinuation of the majority ownership in 1969 is important. After this event the enterprise ceases to exist as a family business already in the first generation and becomes a public company. Later they operate as a foreign subsidiary and in the end, *Horten* becomes a subsidiary company of another German department store chain and gets consolidated.

Despite this comprehensive approach a limitation needs to be mentioned. The historical analysis starts in 1958 with the status quo of the ownership structure. Based on this structure the company type is defined. Furthermore, the year of foundation is collected as part of the variables. Nevertheless, majority ownership changes between the year of foundation and 1958 are not captured in the analysis. Therefore, only a part of a company's development is analyzed. This limitation is partly addressed by capturing the owner generation of all family enterprises which provides insights how long the business is owned by the same family.

Capturing all majority ownership changes in the observation period ensures that not only a change of the type of the company (e.g., family business to public company) is registered but also the discontinuity of the ownership from one family to another family. Contrary to all the described discontinuities, a company can also continue in all three dimensions until 2018 without any change. This development is also highlighted in the results.

3.7.1.3 Step C: Assessing the Status of the 250 Largest Enterprises of 1958 in 2018

In the third and last step of the creation of Dataset I, the status of the 250 largest enterprises of 1958 for the year 2018 is collected. This applies only for the companies which survived over the study period of 60 years. For failed enterprises, the final year of an identified operations or solvency discontinuity is the last year of their existence. In total, 15 variables describe the status of each enterprise in 2018 (see Table 3.3).

Table 3.3 250 Largest Enterprises of 1958: List of 2018 Variables

#	Dataset I 2018 variable	Description
D1-18-01	Official company name	Firm name including legal form (if applicable)
D1-18-02	Headquarters	City of the headquarters in Germany
D1-18-03	Age	Age in 2018 based on the initially collected year of foundation
D1-18-04	Revenue	In million EUR
D1-18-05	Revenue CAGR	CAGR of revenue between 1958 and 2018
D1-18-06	Number of employees	In thousand
D1-18-07	Number of employees CAGR	CAGR of number of employees between 1958 and 2018
D1-18-08	Ownership structure	Identification of shareholders / partners and their voting rights

(continued)

Table 3.3 (continued)

#	Dataset I 2018 variable	Description
D1-18-09	Type of company	Based on ownership structure classification of company type
D1-18-10	Family generation	Number of family generation by which a family business is owned
D1-18-11	Parent enterprise	If the company becomes a subsidiary the name of the parent enterprise is identified
D1-18-12	Stock exchange listing	Identification if company is listed on a stock exchange
D1-18-13	Industry	Main industry affiliation
D1-18-14	Legal form	Identification of legal form (e.g., *AG*, *KGaA*, *GmbH*)
D1-18-15	Downfall	Indicator whether a company fails or survives between 1958 and 2018

Source: Author's own table.

Starting with the last variable in the table, a company from the 1958 list might not exist anymore in 2018 as described above. There can be several reasons why this could be the case and they are discussed in the previous chapter in more detail. For the 2018 status it is primarily important to capture whether a company failed or survived within the study period of 60 years. If a company failed, no other variables need to and can be captured for the 2018 status. Otherwise, if the enterprise survives the company's official name in 2018 is identified. For example, the enterprise *Volkswagenwerk GmbH* in 1958 survived until 2018 and changed their name to *Volkswagen AG.* in 1985.[98]

Using a similar approach like for the 1958 variables the data for the following 2018 variables is collected: Headquarters, age, revenue, number of employees, ownership structure, type of company, family generation, stock exchange listing, industry, and legal form. The key difference are the used sources. For the 2018 status, many more primary sources are available, especially company publications like annual reports and profiles which are often accessible on the firm's website. In addition, the online database *dafne*[99] provides a comprehensive collection of relevant company information for more than one million listed and non-listed firms in Germany. The database, a secondary source, also includes ownership

---

[98] See Lupa (2008, p. 132).

[99] See Bureau van Dijk (2021) for an overview of the database.

structures for several companies and the industry affiliations based on *WZ* codes. For the 2018 industry variable the primary *WZ* code is used. If the primary *WZ* code does not provide sufficient information about the main industry the secondary *WZ* codes are investigated. If the main industry can still not be identified additional research is conducted to capture the industry classification. Among others company websites and industry associations are used. From the identified *WZ* code the first level, e.g., transportation and storage, is used. This industry variable is compared with the 1958 industry affiliation to understand if a company has radically changed its industry focus. A detailed analysis of the entire product and service portfolio of each enterprise cannot be performed in this thesis, but the overall industry affiliation and their changes can be identified. Several examples of radical shifts are presented in the result sections. An additional comprehensive source is the official *Federal Gazette* [*Bundesanzeiger*]. It "is the central platform for pronouncements and announcements, as well as for legally relevant company news"[100] in Germany. Exemplary, according to *§1 PublG* (*Publizitätsgesetz*) companies which are not corporations and fulfill two of the three following criteria in three consecutive financial years are obliged to publish their financial statements in the *Federal Gazette*; (1) balance sheet total greater than EUR 65 million, (2) total revenue greater than EUR 130 million and, (3) on average more than 5,000 employees per financial year. Corporations regardless of their size are generally required to publish their accounting documents. These databases make it easier to extract the relevant data required for the 2018 status. Nevertheless, in some cases more comprehensive research is required to identify certain variables. Exemplary, the family generation is not covered by above-described databases. Furthermore, it is not always mentioned on a family firm's website. Again, newspaper articles and additional publications need to be included in the research to identify and validate the family generation which is the majority owner of a family-owned company. As indicated in Section 2.2.2, besides the already mentioned company types an additional type is introduced in the 2018 status based on the ownership structure in 2018. If another German enterprise is the majority owner of a company from the list of the largest 250 enterprises in 1958, the company is marked as a subsidiary company. Because the company is majority controlled, it is consolidated with the parent enterprise and is not independent anymore. The name of the parent enterprise is also explicitly added to the dataset as a separate variable. If the majority ownership of a company is acquired by another firm and fully integrated their operations discontinue and therefore the company fails. In the case of a subsidiary company the full integration has not happened.

---

[100] Federal Ministry of Justice and for Consumer Protection (2021).

After collecting the 2018 revenue figures, again representing the global revenue, the compound annual growth rate (CAGR) is calculated for the entire study period based on the revenue data from 1958 and 2018 using the following formula:

$$CAGR(1958, 2018) = \left(\frac{R(2018)}{R(1958)}\right)^{\frac{1}{(2018-1958)}} - 1$$

$R(1958) =$ Revenue in 1958 in million EUR
$R(2018) =$ Revenue in 2018 in million EUR

It is noteworthy that both revenue figures are not price adjusted. This allows a comparison with the GDP development at market prices in Germany from 1958 to 2018 (see Section 4.1 and Figure 4.1). A similar calculation is made using the number of employees to obtain the average employee growth rate from 1958 to 2018. Not for all surviving enterprises is this second calculation possible because of missing employee numbers either in 1958 or in 2018. For the revenue growth rate calculation only one CAGR cannot be calculated because a figure for 2018 cannot be identified.[101]

Using the 1958 and 2018 variables as well as the tracking information about the ownership, operations and solvency discontinuities a profile card for each of the 250 largest enterprises of 1958 is created. In the following, three

[101] This is the case for *Heinrich Bergbau AG* (1958) whose name is *Littelfuse GmbH* in 2018. The company experiences two majority ownership changes since 1958. In 1967, Werhahn family acquires the majority after being a minority shareholder in the public company for years. *Heinrich Bergbau AG* becomes a family business. After the foundation of the *Ruhrkohle AG* (*RAG*) and the transfer of coal mining assets from *Heinrich Bergbau* to *RAG* the firm ceases their operations in 1968 but continues to exist as *Heinrich Industrie AG* and acts as an investment company. In 2004, *Littelfuse, Inc.* (USA) takes over the majority from Werhahn family including the portfolio of electronic manufacturers which *Heinrich Industrie* acquires in the meantime. The name changes to *Littelfuse GmbH* and they become a foreign subsidiary which they still are in 2018. *Littelfuse* is specialized in electronic switches, fuses, and sensors. The revenue of *Littelfuse GmbH* is not published because they are consolidated in the annual report of the US entity but not revealed separately. Interestingly, in their 2018 report (Littelfuse, Inc. (2019, p. 47)) they highlight outstanding coal mining liabilities of EUR 1.1 million in connection with their acquisition of *Heinrich Industrie AG* in 2004.

examples of such profile cards[102] are presented and described afterwards; a surviving family-owned enterprise with *Henkel & Cie. GmbH* (Figure 3.3), and two failed companies with *Mannesmann AG* (Figure 3.4) and *Zündapp-Werke GmbH* (Figure 3.5):

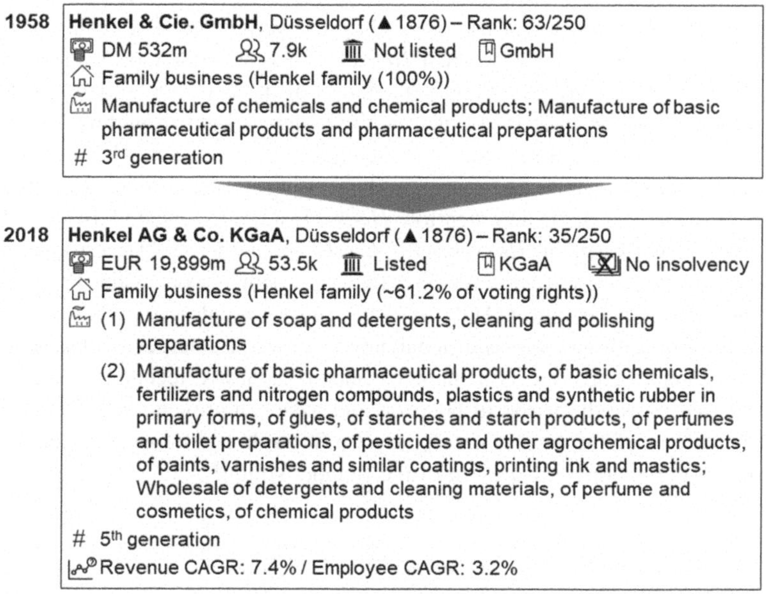

Figure 3.3 *Henkel & Cie. GmbH* Profile Card. (Source: Author's own figure)

Henkel & Cie. GmbH is founded in 1876 in Aachen. Already two years later the company moves to Düsseldorf where it is still headquartered in 1958.[103] With a total revenue of DM 532 million (EUR 272 million) and around 7,900 employees the company is ranked on position 63 of the largest enterprises of 1958. At that time, *Henkel* is fully owned by the Henkel family, descendants of the founder in the third generation. The company operates predominantly as a manufacturer of chemicals and chemical products (e.g., glues and cleaning supplies). Over the

[102] The explanations of the icons can be found in Section 10.1 of the appendix in the electronic supplementary material.

[103] The sources for *Henkel's* data are *HdG*, *Wgzw*, Feldenkirchen and Hilger (2001), Henkel KGaA (2006), and Henkel AG & Co. KGaA (2018, 2019, 2021).

entire study period, no discontinuity of the majority ownership, of the operations or of the solvency is recorded. Nevertheless, *Henkel* change its legal form from a *GmbH* to a *KGaA* in 1975 and goes public ten years later in 1985. Since then, *Henkel* is a listed company. In 2008, the renaming to *Henkel AG & Co. KGaA* takes place after *Henkel Management AG* is appointed the sole personally liable partner of *Henkel KGaA*. Initially, *Henkel* offers only preferential stocks when going public. All common stocks (including the voting rights) remain with the family. This changes in 1996, when *Henkel* also issues common stocks to the public. Over the next years several percentages of these stocks are being sold to non-family members. In 2018, Henkel family members hold around 61.2% of the common stocks which are pooled in a shareholders' agreement. The preferential stocks are all in free float. The family in their fifth generation is still the majority owner of the voting rights and therefore *Henkel* is a family-owned business. With a revenue of EUR 19.9bn *Henkel AG & Co. KGaA* is the 35th largest enterprise in Germany in 2018 and employs 53.5 thousand people worldwide. From 1958 on, this reflects a revenue CAGR of 7.4% and an employee CAGR of 3.2%. The enterprise still operates as a manufacturer of soap, detergents, cleaning and polishing preparations and is a market leader in adhesive technologies. *Henkel* has survived the study period of 60 years and has been growing to improve their ranking as one of the largest enterprises by 28 ranks. Moreover, the company remains in the majority ownership of the founder's family.

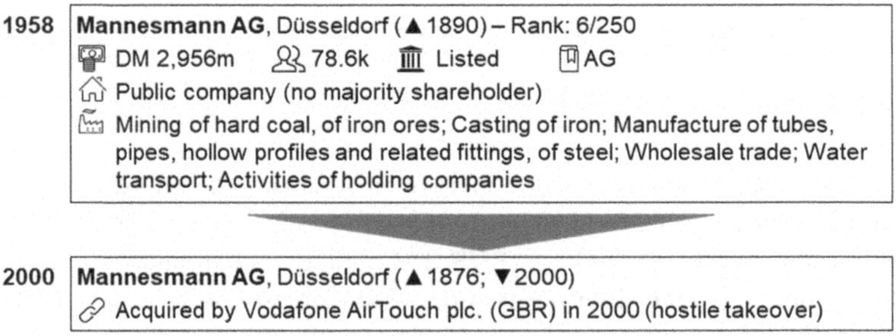

Figure 3.4 *Mannesmann AG* Profile Card. (Source: Author's own figure)

Mannesmann AG, headquartered in Düsseldorf, is ranked the sixth largest enterprise of 1958 with a revenue of DM 2.96bn (EUR 1.51bn) and 78.6 thousand employees.[104] Initially founded in 1890, the company is listed as an *AG* with no majority shareholder in 1958. The shares are free float. At the end of the 1950s, the enterprise is operating in different areas with a strong footprint in mining, manufacturing of tubes and pipes as well as trading. After World War II *Mannesman* is divided into several separate companies to limit their power but most of them are reunited in 1954 which is approved by the Allied Control Council, the governing body of the Allied Occupation Zones in Germany. Later *Mannesmann* expands into the automotive and telecommunications sector, among others. Its strong performance in the second-mentioned area attracts the British mobile operator *Vodafone*. As a listed company *Mannesmann* could become the target of a hostile takeover bid. At the end of the 1990s *Vodafone AirTouch plc.* start their takeover attempt which ends successfully in 2000 after long and controversial negotiations with the highest price of a corporate acquisition to date of around EUR 190bn. After the acquisition *Mannesmann* is split and several business units like the tubes and automotive business are sold to former competitors as well as to a consortium of Siemens and Bosch, among others. The telecommunications business remains with *Vodafone* and gets integrated.[105] Therefore, the ownership as well as the operations discontinue.

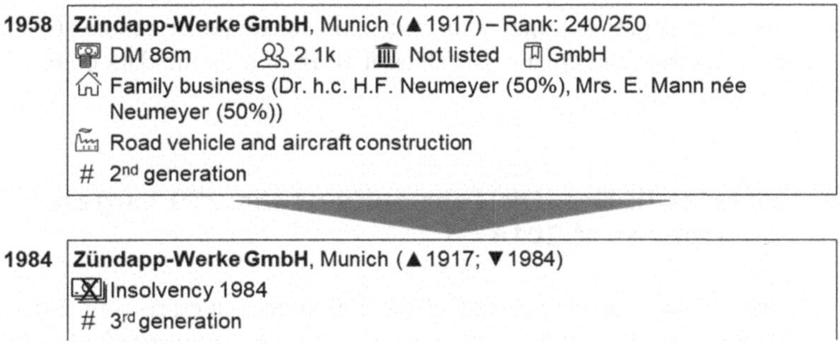

Figure 3.5 *Zündapp-Werke GmbH* Profile Card. (Source: Author's own figure)

[104] The description of *Mannesmann's* development is based on the following sources: *HdG*, *SAf*, Neumann (1959), H. Koch (1965), Müller-Haeseler (1973) and Knipp (2007).

[105] The name *Mannesmann* is still found in some company names which are part of other enterprises like the entire business unit *Mannesmann* as part of *Salzgitter AG*. In contrast, the existing and listed *Brüder Mannesmann AG* is not connected with *Mannesmann AG*.

Zündapp-Werke GmbH are founded in 1917 in Nuremberg and move their headquarters to Munich in 1958.[106] They rank on position 240 of the largest enterprises of 1958 with a revenue of DM 86 million (EUR 44.1 million) and 2,055 employees. The firm operates as a *GmbH* and is accordingly not listed on a stock exchange. The founder's son and daughter own the company in equal shares in 1958.[107] At that time, *Zündapp-Werke GmbH* is one of the largest motorcycle manufacturers in Germany. The family keeps the majority ownership of the company until the insolvency in 1984. The production machinery of the Munich factory is sold to a Chinese company which dismantles the equipment and ships it to China. *Zündapp* fails in the third generation due to the discontinuity of the solvency. It needs to be mentioned that the family divides the company into an operating company and a management company in 1982. The discontinuity is only applicable to the operating company—see Section 2.2.2.3 for the business perspective. The management company including the real estate assets remain with the family and secure their wealth. Moreover, since 2017 several motorcycles and bicycles are again sold under the brand *Zündapp* but the family is not operationally involved.

After creating the unique list of the 250 largest enterprises of 1958 in Germany, tracking the companies' developments over 60 years and finally collecting their 2018 status Dataset I is completed. The descriptive statistics of the 2018 status of the 250 largest enterprises of 1958 can be found in Section 6.1. The next chapters describe the creation of Dataset II as well as the data comparison between both datasets.

3.7.2 Dataset II: The (Dis)Continuity of the 250 Largest Enterprises of 2018

Dataset II is the basis for the analysis of the 250 largest enterprises of 2018 and their development back to 1958 or their year of foundation, respectively, if they were founded after 1958. The sources for the data of the largest companies of 2018 are already much better processed and structured compared to the data for

[106] The sources for the *Zündapp's* development are Verlag Hoppenstedt & Co. (1959b), Goslich (1984), Der Spiegel (1984), Kubisch (1986), Rauch and Kletzke (1996) as well as Zündapp Vertriebsgesellschaft mbH (2021).

[107] Regarding the influence of the family, Elisabeth Mann née Neumayer, the daughter of the founder Friedrich Ludwig Neumeyer, was married to Eitel-Friedrich Mann who was managing director of the Munich factory from 1950 to 1958. Afterwards he became managing director of the entire company until his unexpected death in 1960.

the largest companies of 1958. Nevertheless, the available data needs to be validated and combined. Moreover, the tracking of the development again requires historical sources and analyses to identify the relevant continuities and discontinuities of ownership. In comparison to Step B additional measures are introduced to better understand the origin of newly founded enterprises between 1958 and 2018.

3.7.2.1 Step D: Identifying the 250 Largest Enterprises of 2018

Over the last 60 years the interest in and the availability of corporate data has increased significantly. The media coverage of the performance of companies but also professional service providers and legal requirements have led to more transparency. Enterprises publish and communicate more details of their past performance and their future perspective. The annual report of *August Thyssen-Hütte AG* for the fiscal year 1957/1958 was in total 78 pages long which was already one of the most extensive reports of this fiscal year evaluated for this thesis. In 2019, *thyssenkrupp AG*, the successor company created from the merger of *Thyssen* and *Krupp* in 1999[108], presented their 2017/2018 financial results in a 255-page annual report.[109] An even higher difference can be found for *Damiler-Benz AG*. The 1958 annual report had 48 pages compared to *Daimler AG's* annual report for the financial year 2018 with 353 pages.[110] *Thyssen* and *Daimler* were already listed in 1958 and had to comply with higher disclosure standards than non-listed companies. For private firms, like *Fried. Krupp, Essen* as a sole proprietorship no annual report was published at all in 1958. The same applies for *Oetker*. Only in 1971, *Dr. August Oetker KG* started to publish their annual reports. The one for the financial year 2018 was published on their website, and it is also available via the *Federal Gazette*.[111]

---

[108] Already two years earlier in 1997, *Thyssen Krupp Stahl AG* was created after an attempted hostile takeover of *Thyssen* by smaller *Krupp* was leaked and cancelled due to fierce protests by employees. In the joint company only the flat steel activities were bundled. Nevertheless, it was a first step towards the entire merger which was finalized in *1999*. The full name of *Krupp* at that time was *Fried. Krupp AG Hoesch-Krupp* after the hostile takeover of *Hoesch AG* by *Fried. Krupp AG* in 1992.

In 1958, *Fried. Krupp, Essen*, ranked on fourth position of the largest enterprises, and *August Thyssen-Hütte AG* on position 20. At that time, both companies were family-owned businesses.

[109] See August Thyssen-Hütte AG (1959) and thyssenkrupp AG (2018).

[110] See Daimler-Benz AG (1959) and Daimler AG (2019).

[111] See Dr. August Oetker (1958), Dr. August Oetker KG (1972) and Dr. August Oetker KG (2019).

The comparison of the list of the 100 largest enterprises in Germany of 1958 and 2018 published by *FAZ* serves as an additional and illustrative example of the increased transparency. As described above, Kruk's first list published in 1959 covers the ranking of 100 companies and their largest subsidiaries as well as a short article describing the results and shortcomings. In 2019, the ranking was published in the 61st edition, was in total eight pages long and in a special section of the newspaper.[112] Despite the headline "The 100 Largest" ["*Die 100 Größten*"] the series now covers the 250 largest industry, trade, and services enterprises in Germany as well as several additional rankings of the largest banks, insurance companies, association groups [*Verbundgruppen*], listed companies and family businesses. It further includes a comparison with European and international companies. A mid-term perspective is provided by the presentation of the annual net profits of the Dax companies from 1988 to 2018. In addition to the revenue and employee figures, the relevant list for this thesis with the 250 largest enterprises also contains data on net income. But this information is not available for all companies (e.g., for the supermarket chain *Aldi* and their competitor *Schwarz Group*). The disclosure requirements have not yet reached the point where these enterprises need to publish their net income just due to their size or legal structure.

The *FAZ* publication is not the only ranking of the largest enterprises. There are several other newspapers, publishers and service providers which create similar rankings. Although the methodology is not always the same revenue is often the key indicator to illustrate the size of an enterprise (except for banks and insurance companies). Other exemplary rankings are published by the online portal *boerse.de* or the newspaper *Handelsblatt*.[113] Forbes' *Global 500* list also covers German enterprises but provides only an overview of the largest 32 public companies.[114] A different indicator is used by the Monopolies Commission in their Biennial Report to determine the state and development of concentration among companies in Germany. With this report the commission provides advice to the German government and legislature. Their list of the 100 largest enterprises is based on the total value added.[115] Besides these static rankings published once a year, databases like *dafne* or *Bloomberg* which need to be licensed provide the possibility to extract lists of all covered companies at any time which are entered

112 See Giersberg and F.A.Z.-Archiv (2019).

113 See boerse.de Finanzportal AG (2021) and Handelsblatt (2021).

114 See Fortune Media IP Ltd. (2020b). A more comprehensive list, Fortunes' Global 2000, which covers 54 German enterprises is available only from 2020 on.

115 See Monopolkommission (2020).

in the data pool. Hence, a ranking of the largest enterprises in Germany of 2018 can be created.

When comparing the above-mentioned lists, it becomes clear that there are differences in their composition. For example, some have a strong focus on public companies while others also include private ones. There is not one single truth of a list which is also directly available—similar to the 1958 list. Therefore, a unique and comprehensive list of the 250 largest enterprises of 2018 needs to be created based on the requirements and the research objectives. The ranking published in *FAZ* is again used as the basis to have a similar starting point as for the 1958 list creation. For these 250 enterprises the revenue and employee data is validated using the annual reports and other company publications.[116] Furthermore, the ownership structure is identified similar to the 2018 status of the 1958 enterprises. The *dafne* database provides useful information, which is further validated through, for example, corporate disclosures due to capital market requirements. A total of eleven variables are checked and validated (see Table 3.4).

Table 3.4 250 Largest Enterprises of 2018: List of 2018 Variables

#	Dataset II 2018 variable	Description
D2-18-01	Official company name	Firm name including legal form (if applicable)
D2-18-02	Headquarters	City of the headquarters in Germany
D2-18-03	Year of foundation / Age	Initial year when the company was founded and calculation of age
D2-18-04	Revenue	In million EUR
D2-18-05	Number of employees	In thousand
D2-18-06	Ownership structure	Identification of shareholders / partners and their voting rights
D2-18-07	Type of company	Based on ownership structure classification of company type
D2-18-08	Family generation	Number of family generation by which a family business is owned

(continued)

[116] Annual reports are available for nearly all enterprises of 2018. Exceptions are several foreign subsidiaries (e.g., *Amazon Deutschland*) as well as company constructs which do not have one single legal entity as a holding company (e.g., *Aldi Group*).

Table 3.4 (continued)

#	Dataset II 2018 variable	Description
D2-18-09	Stock exchange listing	Identification if company is listed on a stock exchange
D2-18-10	Industry	Main industry affiliation
D2-18-11	Legal form	Identification of legal form (e.g., *AG*, *KGaA*, *GmbH*)

Source: Author's own table.

After validating the revenue, the order of the firms changes slightly. Among others, the revenue figures for *thyssenkrupp AG*, for *REWE-ZENTRALFINANZ eG* and for *Otto GmbH & Co. KG* are adjusted based on their annual reports. Moreover, after identifying all ownership structures and following the definitions of the company types (see Section 2.2.2.3) *innogy SE*, ranked on position 20 with EUR 35.1bn in revenue, needs to be removed from the list. Despite being listed *innogy* is majority-owned by *RWE AG* (76.8% of share capital) and therefore their subsidiary. A similar case is *Siemens Healthineers AG* which is a spin-off of *Siemens AG* and goes public in March 2018, but *Siemens AG* remains its majority owner with 85% of the share capital. *Siemens Healthineers* is not ranked separately in the *FAZ* list. It is highlighted as a subsidiary of *Siemens AG*. The shareholder structures of public companies are identified using the companies' annual reports as well as the legally required disclosure notifications if an investor reaches or crosses certain thresholds. A second enterprise which is removed from the list is *Deutsche Leasing AG* with a leasing income of EUR 7.1bn.[117] Due to their business model which is mainly focused on leasing services the company is classified as a financial institution and therefore not in the scope of this thesis. *Wirtgen Group* with revenues of EUR 3.0bn also needs to be excluded from the 2018 ranking because the company is acquired by *John Deere* in 2017 and is already consolidated in the 2018 revenue figures of *John Deere GmbH & Co. KG*, the German subsidiary.[118] *Wirtgen* is not independent anymore, they have become a subsidiary of *John Deere*. Overall, three companies are removed which results in a list of 247 companies so far.

An additional adjustment is made related to *Aldi*. In the *FAZ* ranking the discount supermarket chain is listed as one entity on position five with an estimated

[117] *Deutsche Leasing AG* is a 100%-subsidiary of *Deutsche Sparkassen Leasing AG & Co. KG* which as part of the *Sparkassen-Finanzgruppe* is owned by several German saving banks.

[118] See John Deere GmbH & Co. KG (2019).

revenue of EUR 90bn. But *Aldi* comprises two separate companies with two separate ownership structures.[119] Therefore, *Aldi* is split into *Aldi Süd*, owned by the family of Karl Hans Albrecht, and *Aldi Nord*, owned by the family of Theodor Paul Albrecht. *Aldi Süd* has a revenue of approximately EUR 59bn and around 150,600 employees. *Aldi Nord's* revenue is approximately EUR 22.6bn and has around 73,900 employees. Based on these numbers *Aldi Süd* becomes the 11th largest company and *Aldi Nord* number 28 of the list. In 1958, *Aldi*, at that time still one entity called *Albrecht KG Lebensmittel-Filialbetrieb*, is already part of the largest enterprises on rank 235 with a revenue of around DM 90 million (EUR 46 million). The Albrecht family owns the company in the second generation. One succession takes place in both enterprises after the separation in 1961 and during the study period. The companies are now held in the third generation.[120] After this first split the list comprises 248 companies. A second split of a reported company in the *FAZ* ranking is required because at the end of 2018 the merger of the two companies has not yet been closed. *Galeria Karstadt Kaufhof GmbH* are two separate entities on 31st December 2018; first, *Karstadt Warenhaus GmbH* and second, *GALERIA Kaufhof GmbH*.[121] The former is the smaller firm with approximately EUR 2.1bn in revenue and around 12,300 employees while *Kaufhof* has a revenue of approximately EUR 2.6bn and around 15,400 employees. Based on this split *Kaufhof* becomes the 217th largest enterprise while *Karstadt* drops to the end of the current ranking on position 249. Between *Karstadt* and 248th largest enterprise is a revenue gap of around EUR 250 m. There might be larger companies which could replace *Karstadt* on the list. Therefore, and to check

[119] *Aldi Nord* and *Aldi Süd* have different owners but they work quite closely together in certain areas (e.g., in marketing and purchasing, see B. Koch and Scharrenbroch (2018)). Further, the *Bundeskartellamt* sees both companies due to their joint history as a "*faktischen Gleichordnungskonzern*" [jointly dominated groups] (see Bundeskartellamt (2008, p. 37)). In this thesis the different ownership structures are relevant because they ensure the influence on corporate decisions.

[120] *Aldi* was split in two separate entities in 1961 by the brothers Karl Hans Albrecht and Theodor Paul Albrecht who took over the parental business in 1945. Since then, Karl Albrecht was responsible for southern Germany while Theodor Albrecht focused on Northern Germany. Today, both enterprises are organized by decentralized regional companies which make it difficult to validate a consolidated revenue. There is no overall consolidated financial statement for *Aldi Süd* or *Aldi Nord* publicly available. The revenue numbers are rough data points which the companies published on their websites. Further, estimates from industry experts come to similar revenue figures. Today both enterprises are owned by several (family and charitable) foundations.

[121] See the press release in November 2019 which shows that, until then, there were two separate companies (see Karstadt Warenhaus GmbH (2019)).

whether companies have not been considered in the *FAZ* list, the adjusted ranking which covers 249 companies is compared to the other available rankings from online databases, newspapers, service providers and the Monopolies Commission. The revenues and ownership structures of companies which do not appear on the *FAZ* list are checked and validated to decide whether they need to be added or not. Overall, fifteen additional enterprises are identified. After sorting by revenue two new companies appears on the list of the 250 largest enterprises. First, the foreign subsidiary *GAZPROM Germania GmbH* which is owned by the Russian state-owned energy company *PAO GAZPROM* is added with revenues of EUR 27.3bn and around 1,624 employees. The relevant information comes from the database *dafne* as well as the 2019 *FAZ* ranking which includes the company for the first time in the newspaper's list. Based on the large revenue the company is ranked on position 24. Furthermore, the foreign subsidiary *Dell GmbH* with a revenue of EUR 2.37bn joins the ranking on position 247. This also means that *Karstadt Warenhaus GmbH* drops from the list because two additional companies have been added. Moreover, with these additions Step D is completed and the list provides the 250 largest enterprises of 2018 which is used as a basis for the following three steps.

The descriptive statistics of the 250 largest enterprises of 2018 can be found in Chapter 5.

3.7.2.2 Step E: Comparing the 250 Largest Enterprises of 1958 with Those of 2018

Before tracking the development of the 250 largest enterprises of 2018 back to 1958 or their year of foundation their 2018 status is compared with Dataset I. Firms which were already large 60 years ago and survived the study period might reappear on the 2018 list.[122] The 1958 status of the reappearing companies from Step A and their development from Step B are duplicated to Dataset II. An example is *HeidelbergCement AG* founded in 1873 and ranked on position 39 in 2018 with a revenue of EUR 18.1bn and around 57,900 employees.[123] It is a public company with their majority in free float. Largest investor is Ludwig Merckle (via *PH Vermögensverwaltung GmbH*) owning 26.7% of the shares. The company operates as a manufacturer of cement (primary *WZ* code) and is a wholesaler of construction materials and mineral construction elements (secondary *WZ* code).

---

[122] For the numbers and names of the reappearing enterprises see Section 5.5.

[123] Sources of the corporate information of *HeidelbergCement AG* are Verlag Hoppenstedt & Co. (1959a, 1959c), HeidelbergCement AG (2013, 2019), manager magazin new media GmbH & Co. KG (2005), Der Spiegel (2009) and *dafne*.

60 years earlier, the company was called *Portland-Zementwerke Heidelberg AG* and was also a public company with no majority owner. They are ranked on position 112 on the list of the largest enterprises of 1958 generating a revenue of DM 262 million (EUR 134 million) and employing 4,600 people. Back then the company was headquartered in Heidelberg like in 2018 and already operated as a manufacturer of cement as well. The legal form of an *AG* remains over the study period as well as their listing. *HeidelbergCement* has grown by an average of 8.5% annually in terms of revenue and by 4.3% in terms of employees. Despite their similar company type as a public company in 1958 and 2018 two discontinuities of the majority ownership are identified in Step B. In 2005, the Merckle family increases their minority stake to 77.95% through a public takeover offer via *Spohn Cement GmbH*, a subsidiary company of the *Merckle Group* which is led in third and fourth generation. Furthermore, they acquire a two-digit percentage stake from the minority shareholder *Schwenk* which is also a cement manufacturer based in Ulm.[124] With this majority takeover *HeidelbergCement* becomes a family business. Unfortunately, this does not last long. In 2009, the Merckle family loses their majority again after a capital increase and the issuing of new shares which is required because of *HeidelbergCement's* high debts (after several acquisitions in previous years) and refinancing requirements. Due to a liquidity crisis in one of the family's asset management companies at the same time, the family cannot participate in the capital increase. After this move, Ludwig Merckle, fourth generation, holds 24.4% at the end of 2009.[125] Due to these two discontinuities of ownership in the study period *HeidelbergCement* becomes a public company in 2018 again which it already is in 1958.

This development of *HeidelbergCement* from Step B and their 1958 status from Step A captured in Dataset I can also be used for Dataset II. No further work is required for all the duplicates of the largest enterprises of 1958 and of 2018. For all other enterprises which are not already tracked additional research is required to understand their historic development and to identify their status in 1958. These companies are referred to as "new joiners".

---

[124] From a family perspective it might be noteworthy that Adolf Merckle's wife Ruth (third generation) came from the Schwenk/Schleicher family based in Ulm which sold the minority stake to him.

[125] Due to the financial difficulties of the family's asset management company mainly caused by the financial crisis in 2008 Adolf Merckle committed suicide in January 2009. His son, Ludwig Merckle, took over the entire business and restructured it successfully although the family lost the majority in *HeidelbergCement*. Further, the family's second large investment, *Ratiopharm GmbH*, which was founded by Adolf Merckle in 1973 was sold as well.

3.7.2.3 Step F: Tracking the (Dis)Continuity of the 250 Largest Enterprises of 2018 back to 1958

The new joiners on the list of the largest enterprises of 2018 are investigated in Step F. Similar to Step B for the largest enterprises of 1958, Step F tracks the development of the largest enterprises of 2018. This time, the tracking goes back in time from 2018 to 1958. In Dataset I not all enterprises survived the study period of 60 years. In Dataset II not all enterprises already existed in 1958. Therefore, the tracking might end before 1958 in the year of foundation if the firm is younger than 60 years.

The overall framework of the continuity or discontinuity of ownership, operations and solvency is again used to identify the changes in the development. While ownership is the key dimension in these cases, too, solvency, as the third dimension, is not as relevant as in Step B because all enterprises have survived until 2018. Otherwise, they would not be part of the sample. Nevertheless, if a company experienced a discontinuity of solvency but managed to operate and become solvent again this will be tracked, as well which is an exceptional case.

On the other hand, the operations dimension becomes more important. In Step B, enterprises can be acquired and then integrated in the buyer's organization. This is indicated by an ownership as well as an operations discontinuity resulting in the failure of the company. The opposite process which can now occur in Step F is based on the foundation of independent operations. This means, an integrated business unit of a diversified firm becomes operationally independent and in a next step independent of its majority owner, the diversified firm. Such carve-outs became popular in recent years. Several diversified enterprises prepare business units which the management often define as non-core activities to be run independently from the parent company (including the separation of back-office activities like IT and HR or the removal from integrated production systems) and sell them or take them public. With this type of company foundation an independent firm appears (if the unit is not sold to another group) which can already become one of the largest enterprises in the moment of their foundation. Such carve-outs explain to a certain extent the new joiners on the list of the largest enterprises of 2018.

An example of a company which was founded after 1958 and started as a carve-out is *Covestro AG*.[126] The company has experienced a discontinuity of their majority ownership structure since their foundation or the years in which the company became independent, respectively. *Covestro* is ranked on position 46 of

[126] Sources of the corporate information of *Covestro AG* are Covestro AG (2016, 2017, 2018, 2019, 2021), Mußler (2015) and *dafne*.

the largest enterprises of 2018 with a revenue of EUR 14.6bn and around 17,300 employees. Based on their ownership structure with a free float of around 92% the listed firm is classified as a public company. *Covestro* operates in the chemical industry with a focus on polymer products.[127] In 2015, *Bayer AG* carves out its material science business unit and takes the separated company public but remains majority owner with around 69%. Two years later, *Bayer* sells additional shares and gives up the majority in June 2017. The ownership dimension discontinues and *Covestro* becomes a public company in the definition of this thesis. Two examples which are not recognized as fully separated entities as described in Section 3.7.2.1 are *innogy SE* and *Siemens Healthineers AG* which are (to a large extent) operationally independent but are both still majority owned by their parent company *RWE AG* and *Siemens AG*.

Besides the development of the companies which are founded between 1958 and 2018 all other enterprises with a year of foundation before 1958 and which are not covered by Dataset I are also investigated in Step F. The continuities and discontinuities of their majority ownership structure are identified and included in Dataset II. Exemplary, no discontinuities are identified for *Schaeffler AG* founded in 1946 and headquartered in Herzogenaurach even despite their IPO in 2015. The majority ownership remains with the Schaeffler family in the second and third generation.[128] In contrast to the development of *Schaeffler*, one relevant majority discontinuity can be identified for *Rhenus SE & Co. KG* since 1958. In 2018, the family firm is owned by the Rhetmann family and headquartered in Holzwickede. Going back in time, the family acquired the majority in 1998 from *Stinnes AG* which was part of *VEBA AG* at that time. Prior to this change, *Rhenus*, which

[127] This industry classification is based on additional research and not on the *WZ* code classification. Like for several other companies in the sample the primary *WZ* code of *Covestro AG* is "Management activities of holding companies" and no secondary *WZ* code is available. This code does not provide insights into the main industry of the company therefore more sources like annual reports and stock exchange information are used.

[128] In 1946 *Industriewerk Schaeffler oHG* was founded by the two brothers Wilhelm and Georg Schaeffler. Prior to this company, both were owners of the *Davistan AG*, later *Wilhelm Schaeffler AG*, which Wilhelm Schaeffler initially acquired in 1940. It is mentioned that this company also produced war equipment in World War II and was owned by Jews several years before that. Despite a scientific study about the involvement of the Schaeffler family in World War II there is no information about this episode on the official *Schaeffler* website (see Ritzer (2010)).

In this IPO only preferential stocks without voting rights have been issued. At the end of 2018, all 166 million preferential stocks are in free float. All 500 million common stocks are still with the Schaeffler family (via *IHO Verwaltungs GmbH*). Overall, the free float of the entire share capital is 24.9%. The official prospectus of the IPO as well as the annual reports provide useful insights, see Schaeffler AG (2015, 2016, 2019).

was founded as a joint company of *Badische AG für Rheinschifffahrt und Seetransport* and *Rheinschiffahrts AG* in Frankfurt in 1912, was reorganized within the *VEBA Group* several times and had different direct majority owners (e.g., *Fendel Schiffahrts-AG* in 1958) but always within the same group. Overall, until 1998 *Rhenus* was a subsidiary company since the end point of the tracking in 1958.[129]

At the end of Step F, the developments of the largest enterprises of 2018 are captured in Dataset II. Their continuity and discontinuity of the three framework dimensions are used to further understand the long-term developments.

3.7.2.4 Step G: Assessing the Status of the 250 Largest Enterprises of 2018 in 1958

In the last step, Step G, the 1958 statuses of all enterprises which were founded before 1958 and which are not already part of the list of the largest enterprises of 1958 are identified. Similar variables known from Step A are collected using predominantly the same sources (see Table 3.5). Furthermore, the CAGR of revenue and employees is calculated between 1958 and 2018. It needs to be mentioned that the relevant data is often more difficult to find because these companies were smaller in 1958 compared to the ones in Step A. Therefore, the data could not be identified for all enterprises.

Table 3.5 250 Largest Enterprises of 2018: List of 1958 Variables

#	Dataset II 1958 variable	Description
D2-58-01	Official company name	Firm name including legal form (if applicable)
D2-58-02	Headquarters	City of the headquarters in Germany
D2-58-03	Age	Age in 1958 based on the initially collected year of foundation
D2-58-04	Revenue	In million DM and converted to million EUR
D2-58-05	Revenue CAGR	CAGR of revenue between 1958 and 2018
D2-58-06	Number of employees	In thousands

(continued)

[129] See among others Odrich (1976) and Rhenus SE & Co. KG (2018, 2021).

Table 3.5 (continued)

#	Dataset II 1958 variable	Description
D2-58-07	Number of employees CAGR	CAGR of number of employees between 1958 and 2018
D2-58-08	Ownership structure	Identification of shareholders / partners and their voting rights
D2-58-09	Type of company	Based on ownership structure classification of company type
D2-58-10	Family generation	Number of family generation by which a family business is owned
D2-58-11	Parent enterprise	If the company was a subsidiary the name of the parent enterprise is identified
D2-58-12	Stock exchange listing	Identification if company is listed on a stock exchange
D2-58-13	Industry	Main industry affiliation
D2-58-14	Legal form	Identification of legal form (e.g., *AG, KGaA, GmbH*)

Source: Author's own table.

Like in Step C, a profile card for each of the 250 largest enterprises of 2018 is created based on the collected 1958 statuses and development information from Step F.[130] Five examples follow to provide an overview of different developments. The examples include two family-owned businesses (1) *Brose Fahrzeugteile GmbH & Co. KG* (Figure 3.6) and (2) *Dachser Group SE & Co. KG* (Figure 3.7), one public company (3) *Puma SE* (Figure 3.8), one state-owned enterprise (4) *Fraport AG* (Figure 3.9) as well as one foreign subsidiary (5) *KUKA AG* (Figure 3.10).

[130] The explanations of the icons can be found in Section 10.1 of the appendix in the electronic supplementary material. The arrow between the 1958 and 2018 box indicates the direction of the development investigation from 2018 back to 1958.

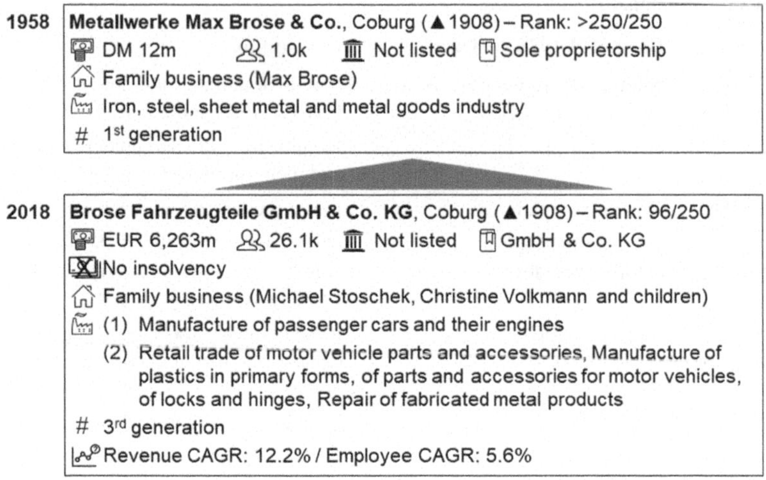

Figure 3.6 *Brose Fahrzeugteile GmbH & Co. KG* Profile Card. (Source: Author's own figure)

In 2018, *Brose Fahrzeugteile GmbH & Co. KG* is ranked on position 96 with a revenue of EUR 6.3bn and around 26,100 employees globally. Operating in the automotive industry this size qualifies for one of the ten largest German suppliers.[131] The company is not listed on a stock exchange and operates as a limited partnership with a *GmbH* as the general partner. *Brose* is fully owned by the Stoschek and Volkmann families, descendants of the founder Max Brose. Accordingly, *Brose* is a family-owned enterprise and in 2018 in the third generation. Since 1958 no discontinuities of ownership, operations or solvency are identified. Also, the headquarters are still in Coburg where they are already in 1958. With a revenue of DM 12 million (EUR 6.1 million) and around 1,000 employees in 1958 *Brose* is not part of the 250 largest enterprises in that year.

[131] The reconstruction of *Brose's* development is based on *HdG*, Wirth (2019), Brose Fahrzeugteile GmbH & Co. KG (2019), Brose Fahrzeugteile SE & Co. KG (2021) and *dafne*. The *Brose Group* does not publish one consolidated financial statement but provides press information about its consolidated performance. *Brose Fahrzeugteile GmbH & Co. KG* in Coburg act as the leading organization. There are several other firms with the same name headquartered in other cities, e.g., Bamberg and Würzburg. They represent the three main divisions: door business, seat structures business and electric motors and drives business.

But with a CAGR of 12.2% in terms of revenue and of 5.6% in terms of employees the firm has become one of the 100 largest enterprises in Germany in 2018. Back in 1958, *Metallwerke Max Brose & Co.* is a sole proprietorship in the hands of the founder and already operating as an automotive supplier.

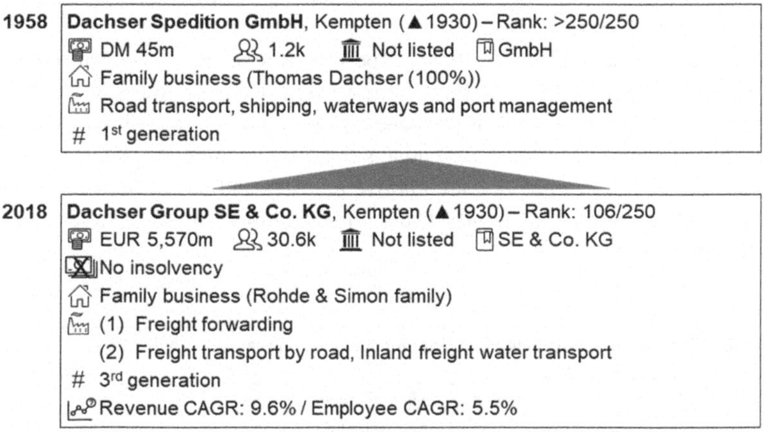

Figure 3.7 *Dachser Group SE & Co. KG* Profile Card. (Source: Author's own figure)

A second example of a family enterprise which has become one of the largest enterprises in 2018 is *Dachser*.[132] The company appears on the 2018 list (Step D) and was also already under investigation in Step A for the 1958 list. The company is founded in 1930. In 2018 they operate under the name *Dachser Group SE & Co. KG* and are ranked on position 105 with a revenue of EUR 5.6bn and 30.6 thousand employees. In 1958, 60 years earlier and operating under the name *Dachser Spedition GmbH*, the company has 1,200 employees as stated in *HdG*. Because this number is above the threshold of 1,000 it was further investigated if it was part of the 250 largest enterprises in 1958. Based on corporate information published in a company history in 2008 the 1958 revenue amounted to DM 44.5 million (EUR 22.8 million). This revenue figure does not qualify for the 250 largest enterprises in 1958. Nevertheless, this information is relevant for this step, Step G, to calculate the revenue CAGR which is 9.6%. In comparison, the employee CAGR is 5.5%. The majority ownership remains in the

[132] See *HdG*. Erker (2008), DACHSER Group SE & Co. KG (2019) and *dafne* for the relevant sources.

founder's family until today. *Dachser* was and is still a family-owned company, today in the third generation. Moreover, no operations or solvency discontinuities have been identified since 1958. Like the majority ownership the headquarters have not change over 60 years and are still in Kempten. The industry in which the company operates has remained identical, as well, in logistics. As the different company names indicate the legal form has changed from a *GmbH* to a *SE & Co. KG* but remained a corporation.

Both above-described family firms experienced a strong growth over the last decades to become the 96th and 105th largest enterprise in Germany in 2018. Furthermore, both have remained in the hands of the founders' families and are now in the third generation. What differentiates these two companies is the respective industry in which they operate—automotive industry and logistics. The following example shows that not all family firms remain family-owned despite a similar growth story.

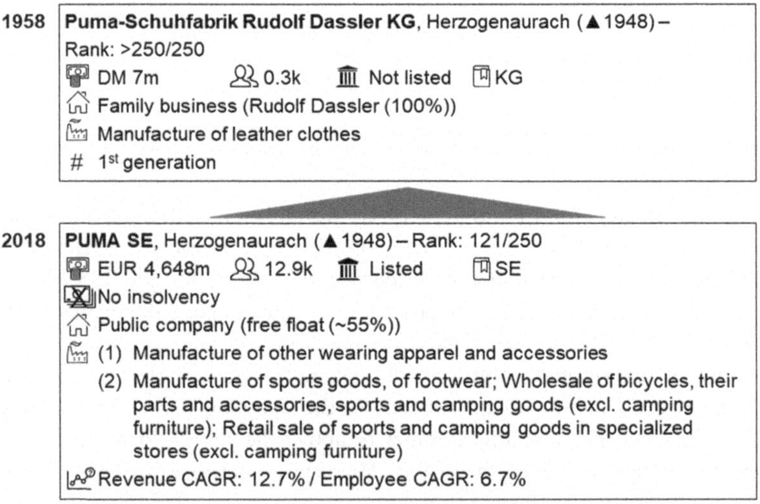

Figure 3.8 *PUMA SE* Profile Card. (Source: Author's own figure)

On rank 121 of the largest enterprises of 2018 is *Puma SE* with a revenue of EUR 4.65bn and around 12,900 employees.[133] The company has grown by a revenue CAGR of 12.7% and an employee CAGR of 6.7% since 1958. Ten years after *PUMA's* foundation in Herzogenaurach where they are still headquartered the company generates around DM 7 million (EUR 3.6 million) in revenue with around 300 employees. At that time, the *KG* (*Kommanditgesellschaft*) is fully owned by the founder Rudolf Dassler.[134] This has changed until 2018 and the company is now a public company (a listed *SE*). In 1986, the family business is in the second generation owned by the two sons of the founder, Armin (70%) and Gerd Dassler (30%), and then makes an IPO. Again, only preferential stocks without voting rights are issued and the brothers keep all the common stocks. But this already changes in 1989 after severe financial issues when the brothers sell their shares to the trading company *Cosa Liebermann* which is owned by several Suisse families. One year later, Swedish *Aritmos AB*, initially a food company then in sports and leisure products, acquires the majority of the common shares before they become the sole owner of the common shares at the beginning of 1991. At that time, *Aritmos* is part of *Proventus*, a family-owned investment company of Robert Weil from Sweden. Five years later, *Proventus* issues the common shares and sells them completely. After several minority shareholders, among others Günter Herz and Daniela Herz-Schnoeckl (heirs of *Tchibo*) and *Monarchy Enterprises*, a US media investor, the French retail and luxury goods group *PPR* (since 2013 *Kering*) acquires the majority in 2007 and keeps it for eleven years. Since the mid of 2018, *PUMA SE* is a public company with a free float of around 55% after *Kering* sells most of their shares or distributes them to their own shareholders, respectively. Overall, five majority ownership discontinuities are identified. After being a family business owned by the founder and his sons for 41 years it is noteworthy that all majority owners were also family enterprises but from Switzerland, Sweden, and France. Nevertheless, compared to *Brose* and *Dachser PUMA* cannot remain a family business over the study period. On the other hand, they are also able to grow by 12.7% annually.

---

[133] Besides *HdG* and *dafne* see Goslich (1986, 1989), Psotta (1991), Knust (1996), Herr (2007), Dommenget (2016), Köhn (2018), PUMA SE (2019) for the relevant sources.

[134] Before Rudolf Dassler founded *PUMA* in 1948, he already produced sport shoes with his brother Adolf since 1919 / 1924 in the joint company *Sportschuhfabrik Gebrüder Dassler*. After the brothers split up, Adolf founded *Adi Dassler adidas Sportschuhfabrik* in 1949 which is today the second largest sportswear and sporting goods company in the world. *adidas* is also a public company in 2018.

1958 **Flughafenaktiengesellschaft Rhein-Main (FAG)**, Frankfurt (Main) (▲1924) – Rank: >250/250
DM 10m | 0.6k | Not listed | AG
State-owned enterprise (State of Hesse (45.2%), City of Frankfurt (Main) (28.9%), Federal Republic of Germany (25.9%))
Operation of airports and airfields

2018 **Fraport AG**, Frankfurt (Main) (▲1924) – Rank: 164/250
EUR 3,478m | 23.3k | Listed | AG
No insolvency
State-owned enterprise (State of Hesse (31.3%), Stadtwerke Frankfurt am Main Holding GmbH (20.16%))
(1) Operation of airports and airfields
Revenue CAGR: 11.5% / Employee CAGR: 6.4%

Figure 3.9 *Fraport AG* Profile Card. (Source: Author's own figure)

In 2018, *Fraport AG* is ranked on position 124 of the largest enterprises with a revenue EUR 3.48bn and around 23,300 employees.[135] The firm is headquartered in Frankfurt (Main) because it started as the operating company of the international airport there which is still the case. In 1958, the company is called *Flughafenaktiengesellschaft Rhein-Main (FAG)* and is founded in 1924.[136] At that time, the revenue is DM 10 million (EUR 5.2 million) and *FAG* has around 600 employees. These numbers do not qualify for one of the 250 largest enterprises in 1958. Despite the legal form of an *AG* the company is not listed. *FAG* is a 100% state-owned enterprise with the State of Hesse as main shareholder as well as the city of Frankfurt (Main) and the Federal Republic of Germany as the other two remaining owners. Despite the IPO and the partial privatization in 2001 *Fraport* remains a state-owned enterprise in 2018 with the State of Hesse and *Stadtwerke Frankfurt am Main Holding GmbH* as the largest shareholders with 31.3% and

[135] The primary and secondary sources for *Fraport AG* are *HdG*, *Wgzw*, Bundesministerium der Finanzen (2017) and Fraport AG (2019, 2021).

[136] In 1924, *Südwestdeutsche Luftverkehrs AG* was founded by the city of Frankfurt (Main), *Junkers Luftverkehr AG* and several private investors as the legal predecessor of *Fraport AG*. After World War II in 1946 *Verkehrsaktiengesellschaft Rhein Main (VAG)* was re-founded and renamed in 1957 to *Flughafenaktiengesellschaft Rhein-Main (FAG)*. Prior to the IPO, the name was changed from *FAG* to *Fraport AG—Frankfurt Airport Services Worldwide* in 2000.

20.2%, respectively. The majority is still with state-owned organizations.[137] Furthermore, the main industry in which *Fraport* operates has not changed since the foundation with the operation of airports and airfields. What has changed is the global footprint. *Fraport* does not only operate the airport in Frankfurt (Main) in Germany but also airports in Greece, Peru, and Brazil among others. Since 1958, *Fraport* has a revenue CAGR of 11.5% and an employee CAGR of 6.4% to become one of the 250 largest enterprises in 2018 as a state-owned enterprise. No discontinuities of the three dimensions have been identified.

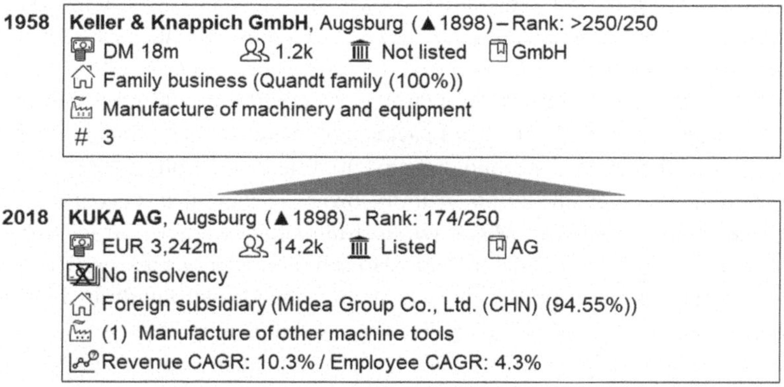

Figure 3.10 *KUKA AG* Profile Card. (Source: Author's own figure)

A last example of a profile card covers *KUKA AG* which has a revenue of EUR 3.24bn and around 14,200 employees in 2018.[138] Based on these numbers the company is ranked on position 174 of the largest enterprises in that year. *KUKA* is a manufacturer of machine tools, especially of industrial robotics and of production machines and systems. They are a listed *AG* but around 94.6% of the shares and thus more than the majority are owned by the Chinese *Midea Group*. Therefore, the Augsburg-headquartered company is categorized as a foreign subsidiary. In 1958, the predecessor company is called *Keller & Knappich GmbH* which is founded in 1898. With a revenue of DM 18 million (EUR 9.2 million) and around 1,200 employees the company is far smaller than the 250th

[137] The Federal Republic of Germany has completely divested their stake since the IPO.

[138] The relevant sources are *HdG*, *Wgzw*, Helmer (1982), Scholtyseck (2011), Paul (2014), Köhn (2015) and KUKA AG (2019, 2021). The name *KUKA* is the abbreviation of the first letters of *Keller und Knappich Augsburg*.

largest enterprise of 1958. At that time, *Keller & Knappich* is owned by the Quandt family and predominantly run by Harald Quandt as managing director. The Quandt family is not related to the founder but already in the third generation in 1958. They acquire the company after World War II and keep the majority until 1980. In that year *KUKA* or *Industrie-Werke Karlsruhe Augsburg AG*[139], respectively, is struggling financially and in the course of a capital reduction followed by a capital increase the Quandt family, still in the third generation, give up their shares. In the following years the shares are in free float with no majority owner. After several restructurings including acquisitions and sales of parts of the company the firm moves back to its old name *KUKA* in 2005. In 2009, the machine manufacturer *Grenzebach* acquires around 25% during the financial crisis in which *KUKA* is struggling financially again. In 2014, the manufacturer of paper machines, hydropower plant equipment and other machinery *Voith* buys 25.1% of *KUKA* (a large package of shares comes from *Grenzebach*) and becomes the largest shareholder next to Friedhelm Loh (~10%). Despite these shareholder movements no majority owner is identified since 1980. This only changes in 2016 when *Midea Group* from China acquires up to 94.6% of the shares.[140] *Voith* and Friedhelm Loh also sell their share packages. This is the second ownership discontinuity since 1958 after the Quandt family in 1980 give up their majority. In 2018, *Midea* still owns a share of more than 90%. Over the study period from 1958 to 2018 *KUKA* has grown annually on average by 10.3% in terms of revenue and by 4.3% in terms of employees. The company changes from a family-owned business to a foreign subsidiary in 60 years with a low two-digit growth rate annually. The industry in which *KUKA* operates remains the same.

The above-mentioned examples of the development of five of the 250 largest enterprises of 2018 back to 1958 illustrate the diverse continuities and discontinuities especially of the ownership dimension. In case of discontinuities this leads to a change of the company type. How the company types have changed and grown for the entire Dataset II over 60 years is analyzed in Chapter 7. Before describing the context in which these corporate developments have occurred in Chapter 4, the following sub-chapter provides an example of the required effort to collect the necessary corporate data.

---

[139] After a merger between *Keller & Knappich GmbH* and *Industrie-Werke Karlsruhe AG (IWK)* which was also owned by the Quandt family in 1970 the company was called *Industrie-Werke Karlsruhe Augsburg AG (IWKA)*.

[140] The acquisition by the Chinese *Midea Group* was seen as controversial. Even the German government discussed a counter offer by a German or European organization to avoid a potential drain of key industry knowledge in automation to China (e.g., see Köhn (2016)).

3.7.3 Interlude: The Unknown Voting Rights of the Siemens Family

Besides the characteristic of long-term orientation many family enterprises and their owning families are cautious in providing information and transparency about their business performance or ownership and investment structure compared to other types of companies. This was the case in 1958 and is still the case today despite the stricter disclosure requirements. A stunning example is *Siemens AG* and the Siemens family. Lots of researchers from different disciplines have written about Siemens family members, about certain periods of the company's development and even about management systems in the company.[141] There is also a dedicated *Siemens Historical Institute* run by *Siemens AG* with an outstanding archive in Berlin which allows researchers to study thousands of analogue and digital files and thus the almost 175-year history of the company.[142] Although comprehensive financial data and information about products of *Siemens AG* are accessible quite easily, it is very difficult to get access to reliable sources with the necessary information about the development of *Siemens'* ownership structure and the related voting rights. For this thesis, the structure of 1958 and 2018 as well as the changes of the majority ownership are relevant.

In 1960, a member of the board of directors of *Siemens & Halske AG* mentions in the course of a pending capital increase that they want to keep their existing shareholder structure, and this requires certain considerations especially when increasing the share capital. It is further mentioned that the Siemens family owns *a not inconsiderable part* of shares.[143] Other sources from the time repeat that the family has a major shareholding but no information about the percentage share are available.[144] In addition to the absolute share ownership, the Siemens family

[141] For studies about single family members see, among others, Bähr (2016) for Werner von Siemens (1816–1892) and Lutz (2013) for Carl von Siemens (1829–1906). Further, see Roth (1996) for *Siemens* during World War II and Kocka (1969) for the enterprise management between 1847 and 1914. Further, Neubürger (2000) investigates the established management system focusing on Economic Value Added (EVA) / *Geschäftswertbeitrag (GWB).*

[142] See Siemens AG (2021b).

[143] See Kruk (1960).

[144] See, among others, Frankfurter Allgemeine Zeitung (1962) in which the family is called a *major shareholder* (*"Großaktionär"*). The regular sources like *Saling Aktienführer* and *Wgzw* do not provide a percentage share for the family.

had the privilege of a sixfold voting right associated with their preferential stocks since the 1920s.[145] However, these multiple voting rights were only applicable to certain strategic decisions and provided a protection against "*Überfremdung*"—in essence the family was an anchor shareholder which made it nearly impossible for other companies to acquire *Siemens AG*.[146] That the family has a significant influence in 1958 is also visible by the two family members active in the supervisory board of *Siemens & Halske AG* (out of 12 seats) as well as by one family member active in the supervisory board of *Siemens-Schuckertwerke AG*.[147] Overall, in 1958 *Siemens* can be categorized as a family enterprise due to the family's major shareholding and the multiple voting rights which most likely provide a majority in critical strategic questions. The two family members in the supervisory board also indicate a significant influence of the family. In 2018, the family's shareholdings in *Siemens AG* are reported at 6%.[148] Furthermore, the sixfold voting right for the family does not exist anymore. It was abolished in 1999 to simplify the capital and ownership structure before *Siemens AG* started to offer their shares in the US in 2001 (which was stopped again in 2014).[149] Therefore, in 2018 *Siemens AG* is categorized as a public company. Compared to all other companies in the datasets of this thesis the date when *Siemens* became a public company or in other words when the family lost their voting right majority cannot be identified because available information do not provide the necessary share distribution.[150] Secondary sources show that the family owns around 10% of *Siemens* in 1980. It is assumed that in combination with the multiple voting

---

145 See taz (1993) and Der Spiegel (1995).

146 See Bößenecker (1980).

147 See Verlag Hoppenstedt & Co. (1958). In 1958, Ernst and Hermann von Siemens were in the supervisory board of *Siemens & Halske AG*. Ernst von Siemens was also in the supervisory board of *Siemens-Schuckertwerke AG* which was a 100% subsidiary of *Siemens & Halske*. One year later in 1959, Peter von Siemens was elected in the board of directors of *Siemens-Schuckertwerke*.

148 See Siemens AG (2021a) and the published Voting Rights Announcements since 2018.

149 See Hegmann (2014) as well as the described court rulings regarding the termination of multiple voting rights in the case of the Siemens family in Daske (2019, pp. 273–274). In addition, the sources indicate that the family never used their multiple voting right privilege because it was not necessary (see, among others, Bößenecker (1980)).

150 For the majority shareholder structure in a much earlier period, between 1905 and 1914, see Müller (2018, pp. 187–189).

rights they could have achieved a blocking minority in the shareholder meeting but no majority.[151] Therefore, the discontinuity as a family business occurs already earlier.

The case of *Siemens* shows the difficulties of historical analysis especially the search for the right sources to get the necessary information. In this dissertation, *Siemens* is only one of 250 enterprises of which such detailed data needs to be gathered.

[151] See Bößenecker (1980).

History of the German Industrial Landscape between 1958 and 2018

4

The historical development of companies like all other historical phenomena is determined by five dimensions which need to be considered in the analysis: (1) economic, (2), political, (3) legal, (4) social, and (5) cultural factors.[1] In the following, the first three dimensions are discussed in more detail in which references of the last two dimensions are embedded. Due to the research question and the quantitative approach of this thesis the economic, political, and legal frames are key for the analysis.

4.1 Economic Developments: Overall Growth with Structural Changes

After World War II, Germany develops to one of the largest economies in the world and several German enterprises are market leaders in their industries. Despite this continuous upward trend (without a war), the structure of the economy has changed drastically within just a few decades. Entrepreneurs as well as the enterprises investigated in this thesis have to navigate through these economic developments to survive in the long-term.

The economist and political scientist Philipp Lepenies calls the gross domestic product (GDP) "the most powerful statistical figure in human history"[2]. Based on this indicator politicians, economists, managers, entrepreneurs as well as consumers take decisions. It displays the development and progress of entire nations

---

[1] See Berghoff (2016b, pp. 15–26) as well as Section 3.1 for the methodological concepts.

[2] Lepenies (2016, p. ix), as well as the entire book for the overall historical development and the importance of the concept of the GDP from its origins until today in Great Britain, the USA and Germany.

M. Lantelme, *The Continuity and Discontinuity of the 250 Largest Enterprises in Germany*, Familienunternehmen und KMU,
https://doi.org/10.1007/978-3-658-42375-9_4

by translating economic activities into figures. The International Monetary Fund defines it as follows: "GDP measures the market value of goods and services that are produced in Germany after deduction of intermediate consumption but before deduction of consumption of fixed capital."[3] Despite all critics[4] it remains the most widely used measure of economic activity and provides valuable insights into the economic environment enterprises operate in. The value represents all enterprises in an economy by aggregating all individual performances. Therefore, it is a measure of the average including well and poor performing companies. The growth rate of an individual company compared to the one of the GDP shows if the firm grows faster than the entire economy or not. A firm's growth rate below the one of the entire economy can lead to a disappearance of the firm in the long-term. Therefore, the development and growth of the German GDP is described in the following.

The official statistical data of the GDP for Germany after World War II starts in 1950 and shows an increase by 230% in market prices until 1958—from EUR 49.69bn to EUR 118.95bn. This reflects a CAGR of 11.5%. The further GDP development in market prices in Germany between 1958 and 2018 is displayed in Figure 4.1. In 2018, the GDP reaches a total value of EUR 3,356bn based on which Germany represents the largest economy in the European Union (EU) and the fourth largest in this particular year.[5] Over the entire timeframe of 60 years the German GDP at market prices grows with a CAGR of 5.7%. To provide more insights into the dynamics of the GDP development the timeframe is split in shorter periods of ten years. The first two periods show the highest rates of 8.6% and 9.6%, respectively. The rates drop to 5.2% and 6.0% in the following two periods and even further between 1998 and 2008 as well as 2008 and 2018 to 2.4% and 2.8% (see Table 4.1).

---

[3] International Monetary Fund (2021).

[4] See among others the critics by the Nobel Prize-winning economists Joseph Stiglitz and Amartya Sen as well as French economist Jean Paul Fitoussi (Stiglitz, Sen, & Fitoussi, 2010).

[5] See International Monetary Fund (2019).

Table 4.1 10-Year CAGR of GDP in Germany between 1958 & 2018

Year	1958	1968	1978	1988	1998	2008	2018
GDP [EUR bn]	118.95	272.66	678.94	1,123.29	2,014.42	2,546.49	3,356.41
10-year CAGR	–	*8.6%*	*9.6%*	*5.2%*	*6.0%*	*2.4%*	*2.8%*

Source: Author's own table based on German Federal Statistical Office (2020a). Note: GDP figures at market prices.

Going one level deeper and looking at each single year, it can be shown that for the GDP development at market prices there is only one year over the entire study period, namely 2009, in which the indicator drops. In all other years, the GDP is growing. Nevertheless, it needs to be considered that these rates are not price-adjusted, and inflation is included. Therefore, an increase of the GDP could be the result of higher prices instead of additional generated economic output. Adjusting the GDP growth rates by inflation lowers them in nearly all cases. A comparison of the 10-year CAGR of the GDP at market prices and the price-adjusted rates can be found in Table 4.2. A flattening of the growth over the decades can also be observed for the price-adjusted figures.

Table 4.2 10-Year CAGR of GDP in Germany between 1950 & 2020

Year	1950	1960	1970	1980	1990	2000	2010	2020
10-year CAGR [at market prices]	–	*11.4%*	*8.4%*	*8.1%*	*5.2%*	*4.9%*	*2.0%*	*2.7%*
10-year CAGR [price-adjusted]	–	*8.2%*	*4.4%*	*2.9%*	*2.3%*	*1.6%**	*0.9%*	*1.0%*

Source: Author's own table based on German Federal Statistical Office (2020a). Note: Due to data availability a comparison starting with 1958 is not possible. *Rate is calculated from 1991 to 2000 because of official measurement changes in 1991.

Figure 4.2 shows the development of the price-adjusted GDP growth rates in more detail as well as the inflation and unemployment rates. The strong economic growth in the 1950s and at the beginning of the 1960s with low inflation rates becomes visible. The German economy was experiencing a remarkable upswing after World War II including continuous salary increases and full employment. Nevertheless, this development weakened in the late 1960s. The negative price-adjusted growth rate in 1967 was the first indicator for a rising tougher economic environment. Although the economy grew again in the following years the trend came to an end with the economic crisis in 1974/1975 (with growth rates of 0.9% / −0.9%). Both, economic and political changes contributed to this development including stronger international competitors especially on mass markets—strengthened by the opening of global markets based, among others, on the General Agreement on Tariffs and Trade (GATT) –, the breakdown of the Bretton Woods system at the beginning of the 1970s as well as the 1973 oil crisis as a consequence of the Yom Kippur War. The termination of the convertibility of the US dollar to gold and the change to free-floating currencies with the end of the Bretton Woods systems dramatically changed the institutional structures of the global economy. Governments around the world and the German government as well increased their spending following Keynesian economics due to the weakening economy which led to drastic increases in government debts.[6] In addition, the German government spending ratio (spending as percentage of GDP) increased from 32.9% in 1960 to 38.5% in 1970 and to 48.8% in 1975.[7] The state as an economic player became more important. Later, the Keynesian economics was more and more rejected, and governments supported the way towards a free-market capitalism (neoliberalism). In the same period of economic weakness inflation went up to a peak of 7.1% in 1973. Combined with the low GDP growth rates as well as the increasing unemployment rates in the mid-1970s the German economy slipped into a stagflation.[8] The following upswing in the second half of the 1970s was short-lived. GDP growth rates started to drop again in 1980 including a third decline of the economic output in 1982 (-0.4%) while inflation rates were on the rise, peaking in 1981 with 6.3%. The 1979 oil crisis was one of the reasons for this downturn. Enterprises had to adapt to these changing conditions by accelerated internationalization, implementing rationalization measures, and diversifying their product and service portfolios.[9]

The economic model in Germany so far often referred to as *cooperative capitalism* (which is also linked to *Deutschland AG*) in which the long-term development of the enterprises and the shielding from the stock market were

---

[6] See German Federal Statistical Office (2020b, p. 41) for the exact figures of government spending and Giersch, Paqué, and Schmieding (1992) as well as Plumpe (2018, pp. 70–71) for an overview of the economic development in Germany at this period. For an European perspective see Eichengreen (1995).

[7] See Bundesministerium der Finanzen (2021).

[8] For the unemployment rates since 1951 see German Federal Statistical Office (2021c).

[9] As a result of the required corporate changes in the 1970 s / 1980 s the consulting business became more and more relevant in supporting enterprises. For its development in Germany and Western Europe see Kipping (1996, 1999) and for a self-description see Berger (2015).

key was questioned. Because markets did not expand as in previous years companies focused more on gaining market shares which led to stronger mergers and acquisitions (M&A) activities. This has increased the relevance of the financial market also in Germany (e.g., raising capital or acquiring companies with the acquirer's own shares).

The changing conditions resulted in relatively low economic growth since the mid-1980s which was only overcome by the German reunification after 1989. These years with growth rates around 5.0% were followed by an economic crisis in 1993 (-1.0%) again with a high inflation rate of 4.5%. While the inflation rate started to become more stable after the crisis in 1993 oscillating between 0.5% and 2.6% until 2018 the GDP development was much more volatile. In 2002 and 2003 the GDP declined again by 0.2% and 0.7%, respectively, because of the effects of the dot-com bubble as well as the September 11 attacks in 2001. The German economy recovered over the next five years until the effects of the financial crisis of 2007 to 2008 resulted in a GDP decline of 5.7% (the highest ever recorded) in 2009.[10] The upswing quickly followed in 2010 with a rise in the GDP of 4.2% and 3.9% in the subsequent year. Until 2018, the end of the study period of this thesis, the growth rates varied between 0.4% and 2.6%.

A large contribution of the overall GDP growth can be allocated to foreign trade which becomes a major pillar for the German economy. The export quota which is the share of exports in GDP increased significantly from 21.8% in 1958 to 47.3% in 2018.[11] Nearly half of the GDP is linked to exports. They include, for example, the products of the German automotive industry which has a strong presence in global markets as well as of the mechanical engineering industry.

In summary, the German economy shows a continuous development with a CAGR of 5.7% between 1958 and 2018 without experiencing war. It has strong growth until the end of the 1960s with full employment and low inflation rates. This phase is followed by years of stagflation increasing the government's debts and spending ratio dramatically. Various global economic crises and political clashes cause a longer period of little economic growth and a rising unemployment rate which accelerates after the German reunification. While the inflation rate stabilizes from the mid-1990s until today the GDP experiences several setbacks especially in 1993, in 2002 / 2003 and in 2009. Nevertheless, in 2010 the recovery follows immediately and since then the German economy has again

[10] The financial crisis has led to many dramatic fates such as the suicide of Adolf Merckle due to a liquidity crisis of one of his main asset management companies (see Section 3.7.2.2).

[11] See J. Hiemer (personal communication, 2022) and German Federal Statistical Office (2021a).

continuously gained strength. After World War II and within 60 years, Germany has become the fourth largest economy in the world. Exports play a significant role in this success. German enterprises have to adapt to the shifting conditions and simultaneously have shaped this development. As highlighted in Section 1.1 family businesses contribute to a large extent to the overall economic development and prosperity in Germany.[12] However, not all companies have managed this overall growth path successfully because the economic development is not as linear as Figure 4.1 suggests. It has been more like a roller coaster ride over the last 60 years and some industries have almost completely disappeared on this dynamic journey.

Despite the overall positive development of the German economy there have been massive shifts from one sector to another. Following the three-sector model the change within the German economy becomes visible (see Table 4.3).[13] In 1958, 16.2% of all employed people work in the primary sector which includes agriculture, forestry and fishing. Its share drops to 1.4% in 2018. The share of the secondary sector which covers manufacturing also decreases from 47.3% to 24.1% although the absolute number of employed people decreases only slightly from 11.3 million to 10.8 million. On the other hand, the tertiary sector, services, information sector and remaining industries[14], increases from 36.5% to 74.5% which corresponds to a change from 8.7 million employed people to 33.4 million.[15] The numbers look similar for the share of the sectors based on Gross Value Added (GVA) contribution. The first and third sector have a slightly smaller contribution compared to employed people and the secondary sector has a higher share.[16] Overall, there has been a major shift from agriculture and a smaller shift from manufacturing towards services. Therefore, the tertiary sector has become more important for the German economy over the last 60 years. The changes are caused by various reasons including technological progress, productivity gains

---

[12] See Gottschalk et al. (2019, p. 6). Further, see La Porta et al. (1999) for a global perspective.

[13] See Steiner (2016, pp. 15–23) for a critical review of the three-sector model developed in the 1930 s and 1940 s and its use in historical sciences.

[14] Steiner mentions that the tertiary sector is a residual size [*Restgröße*] and sees difficulties in the definition of the sectors in detail (see Steiner (2016, pp. 17–18)).

[15] See J. Hiemer (personal communication, 2022) as well as Köster (2020, pp. 49–60).

[16] See German Federal Statistical Office (2020b, p. 56). GVA can be seen as a proxy for GDP. For 2018, the shares are 0.8% for the primary, 30.3% for the secondary and 68.9% for the tertiary sector.

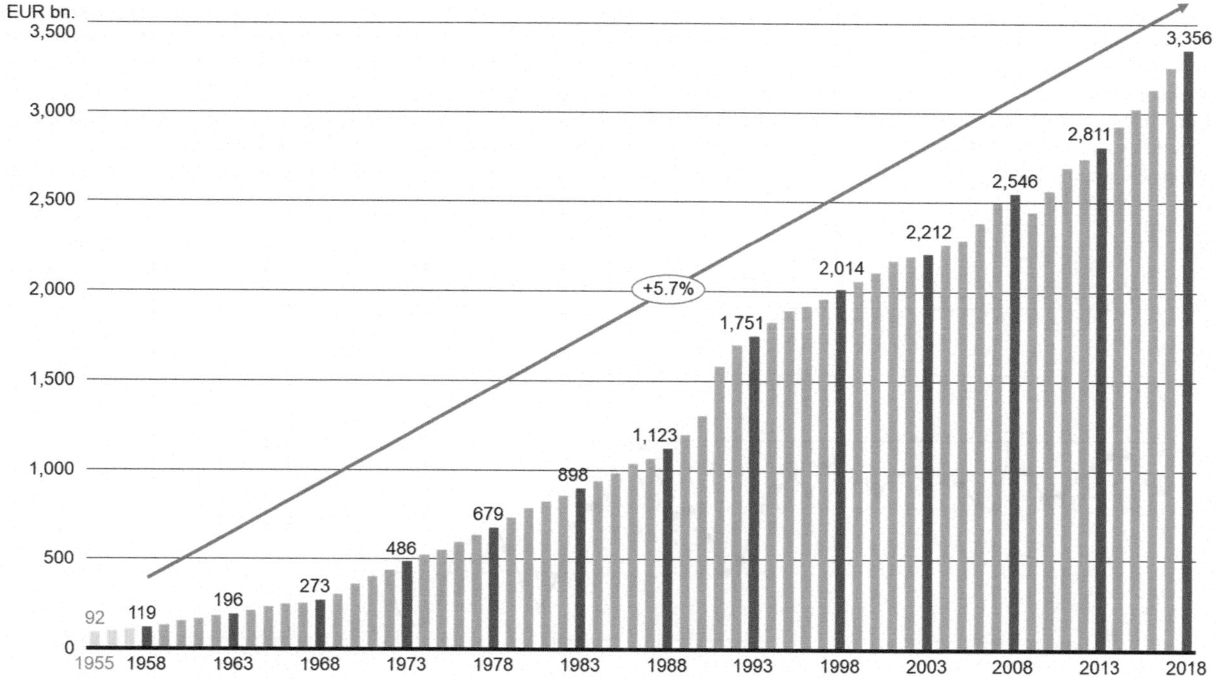

Figure 4.1 GDP Development at Market Prices in Germany from 1958 to 2018. (Source: Author's own figure based on German Federal Statistical Office (2020a). Note: Data until 1959 consider the former federal territory without Saarland and West-Berlin. Data from 1960 to 1969 considers the former federal territory. Data from 1970 to 1990 consider the former federal territory based on the 2005 revision of the National Accounts. Data from 1991 onwards consider the reunified German Federal Republic. Due to conceptual and definitional differences, the data from 1970 onward and those from 1991 onward are not fully comparable with those of previous years)

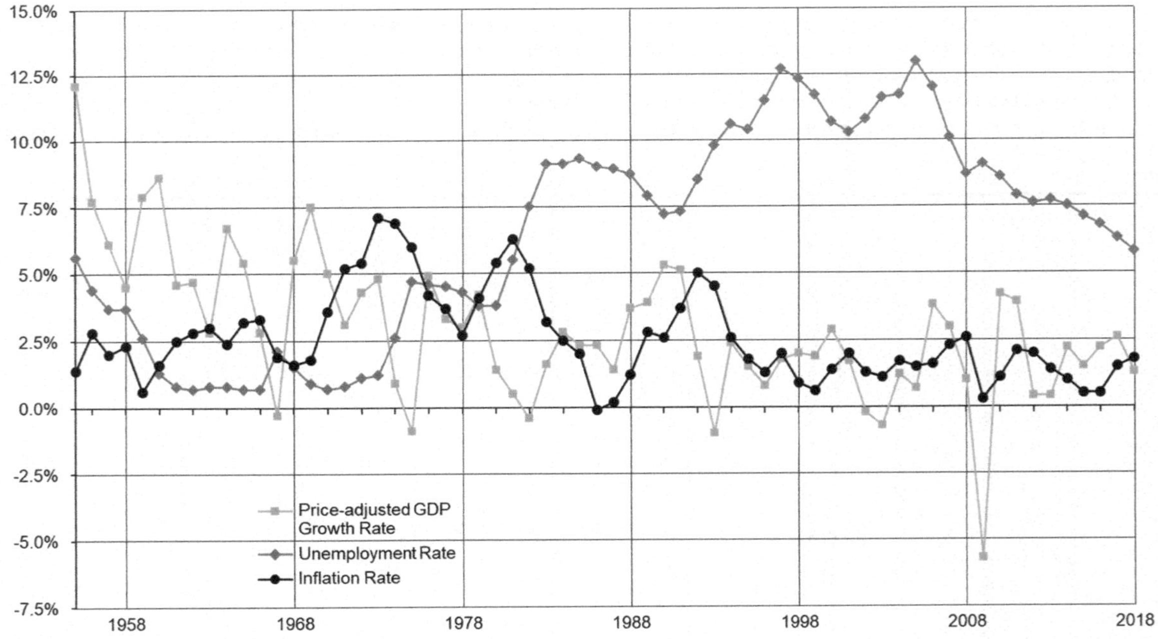

Figure 4.2 Price-Adjusted GDP Growth, Unemployment & Inflation Rates in Germany from 1958 to 2018. (Source: Author's own figure based on German Federal Statistical Office (2020a), German Federal Statistical Office (2021b) and German Federal Statistical Office (2021c). Note (GDP): See Figure 4.1. Note (inflation): Until 1991, the figures consider the former federal territory; from 1992, the reunified German Federal Republic. From 1950 to 1962, the data refer to the price index of four-person households of blue- and white-collar workers with medium incomes, from 1963 to 1991 to the price index for all private households, and from 1992 to the consumer price index. The comparability over time of the values from 1992 onward with those from the years up to 1991 is limited due to conceptual changes. Note (unemployment): Unemployment rate of dependent civilian labor force. Until 1990, the figures consider the former federal territory; from 1991, the reunified German Federal Republic. Figures between 1955 to 1958 without Saarland)

and international competition.[17] It needs to be highlighted that the number of employed people has increased by 87.7% from 23.9 million to 44.9 million over the last six decades. The economic growth described above is also possible due to this increase. Overall, the structural changes have been a success for the overall economic development of Germany despite regional declines.[18]

The dramatic shifts between the sectors are also reflected in the development of specific industries, for example, the coal and steel industry, the automotive industry as well as food retailing and the information and communication industry. These developments will be further outlined in the quantitative as well as the long-term analyses of the datasets and their observations including the identification of the company types which foster the changes.

Table 4.3 Development of Primary, Secondary & Tertiary Sector from 1958 to 2018

Year	Employed persons [in million]	Agriculture, forestry and fishing (primary sector)	Manufacturing (secondary sector)	Services and remaining industries (tertiary sector)
1958	23.9	3.9	11.3	8.7
	100%	*16.2%*	*47.3%*	*36.5%*
2018	44.9	0.6	10.8	33.4
	100%	*1.4%*	*24.1%*	*74.5%*

Source: Author's own table based on German Federal Statistical Office (2022a).

Two major developments at the intersection of economic and political factors which have an impact on the long-term development of the German economy and enterprises are, first, the privatization efforts of state-owned enterprises between 1958 and 2018 and, second, the evolvement of public utilities which is also linked to the first point.

Overall, the industrial holdings of the German state steadily decline between 1958 and 2018. At the end of the 1950s the Federal Republic of Germany has a separate ministry which is responsible for the various (industrial) assets owned by the state—the *Bundesministerium für wirtschaftlichen Besitz des Bundes*. Among them are *Vereinigte Elektrizitäts- und Bergwerks-AG* (*VEBA*) and

[17] For an analysis of the structural changes and their root causes see, among others, the early publication by Donges (1986) as well as the historical analysis by Steiner (2016, pp. 23–34).

[18] See Plumpe and Steiner (2016, pp. 13–14).

Vereinigte Industrie-Unternehmungen AG (*VIAG*) as holding companies of several state-owned enterprises including *Preußische Bergwerks- und Hütten AG* (*Preussag*) as well as the large enterprises *Hüttenwerk Salzgitter AG*, *Bergwerksgesellschaft Hibernia AG*, *Kieler Howaldtswerke AG* and *Volkswagenwerk AG*. Smaller companies are also part of the state's ownership like *Holzverzuckerungs-GmbH* and *Deutsche Wochenschau GmbH*.[19] Sack mentions that the industrial holdings of the state are mainly inherited from the German Reich and Prussia and a random composition.[20] A first privatization wave can be seen until 1965 based on the IPOs of *Preussag* in 1959 (~21.0% remain with *VEBA*), of *Volkswagenwerk AG* in 1961 (~20.0% remain with the German state) and of *VEBA* in 1965 (~43.8% remain with the German state). Drivers of going public are the ideas to spread the ownership widely and let citizens participate in the dividends of the companies. In the 1970s, political discussions start to move away from Keynesian positions and transfer more economic activities to private companies. Nevertheless, further divestments of the German state only take place in the 1980s with additional sales of *VEBA* and *Volkswagen* shares, the IPOs of *VIAG* and *Deutsche Verkehrs-Kredit-Bank AG* and the sale of *Deutsche Lufthansa AG* shares. By the late 1980s, *Salzgitter AG*, *Volkswagen AG*, *VIAG* and *VEBA* are completely privatized. In the 1990s, the efforts are driven by the privatization of the state-owned *companies* of the former GDR after the reunification as well as by the privatization of *Deutsche Telekom AG* and *Deutsche Post AG*. Again, the ownership of the companies should be widely distributed with the participation of many citizens ("*Volksaktie*"). The further reduction of the state to the core of its tasks is another key objective of the privatizations, i.e., that the companies become more competitive and the market more open.[21] In the 2000s, mainly rental housing stocks are sold as well as remaining stakes in the companies already mentioned.[22] Overall, the industrial ownership of the German state has been reduced in the observation

[19] See Bundesministerium für wirtschaftlichen Besitz des Bundes (1959) including an overview of the industrial assets. The ministry was renamed the *Bundesschatzministerium* in 1961 and dissolved in 1969. In addition, see Zugehör (2003, pp. 71–74) for the privatizations in the 1980 s and 1990 s. Other federal ministries were directly responsible for *Deutsche Bundesbahn* and *Deutsche Bundespost*.

[20] See Sack (2019, p. 147).

[21] See Sack (2019, pp. 157–158).

[22] For an overview of the development of the direct ownerships of the Federal Republic of Germany between 1959 and 2016 see Bundesministerium der Finanzen (2017).

period to enable citizens to participate in the development of the enterprises but also due to the political conviction of a leaner state.[23]

The second state-related companies are public utilities. Compared to the previously analyzed enterprises they are mainly owned by cities or municipalities. Their origins are often related to the establishment of a gas or water supply in smaller or bigger cities in the 19th century.[24] Although larger municipal organizations already exist at the end of the 19th century which, among others, combine municipal electricity and gas works as well as gas lighting as in Munich[25] organizations with the designation *public utilities* [*Stadtwerke*] first emerge towards the end of the 1930s based on the adoption of the *Deutsche Gemeindeordnung* (*DGO*) in 1935 and the *Eigenbetriebsverordnung* (*EigVO*) in 1938. Since then, municipal companies can be established as *Eigenbetrieb*.[26] Despite a municipal organization *Stadtwerke München*, for example, are officially founded in 1939 combining the electricity utilities, the gas and water utilities and the transport utilities. The dataset with the 250 largest enterprises of 1958 includes several *Eigenbetriebe* like *Stadtwerke Düsseldorf* and *Städtische Werke Nürnberg*. After World War II the German federal states established their own *Eigenbetriesverordnung* but in terms of content, the regulations remain mostly identical to the one from 1938. In the second half of the 20th century more and more municipal companies start to change their legal form from *Eigenbetrieb* to one of the legal forms of German Commercial Law like *GmbH* or *AG* or to the newly established form of *Anstalt des öffentlichen Rechts*.[27] Today, they are competing with private companies on liberalized markets in several areas like energy or telecommunications. Nevertheless, they remain in the hands of municipalities or cities to fulfill their legal duties. The ownership development as well as the performance of these

[23] During the financial crisis at the end of the 2000 s the German state became part owner of, for example, *Commerzbank AG*. This was a temporary engagement and acted as a lender of last resort.

[24] See for example the existence of a gas supply in 1838 and the first gas plant in 1868 in Elberfeld which is the basis for today's *Wuppertaler Stadtwerke AG* (see WSW Wuppertaler Stadtwerke GmbH (2021)).

[25] See Bähr and Erker (2017) for the history of *Stadtwerke München*, Munich ' s municipal utilities company.

[26] See Cronauge and Pieck (2016, pp. 58–59) for a more detailed description of the history of municipal companies including the legal basis.

[27] An overview of the legal forms and their advantages as well as disadvantages for municipalities can be found in Fabry and Appel (2011, pp. 43–56). Further, see Cronauge and Pieck (2016, pp. 61–62) and their overview of the development of legal forms.

state-owned companies is analyzed based on the datasets of this dissertation as well.

In summary, the German state was the owner of some of the largest enterprises in Germany several decades ago. Although most of the holdings have been sold to date the German state as the majority owner plays a significant role in the development of several companies and remains a key shareholder of infrastructure companies like the *Deutsche Bahn AG* despite more liberalized markets. In addition, lots of the utilities are further state-owned. They compete with private companies on liberalized markets but continue to secure basic services. Both company types have contributed and continue to contribute to the economic development of Germany.

4.2 Political Developments: From Nations to a Union

Politically, Germany has developed from a defeated and occupied nation after World War II to one of the leading members of the European Union (EU). European integration as a key priority of most German governments affects, in addition to the political realm, other areas like the economic and legal one as well. In the same decades, Germany is reunited, and it is not until the late 1950s that the Saarland joins the Federal Republic. Both political events also have economic consequences.

Although the political integration of the Saarland into the Federal Republic of Germany already happens in 1957 it takes more than two more years for the economic integration. The 1956 Saar Treaty between France and Germany changes the status of the French protectorate which it was since the end of World War II.[28] The Saarland is the second smallest German state. Nevertheless, it is of importance due to its coal deposits. Therefore, several of the largest German enterprises of 1958 are located there (e.g., *Saarbergwerke AG*). Their revenues have to be converted from *Francs* to *DM* for the calculations of this dissertation due to the economic integration in 1959 when also the *DM* is introduced. Joining the Federal Republic is of economic and of historical importance for the Saarland but also for the Federal Republic.

The second *reunification* in Germany is the integration of the former German Democratic Republic (GDR) into the Federal Republic of Germany after the peaceful revolution in 1989. From a political perspective the reunification also marks the end of reunification efforts which started with the occupation after

[28] See Linsmayer and Reicherlt (2012) as well as Herrmann (2012).

World War II and the separation into four occupation zones.[29] It also creates a larger economic area with new market opportunities mainly for Western companies. Due to different economic systems the opportunities for Eastern *companies* are limited which can also be seen by the very limited number of companies located in the new federal states which make it to the list of the largest enterprises.[30] The extent to which the politically and socially necessary reunification has succeeded economically is disputed.[31]

A political development which started with a kind of economic initiative shortly after World War II is the ongoing European integration. In 1951, the "Treaty of Paris" is signed by Belgium, France, Italy, Luxembourg, the Netherlands and West Germany to establish the "European Coal and Steel Community" (ECSC). It is an initiative by the French Foreign Minister Robert Schuman. A political objective is to secure peace in Europe after the devastating historical experiences of World War I and World War II. The ECSC as a supranational organization is responsible for the joint regulation of the coal and steel industries of the participating countries. The regulatory measures include, among others, the creation of a common market as well as the approval of mergers and acquisitions in the industries.[32] For example, the *High Authority* of the ECSC approves the acquisition of *Bochumer Verein für Gußstahlfabrikation AG* by *Hütten- und Bergwerke Rheinhausen AG* (part of *Krupp*) in 1959 after several negotiation rounds.[33] Despite several setbacks (e.g., European Defense Community and European Political Community) the integration continues. The economic collaboration deepens between the six founding members of the ECSC with the establishment of the European Atomic Energy Community (EAEC / Euratom) and the European Economic Community (EEC) in 1958. At that time the countries are already striving for a common market with free movement of people, services and capital as well as a customs union. The ECSC, EAEC and EEC are merged in 1967 into the European Communities (EC). Although most of these initiatives are focused on the economic integration of the member states, the political integration (including a common legislative) is not given up.[34] Further developments around the Economic and Monetary Union (EMU) as well as the *Mauerfall* in 1989 accelerate

---

[29] See MacAdams (1993, pp. 152–157).

[30] See the remarks by Joly (1998, pp. 14–15).

[31] See among others the latest research on the *Treuhandanstalt* by Malycha (2022). The institution was responsible for the privatization of the state-owned *companies* after 1989.

[32] See Weidenfeld (2020, pp. 13–14).

[33] See FAZ (1959) and Section 3.7.1.1.

[34] See Weidenfeld (2020, pp. 14–15).

the integration and several new candidates for a unified Europe in Central and Eastern Europe appear. Finally, in 1992, the European Union (EU) is founded based on the Maastricht Treaty. Since then, several adjustments have been made to the supranational organization and it has grown to 27 member states of which 19 are part of the euro area with a common currency. All member states are linked by a common European market with (almost) no trade barriers.[35] This common market which was already a key objective of predecessor organizations is one reason for the high export quota of Germany which was mentioned in the previous chapter.

Overall, the political developments in Germany including the reunifications have led to an overall European integration which has also improved the economic conditions for enterprises based on a common European market. Furthermore, the EU can speak with one voice for its 27 member states and with a joint GDP of EUR 16.0bn in 2018 represents the second largest economic area behind the USA.[36]

4.3 Legal Developments: Increasing Transparency and Competition

Besides the highlighted economic and political factors there are legislative changes between 1958 and 2018 which have an impact on the development of German enterprises. New German and European legal forms are introduced which provide a broader range of possibilities for the development of companies. On the other hand, enterprises are legally obliged to publish (more detailed) corporate data to provide greater transparency to shareholders and the public. Such demands were strictly rejected 60 years ago.

At the annual general meeting of *Schering AG* on 10th June 1959 the chairman of the management board at the time, Dr. Wilhelm Borner, held a lively discussion with a shareholder about the disclosure requirements. Despite an explicit request from the shareholder Dr. Borner refused to provide the revenue figure for the financial year 1958. He argued that this was neither in the interest of the company nor of the shareholders and that they would only provide the figure if they were legally obliged to do so.[37] And at that time, stock corporations were not.

---

[35] See.

[36] Including the United Kingdom which left the EU in 2020. See European Statistical Office (2022).

[37] See Frankfurter Allgemeine Zeitung (1959b).

The concerns, shared by many other industry representatives as well, were mainly directed against feared competitive disadvantage because competitors (especially from abroad) might gain valuable insights into the cost calculations of the companies. Nevertheless, besides ongoing discussions in the media at that time there was already a draft law of the *AktG* under review, proposing to implement a more detailed profit and loss statement in the annual reports.[38] The revised version of the *AktG* with the obligation to report the total revenue figure came into force in December 1959 with a majority in the *Bundestag* and *Bundesrat* based on the ruling Christian Democratic parties (*Christian Democratic Union* (*CDU*) and *Christian Social Union* (*CSU*)).[39] This adoption of the law was only the first step towards a more extensive reform of the *AktG* in 1965which is still the basis of today's law.[40] The revision of the existing 1937 *AktG* was considered after World War II for several reasons; among others the general (political) view to eliminate National Socialist ideas in German legislation (e.g., *Führerprinzip* in the management board) as well the improvement of conditions for the *AG* on the financial market (e.g., extended shareholders' profit rights and increased disclosure requirements).[41] On the other hand, not all reform proposals made it into the new law. Although shares with multiple voting rights were forbidden in principle since the 1937 reform of the *AktG* several exceptions (justified for the good of society or because of economic interests) have been granted by the responsible authority since then. Furthermore, existing multiple voting shares could be continued without a due date. For the reform in 1965 several attempts were made to include a phase out of existing multiple voting shares and a definitive prohibition of them, but it failed due to the influence of leading business associations which wanted to keep the status quo. Multiple voting shares were introduced in 1900 but remained exceptional, e.g., in restructuring cases, until after World War I. Then, politically supported, they were used to avoid losing control of companies to foreign investors. Rising inflation and the depreciation of the *Mark* against the dollar led to multiple (hostile) takeovers of German firms by foreign companies. This should be prevented. But the shares also became an instrument for the existing management and owners to consolidate their power despite increasing capital requirements. The following public debate ended with the prohibition of

---

[38] See Kropff (2007, pp. 732–733).

[39] See BGBl. I 1959 p. 789 with the revised version of § 132 AktG (as of 1959) outlining the structure of the profit and loss statement including the total revenue.

[40] See BGBl. I 1965 p. 1089 as well as BGBl. I 1965 p. 1185.

[41] See Kropff (2007, pp. 697–720).

new multiple voting shares in 1937 but this law had no impact on existing ones. It was not until the late 1990s that multiple voting rights were finally abolished.[42]

Besides the mentioned reforms after World War II the development of the German corporation law in the 19th century already had a major impact on the emergence of large stock corporations and enterprises. The first German Corporation Law (*Aktienrecht*) was established in 1870[43] one year before the Proclamation of the German Empire [*Deutsche Reichsgründung*] and the foundation of the new German state[44]. It was built on the German Commercial Code (*Allgemeines Deutsches Handelsgesetzbuch, ADHGB*) of 1861[45]. With the reform in 1870 which included *Kommanditgesellschaften auf Aktien* (*KGaA*) as well as *AG*s the concession system was abolished. The authorization by the state for the foundation of one of the two types of firms was discarded and their oversight by the state was replaced by the introduction of the supervisory board (*Aufsichtsrat*).[46] Plumpe sees in this new opportunity to found an organization without state interference the requirement for the development of the modern firm besides required free markets.[47] Nevertheless, the fact that the 1870 reform was insufficient became apparent in the Founders' Crash in the following years when lots of the newly founded corporations went bankrupt due to heavy speculations and consequently many shareholders lost their investments. Legislators saw the need for new laws that would provide better protection for shareholders and increase the transparency of the foundation process and the annual reporting. For this reason, the first proposals for a reform of the German Corporation Law were developed in the early- and mid-1870s. Nevertheless, it took several years and discussions before the adapted law was introduced in 1884 of which certain parts can still be found in the current *AktG*. The legislator found (impactful) solutions to the identified weaknesses especially in the formalization of the founding process and the strengthening of the general assembly (*Generalversammlung*).[48] Overall, in

---

[42] See Selgert (2018, pp. 80–88) and Kropff (2007, p. 794).

[43] Mainly driven by the Hanseatic cities and Prussia although a compromise between their different views on the degree of liberalization had to be negotiated—see Schubert (1981) for an analysis of the legislative procedure.

[44] See Abrams (2006) for an overview of the proclamation and Wehler (2006) for a detailed analysis.

[45] See Pahlow (2007) for a comprehensive review of the ADHGB.

[46] See Lieder (2007, pp. 321–333).

[47] See Plumpe (2018, p. 1).

[48] See Schubert and Hommelhoff (1985, pp. 55–102) for the evaluation of the reform of the German Corporation Law (*Gesetz betreffend die Kommanditgesellschaft auf Aktien und die Aktiengesellschaft*) in 1884 and its detailed impact.

1887 as well as in 1907 around 80% of the largest enterprises in Germany had the legal form of an *AG*.[49]

Furthermore, at the end of the 19th century a totally new type of company was adopted. In 1892 the German legislator introduced the *Gesellschaft mit beschränkter Haftung* (*GmbH*)—a limited company. The objective was to close the gap between the *AG* and partnerships because the *AG* became more expensive and complicated in regards of foundation and administration with the 1884 reform of the Corporation Law and partnerships had unlimited liability of the partners.[50] The *GmbH* with its limited liability became a major success and supported the economic upswing in the late 19th century. While in 1882 around 95% of German enterprises were private firms[51] the *GmbH* as a corporation has become the most common legal form for firms in Germany in the late 20th century.[52] In the dataset of this thesis several of the largest enterprises of 1958 have the legal form of a *GmbH*, especially family-owned firms like *Franz Haniel & Cie. GmbH*, *Helmut Horten GmbH* and *Grundig-Radio-Werke GmbH*.

Although the legislator made additional changes to the *AktG* after the reforms of 1959 and 1965 the core remains as of 1965 until 2018.[53] In addition, the obligation to publish the financial statements for the *AG* are now further regulated in the *Handelsgesetzbuch* (*HGB*)—Commercial Code. There, also the disclosure requirements for all other corporations (i.e., *KGaA*, *GmbH* and *GmbH & Co. KG*) as well as companies which exceed a certain size are regulated.[54]

The development of the *AktG* until the mid-1960s is of importance for the research questions in this thesis because of two main reasons. First, based on the reform of 1959 listed companies were legally obliged to publish their annual revenue figures which further improved the monitoring possibilities of the shareholders, and the published data is a major component for historical long-term analysis like the one of this thesis. Second, with the 1870 and 1884 reform the *AG* became a driver for the evolution of the modern firm with its bureaucratic and functional divisions as well as the adjusted corporate governance system. This type of company shaped the German economy over the next century.

Over the last decades similar legislative adjustments have been made related to the *Depotstimmrechte* mentioned in Section 2.2.2.4. The legislator saw the

49 See Fohlin (2005, p. 228).

50 See Fastrich (2017, p. 9).

51 See Pohl (1991, p. 35).

52 See Grziwotz (2018, pp. 2–9).

53 See Bayer and Habersack (2007), especially Chapter IV.

54 See, among others, §§ 325 onwards HGB, $ 264a HGB and §§ 326–327 HGB.

necessity to further regulate the ways how banks were able to exert influence on listed enterprises apart from direct ownership. In the 1950s banks were able to vote on behalf of their depositors which was offered as a service to their clients that shareholders did not have to attend the general meetings in person. However, the shareholders only rarely acted on their voting requests, which is why banks were able to vote in their favor. Therefore, the influence of banks on the votes at shareholders' meetings in the late 1950s can be assumed to be greater than the data of the shareholder structure of the listed companies suggest.[55]

Reforms of existing legal forms are not the only legislative change which have an impact on the development of enterprises. New legal forms have been introduced as well and companies are making use of them. In 2004, the *Societas Europaea* (*SE*) was introduced as a corporation in accordance with the corporate law of the EU. A similar form for cooperatives is the *Societas Cooperativa Europaea* (*SCE*) which was launched in 2006. In the course of European integration these legal forms follow largely uniform legal principles across the European Union. In Germany, the SE is basically treated like an *AG* with differences, among others, in participation.[56] Several years earlier, the German Federal Court of Justice confirmed in 1997 that a corporation like the *AG* or *GmbH* (and later on also the *SE*) can be a general partner in a *KGaA*.[57] After this judgement, the number of *KGaA* increased significantly and more companies went public using this legal form.[58] In the 2018 dataset of this thesis, it will be shown that several of the largest enterprises operate as *SE* or *KGaA*. Due to these legislative changes, enterprises can choose a legal form which best suits them from a larger portfolio. The legal form provides the framework for the development of the company.

In contrast to these expanded development opportunities, stricter requirements with regard to the cooperation between companies have emerged over the last decades. In 1958, the same year the study period of this dissertation starts, the Federal Cartel Office [*Bundeskartellamt*] was established. Its main tasks include the implementation of the ban on cartels, merger control as well as the control of abusive practices of dominant or powerful companies.[59] The ban of cartels similar to the disentanglement of certain industries (e.g., coal and steel, chemical industry) was a key objective of the Allies after World War II to ensure that German enterprises do not become as powerful as before. Hundreds of cartels existed

---

[55] See Denton et al. (2017, p. 69).

[56] See Theisen and Wenz (2005) for an overview of the *SE* development.

[57] See BGH II ZB 11/96.

[58] See Fett and Stütz (2017).

[59] See Bundeskartellamt (2018).

in Germany in the first half of the 20th century.[60] The increase of competition and the limitation of coordination between market players are essentials of the German economic system. The Federal Cartel Office has the oversight of these principles. Over the last decades, this tightening development is also connected to European integration because today the Directorate-General for Competition within the European Commission works with the national competition authorities to further enforce EU competition rules.

4.4 Summary: The Continuous and Dynamic Development of the German Economy

Over the last six decades Germany has experienced a continuous development to become the fourth largest industrial nation. Despite this steady path the economy has changed drastically. The development with a GDP CAGR of 5.7% between 1958 and 2018 is characterized by structural changes. The economy shifts towards services and the importance of the first and second sector is declining. In this context, enterprises can be described as agents of change in the German economy. At the same time, political and legal developments have created new opportunities for enterprises like the common European market with its extended export possibilities and the new German and European legal forms with their updated governance structures. New institutions like the Federal Cartel Office and the supranational organizations of the EU secure the advantages of competition and form a counterweight to other major economies. Furthermore, the German state has withdrawn from direct ownership of companies at that time, but cities and municipalities remain an important owner of utilities for basic services.

But how do the enterprises develop within this continuous but also dynamic economy? How do they get impacted by the political and legal changes over the last decades? And what are the differences between the various company types? To further analyze these questions as well as the overarching research questions the long-term development of the affected companies needs to be investigated. Therefore, Chapter 5 analyzes the 250 largest enterprises of 1958 and their development until 2018. Furthermore, in Chapter 6 the 250 largest enterprises of 2018 are investigated back to 1958 or their foundation. The historical context described in this chapter is used for the interpretation of the results based on the analyses of the datasets which follow in the next chapters.

[60] See Kurzlechner (2009, pp. 28–77).

Quantitative Analysis: The 250 Largest Enterprises of 1958 and 2018

5

After providing the context in the form of relevant economic, political, and legal developments in Germany over 60 years the two samples with the 250 largest enterprises of 1958 and 2018 are analyzed.[1] This chapter provides an overview of both datasets and their included companies. As highlighted in Section 2.1.1 and 2.1.2 there are several conditions like age, growth and ownership structure which are expected to impact the continuity of companies. Therefore, this chapter analyzes these conditions step by step. It further compares the datasets to extract initial observations and patterns of key developments which are put into the described historical context. The derived definitions of the various company types from Section 2.2.2.4 are applied to both rankings which ensures that the two observed statuses in 1958 and 2018 can be compared as outlined in this chapter. Predominantly the companies are compared on an aggregated level, e.g., different company types. This ensures that the modeled developments in this chapter are not confused with the actual development of a specific company. Nevertheless, in several cases, specific company names are highlighted to provide a glimpse into the development of specific enterprises included in the datasets, e.g., naming the largest and smallest or the oldest and youngest companies of the samples. The

---

[1] As a reference of this thesis' sample, in total 3,483,691 enterprises exist in Germany in 2018 of which 15,452 (0.4%) have more than 250 employees (see German Federal Statistical Office (2019)).

Supplementary Information The online version contains supplementary material available at https://doi.org/10.1007/978-3-658-42375-9_5.

M. Lantelme, *The Continuity and Discontinuity of the 250 Largest Enterprises in Germany*, Familienunternehmen und KMU,
https://doi.org/10.1007/978-3-658-42375-9_5

detailed developments of individual enterprises are analyzed in the subsequent two chapters.

Overall, it can already be highlighted that there are tremendous changes between the two datasets although some enterprises appear in both datasets.

5.1 Enterprise Size Ranges and Modeled Growth Rates: Growing Bigger—Fast

In a first step, the enterprises' sizes and ranges within the samples as well as the modeled growth rates to remain one of the 250 largest enterprises over 60 years are provided (see Table 5.1). A certain growth rate is expected to be required to survive in the long-term. Overall, the average company grew by 6.6% and the spread between the largest and smallest enterprises in the sample increased tremendously. This indicates a growing gap between the developments of the investigated enterprises.

The 250 companies of 1958 generated a total revenue of EUR 67.7bn (DM 132.3bn). At that time, the largest enterprise based on revenue is *Deutsche Bundesbahn* with a revenue of EUR 3,493 m (DM 6,831 m) which corresponds to a share of 5.2% of the samples' total revenue. Moreover, *Deutsche Bundesbahn* has around 519,300 employees.[2] In comparison, the company on position 250 and therefore the smallest one in the 1958 list is *Saar-Ferngas AG* which generates EUR 41 m (DM 79 m) in revenue and employs around 500 employees. Thus, the list covers a revenue range of EUR 3,452 m (DM 6,752 m) which also means that the largest company has 85.9 times the revenue of the smallest company or, vice versa, *Saar-Ferngas* generates 1.2% of the revenue of *Deutsche Bundesbahn*. Furthermore, the revenue average of all 250 enterprises is EUR 271 m (DM 529 m) while the median is EUR 108 m (DM 211).[3] With a standard deviation of EUR 407 m (DM 796 m) the company sizes are quite different which also shows that the very top companies are very rare exceptions.

In comparison, the total revenue of the 250 largest enterprises of 2018 in Germany is EUR 3,065.3bn. In this dataset *Volkswagen AG* is on top with a revenue

[2] The largest non-state-owned enterprise is *Siemens AG* on third position with a revenue of EUR 1.7bn (DM 3.3bn) and around 179,000 employees. For more company examples see Section 5.6.

[3] The two companies which determine the median of the 1958 list are *Howaldtswerke Hamburg AG* and *Knorr-Bremse AG* on position 125 and 126 with a revenue of EUR 109 m and EUR 106 m.

of EUR 235.9bn which corresponds to 7.7% of the total revenue of the 250 companies. Moreover, *Volkswagen* employs around 664,500 people worldwide which also makes it the largest employer of the 2018 sample. On the other end of the ranking is *Dussmann Stiftung & Co. KGaA* as the smallest of the 250 companies which generates a revenue of EUR 2.3bn with around 66,100 employees. This results in a revenue range of EUR 233.5bn with *Volkswagen* having 100.7 times the revenue of *Dussmann* or, vice versa, *Dussmann* generates 1.0% of *Volkswagen's* revenue. The revenue average of the 250 largest enterprises of 2018 is EUR 12.3bn while the median is lower with EUR 4.6bn.[4] Furthermore, the sample has a standard deviation of EUR 23.6bn which is a high value due to the broad range of company sizes in the sample.

The descriptive results of the two datasets so far show that the ratio between the largest and the smallest enterprise increases from 1958 to 2018. The company on position one becomes larger relative to the company on position 250. Additionally, even within the relatively small group of the 250 largest enterprises the diversity in terms of size is enormous.

This increasing gap between the largest and the smallest enterprise of the sample can also be confirmed when looking not only at the 1st and 250th company but also when considering larger groups at the top and bottom of the samples. In 1958, the three largest and smallest companies have a share of the sample's total revenue of 11.1% and 0.18%, respectively. 60 years later this share rises to 16.6% and 0.23%. Similar results are found when increasing the number of enterprises to ten. The share goes up from 26.23% for the ten largest and 0.63% for the ten smallest companies in 1958 to 34.08% and 0.77%, respectively, in 2018. The share of the three largest enterprises increases from 10.9% to 16.3%. The share of the three smallest companies in the sample even decreases slightly from 0.47% to 0.44%. A similar comparison by Lantelme for the period from 1971 to 2011 based on 143 companies in each year provides similar findings.[5] The share of the three largest enterprises increases from 10.9% in 1971 to 16.3% in 2011.

The observation of increasing shares of the top companies stops when splitting the entire sample in two. In 1958, the first half with 125 enterprises generates 87.6% of the total revenue while the second half is responsible for 12.4%. In 2018, these number move slightly to 87.3% and 12.7%.[6] These comparisons

---

[4] For 2018, *Gebr. Heinemann SE & Co.* KG and MTU *Aero Engines AG* determine the median with a revenue of EUR 4,600 m and EUR 4,567 m.

[5] See Lantelme (2017, p. 60).

[6] These numbers are not included in Table 5.1 to increase its readability.

also show the importance of the very largest enterprises and their exceptional performance within the group of the largest 250 companies. Furthermore, while the companies at the top become bigger—in absolute and relative terms—the size differences of the companies at the end of the ranking become smaller.

But what do these figures mean for the development of the enterprises in the samples? To get a first idea of the required growth to remain one of the 250 largest enterprises the necessary growth rates are modeled independent of the actual growth of a specific company over the observed 60 years. The largest enterprise of 1958 must grow at an annual rate of 7.3% to defend its top spot in 2018. This would lead from a revenue of EUR 3.5bn in 1958 to a revenue of 235.9bn in 2018. If the smallest enterprise of 1958 wants to remain the 250th largest enterprise of 2018 it requires a CAGR of 7.0%, growing from EUR 41 m to EUR 2,341 m. To further improve the initial understanding of the required developments a closer look is taken at the 50th, 100th, 150th and 200th largest enterprises of 1958 and at their counterparts of 2018.[7] As 50th largest company in 1958 an annual growth rate of 6.3% is required to stay at position 50 in 2018. A slightly higher growth rate of 6.4% is necessary for the 100th largest company. This trend of a slightly higher growth rate goes on, for position 150 a rate of 6.5% is required and on position 200 the rate needs to be 6.6%.

These growth rates also show that if a company other than the largest one of 1958 reaches the top spot in 2018 it needs to grow by a larger annual rate than 7.3%. Similarly, a company from the sample other than the one on position 250 can have a smaller CAGR than 7.0% and still remain in the ranking of 2018 provided the company is not acquired or split.

For the *average* company of the 1958 sample with a revenue of EUR 271 m (DM 529 m) a CAGR of 6.6% is required to become the average company of the 2018 list of the 250 largest enterprises with revenues of EUR 12.3bn. This rate is mathematically identical to the growth rate of the total revenue from EUR 67.7bn to EUR 3,065.3bn because the number of companies is identical in both calculations. A slightly smaller growth rate of 6.5% is needed to remain the median company in both datasets growing from EUR 108 m (DM 211 m) to EUR 4.6bn which confirms the superior performance of the top companies of the sample.

An additional thought experiment is the calculation of the hypothetical CAGR which the smallest enterprise of 1958 requires to become the largest company of

[7] In 1958, the following companies are ranked on position 50, 100, 150 and 200: *Klöckner-Humboldt-Deutz AG*, *Duisburger Kupferhütte AG*, *Deutsche Lufthansa AG* and *G. M. Pfaff AG Nähmaschinenfabrik*. Their counterparts in 2018 are *Otto GmbH & Co. KG*, *Unternehmensgruppe Theo Müller S.e.c.s.*, *Gas-Union GmbH* and *SMS group GmbH*.

2018. From EUR 41 m of revenues in 1958 it needs an annual growth rate of 15.5% to generate revenues of EUR 235.9bn 60 years later. A double-digit rate over six decades seems to be very difficult especially as soon as the economic cycles are considered, and the market conditions become tougher in recessions as the historical development in Section 4.1 shows. On the other hand, the largest company of 1958 would even remain in the top 250 enterprises of 2018 if it had no growth at all. Its revenue of EUR 3.5bn could decline annually by 0.7% and it would become the 250 largest enterprise of 2018 with a total of EUR 2.3bn in revenues. This shows that if a company has received a certain size it could remain among the largest enterprises even without growth for decades.

Table 5.1 Enterprise Size Ranges & Modeled Growth Rates 1958 & 2018

250 largest enterprises	1958		2018	1958–2018
	Revenue [mEUR]	**Revenue** [mDM]	**Revenue** [mEUR]	**CAGR**
Total	67,662	132,336	3,065,296	*6.6%*
Largest	3,493	6,831	235,849	*7.3%*
Smallest	41	79	2,341	*7.0%*
Range	3,452	6,752	233,508	–
Range (multiple)	*85.9*	*85.9*	*100.7*	–
Average	271	529	12,261	*6.6%*
Median	108	211	4,584	*6.5%*
Standard deviation	407	796	23,572	–
50th largest	352	688	13,653	*6.3%*
100th largest	147	287	5,900	*6.4%*
150th largest	87	170	3,807	*6.5%*
200th largest	59	116	2,805	*6.6%*

Source: Author's own table.

The modeled annual growth rates show that the average company of the 250 largest enterprises of 1958 and 2018 grows by 6.6%. The rates of the largest and smallest companies confirm that at the top the enterprises become bigger while at the end the smaller ones are moving closer together in terms of their size. Additionally, these rates are put in perspective by comparing them with the historical development of the German economy as outlined in Section 4.1. The GDP at market prices grows by 5.7% annually between 1958 and 2018. This means that the average companies of the 1958 and 2018 samples with a CAGR of 6.6% outperform the German economy by 1.1 times, the smallest enterprises with a CAGR of 7.0% and the largest ones with 7.3% by 1.2 and by 1.3 times, respectively. In addition, it is worthwhile to mention that a rate of 7.3% like the one to remain the largest enterprise in the datasets means a doubling of revenues in just under ten years (9.9 years)—over six decades. With a 7.0% growth rate, which is required to remain the 250th largest enterprise, it takes just over ten years (10.3 years) to double revenues. Finally, the average company with a growth rate of 6.6% would double its revenue within 10.8 years. Such a growth can stress the organization heavily and requires a vast number of resources especially over such a long period.

The findings show that the 250 largest enterprises grow on average more than the German economy and therefore achieve a position in the ranking. Taking into account that the companies in both datasets are not identical suggests that the 2018 enterprises have achieved even higher growth rates than the calculated average. This is further investigated in Chapter 6.

5.2 Types of Companies: Reshuffling the Composition with One Constant

After comparing the entire samples, the distribution of the different company types is analyzed which provides the baseline for the upcoming comparisons on company type level. The company type is determined by the ownership structure of the enterprise as explained in Section 2.2.2.4. Ownership is seen as an important condition for a company's long-term development especially in family business research. Overall, the company type composition of the 250 largest enterprises changed drastically between 1958 and 2018 except family businesses.

In 1958, family-owned businesses represent the biggest group of company types with 87 (34.8%) of the 250 largest enterprises. Additional eight companies (3.2%) are held by foreign families. Public companies and state-owned enterprises follow as the second and third largest type with 56 (22.4%) and 39 (15.6%) firms, respectively. Foreign subsidiaries are the fourth largest group with 22 entities (8.8%). Moreover, the two foundation-owned enterprises (0.8%), *Carl Zeiss* and *Zahnradfabrik Friedrichshafen AG*, made it onto the list of the largest companies of 1958 representing the smallest company type. In between are the types of multiple companies-owned enterprises with 20 (8.0%) and cooperatives with 16 (6.4%) entities (see Figure 5.1).

In comparison with the 2018 ranking, family firms remain the biggest group with again 87 (34.8%) entities, but all other company types gain or lose shares. The second biggest group has changed with 55 foreign subsidiaries (22.0%) instead of public companies which are now the third biggest type with 47 entities (18.8%). The additional five company types follow with foreign family-owned enterprises with 18 (7.2%), state-owned enterprises with 14 (5.6%), foundation-owned enterprises with twelve (4.8%), cooperatives with ten (4.0%), and multiple companies-owned enterprises with seven (2.8%) entities.

Looking at the entire German economy, studies estimate the share of family firms at 90.0%. This figure is much larger than the share of family businesses in the datasets of this thesis with 34.8% in both years. The reason is that the majority of the entire family businesses are smaller firms with less than ten employees.[8] Due to the research question and the resulting focus on the largest enterprises in Germany the share of family firms is expected to be lower than the one of the total population.

Overall, when comparing the list of the 250 largest enterprises of 2018 with 1958, state-owned (−25 / −10.0 percentage points (pp)) and multiple companies-owned (−13 / −5.2pp) enterprises as well as public companies (−9 / −3.6pp) and cooperatives (−6 /−2.4pp) have lost share. In contrast, the number of foreign subsidiaries (+33 / 13.2pp), foreign family-owned (+10 / 4.0pp) and foundation-owned enterprises (+10 / 4.0pp) has increased. The number of family firms remains the same in both datasets (+/−0).

As a brief digression, a closer look is taken at the company type with the second largest loss of entities, the multiple companies-owned enterprises. Major changes in their ownership structures are noticeable. In 1958, three main ownership categories can be identified. First, the majority of this company type in the sample is owned by several other large enterprises which are—to a great extent—also part of the ranking. They can be classified as joint ventures. An example is *Duisburger Kupferhütte AG* (#100) founded in 1876 which is owned by *Farbwerke Hoechst AG* (30.33%, #19), *Farbenfabriken Bayer AG* (30.33%, #14), *BASF Badische Anilin- & Soda-Fabrik AG* (30.33%, #17), *Gebrüder Giulini*

[8] See Gottschalk et al. (2019, p. V) also for the share of 90.0%.

GmbH (4.4%), *Chemische Werke Albert AG* (2.4%, #243), *Chemische Fabrik Curtius GmbH* (~1.0%) as well as *E. Matthes & Weber GmbH* (~1.0%). Four of the owners can be found in the 1958 dataset as well. A second example is *Eisen und Metall AG* (#109) also founded in 1876 whose owners are *Hoesch AG* (33.33%, #22), *Rheinmetall Berlin AG* (33.33%) which in turn is part of *Röchling'sche Eisen- und Stahlwerke GmbH* (#61) and *Mannesmann AG* (33.33%, #6). With the participation of a family *Wacker Chemie GmbH* is also classified as a multiple companies-owned enterprise. The family Wacker and *Farbwerke Hoechst AG* (#19) own 50.0% each. A second category of this company type are joint ventures with the participation of foreign enterprises. Examples are *Norddeutsche Affinerie AG* (#89) owned by *Metallgesellschaft AG* (40.0%, #31), *Degussa AG* (40.0%, #46) and *The British Metal Corporation* (20.0%). Furthermore, *Osram GmbH* (#140) is a second example which is owned by *Siemens AG* (42.8%, #3), *AEG Allgemeine Electricitäts-Gesellschaft* (35.8%, #16), and US-based *International General Electric Company* (21.5%). The third category are syndicates and / or purchasing groups. An example is *Verkaufsvereinigung für Teererzeugnisse (VfT) AG* (#107) owned by numerous mining companies, of which some are also part of the 1958 sample, to sell the byproduct of coal tar which is formed during the production of coke and coal gas from coal.[9] A purchasing syndicate / group is *GEDELAG Gemeinschaft Deutscher Lebensmittel-Großhändler AG* whose owners are hundreds of wholesale companies. The objective is to bundle their purchasing power and to achieve better purchasing conditions from producers. In general, these categories of multiple companies-owned enterprises do not exist anymore in 2018. Syndicates and cartels are prohibited and joint ventures between large companies which operate in the same economic or regional area are much more difficult to establish due to stricter competition policies not only in Germany (see also Section 4.3). Therefore, the existing seven multiple companies-owned enterprises in 2018 are mainly in the hands of financial investors like *Amprion GmbH* (#49) owned by German institutional financial investors via *M 31 Beteiligungsgesellschaft mbH & Co. Energie KG* (74.9%) and the strategic investor *RWE AG* (25.1%). A second example is *Auto1 Group GmbH* (#192) which is owned by several investor funds. *Hapag-Lloyd AG* (#60) is also owned by financial investors which are *Qatar Holding Germany GmbH* (14.5%) and *The Public Investment Fund of the Kingdom of Saudi Arabia* (10.2%) as well as by strategic investors

[9] The mining companies include, among others, *Gelsenkirchener Bergwerks-AG* (#10), *Steinkohlenwerke Mathias Stinnes AG* (#67), *Rütgerswerke AG* (#146) and Bergbau AG Ewald-König-Ludwig (subsidiary of *Salzgitter-Konzern*). In total, ten companies are named as members of the *VfT* in their commemorative publication for the 50th anniversary in 1955 (see Verkaufsvereinigung für Teererzeugnisse (VfT) AG (1955)).

which are *CSAV Germany Container Holding GmbH* (25.8%) and *Kühne Holding AG* (~25.0%). Companies with multiple pure strategic investors are rare. These are most likely *Lekkerland AG & Co. KG* (#59) which is owned by several international wholesalers and *Gas-Union GmbH* (#150) whose owners are, among smaller utilities ones, *Mainova AG* (34.3%) which is majority owned by the city of Frankfurt and *Uniper SE* (23.6%, #7). Both are active in energy trading and distribution. Overall, multiple companies-owned enterprises like in 1958 do not exist anymore in 2018. This is in line with the highlighted legal historical context in Section 4.3. Stricter national and European competition laws have banned cartels and increased the barriers for a collaboration between enterprises. On the other hand, more financial investors own substantial stakes in non-listed enterprises.[10]

Coming back to the company types, from an ownership perspective the data shows that German family firms remain a significant company type even in the group of the largest enterprises in Germany over 60 years. This company type seems to be as relevant as decades earlier. The number of foreign family firms (which are further investigated later) even increases. Furthermore, foundations which are associated with families in several cases have gained in importance as well. In contrast, the relevance of state-owned enterprises decreases over the observation period which is in line with the described privatization efforts in the last decades. The type of foreign subsidiaries noticeably increases its relevance. This development reflects the economic liberalization after World War II and the attractiveness of the German market as the fourth largest economy in the world. Based on absolute numbers the relevance of public companies in the lists of the 250 largest enterprises also decreases in 2018 compared to 1958 which needs further investigation by looking at revenue and the number of employees. The development of the number of multiple companies-owned enterprises is linked to the stricter competition policies and the development of cooperatives might be linked to certain industries which are described in Section 6.1.5.

It is noteworthy that previously described numbers provide an aggregated overview of the different company types which means that, e.g., the 87 family firms of 1958 do not need to be identical with the 87 family firms of 2018. As it will be shown later in this chapter as well as in Chapter 6, the 2018 list includes *Reappearers* from the 1958 list as well as *New Joiners*.

Taking a closer look at the different types of companies, their revenue and number of employees are compared to better understand their dimensions and

[10] In the case of public companies, financial investors like *Blackrock* also own several stakes. However, they rarely exceed single-digit percentages, e.g., see *Blackrock's* share in the DAX 30 companies (see Statista GmbH (2021)).

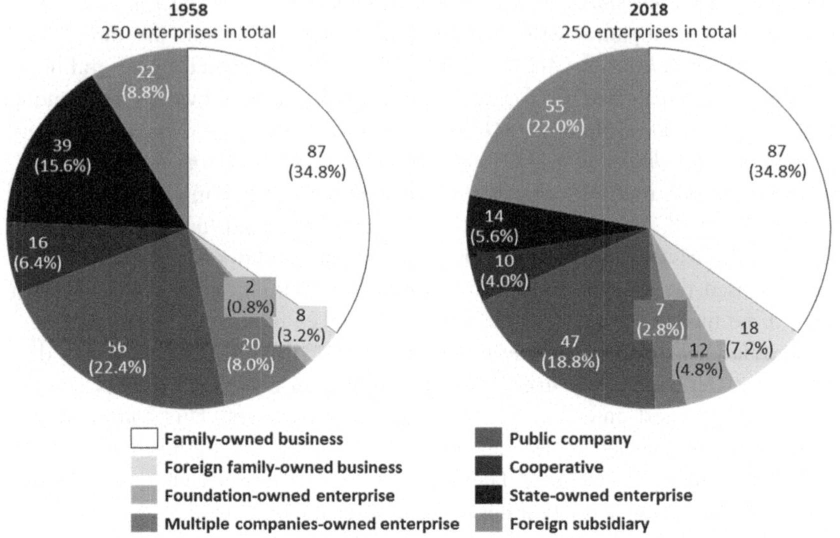

Figure 5.1 Type of Company Distribution 1958 & 2018. (Source: Author's own figure)

relative sizes (see Table 5.2). As mentioned in the previous sub-chapter, the 250 enterprises have a total revenue of EUR 67.7bn in 1958 compared to EUR 3,065.3bn in 2018 which corresponds to a CAGR of 6.6% (not adjusted for inflation). Now the number of employees is also considered. The figure grows from 3.8 million to 9.9 million in the same period. This increase corresponds to a CAGR of 1.6%.[11] Despite the same number the enterprises become larger in terms of employees and of revenue.

Family firms increase their revenue share slightly by 1.3pp from 27.8% to 29.1% although their number remains the same in both datasets.[12] Nevertheless, this figure is still smaller than their share in the number of all companies with

[11] Overall, all 3,483,691 enterprises in Germany in 2018 generate a revenue of EUR 6,968bn and employ 30.9 million people. The 15,452 companies with more than 250 employees have a revenue share of 51.5% (EUR 3,589bn) and an employee share of 45.6% (14.1 million) (German Federal Statistical Office (2019)). Note: The provided employee number of the 250 companies in this thesis includes the enterprises global workforce and not only the employees in Germany.

[12] Possible discrepancies between the percentages and percentage points in the text and the differences in the tables are due to rounding differences.

34.8%. Their gain in the share of employees is even higher with a plus of 7.5pp. In line with the increased number of foreign family firms (+10) and foundations (+10) in the 2018 dataset their shares of revenue increase as well, by 1.3pp and 6.7pp. While for foreign family firms the share of employees remains stable (+ / −0) foundations increase their share by 10.7pp. These numbers show that foundations gain considerably more—disproportionately more to the increase of their number of companies. Moreover, it stands out that the share of revenue generated by public companies and their share of employees increase by 9.2pp and 7.8pp, respectively, although their number decreases from 56 to 47 in the two datasets. This indicates that the relative size of a public company in 2018 is bigger than in 1958. An almost contrary development can be observed in the case of foreign subsidiaries. Their number more than doubles from 22 to 55 but their share in revenue increases only slightly (+1.2pp) and their share in employees even decreases (−2.2pp). Their relative size must shrink as well, from 1958 to 2018 compared to the other company types. Multiple companies-owned firms and state-owned enterprises both lose revenue (−3.6pp / −16.7pp) and employee (−0.7pp / −29.4pp) shares which is in line with their decreasing number in the 2018 ranking although not always exactly proportionally. The strong decline in state-owned enterprises can be seen in the decline from strong double-digit revenue and employee shares in 1958 to low one-digit shares in 2018. Cooperatives, similar to public companies, increase their share in revenue (+0.7pp) and employees (+6.3pp) although their number drops from 16 to ten between 1958 and 2018. Again, their relative size increases compared to the other company types. These described developments of the relative size of the different company types can also be seen when comparing the average size of an enterprise. As an example, overall, the average revenue per firm is EUR 0.27bn in 1958 and EUR 12.26bn in 2018. For cooperatives the average is EUR 0.19bn and EUR 16.03bn, respectively. Cooperatives move from below the overall average in 1958 to above the average in 2018. The opposite development, from above the average to below the average, can be found with foreign subsidiaries with an average revenue of EUR 0.35bn in 1958 and EUR 7.05bn in 2018. As previously indicated, the average size of a public company increases tremendously compared to the overall average firm. While the average public company has revenues of EUR 0.34bn in 1958 which is slightly above the overall enterprises' average of EUR 0.27bn this company type generates revenues of EUR 24.12bn on average in 2018 compared to the overall average of EUR 12.26bn. The average public company is nearly twice the size of an overall average enterprise.

Similar to the number of companies in the datasets the revenue and employee share of family businesses in this thesis is much lower than their share which studies estimate for the entire German economy. Approximately 53.5% of all employees work in family firms which are responsible for around 52.0% of the entire revenue generated in the private sector.[13] Again, because this thesis focuses on the largest enterprises in Germany the total revenue and employee share of family firms in the used datasets is expected to be smaller. The majority of family firms are small firms with fewer than ten employees as further highlighted by Gottschalk et al.

What can be learned from these findings? Overall, the observed changes among the 250 largest enterprises confirm the historical context of the privatization efforts of the German state as well as of the tightening regulations on cartels and competition. The number of state-owned and of multiple companies-owned enterprises as well as their revenue and employee share decrease drastically. On the other hand, the number of foreign subsidiaries increases significantly (but there is only a small increase in revenue and employees) and foster the structural change towards the tertiary sector. Public companies contribute the largest share to overall revenues and employees of the 250 largest enterprises of 1958 and 2018 although their number decreases over the 60 years. On average, they become bigger which implies that a listing can lead to above average growth and size. Family firms slightly increase their shares while their number remains stable in the samples. They are a constant in the overall changing conditions of the other company types over the last 60 years.

[13] See Gottschalk et al. (2019, pp. 5–6).

Table 5.2 Overview Revenue & Employees per Company Type 1958 & 2018

#	Type of company	Revenue [bnEUR]				Employees [thousands]			
		1958		**2018**		**1958**		**2018**	
1	Family-owned business	18.8	*27.8%*	891.5	*29.1%*	982.6	*25.7%*	3,300.0	*33.2%*
2	Foreign family-owned business	1.6	*2.4%*	112.1	*3.7%*	94.6	*2.5%*	248.7	*2.5%*
3	Foundation-owned enterprise	0.3	*0.4%*	218.0	*7.1%*	30.9	*0.8%*	1,147.7	*11.5%*
4	Multiple companies-owned enterprise	3.5	*5.2%*	50.4	*1.6%*	58.4	*1.5%*	77.5	*0.8%*
5	Public company	18.8	*27.8%*	1,133.6	*37.0%*	1,024.6	*26.8%*	3,436.9	*34.6%*
6	Cooperative	3.0	*4.5%*	160.3	*5.2%*	33.2	*0.9%*	715.1	*7.2%*
7	State-owned enterprise	13.8	*20.3%*	111.8	*3.6%*	1,306.0	*34.2%*	472.4	*4.8%*
8	Foreign subsidiary	7.8	*11.5%*	387.6	*12.6%*	292.1	*7.6%*	538.2	*5.4%*
	Total	**67.7**	***100.0%***	**3,065.3**	***100.0%***	**3,822.4**	***100.0%***	**9,936.5**	***100.0%***

Source: Author's own table.

5.3 Legal Forms: Using the Broader Selection of Available Legal Forms

The legal form of a company provides the basis for its governance structure. Therefore, it is expected to have an impact on the development of a company. In the following, the distribution of the legal forms in the two datasets from 1958 and 2018 are compared (Table 5.3). As highlighted in the legal historical context new legal forms have been introduced and jurisprudence has allowed new combinations over the course of the last 60 years. Therefore, not all forms of 2018 were available in 1958. Overall, enterprises make use of the newly introduced legal forms like the *SE* and the *Co. KG. / KGaA*. Forms with unlimited liability have nearly disappeared among the 250 largest companies in 2018. This suggests that the personal responsibility of single or multiple entrepreneurs has given way to organizational structures and responsibility.

Table 5.3 Distribution of Legal Forms 1958 & 2018

Legal form	**Number of enterprises**			
	1958		**2018**	
AG	163	*65.2%*	81	*32.4%*
GmbH	46	*18.4%*	69	*27.6%*
KGaA	2	*0.8%*	1	*0.4%*
Co. KGaA	–	–	12	*4.8%*
SE	–	–	21	*8.4%*
Sole proprietorship	5	*2.0%*	–	–
oHG	4	*1.6%*	–	–
KG	11	*4.4%*	13	*5.2%*
Co. KG	–	–	48	*19.2%*
Eigenbetrieb / Sondervermögen	7	*2.8%*	–	–
eGmbH / eG	12	*4.8%*	3	*1.2%*
SCE	–	–	1	*0.4%*
LLC	–	–	1	*0.4%*
Total	**250**	***100.0%***	**250**	***100.0%***

Source: Author's own table.

In both years the *AG* is the most common legal form among the 250 largest companies. Nevertheless, with 81 (32.4%) in 2018 compared to 163 (65.2%) in

1958 the number drops by more than half (−50.3%). Within the 60 years alternative legal forms which can also be listed on a stock exchange are introduced like the *SE* in 2004 as well as the *KGaA* with a legal entity as general partner (*Co. KGaA*) which is confirmed by the Federal Court of Justice in 1997.[14] In 2018, there are 21 *SEs* (8.4%) and 12 *Co. KGaAs* (4.8%) in the sample. The latter group of *Co. KGaAs* includes in total four combinations: two cases with the limited company *AG* (*AG & Co. KGaA*), four with the *GmbH* (*GmbH & Co. KGaA*), five with the *SE* (*SE & Co. KGaA*) and one with a foundation (*Stiftung & Co. KGaA*). The latter one was chosen by *Dussmann Stiftung & Co. KGaA*. The number of *KGaAs* as a corporation with personally liable partners as general partners decreases from two (0.8%) to one (0.4%). In 1958, *Carl Freudenberg KGaA* and *Heinr. Auer Mühlenwerke KGaA* use this legal form while in 2018 only *Merck KGaA* does so. It stands out that *Merck* is also listed and a family-owned enterprise. But not all of the *AGs*, *SEs* or *KGaA* and *Co. KGaAs* are listed as the analysis in the next chapter shows. The last type of a corporation is the *GmbH* whose number increases from 46 (18.4%) to 69 (27.6%) over the 60 years. The *GmbH* is further institutionalized within the largest companies after this legal form was established in 1892. Nevertheless, the total number of corporations decreases from 211 (84.4%) to 184 (73.6%) including *AGs*, *GmbHs*, *KGaAs*, *Co. KGaAs* and *SEs*.

One remarkable legal form which does not appear in the 2018 list of the 250 largest enterprises anymore but is used five times (2.0%) in 1958 is the *Sole Proprietorship* (*Einzelunternehmen*). As fourth largest enterprise in 1958 with a revenue of DM 3.3bn and more than 105,000 employees *Fried. Krupp, Essen* is fully owned by Alfried Krupp von Bohlen und Halbach who is exclusively liable for all corporate activities, as well.[15] The similar legal form is used by *Wilhelm Grillo Handelsgesellschaft*, *C. Bertelsmann Verlag*, *Werner Otto Versandhandel* and *Carl Zeiss*. Their sole owners are single individuals with Herbert Grillo, Reinhard Mohn and Werner Otto. *Carl Zeiss* is a special case because the sole owner of the sole proprietorship is the *Carl Zeiss Foundation* and no natural person. The firm was transferred from Ernst Abbe and Roderich Zeiss to the

[14] See Section 4.3 for more details.

[15] *Fried. Krupp* was founded in 1811 and experienced a rapid development between the end of the 1840s until 1873, increasing their number of employees from less than 100 to around 12,000 (see Plumpe (2018), p. 16). At that time, factories were just starting to become relevant in the production of materials and goods. For the overall development of *Fried. Krupp* from their foundation and difficulties in the early stage see Gall (2000) and James (2012) for the later developments until the merger with Thyssen.

foundation in 1891.[16] Besides sole proprietorships and corporations there are several types of partnerships (*Personengesellschaften*). One partnership which does also not appear in the 2018 list is the *General Commercial Partnership* (*offene Handelsgesellschaft—oHG*). In 1958, four companies (1.6%) have the form of an *oHG* namely *Spiesshofer & Braun oHG (Triumph), Peter Eckes oHG*[17]*, TOUROPA oHG and "Der Photo Porst" Hanns Porst oHG*. Reasons for the decline of *oHGs* in the datasets can be assumed to be the unlimited liability of the owners who are natural persons as well as the few governance structures determined by law. In contrast to this development, the number of *KGs* has increased slightly from eleven (4.4%) to 13 (5.2%). In 1958, companies like *H. F. & P. F. Reemtsma KG, Neckermann Versand KG, Miele & Cie. KG, B. Rawe & Co. KG* as well as *Albrecht KG Lebensmittel-Filialbetrieb* use this legal form. In 2018, *Gebr. Knauf KG, Dr. August Oetker KG, Wilh. Werhahn KG*, Vorwerk *& Co. KG* and *Muhr und Bender KG* are among the companies which operate as a *KG*. All of the *KGs* in 1958 and 2018 are family businesses without exceptions due to the legal requirement that at least one natural person needs to be the general partner who is fully liable. This risk goes hand in hand with the advantage that there are only few obligations to publish corporate or financial information. This advantage but also the risk of full liability disappears if the general partner is a legal entity like a *GmbH* or *AG* similar to the *Co. KGaA*. With 48 companies (19.2%) using the legal form of a *Co. KG* in 2018 it becomes the third largest type. Moreover, the variety of combinations is greater with the KG. Ten enterprises chose the *AG* (*AG & Co. KG*), 29 the *GmbH* (*GmbH & Co. KG*), three the *SE* (*SE & Co. KG*), four a foundation (*Stiftung & Co. KG*), and one enterprise each a British private company limited by shares (*Ltd.*) (*Ltd. & Co. KG*) and a Dutch private limited liability company (*B.V.*) (*B.V. & Co. KG*) as the general partner. The last two legal forms is chosen by *Müller Holding Ltd. & Co. KG* and *H & M Hennes & Mauritz BV & Co. KG*. Since German law does not recognize these legal forms, their use is more complicated and accordingly only worthwhile in individual cases. Foundations as general partner are used by *Schwarz-Gruppe*[18], *Diehl Stiftung & Co. KG,*

---

[16] See Mühlfriedel, Walter, and Hellmuth (1996). Later in 2004, *Carl Zeiss* changes its legal form to an AG.

[17] Besides the *Peter Eckes oHG* there are two additional companies in 1958 which are associated with the Eckes family and their business activities: *Chantré & Cie GmbH* and *ECKES Übersee-Fruchtsaft KG*. The revenue of DM 141 m relates to all three companies of which the *oHG* appears to be the largest one. Therefore, this legal form was chosen to represent *Eckes* (see Verlag Hoppenstedt & Co. (1959b, p. 1567)).

[18] The identification of the legal form of the *Schwarz-Gruppe* turns out to be difficult. Similar cases are *Aldi Süd* and *Aldi Nord* as well as other mainly retail chains. They do not have

Norma Lebensmittelfilialbetrieb Stiftung & Co. KG and *Friedhelm Loh Stiftung & Co. KG*. Such structures do not imply that the enterprises are foundation owned. Ultimately, a foundation can also largely benefit the family (family foundation) and not the common good like the *Körber Foundation*.

In 1958, seven of the 39 state-owned enterprises have specific legal forms which are limited to this company type. *Deutsche Bundesbahn* and *Deutsche Bundespost* are both special assets of the German government (*Sondervermögen des Bundes*) while additional five companies have the form of an *Eigenbetrieb* which are municipal-owned and have an independent corporate status. The latter ones are all public utilities from the cities Munich, Dusseldorf, Nuremberg, and Frankfurt (Main) as well as the *Berliner Gaswerke (GASAG)*. None of the 14 state-owned enterprises in 2018 has such a special legal form. They all operate as *AG* or *GmbH*. This supports the highlighted trend in Section 4.1 that more common legal forms are used by the state, municipalities and cities.

Twelve cooperatives (4.8%) also use the legal form of the *eGmbH* (*eingetragene Genossenschaft mit beschränkter Haftpflicht*) in 1958. They are mainly consumers' co-operatives like the *Konsumgenossenschaft Wuppertal eGmbH* and the *Konsumgenossenschaft Stuttgart eGmbH* or retailers' cooperatives like *Edeka eGmbH* and *Nürnberger Bund Grosseinkaufsverbund eGmbH*. The form of the *eGmbH* was changed to *eG* (*eingetragene Genossenschaft*) in 1973.[19] In 2018, this legal form is used by three cooperatives (1.2%) among the 250 largest enterprises. Similar to the *SE* a cooperative can also operate as a *Societas Cooperativa Europaea* (*SCE*). In the 2018 dataset only *Westfleisch Gruppe* use this legal form which was established in 2006.

The last legal form which appears once (0.4%) in the sample is a US limited liability company (LLC of the US state of Delaware) under which *McDonald's Deutschland LLC* operates. This is a rare exception and applied by a foreign subsidiary whose parent company is also headquartered in the US.

Overall, the comparison of the legal forms of the 250 largest enterprises of 1958 and 2018 shows that the number of corporations decreases while the number of partnerships increases over 60 years. Nevertheless, the liability is limited in most cases in 2018. New legal forms are established over time which are also

---

a single legal entity which owns all subsidiaries. It is a network of different entities (often split by region). These entities are then owned by different foundations, e.g., in the case of *Schwarz* there are at least three foundations with *Lidl Stiftung & Co. KG*, *Kaufland Stiftung & Co. KG* and *PreZero Stiftung & Co. KG* as well as the *Schwarz Produktion GmbH & Co. KG* which are all controlled by the *Dieter Schwarz Stiftung*.

[19] See Gesetz zur Änderung des Gesetzes betreffend die Erwerbs- und Wirtschaftsgenossenschaften, 1973.

used by the largest enterprises. This is not only driven by national legislation but also by the development of the European integration. In contrast, there are only individual cases of the use of foreign (especially European) legal forms. Furthermore, the legal form of sole proprietorship completely disappears in 2018 compared to 1958. Section 5.8 further analyses the legal forms of family firms for a better understanding which governance basis this company type choses.

5.4 Listings: Declining Importance of the Capital Market

After introducing the different legal forms of the enterprises, some of which are necessary to be listed on a stock exchange, their actual listing status in both datasets is analyzed as a next logical step. Based on a listing a company has broader access to the capital market, but it must also comply with listing and higher disclosure requirements. Moreover, its shares can be traded publicly which could lead to takeover attempts even hostile ones depending on the ownership structure. Therefore, a listing can have an impact on the continuity of an enterprise. Overall, the importance of the capital market decreases among the 250 largest enterprises between 1958 and 2018. Especially family firms and foreign subsidiaries refrain from listing.

100 (40.0%) of the 250 largest enterprises of 1958 are listed on a German stock exchange compared to 72 (28.8%) of the 250 enterprises of 2018. The rest of the 250 companies, 150 in 1958 and 178 in 2018, are not listed (Figure 5.2). The number of listed entities decreases accordingly by 11.2pp in the samples.

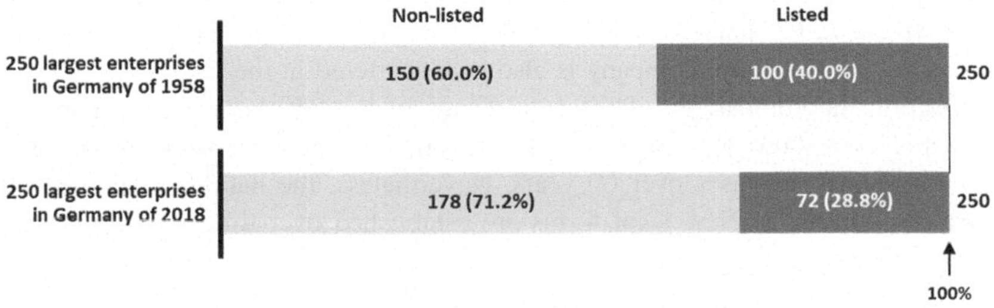

Figure 5.2 Listing Distribution 1958 & 2018. (Source: Author's own figure)

These figures are compared to the total number of listed companies in Germany in 1958 and 2018 to better understand the observed development in the broader context. Depending on the source the number varies for 1958. *SAf* covers 803 companies in the 1958 edition (end of October 1958 as cut-off date) and 788 companies in the 1959 edition (end of October 1959 as cut-off date) including foreign enterprises which are also listed on a German stock exchange. Excluding them the numbers decrease slightly to 802 and 783.[20] The Federal Statistical Office reports 659 listed companies for the end of November 1958.[21] This figure already covers only companies which are headquartered in Germany. Because the Federal Statistical Office does not provide a full list with the names of the companies included in their list a direct comparison is not possible. The gap of 143 and 124, respectively, cannot be identified. Nevertheless, both editors provide higher figures for 1958 than the reported figure 60 years later. In 2018, 465 companies with their headquarters in Germany are reported to be listed at a German stock exchange by The World Bank.[22] There are fewer listed enterprises in 2018 compared to 1958.[23] The number decreases by 42.0% (802 in 1958), 40.6% (783 in 1958) or 29.4% (659 in 1958), respectively. The decline of listed companies in the sample of the 250 largest enterprises of 1958 compared to 2018 is 28.0% (from 100 to 72 companies). This value is similar to the decline of 29.4% based on the reported figure from the Federal Statistical Office in 1958. The trend of fewer listed companies over the last decades in the datasets of this thesis is in line with the overall decline of listed companies in Germany.

All 100 listed companies in 1958 have the legal form of an *AG* while in 2018 only 53 (73.6%) of the 72 listed enterprises are an *AG*. Additional legal forms in 2018 are the *SE* (14 / 19.4%) and the *KGaA* (5 / 6.9%) including various types with other legal forms as general partners like the *AG*, *SE* or *GmbH*.[24] In 2018, companies also take advantage of the possibility of a broader selection of legal forms that can be listed on the stock exchange like the *SE* and the *KGaA* with a

---

[20] For 1958, only *Philips' Gloeilampenfabrieken* (NED) is covered as a foreign entity listed on a German stock exchange. For 1959, *Anglo American Corporation of South Africa Ltd.* (ZAF), *Banque des Paris et des Pays-Bas* (FRA), *Philips' Gloeilampenfabrieken* (NED), *Royal Dutch Petroleum Company* (NED) and *MONTECATINI* (ITA) are covered.

[21] See German Federal Statistical Office (1958). A similar report for December 1958 is not available.

[22] See The World Bank (2021).

[23] A similar decline is reported for the US (see Gupta, Koller, and Stumpner (2021)) The number dropped from 5,500 in 2000 to around 4,000 in 2020.

[24] Four of the five listed *KGaAs* are family firms which are *Henkel AG & Co. KGaA*, *Merck KGaA*, *Hella GmbH & Co. KGaA* and *Hornbach Holding AG & Co. KGaA* while the fifth enterprise, *Fresenius SE & Co. KGaA*, is majority-owned by a foundation.

corporation as general partner.[25] Presumably the different governance structures of the legal forms are the reason for broader range. These possibilities are not available for the enterprises in 1958.

The used definition of a public company leads to the fact that all these companies are listed (and have no majority owner). The 56 and 47 public companies from 1958 and 2018 are included in the total numbers of 100 and 72 listed entities, respectively. In addition, other types of companies are also listed but they have a majority owner including family-owned enterprises or state-owned enterprises like *Pintsch Bamag AG* and *Rheinisch-Westfälisches Elektrizitätswerk AG* in 1958 as well as *Volkswagen AG* and *Fraport AG* in 2018. When comparing the share of non-listed and listed enterprises per company type in 1958 foreign family firms (50.0%) and foreign subsidiaries (36.4%) have the highest share of listed entities (of course behind public companies with a share of 100%). Foundation-owned and multiple companies-owned enterprises have no listed entity at all. Cooperatives and state-owned enterprises have a relatively low share of listed entities with 6.3% and 12.8%. Their share of listed entities grows in 2018 to 20.0% and 21.4% but their total numbers decrease (see Table 5.4). Two foundation-owned enterprises, *Fresenius SE & Co. KGaA* and *Evonik Industries AG*, and one multiple companies-owned enterprise, *Hapag-Lloyd AG*, are listed in 2018 which increases their share from 0% to 16.7% and 14.3%. They can be labelled as single cases but are worthwhile to mention as special exceptions. Similar to the share of employees the share of listed foreign subsidiaries drops to 7.3% although the absolute number increases substantially.

[25] See Section 4.3 for more details of the legislative changes.

Table 5.4 Listings per Company Type 1958 & 2018

#	Type of company	Number of enterprises									
		1958					**2018**				
		Non-listed		**Listed**		**Total**	**Non-listed**		**Listed**		**Total**
1	Family-owned business	61	*70.1%*	26	*29.9%*	87	74	*85.1%*	13	*14.9%*	87
2	Foreign family-owned business	4	*50.0%*	4	*50.0%*	8	18	*100.0%*	–	–	18
3	Foundation-owned enterprise	2	*100.0%*	–	–	2	10	*83.3%*	2	*16.7%*	12
4	Multiple companies-owned enterprise	20	*100.0%*	–	–	20	6	*85.7%*	1	*14.3%*	7
5	Public company	–	–	56	*100.0%*	56	–	–	47	*100.0%*	47
6	Cooperative	15	*93.8%*	1	*6.3%*	16	8	*80.0%*	2	*20.0%*	10
7	State-owned enterprise	34	*87.2%*	5	*12.8%*	39	11	*78.6%*	3	*21.4%*	14
8	Foreign subsidiary	14	*63.6%*	8	*36.4%*	22	51	*92.7%*	4	*7.3%*	55
	Total	**150**	***60.0%***	**100**	***40.0%***	**250**	**178**	***71.2%***	**72**	***28.8%***	**250**

Source: Author's own table.

Overall, the decrease in public companies between 1958 and 2018 does not account for the entire decline of listed entities. Especially family firms with a decreasing share of listed entities as well as foreign subsidiaries whose share drops tremendously although their total number increases contribute to this development. The overall trend of the decreasing importance of the capital market which can be observed in Germany over the last 60 years is also visible among the largest enterprises of the country. Furthermore, because listed companies are an easier target for acquisitions the consolidation of industries can result in fewer listed companies due to the acquisitions between listed companies. This will be investigated in more detail in the industry section.

5.5 Age: Getting Older and More Evenly Distributed

Age is expected to have an impact on the mortality and survival of companies and therefore on a company's long-term development as highlighted in Chapter 1.Therefore, an overview of the average age for each company type in 1958 and 2018 is provided (see Table 5.5).[26] Additionally, the enterprises year of foundation is displayed in an overview of the founding decades in a first step to provide insights into the historical context of the largest companies of 1958 and 2018 (Figure 5.3). Overall, the average age of all company types increases except for foreign subsidiaries. However, public companies experience a below average increase which suggests a high fluctuation.

Of the 250 largest enterprises of 1958 the highest number was founded in the 1890s with 34 companies (13.6%). Among them are, e.g., *Mannesmann AG* (1890), *Brown, Boveri & Cie. AG* (1891), *Fichtel & Sachs AG* (1895), *Miele & Cie.* KG (1899) and *Deutsche Linoleum-Werke AG* (1899). These fall in the period of high industrialization in Germany. 29 of the sample's companies (11.6%) were each founded in the 1870s and the 1920s. The former decade is characterized as the *Gründerzeit* in which hundreds of new *AGs* were established but which also ended in a stock market crash in 1873. Nevertheless, *Maschinenfabrik Fahr AG* (1870), *Schering AG* (1871) and *Wilhelm Karmann GmbH* (1874) as well as *Henkel & Cie. GmbH* (1876) and *Gesellschaft für Linde's Eismaschinen AG* (1879) are among the foundations which make it to the list of the largest enterprises of 1958. The 1920s (*Golden Twenties*) were also characterized by a great economic upswing until the stock market crash in 1929. Also, foreign companies founded subsidiaries in Germany at that time like *Deutsche FIAT-Gruppe*

[26] Furthermore, see the explanations of the liability of newness in Section 2.1.1.

(1922) and *Ford-Werke AG* (1925) similar to the foundations of *Heinrich Lanz AG* (1925), *Großversandhaus Quelle Gustav Schickedanz K.G.* (1927) and *Eternit AG* (1929). In addition, the twelve foundations (4.8%) in the 1950s which become one of the 250 largest enterprises of 1958 within only a couple of years stand out. Some of them are related to the deconcentration of the coal and steel industry based on the decisions of the Allied High Commission. Companies like *Hüttenwerke Siegerland AG* (1952), *Friedrich Thyssen Bergbau AG* (1953) and *Hamborner Bergbau AG* (1953) were founded to receive certain assets which were split from, e.g., *Vereinigte Stahlwerke* and *Gelsenkirchener Bergwerks-AG*. Therefore, these companies were able to reach a considerable size in a very short time. But entrepreneurs like Josef Neckermann and Willy H. Schlieker also developed their companies, *Neckermann Versand KG* (1950) and *Willy H. Schlieker KG* (1951), into one of the largest in Germany within just a few years without receiving assets due to deconcentration activities.

The foundations of the 250 largest enterprises of 2018 are more evenly distributed over the decades than the ones of the 1958 companies. The 2018 distribution has a lower standard deviation. In six additional decades, from the 1960s to the 2010s, companies were founded. Once again, the 1920s decade stands out, this time with the highest number of foundations—25 (10.0%) in total. Besides the already mentioned companies *Mahle GmbH* (1920), *Haribo GmbH & Co. KG* (1920), *BayWa AG* (1923), *Stihl Holding AG & Co. KG* (1926) and *REWE-ZENTRALFINANZ eG* (1927) are established in this decade as well.[27] Moreover, there are more companies in the 2018 dataset which were founded in the 1910s than in the 1958 sample—21 compared to 18 enterprises. Overall, 107 companies were founded earlier than 1920 which shows the importance of companies with an age of around 100 years and older.[28] The number of companies founded in the 1850s decreases sharply from 17 (6.8%) to three (1.2%). In comparison, more companies make it to the list of the largest 250 enterprises of 2018 which are founded in the 1930s (15 / 6.0%) and 1940s (14 / 5.6%). In the same list companies with a founding year also after the 1950s are included and even eight companies (3.2%) which are eight years old or less are part of the ranking.[29]

Besides the comparison of the actual decades the foundations can also be compared looking at the relative decades prior to the years 1958 and 2018. Looking

[27] The company names refer to the names in 2018 and not to the names in the year of foundation or in 1958.

[28] See Fernandez Moya, Fernandez-Perez, and Lubinski (2020) who show that 54 of the 100 largest family businesses in Germany in 2005 were founded before 1913.

[29] See Section 5.7.2 for more details of the youngest enterprises in the datasets.

at Figure 5.3 this would mean that the entire bars of the 2018 datasets move six decades to the left. Then the eight companies (3.2%) from the 2010s (2018 dataset) are compared with the twelve companies (4.8%) from the 1950s (1958 dataset). Both figures represent the number of companies which were founded in the same decade of the observation years 1958 and 2018. Comparing a relative decade earlier the figures are nine foundations (3.6%) for the 250 largest enterprises of 1958 and 17 (6.8%) for the companies of 2018. This comparison also shows that in 1958 six companies (2.4%) were founded more than 15 decades ago (prior to 1800). This number increases to 18 (7.2%) for the 2018 list.[30] There are much more older companies in the 2018 sample than in the 1958 dataset which overall makes the distribution of the founding decade more evenly distributed.

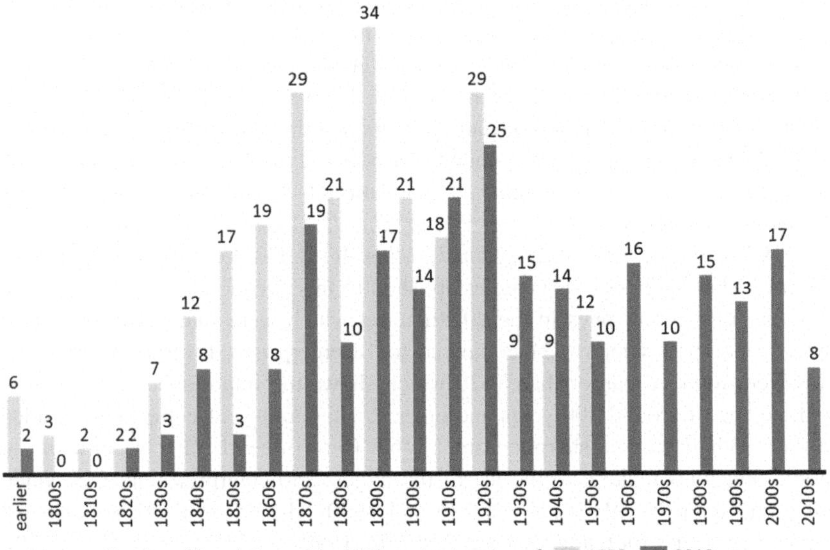

Figure 5.3 Foundation Decade Distribution of the Largest Enterprises of 1958 & 2018. (Source: Author's own figure)

Overall, the data shows that even in 2018 some of the largest enterprises in Germany are several centuries old. This suggests that size comes with age—if the

[30] Including the actual decades for the 2018 dataset of 1850, 1840, 1830, 1820, 1810, 1800 and earlier.

company survives. On the other hand, companies can also reach a considerable size within just a few years. Nevertheless, these extreme developments remain isolated cases—sometimes due to political action or management trends. The majority of the large enterprises was founded a couple of decades before the year of observation. Furthermore, based on the relative comparison and the increased number of very old enterprises in the 2018 dataset it is expected that the average age of a company increases from 1958 to 2018.

To further investigate this observation, the average age is calculated based on the founding years of the companies. It is presented both on an aggregated level per company type as well as across all companies in the datasets of 1958 and 2018. A further distinction is made on the basis of the enterprises' listing status to investigate the differences between non-listed and listed companies because the importance of the capital market has decreased as highlighted in the previous sub-chapter.

The average age of the 250 largest companies of 1958 is 70.0 years which corresponds to more than two generations. This value increases to 89.0 years looking at the 250 largest enterprises of 2018 which is close to three generations. The average age increases by 19 years over the observation period of 60 years. This trend towards older firms is observed for all company types except for foreign subsidiaries. In this group, the average age decreases by 4.4 years from 73.3 to 67.0 over 60 years. This decrease can be associated with the large increase in the number of enterprises within this group of company types comparing the 1958 and 2018 datasets. The decrease indicates that over the last 60 years more and more international companies have founded and built their subsidiaries in Germany which then became part of the largest enterprises in Germany as well. Building a company with the support of a foreign parent company ensures that resources are available which are not accessible for entrepreneurs who found their firm from scratch.

Public companies are the oldest company type in 1958 with on average 80.8 years followed by family firms and foundations with 78.9 and 77.5 years, respectively. These values are close together and indicate similar years of foundation which is supported by the actual founding years of these enterprises. The described order of the oldest company types changes in 2018. Then, the foundations are the oldest company type in the sample with 106.8 years closely followed by family-owned businesses with an average of 105.2 years. The average age of both company types rises considerably by 29.3 and 26.3 years. Public companies follow in third place with 89.3 years which corresponds to the smallest positive change by far of 8.5 years. In combination with the observation of the smaller number of public companies in the 2018 dataset this indicates that only a small portion of the companies from the 1958 list are also included in the 2018 list. Additionally, younger public companies might replace old ones which, put together, leads to such a small increase over 60 years. The youngest company type in 1958 as well as in 2018 are multiple companies-owned enterprises with 45.4 and 64.4 years, respectively. As highlighted earlier, these firms are often joint ventures which means that established enterprises provide certain assets and relationships to the company to achieve a predefined objective. Therefore, joint ventures can achieve a considerable size within a short period of time.

Taking into consideration the listing status of the enterprises it stands out that on average listed companies are older than non-listed ones. With an average age for listed companies of 80.0 in 1958 and of 96.8 in 2018 compared to 63.4 and 85.9 years for non-listed enterprises it is the case in both years. But the values also show that the discrepancy between non-listed and listed enterprises decreases from 16.5 to 10.9 years. Also listed family-owned companies are on average older than non-listed family firms. Exceptions where non-listed enterprises are younger than listed ones are cooperatives and state-owned enterprises in 1958 as well as foundation-owned companies in 2018. Looking at the group of listed cooperatives it comprises only *Bayerische Warenvermittlung landwirtschaftlicher Genossenschaften AG (BayWa)* which was founded in 1923. It is a single case compared to the average of 15 non-listed cooperatives in 1958. Of the state-owned enterprises five are listed compared to 34 non-listed ones. Of the latter ones seven are more than 100 years old while the oldest listed state-owned company is 74 years old. The sub-sample of listed foundation-owned enterprises in 2018 only consists of two companies, *Fresenius SE & Co. KGaA* and *Evonik Industries AG*. *Evonik* was just founded in 2007 although its operations are based on certain parts of *RAG AG*. Due to this recent foundation the average age of this listed company type (58.5 years) is much lower than the overall average (106.8 years).

That in 1958 public companies are the oldest company type and that listed enterprises are in most of the cases older than non-listed ones supports the initially presented view of Chandler that public companies are seen as the next logical development stage of companies after the founder and his or her family is not able to manage or finance the company anymore. The ownership majority of public companies is in free float. Based on the 2018 data Chandler's development is not fully supported because the average age of family firms rises considerably and is far ahead of the average age of public companies. However, listed family firms—the majority of stocks is with a family—are older than non-listed family businesses.

Based on the average age of 70 and 80 years, respectively, it can be concluded that the enterprises of the two datasets "[...] had already stood the test

Table 5.5 Average Age per Company Type 1958 & 2018

#	Type of company	Average age [years]					
		1958			2018		
		Non-listed	Listed	Total	Non-listed	Listed	Total
1	Family-owned business	75.2	87.4	78.9	103.1	116.8	105.2
2	Foreign family-owned business	51.0	57.0	54.0	79.4	–	79.4
3	Foundation-owned enterprise	77.5	–	77.5	116.4	58.5	106.8
4	Multiple companies-owned enterprise	45.4	–	45.4	46.7	171.0	64.4
5	Public company	–	80.8	80.8	–	89.3	89.3
6	Cooperative	48.7	35.0	47.9	80.4	93.5	83.0
7	State-owned enterprise	58.1	56.0	57.8	80.9	116.0	88.4
8	Foreign subsidiary	68.2	82.1	73.3	63.8	108.0	67.0
	Total	**63.4**	**80.0**	**70.0**	**85.9**	**96.8**	**89.0**

Source: Author's own table.

of time […]"[31] as historian Leslie Hannah describes his sample of the largest public companies of 1912 with an average age of 32 years.[32] He continues that his analyzed companies at the beginning of the 20th century "[…] were not the outcome of temporary stock market bubbles: these were the survivors of a brutal shakeout process after the global turn-of-the-century stock market booms and merger waves, in which many giants with watered stock but few capabilities had drastically declined"[33]. Considering the average age of the companies included in this thesis' datasets as well as the historical events during the past seven and roughly nine decades these enterprises are also well tested. With two World Wars in the first half of the 20th century they either survived this horrible time or were

[31] Hannah (1999, p. 255).

[32] Hannah does not consider, e.g., the time as partnerships in his calculation of the average age. He points out that the firms are "[…] on average thirty-two years old in the corporate sense […]" Hannah (1999, p. 255).

[33] Hannah (1999, p. 255).

founded afterwards when resources were scarce. In addition, stock market crashes and economic downturns could not eliminate these companies. The listing of a company appears to happen when the company is already older or mature. Therefore, the average age of listed companies is higher. But this does not mean that the company is in free float. Listed enterprises with an anchor shareholder who owns more than the majority achieve on average a higher age. In addition, foundations as the oldest company type in 2018 confirm their objective to perpetuate the firm.

Besides the comparison on an aggregated level the oldest and youngest companies are analyzed in Section 5.7.2 because of their outstanding age.

5.6 Industry: The Rise and Fall of Entire Industries

After the enterprises' sizes, modeled growth rates, company types, legal forms including the listing status as well as their age, the industry classifications for both rankings are introduced. The industry determines the general conditions in which a company operates and therefore is expected to impact the company's continuity and development. Overall, in accordance with the identified structural change entire industries nearly disappear and others rise substantially. Therefore, the chosen industry a company operates in poses a great threat to an enterprise.

The industries are based on the 2008 *WZ* codes as described in Sections 3.7.1.1 and 3.7.1.3 to ensure comparability. Table 5.6 provides an overview of the industry distributions of the 250 largest enterprises of 1958 and 2018.[34] From the enterprises of 1958 the majority of 145 companies (58.0%) operates in manufacturing which is clearly the dominating category with, among others, *Siemens AG* (#3), *Fried. Krupp, Essen* (#4) as well as the much smaller *Schubert & Salzer Maschinenfabrik AG* (#234) and *Ludwigshafener Walzmühle AG* (#240). The share is already higher than the secondary sector in 1958 with 47.3%. The second largest industry with 36 enterprises (14.6%) is commerce which includes the grocery chains *Heinrich Hill AG* (#208) and *Albrecht KG Lebensmittel-Filialbetrieb* (#235) as well as wholesalers of fuels like *BV-Aral AG* (#11) and the German subsidiary *Swift & Company GmbH* (#201) of the US meat processor *Swift & Company*. This category is followed by mining and quarrying with 29 entities (11.6%). *Steinkohlenwerke Mathias Stinnes AG* (#67), *Bayerische*

[34] Additional *WZ* industries classifications in which none of the 250 companies of 1958 and 2018 operate are (A) agriculture, forestry and fishing, (P) education, (R) arts, entertainment and recreation, (T) activities of households as employers, and (U) activities of extraterritorial organizations and bodies.

Berg-, Hütten- und Salzwerke AG (#232) and *Rheinische Kalksteinwerke GmbH* (#242) are part of this third largest industry category. The 23 companies (9.2%) in the energy and water industry are exclusively state-owned like *Berliner Kraft- und Licht (Bewag)-AG* (#119), *Bayernwerk AG Bayerische Landeselektrizitätsversorgung* (#120) and *Badenwerk AG* (#141). There is only one exception with listed *Neckarwerke Elektrizitätsversorgungs-AG* (#211) which is a public company in 1958 due to a minority stake of *AEG* and *Neckar-Elektrizitätsverband* while the remaining shares are in free float.[35] Transportation and storage as fifth largest industry category includes seven firms (2.8%) of which five are also state-owned, including the largest of all enterprises *Deutsche Bundesbahn* (#1) as well as *Deutsche Lufthansa AG* (#150). The remaining two are one public company, *Hamburg-Amerikanische Packetfahrt-AG* (#108), and one cooperative, *FERN-SVG-NORD Strassenfernverkehr-Genossenschaft Hamburg und Schleswig Holstein eGmbH* (#159). Five construction enterprises are in the sample of the 250 largest companies of 1958 as well, with *Philipp Holzmann AG* (#103), *Hochtief AG für Hoch- und Tiefbauten vorm. Gebr. Helfmann* (#113), *Beton- und Monierbau AG* (#145), *Ed. Züblin AG* (#195) and *Grün & Bilfinger AG Bauunternehmung* (#206). The remaining five entities are the two publishers (0.8%) *Axel Springer Verlag GmbH* (#115) and *C. Bertelsmann Verlag* (#181) in the category "information and communication", the two state-owned real estate companies (0.8%) *Deutsche Gesellschaft für öffentliche Arbeiten AG* (#38) and *"Neue Heimat" Gemeinnützige Wohnungs- und Siedlungsgesellschaft mbH* (#90) as well as the one tourism firm (0.4%) *TOUROPA oHG* categorized as "service activities" on position 213. Overall, manufacturing is the dominant industry in 1958 followed by its upstream and downstream industries like mining and steel trade, respectively.

[35] The company becomes state-owned in 1966 when *Neckar-Elektrizitätsverband* acquires the majority. Later on in 1997, *Neckarwerke Elektrizitätsversorgungs-AG* merge with *Technische Werke der Stadt Stuttgart AG*.

Table 5.6 Industry Distribution of the 250 Largest Enterprises of 1958 & 2018

Industry	**Number of enterprises**					
	1958		**2018**		**Change**	
Accommodation & food service activities	–	–	1	0.4%	1	*0.4pp*
Commerce	36	*14.4%*	65	*26.0%*	29	*11.6pp*
Construction	5	*2.0%*	6	*2.4%*	1	*0.4pp*
Energy & water	23	*9.2%*	20	*8.0%*	−3	*−1.2pp*
Financial & insurance activities	–	–	1	*0.4%*	1	*0.4pp*
Human health & social work activities	–	–	2	*0.8%*	2	*0.8pp*
Information & communication	2	*0.8%*	17	*6.8%*	15	*6.0pp*
Manufacturing	145	*58.0%*	117	*46.8%*	−28	*−11.2pp*
Mining & quarrying	29	*11.6%*	2	*0.8%*	−27	*−10.8pp*
Public administration & defense	–	–	1	*0.4%*	1	*0.4pp*
Real estate	2	*0.8%*	1	*0.4%*	−1	*−0.4pp*
Service activities	1	*0.4%*	7	*2.8%*	6	*2.4pp*
Transportation & storage	7	*2.8%*	10	*4.0%*	3	*1.2pp*
Total	**250**	***100.0%***	**250**	***100.0%***	–	–

Source: Author's own table.

The distribution of the industry affiliation of the enterprises of the 2018 dataset changes tremendously compared to the one of 1958 although the largest industry is still manufacturing with 117 entities (46.8%). This number decreases by 28 companies (−11.2pp) from 145. A similar decrease of 10.8pp is seen for mining and quarrying which leads to only two companies (0.8%) remaining in this industry. These are *K + S AG* with EUR 4.0bn in revenues on position 137 and *Aton GmbH* with EUR 2.5bn on position 236.[36] Additional industries with a decreasing share are "energy and water" with minus three (−1.2pp) and "real estate"

[36] *Aton GmbH* is the holding company of the former principal shareholder and founder of *Helios Kliniken*, Lutz Helmig, and his family. The holding has several portfolio companies in engineering, mining, medical technology, aviation, and digital services. Mining accounts for the largest revenue share. However, the mining activities are not located in Germany but

with minus one (−0.4pp). Accordingly, their total share changes only slightly to 8.0% and 0.4%. The only enterprise in the latter category is the public company *Vonovia SE* (#94) with revenues of EUR 6.5bn and a free float of around 77.5%. In energy and water the big power producers like *E.ON SE* (#22), *EnBW Energie Baden-Württemberg AG* (#33) and *RWE AG* (#52) are included but also the utility *Stadtwerke Köln GmbH* (#103) as well as the family-owned recycling company *Remondis SE & Co. KG* on position 77. These declining categories contrast with industries in which no companies in the top 250 were active 60 years ago. These are "accommodation and food service activities" and "public administration and defense" with one entity (0.4%) each as well as "human health and social work activities" with two entities (0.8%). The included enterprises are *McDonald's Deutschland LLC* (#165) in the first category, *Deutsche Gesellschaft für Internationale Zusammenarbeit GmbH* (#199) in the second as well as *Asklepios Kliniken GmbH & Co. KGaA* (#168) and *Sana Kliniken AG* (#208) in the latter one. In addition, one company (0.4%) in "financial and insurance activities" joins the 2018 ranking which is *Deutsche Börse AG* (#197). This public company does not provide financial or insurance services but the administration of financial markets via stock exchanges. This activity is also part of the mentioned *WZ* code and therefore included in the sample. Additional small increases of one and three entities can be seen in "construction" and "transportation and storage" leading to in total six (2.4%) and ten (4.0%) companies. The former category includes *HOCHTIEF AG* (#27) again, *Strabag AG* (#190) and *Goldbeck GmbH* (#207). *Deutsche Post AG* (#10), *Oldendorff Carriers GmbH & Co. KG* (#130) and *Hellmann Worldwide Logistics SE & Co. KG* (#227) are part of the latter category. A sevenfold increase can be observed in "service activities" from one (0,4%) to seven (2.8%) entities. Again, tourism enterprises like *TUI AG* (#37) and *FTI Touristik GmbH* (#159) are included but also companies which provide technical services like *M + W Group GmbH* (#155) and *Dekra SE* (#170) as well as the temporary employment agency *Randstad Deutschland GmbH & Co. KG* (#244) and the facility management company *Dussmann Stiftung & Co. KGaA* (#250). The information and communication industry has the second largest relative and absolute increase of 15 entities from two (0.8%) to 17 (6.8%). Among the 250 largest enterprises of 2018 again *Bertelsmann SE & Co. KGaA* (#41) and *Axel Springer SE* (#177) but also *SAP SE* (#26), *Amazon Deutschland* (#43), *Vodafone GmbH* (#64), *Bechtle AG* (#129) and *freenet AG* (#195) are part of this industry. These companies are software developers, e-commerce and cloud computing as

---

in Canada and South Africa. This means that only *K + S AG* is categorized as mining and quarrying company in the dataset of the 250 largest enterprises of 2018.

well as internet providers. The largest absolute increase with 29 entities can be observed for commerce from 36 (14.4%) to 65 (26.0%). In this category, the five companies with the highest revenue numbers *Schwarz-Gruppe* (#3), *Aldi Süd* (#11), *Edeka Zentrale AG & Co. KG* (#12), *REWE-ZENTRALFINANZ eG* (#13) and *Metro AG* (#19) all operate supermarkets and are wholesalers. Additional companies in commerce are the drugstore chains *dm-drogerie markt GmbH + Co. KG* (#61), *Dirk Rossmann GmbH* (#68) and *Müller Holding Ltd. & Co. KG* (#144) as well as *Zalando SE* (#107) which sell clothes online and *Ikea Holding Deutschland GmbH & Co. KG* (#114) the furniture retailer. But also wholesalers of fuels like *Marquard & Bahls AG* (#53) and *JET Tankstellen Deutschland GmbH* (#157) as well as of metals and steal like *Heraeus Holding GmbH* (#35) and *Schmolz + Bickenbach Edelstahl GmbH* (#171) are included. The diversity in commerce is high.

From a revenue and employee perspective the distribution is slightly different (Table 5.7). Substantial increases can be seen in commerce as well as information and communication according to their growing number of enterprises. However, in commerce the number of employees rises much more sharply. This can be traced back to the supermarket chains with their hundreds of thousands of employees while in 1958 the trading companies often had a small number of employees but large revenues like *Getreide-Import-Gesellschaft mbH* with EUR 210 m [DM 411 m] in revenue but only around 60 employees. In addition, the manufacturing industry's share in revenue decreases from 55.4% to 49.8% which is in accordance with the decreasing number of enterprises in this category from 145 to 117 but the share of employees increases slightly from 51.8% to 52.0%. This industry remains labor-intensive or at least the productivity compared to other industries appears to have risen less sharply. In contrast, in energy and water the employee share of 2.0% is relatively low compared to the revenue share of 9.0% in 2018. This indicates a high productivity. The strong decrease in mining and quarrying companies is also reflected in the industry's revenue and employee shares dropping from 14.2% in 1958 to 0.2% in 2018 and from 18.4% to 0.3%, respectively. Mainly public companies are affected by this decline because they account for twelve of the 26 companies in this industry in 1958. It is noteworthy that the same number of companies employs more than three times as many employees in 2018 compared to 1958. The enterprises become much bigger which also requires new or adapted forms of organizations and management.

Overall, the changes among the 250 largest enterprises between 1958 and 2018 reflect the structural changes highlighted in Section 4.1—a shift from manufacturing towards the services sector which also includes, e.g., the information and communication industry as well as commerce. Furthermore, some industries like

Table 5.7 Revenue & Employee Distribution per Industry Category of 1958 & 2018

Industry	**Revenue** [bnEUR]				**Employees** [thousands]			
	1958		**2018**		**1958**		**2018**	
Accommodation & food service activities	–	–	3.5	*0.1%*	–	–	60.0	*0.6%*
Commerce	10.0	*14.8%*	729.7	*23.8%*	162.0	*4.2%*	2,257.9	*22.7%*
Construction	0.5	*0.7%*	40.8	*1.3%*	43.6	*1.1%*	137.5	*1.4%*
Energy & water	3.0	*4.4%*	274.4	*9.0%*	89.9	*2.4%*	198.3	*2.0%*
Financial & insurance activities	–	–	2.9	*0.1%*	–	–	6.0	*0.1%*
Human health & social work activities	–	–	6.1	*0.2%*	–	–	81.3	*0.8%*
Information & communication	0.2	*0.3%*	188.9	*6.2%*	3.5	*0.1%*	552.3	*5.6%*
Manufacturing	37.5	*55.4%*	1,587.4	*51.8%*	1,901.9	*49.8%*	5,171.3	*52.0%*
Mining & quarrying	9.6	*14.2%*	6.5	*0.2%*	702.6	*18.4%*	33.6	*0.3%*
Public administration & defense	–	–	2.8	*0.1%*	–	–	21.0	*0.2%*
Real estate	0.6	*0.9%*	6.5	*0.2%*	0.4	*0.0%*	9.9	*0.1%*
Service activities	0.1	*0.1%*	37.9	*1.2%*	0.7	*0.0%*	253.8	*2.6%*
Transportation & storage	6.2	*9.2%*	177.9	*5.8%*	917.9	*24.0%*	1,153.5	*11.6%*
Total	**67.7**	***100.0%***	**3,065.3**	***100.0%***	**3,822.4**	***100.0%***	**9,936.5**	***100.0%***

Source: Author's own table.

mining and quarrying nearly disappear while others like commerce become more important. Despite all the changes manufacturing remains the largest industry of the 250 largest enterprises. Operating in one industry means being exposed to these overall economic trends which is a major threat for a company. A more detailed look at the industries of the family-owned enterprises is given in Section 5.8.

As a critical remark it is noteworthy that the industry categorization of diversified enterprises is based on the assessment of the companies' business units if multiple exist. Each business unit gets an industry affiliation. Ultimately, an enterprise is categorized based on the industry affiliation with the largest revenue. In 1958, for example, *Salzgitter Konzern* (*AG für Berg- und Hüttenbetriebe*) has several subsidiaries some of which operate mainly in mining and quarrying, like *Bergbau-AG Ewald-König Ludwig* and *Erzbergbau Salzgitter AG*, others in manufacturing like *Hüttenwerk Salzgitter AG* and *Linke-Hofmann-Busch Waggon-Fahrzeug-Maschinen GmbH*. Some subsidiaries even manage real estate. Looking at the revenue figures the first area, mining and quarrying, is the largest one. Therefore, *Salzgitter Konzern* is categorized as a company which operates in the mining and quarrying industry. Similarly, if a company has the *WZ* code of holding activities the underlying business units are analyzed and the industry category with the highest revenue share determines the holding's industry affiliation. This described procedure is required much more often for companies of the 2018 dataset. Without analyzing every company in detail regarding their business units it is proposed that the 250 largest enterprises of 2018 have more operations in various industries than their 1958 counterparts. The former are more diversified.

5.7 Company Insights: From Large to Small and from Old to Young

After providing an overview of the aggregated findings on company type level the following comparisons also name the relevant enterprises which are included in the rankings of 1958 and 2018.[37] These insights are intended to improve the historical understanding of corporate developments within the German economy by not only providing averages and modeled developments but by giving the enterprises names and actual statuses for the years 1958 and 2018.

5.7.1 The 25 Largest and Smallest Enterprises: The Increasing Strength of Large Companies

The largest and the smallest enterprise of the 1958 and 2018 dataset is already named in Section 5.1. The present chapter provides more insights into the 25

[37] Some of the enterprises are well-known to the interested reader others might surprise her or him because they do not appear in the daily media or disappear over the last 60 years.

largest and smallest enterprises of the two rankings on company level.[38] The previously presented development conditions of industry, age, listing and ownership structure are part of the company analysis. Overall, the largest enterprises are gaining in importance and the smaller ones are moving closer together.

25 enterprises represent 10.0% of the sample size. In the ranking of the 250 largest enterprises of 1958 the first 25 companies account for 47.1% of the revenue of the entire sample. The last 25 enterprises are responsible for 1.7%.[39] These numbers show the importance of the major companies for the economic performance in the sample but also in the overall economy.

The two state-owned entities [SOE] *Deutsche Bundesbahn* and *Deutsche Bundespost* lead the 1958 ranking (see Table 5.8) with revenues of EUR 3.4bn [DM 6.8bn] and EUR 2.3bn [DM 4.5bn]. *Deutsche Bundesbahn* has twice the size of the first non-state-owned company *Siemens AG* with EUR 1.7bn [DM 3.3bn] on position three which is categorized as family business [FB] and listed at that time.[40] *Deutsche Bundespost* with EUR 2.3bn [DM 4.5bn] in revenues is still around one third larger than *Siemens*. It is noteworthy that these two state-owned enterprises employ around 519,300 and 378,500 people in 1958 making them the largest employers in the sample by far as well. The two enterprises on position four and five based on revenue, *Fried. Krupp, Essen* with EUR 1.7bn [DM 3.3bn] and *Daimler-Benz AG* with EUR 1.6bn [DM 3.2bn], are also family-owned like *Siemens* but only the latter one is also listed. Number six, *Mannesmann AG* with EUR 1.5bn [DM 3.0bn], is the largest public company [PC]. The majority of its shares is in free float. The first and only multiple companies-owned enterprise [MCE] among the 25 largest companies is *BV-Aral AG* on position eleven with EUR 1.1bn [DM 2.1bn] which is closely linked to the *Benzin-Benzol-Verband (BV)* and acts as its managing body. The enterprise is owned by several benzene and gasoline producers including *Bergwerksgesellschaft Hibernia AG, Gelsenberg*

---

[38] As a brief country comparison, FORTUNE lists *General Motors* as the largest corporation in the US in 1958 with a total revenue of USD 11.0bn and 588,160 employees (see CNN (2021)). In 2018, *Walmart* is at the top of the list with a total revenue of USD 500.3bn and 2.3 million employees (see Walmart Inc. (2019)). The American companies are larger than the biggest German enterprise in both years.

[39] The 25 largest enterprises of 1958 generate EUR 31.9bn [DM 62.4bn] of the total revenue of the sample which is EUR 67.7bn [DM 132.3bn] and the 25 smallest enterprises generate EUR 1.1bn [DM 2.2bn].

[40] For the financials of *Deutsche Bundesbahn* see the 295 page report of 1960 to the German Parliament (see Deutscher Bundestag (1960)) which already proposes measures to reduce the company's losses. Further, see Section 3.7.3 the difficulties to determine the company type of *Siemen AG*.

Benzin AG, *Harpener Bergbau-AG*, *Mannesmann AG* and *Wintershall AG*.[41] As part of the Dutch *Unilever Group* the foreign subsidiary [FS] *Deutsche Unilever AG* is the twelfth largest company in the sample of 1958 with a revenue of EUR 1.1bn [DM 2.1bn]. No enterprise of the remaining company types which include cooperatives [COOP], foundations [FD] and foreign family businesses [FFB] is part of the 25 largest enterprises of 1958. They follow on position 26 with *GEG Großeinkaufs-Gesellschaft Deutscher Konsumgenossenschaften* (EUR 0.7bn [DM 1.5bn]), on position 84 with *Carl Zeiss* (EUR 0.2bn [DM 0.4bn]) and on position 28 with *Klöckner-Werke AG* (EUR 0.7bn [DM 1.4bn]). Public companies are the largest group with eight (32.0%) of the 25 entities followed by family businesses with seven (28.0%), state-owned enterprises with five (20.0%) and foreign subsidiaries with four (16.0%). Due to the high number of public companies, it is not surprising that 15 (60.0%) of the 25 largest enterprises are listed and a minority of ten (40.0%) is non-listed.[42] In addition, there is a clear majority of companies in the manufacturing industry with 15 (60.0%) out of the 25 enterprises. Yet, the share is only slightly higher than the one in the overall sample with 250 enterprises which is 58.0%. Four additional enterprises (16.0%) have their main operations in mining and quarrying followed by three (12.0%) in commerce with *BV-Aral AG*, *Deutsche Unilever AG* and *Handelsunion AG*. The two largest companies, *Deutsche Bundesbahn* and *Deutsche Bundespost*, are also the only two (8.0%) in the extract of the top 25 enterprises of 1958 in the transportation and storage industry. Even only one company (4.0%), *Rheinisch-Westfälisches Elektrizitätswerk AG*, is active in the field of energy and water. Nevertheless, as highlighted in Section 5.6 some of the companies also have business activities in other industry areas. The industry categorization is based on the largest business unit of a diversified enterprise. Overall, public companies have a proportionally higher share among the 25 largest companies compared to the overall sample. The same applies for the listing of a company which appear to be attributes for to be or become one of the largest 25 enterprises.

---

[41] See Die Zeit (1960) for more details.

[42] The share of listed companies in all 250 enterprises is 40.0%. Therefore, the percentages have swapped in this smaller sample of 25.

Table 5.8 The 25 Largest Enterprises of 1958

#	Company name 1958	Founding year	Rev. 1958 [mEUR]	Empl. 1958 [thousands]	Company type[43]	Industry
1	Deutsche Bundesbahn	1920	3,492.8	519.3	SOE	Transportation & storage
2	Deutsche Bundespost	1868	2,293.6	378.5	SOE	Transportation & storage
3	Siemens AG	1847	1,706.2	179.0	FB	Manufacturing
4	Fried. Krupp, Essen	1811	1,703.1	105.2	FB	Manufacturing
5	Daimler-Benz AG	1883	1,610.6	80.0	FB	Manufacturing
6	Mannesmann AG	1890	1,511.4	78.6	PC	Mining & quarrying
7	Volkswagenwerk GmbH	1937	1,390.2	47.9	SOE	Manufacturing
8	Gutehoffnungshütte Aktienverein	1758	1,386.6	71.8	FB	Manufacturing
9	Rheinische Stahlwerke	1870	1,362.6	81.6	PC	Manufacturing
10	Gelsenkirchener Bergwerks-AG	1873	1,288.5	83.5	PC	Mining & quarrying
11	BV-Aral AG	1898	1,094.2	5.8	MCE	Commerce
12	Deutsche Unilever AG	1930	1,078.8	32.0	FS	Commerce
13	Adam Opel AG	1862	1,073.7	33.3	FS	Manufacturing
14	Farbenfabriken Bayer AG	1863 / 1951	1,027.7	52.5	PC	Manufacturing
15	Handelsunion AG	1954	1,022.6	6.1	FB	Commerce
16	AEG Allgemeine Elektricitäts-Gesellschaft AG	1883	999.6	105.6	PC	Manufacturing
17	BASF Badische Anilin- & Soda-Fabrik AG	1865 / 1952	986.8	52.1	PC	Manufacturing
18	Esso AG	1890	974.5	5.1	FS	Manufacturing
19	Farbwerke Hoechst AG vormals Meister Lucius & Brüning	1863 / 1951	965.8	43.3	PC	Manufacturing
20	August Thyssen-Hütte AG	1891 / 1953	908.1	33.4	FB	Manufacturing

(continued)

[43] The explanations of the company type abbreviations can be found in Table 60 of the appendix in the electronic supplementary material.

Table 5.8 (continued)

#	Company name 1958	Founding year	Rev. 1958 [mEUR]	Empl. 1958 [thousands]	Company type	Industry
21	Salzgitter-Konzern[44]	1858	889.1	72.7	SOE	Mining & quarrying
22	Hoesch AG	1871	827.8	51.6	PC	Mining & quarrying
23	Deutsche Shell AG	1902	780.7	7.1	FS	Manufacturing
24	Phoenix-Rheinrohr AG	1852	768.0	30.0	FB	Manufacturing
25	Rheinisch-Westfälisches Elektrizitätswerk AG	1898	751.6	13.8	SOE	Energy & water

Source: Author's own table.

In the 2018 sample, the first 25 companies account for 53.4% of the revenue of the entire sample which is an increase of 6.2% compared to 1958. The last 25 enterprises are responsible for 2.0%, an increase of 0.3%.[45] The importance of the largest enterprises has grown over the last 60 years. 10.0% of the companies generate more than half of the entire revenue of the sample. However, the share of the smallest 25 has also increased which shows that the revenue of the smaller companies has become a little bit more equally distributed.

A second car manufacturer, *Daimler AG*, follows *Volkswagen AG* as second largest enterprise with revenues of EUR 167.4bn (see Table 5.9). Compared to the listed family business *Volkswagen Daimler* is a public company similar to *Bayerische Motoren Werke AG*, a third car manufacturer, which is the fourth largest enterprise with EUR 97.5bn.[46] Between the car manufacturers the retail group *Schwarz* can be found on position three with revenues of around EUR 104.4bn and around 429,000 employees. Compared to 1958, three foundations (12.0%) as well as two cooperatives (8.0%) are among the 25 largest enterprises 60 years later. *Robert Bosch GmbH*, *ZF Friedrichshafen AG* and *Fresenius SE & Co. KGaA* are the sixth, 18th and 21st largest enterprise with revenues of EUR 78.5bn, EUR

---

44 In 1958, the legal name of *Salzgitter* was *AG für Berg- und Hüttenbetriebe* but it was hardly used. Most likely because of the reference to its name *Reichswerke für Berg- und Hüttenbetriebe "Hermann Göring"* during the Third Reich. The name was officially changed to *Salzgitter AG* in 1961 (see Wessel (2008) as company publication).

45 The 25 largest enterprises of 2018 generate EUR 1,636.1bn of the total revenue of the sample which is EUR 3,065.3bn and the 25 smallest enterprises generate EUR 61.1bn.

46 *BMW AG* is categorized as public company. See Section 5.8 for a critical discussion.

36.9bn and EUR 33.5bn. The two cooperatives also operate supermarkets like *Schwarz*. *Edeka Zentrale AG & Co. KG* and *REWE-ZENTRALFINANZ eG* are two holding organizations with total revenues of EUR 53.6bn and EUR 53.4bn making them the twelfth and 13th largest enterprise of 2018. Foreign subsidiaries and state-owned enterprises occur with two entities (8.0%) and one (4.0%), respectively, in the sub-sample. The former ones are *BP Europa SE*, ultimately owned by *BP plc.* from Great Britain and generating EUR 29.3bn on position 23, as well as *GAZPROM Germania GmbH*, ultimately owned by Russian *PAO GAZPROM* with revenues of EUR 27.3bn on position 24. *Deutsche Bahn AG* still state-owned and in 1958 the largest enterprise appears on position 15 with revenues of EUR 44.1bn. No foreign family business and multiple companies-owned enterprise is part of the sub-sample. The largest of the first company type follows on position 31 with *Ford-Werke GmbH* (EUR 21.1bn) owned by the US car manufacturer *Ford Motor Company*. *Amprion GmbH*, a transmission system operator, with revenues of EUR 13.8bn on position 49 is the largest multiple companies-owned enterprise. Several German institutional investors as well as *RWE AG* each own a part of the company. Overall, the share of public companies in the 25 largest enterprises of 2018 has increased to 52.0% (13) making them the most common company type by far. Family businesses follow with four (16.0%) entities. The observation that there is no multiple companies-owned enterprise in the sub-sample of 2018 is in line with the overall decrease of this company type since 1958 and the tightened competition laws. The number of listed companies within the 25 largest enterprises does not change and remains at 15 (60.0%) while ten (40.0%) are non-listed. In 2018, the difference to the percentage of the entire sample is even higher because the share of listed companies in the entire sample of 250 enterprises is only 28.8%. From an industry perspective, manufacturing is again the largest category with twelve entities (48.0%) while commerce follows with six companies (24.0%) on second place. Energy and water as well as transportation and storage account for three enterprises (12.0%) each. The latter one exceeds its share in the overall sample substantially suggesting that in this industry size is essential for the business model. All other industry shares are similar to their shares in the overall 2018 sample. Furthermore, *Deutsche Telekom AG* is the only information and communication company among the 25 largest enterprises of 2018. Overall, public companies whose share increases to more than half of the 25, and a listing remain key attributes among the largest companies. Furthermore, the largest 10.0% of the companies of the sample combine more than half of the sample's revenue which increases their economic power.

In 1958 and even more clearly in 2018, the company type distributions in the samples of the 25 largest enterprises show that public companies have a higher

Table 5.9 The 25 Largest Enterprises of 2018

#	Company name 2018	Founding year	Rev. 2018 [mEUR]	Empl. 2018 [thousands]	Company type	Industry
1	Volkswagen AG	1937	235,849.0	664.5	FB	Manufacturing
2	Daimler AG	1883	167,362.0	298.7	PC	Manufacturing
3	Schwarz-Gruppe	1930	104,300.0	429.0	FB	Commerce
4	Bayerische Motoren Werke AG	1916	97,480.0	134.7	PC	Manufacturing
5	Siemens AG	1847	83,044.0	379.0	PC	Manufacturing
6	Robert Bosch GmbH	1886	78,465.0	409.9	FD	Manufacturing
7	Uniper SE	2016	78,176.0	11.8	PC	Energy & water
8	Deutsche Telekom AG	1995	75,656.0	215.7	PC	Information & communication
9	BASF SE	1865 / 1952	62,675.0	122.4	PC	Manufacturing
10	Deutsche Post AG	1868	61,550.0	547.5	PC	Transportation & storage
11	Aldi Süd	1913	59,000.0	150.6	FB	Commerce
12	Edeka Zentrale AG & Co. KG	1907	53,600.0	376.0	COOP	Commerce
13	REWE-ZENTRALFINANZ eG	1927	53,377.8	234.0	COOP	Commerce
14	Continental AG	1871	44,404.0	243.2	PC	Manufacturing
15	Deutsche Bahn AG	1920	44,065.0	342.6	SOE	Transportation & storage
16	thyssenkrupp AG	1891 / 1953	42,745.0	161.1	PC	Manufacturing
17	Bayer AG	1863 / 1951	39,586.0	117.0	PC	Manufacturing
18	ZF Friedrichshafen AG	1915	36,929.0	149.0	FD	Manufacturing
19	Metro AG	1964	36,543.0	146.3	PC	Commerce

(continued)

Table 5.9 (continued)

#	Company name 2018	Founding year	Rev. 2018 [mEUR]	Empl. 2018 [thousands]	Company type	Industry
20	Deutsche Lufthansa AG	1926 / 1953	35,844.0	135.5	PC	Transportation & storage
21	Fresenius SE & Co. KGaA	1912	33,530.0	276.8	FD	Manufacturing
22	E.ON SE	1929	29,565.0	43.3	PC	Energy & water
23	BP Europa SE	1904	29,279.9	10.5	FS	Manufacturing
24	Gazprom Germania GmbH	1990	27,275.0	1.6	FS	Energy & water
25	Phoenix Pharma SE	1994	25,812.0	37.1	FB	Commerce

Source: Author's own table.

share in the top decile with 32.0% and 52.0% compared to their share of 22.4% and 18.8%, respectively, in the total sample with 250 companies. Therefore, public companies with their scattered ownership structure seem to be more suited for the largest of the large enterprises than any other type. Nevertheless, it can be seen that family-owned businesses can also be large with *Volkswagen* and *Schwarz* as the outstanding examples. From an industry perspective manufacturing remains the dominant category in both years while commerce increases its share like in the overall sample. The development mirrors the structural change although manufacturing remains above average.

In comparison to the 25 largest enterprises Table 5.10 and Table 5.11 provide an overview of the 25 smallest enterprises of the 1958 and 2018 samples. Therefore, the positions 226 to 250 are included. These companies may not be as well-known as the ones described previously but they are still much larger than the majority of companies in their time. Overall, they are dominated by family- and state-owned companies. No public company is among the smallest of the sample.

Saarferngas AG was already mentioned as the smallest company of the 1958 sample. It is followed by *WEDAG Westfalia Dinnendahl Gröppel AG* with only a little more revenue—in total EUR 41.7 m [DM 81.5 m]. *WEDAG* is one of five (20.0%) public companies within the sub-sample of the 25 smallest companies. The most common company type are family-owned businesses with nine entities (36.0%) including *Norddeutsche Zucker-Raffinerie AG* with EUR 42.0 m [DM 82.1 m] in revenues and *Friedrich Baur GmbH* with EUR 48.1 m [DM94.0 m]. Seven enterprises (28.0%) which are state-owned follow with entities like *Elektrizitäts-AG Mitteldeutschland* (EUR 41.9 m [DM 82.0 m]) and *Wuppertaler Stadtwerke AG* (EUR 47.2 m [DM 92.3 m]). The rest of the 25 companies is distributed among two cooperative (8.0%) and one foreign subsidiary (4.0%) and multiple company-owned enterprise (4.0%) each. The first company type includes *Ein- und Verkaufsgenossenschaft Westfälischer Molkereien eGmbH* (EUR 42.9 m [DM 84.0 m]) and *Konsumgenossenschaft Stuttgart eGmbH* (EUR 47.0 m [DM 91.9 m]), the middle one *Oelwerke Julius Schindler GmbH* (EUR 45.0 m [DM 88.0 m]) which is owned by *British Petroleum Ltd.* (Great Britain) in 1958 and the last one includes *Süddeutsche Zellwolle AG* (EUR 46.8 m [DM 91.6 m]) whose owners are *Bayerische Vereinsbank* as well as several spinning and weaving mills. There are no foreign family businesses and foundations in the sub-sample. Overall, 18 (72.0%) of the 25 enterprises are non-listed and seven (28.0%) are listed. The share of non-listed companies is 12.0pp higher than the share in the total sample with 60.0%. Due to the high share of state-owned enterprises five (20.0%) enterprises operate in the energy and water industry. The

Table 5.10 The 25 Smallest Enterprises of 1958

#	Company name 1958	Founding year	Rev. 1958 [mEUR]	Empl. 1958 [thousands]	Company type	Industry
226	Friedrich Baur GmbH	1925	48.1	0.0	FB	Commerce
227	Heinrich Bergbau AG	1951	47.6	6.0	PC	Mining & quarrying
228	Kabelwerk Rheydt AG (KWR)	1898	47.3	2.3	PC	Manufacturing
229	Wuppertaler Stadtwerke AG	1838	47.2	4.8	SOE	Energy & water
230	Konsumgenossenschaft Stuttgart eGmbH	1864	47.0	2.1	COOP	Commerce
231	Süddeutsche Zellwolle AG	1935	46.8	2.2	MCE	Manufacturing
232	Bayerische Berg-, Hütten- und Salzwerke AG	1927	46.7	5.3	SOE	Mining & quarrying
233	Wilhelm Karmann GmbH	1874	46.5	3.4	FB	Manufacturing
234	Schubert & Salzer Maschinenfabrik AG	1883	46.5	0.5	PC	Manufacturing
235	Albrecht KG Lebensmittel-Filialbetrieb	1913	46.0	0.0	FB	Commerce
236	Rheinisch-Westfälische Kalkwerke AG	1953	45.2	2.7	PC	Mining & quarrying
237	"Der Photo Porst" Hanns Porst	1919	45.0	1.6	FB	Commerce
238	Oelwerke Julius Schindler GmbH	1908	45.0	0.8	FS	Manufacturing

(continued)

Table 5.10 (continued)

#	Company name 1958	Founding year	Rev. 1958 [mEUR]	Empl. 1958 [thousands]	Company type	Industry
239	Energieversorgung Weser-Ems AG	1930	44.8	1.8	SOE	Energy & water
240	Ludwigshafener Walzmühle AG	1894	44.5	0.4	FB	Manufacturing
241	Zündapp-Werke GmbH	1917	44.1	2.1	FB	Manufacturing
242	Rheinische Kalksteinwerke GmbH	1903	44.0	2.2	FB	Mining & quarrying
243	Chemische Werke Albert AG	1858	43.3	1.9	FB	Manufacturing
244	Ein- und Verkaufsgenossen-schaft Westfälischer Molkereien eGmbH	1921	42.9	0.2	COOP	Commerce
245	Bayerische Milchversorgung GmbH	1915	42.9	1.2	SOE	Manufacturing
246	Pfalzwerke AG	1912	42.1	1.0	SOE	Energy & water
247	Norddeutsche Zucker-Raffinerie AG	1885	42.0	0.8	FB	Manufacturing
248	Elektrizitäts-AG Mitteldeutschland	1923	41.9	1.6	SOE	Energy & water
249	WEDAG Westfalia Dinnendahl Gröppel AG	1881	41.7	2.8	PC	Manufacturing
250	Saar-Ferngas AG	1929	40.6	0.5	SOE	Energy & water

Source: Author's own table.

Table 5.11 The 25 Smallest Enterprises of 2018

#	Company name 2018	Founding year	Rev. 2018 [mEUR]	Empl. 2018 [thousands]	Company type	Industry
226	Körber AG	1946	2,545.0	10.5	FD	Manufacturing
227	Hellmann Worldwide Logistics SE & Co. KG	1871	2,540.0	10.7	FB	Transportation & storage
228	Comparex AG	2011	2,533.0	2.4	FS	Information & communication
229	Saarstahl AG	1873	2,528.0	6.7	FD	Manufacturing
230	Alfred Kärcher SE & Co. KG	1935	2,525.0	13.0	FB	Manufacturing
231	Cronimet Holding GmbH	1980	2,510.0	1.7	FB	Commerce
232	Joh. Vaillant GmbH & Co. KG	1874	2,501.0	13.0	FB	Manufacturing
233	Viessmann Werke GmbH & Co. KG	1917	2,500.0	12.0	FB	Manufacturing
234	Heidelberger Druckmaschinen AG	1850	2,490.0	11.9	PC	Manufacturing
235	Unitymedia GmbH	2005	2,477.0	2.8	FS	Information & communication
236	Aton GmbH	2001	2,462.0	18.7	FB	Mining & quarrying
237	Nordex SE	1985	2,459.0	5.7	PC	Manufacturing
238	Enercity AG	1952	2,440.0	2.8	SOE	Energy & water
239	Wilhelm Hoyer GmbH & Co. KG	1924	2,430.0	1.5	FB	Commerce
240	Neumann Gruppe GmbH	1934	2,405.0	2.4	FB	Commerce

(continued)

Table 5.11 (continued)

#	Company name 2018	Founding year	Rev. 2018 [mEUR]	Empl. 2018 [thousands]	Company type	Industry
241	Diebold Nixdorf AG	1999	2,400.0	8.7	FS	Commerce
242	Muhr und Bender KG	1916	2,400.0	15.0	FB	Manufacturing
243	GE Deutschland Holding GmbH	1883	2,393.0	4.2	FS	Manufacturing
244	Randstad Deutschland GmbH & Co. KG	1968	2,383.0	49.9	FS	Service activities
245	Phoenix Contact GmbH & Co. KG	1923	2,380.0	17.4	FB	Manufacturing
246	3M Deutschland GmbH	1951	2,370.0	6.7	FS	Manufacturing
247	Dell GmbH	1988	2,369.2	2.7	FS	Commerce
248	Hydro Aluminium Rolled Products GmbH	2002	2,360.0	3.6	FS	Manufacturing
249	Heinrich Bauer Verlag KG	1875	2,354.0	10.8	FB	Information & communication
250	Dussmann Stiftung & Co. KGaA	1963	2,341.0	66.1	FB	Service activities

Source: Author's own table.

similar number is in commerce and four (16.0%) in mining and quarrying. Manufacturing is again the biggest industry category with eleven companies (44.0%). Nevertheless, this share is below the overall sample's value of 58.0%.

Dussmann Stiftung & Co. KGaA is the smallest of the overall 2018 sample and one of twelve family businesses (48.0%) in the sub-sample of the 25 smallest companies.[47] Thus, this company type represents the most enterprises. Additional family-owned businesses are *Muhr und Bender KG* (EUR 2.4bn), *Wilhelm Hoyer GmbH & Co. KG* (EUR 2.4bn) and *Viessmann Werke GmbH & Co. KG* (EUR 2.5bn). Foreign subsidiaries are the second largest company type and have a comparatively high proportion with eight entities (32.0%) including companies like *Hydro Aluminium Rolled Products GmbH*, fully owned by Norwegian *Norsk Hydro ASA*, *Randstad Deutschland GmbH & Co. KG*, a subsidiary of Dutch *Randstad N.V.*, and the cable network operator *Unitymedia GmbH* owned by the British multinational telecommunications company *Liberty Global plc*. Two enterprises (8.0%) each are foundations and public companies. *Saarstahl AG* on position 229 and *Körber AG* on position 226 with revenues of EUR 2.5bn and EUR 2.6bn, respectively, are both owned by non-profit foundations. The public companies are *Nordex SE* and *Heidelberger Druckmaschinen AG*. They both generate revenues of around EUR 2.5bn and are ranked on position 237 and 234, respectively. Of all 25 companies only three (12.0%) are listed which is far below the overall average of 28.8% and the remaining 22 entities (88.0%) are non-listed. Like in the sample of the 25 largest enterprises of 2018 twelve (48.0%) of the smallest companies operate in manufacturing. Commerce with five entities (20.0%) as well as information and communication with three (12.0%) follow on second and third place. The remaining companies are distributed among service activities with two entities (8.0%) which are *Randstad Deutschland GmbH & Co. KG* and *Dussmann Stiftung & Co. KGaA*, energy and water, mining and quarrying as well as transportation and storage with one entity (4.0%) each. The latter three are *Enercity AG*, *Aton GmbH* and *Hellmann Worldwide Logistics SE & Co. KG*.

Overall, family businesses are the largest company type of the 25 smallest enterprises in 1958 but also in 2018. While their share in 1958 is close to their share in the overall sample in 2018 they exceed it. Moreover, foreign subsidiaries gain in importance over the 60 years similar to the industries of information and communication, service activities and transportation and storage. These smaller companies are on average less often listed than the overall sample. This confirms the finding from the 25 largest enterprises that being a public company and being listed as another company type are attributes for the major enterprises at the top of the ranking.

When providing the names of the enterprises in these lists of 1958 and 2018 it stands out that some of them appear in both years. Others do not and the reader

---

[47] *Dussmann Stiftung & Co. KGaA* is categorized as family-owned enterprise because ultimately the Dussmann family (often represented by Catherine von Fürstenberg-Dussmann) owns the company. The foundation only acts as general partner of the *Co. KGaA*.

might know or might not know that some of them still exist. Which companies survive the observation period of 60 years and which do not as well as how they grow, decline or disappear is further investigated in Chapter 6 and 7.

The lists with all 250 enterprises of 1958 and 2018 and their corresponding revenue figures can be found in Table 61 and Table 62 of the appendix in the electronic supplementary material.

5.7.2 The 25 Oldest and Youngest Enterprises: Spanning 289 and 349 Years

Specific companies which stand out from the datasets except the largest and smallest ones are the oldest and youngest enterprises because they have either survived several generations or have become one of the largest companies in Germany within a few years.

In 1958, *E. Merck AG*, the pharmaceutical company based in Darmstadt, is already 290 years old, making it the oldest enterprise of the sample (see Table 5.12). The company generates EUR 94.1 m [DM 184.0 m] in revenues in 1958 and appears on position 142. Because *Merck*, founded in 1668, reappears in the 2018 list and no older company joins it *Merck KGaA* remains the oldest entity also in the 2018 sample with revenues of EUR 14.8bn (see Table 5.13) on position 46.[48] Additional companies of the 250 largest of 1958 which have a similarly long history like *Merck* are *Aktien-Gesellschaft der Dillinger Hüttenwerke* (founded in 1685), *Buderus'sche Eisenwerke AG* (1731), *Franz Haniel & Cie. GmbH* (1756), *Gutehoffnungshütte Aktienverein* (1758) and *Stahl- u. Walzwerke Rasselstein-Andernach AG* (1760). These six were all founded before 1800 which is more than 15 decades before the decade of the observation year 1958. As highlighted in Section 5.5, the dataset of the 250 largest enterprises of 2018 includes 18 companies which were founded more than 15 decades ago. Therefore, the number of companies older than 160 years triples and includes, e.g., *Wieland-Werke AG* (1820), *Bertelsmann SE & Co. KGaA* (1835), *B. Braun Melsungen AG* (1839), *Hapag-Lloyd AG* (1847) and *Heidelberger Druckmaschinen AG* (1850). Coming back to the 25 oldest enterprises of 1958, twelve (48.0%) are family-owned which means that this company type dominates with reference to age. Besides some of the above-mentioned enterprises *Christian Dierig AG* (1805),

48 *Merck's* development can be traced back to1668 when Friedrich Jacob Merck takes over a pharmacy in Darmstadt. It is noteworthy that at that time no industrial production took place. This first changed in 1827. Nevertheless, the origin of today's company *Merck KGaA* goes back to the 17th century.

Table 5.12 The 25 Oldest Enterprises of 1958

#[49]	Company name 1958	Founding year	Rev. 1958 [mEUR]	Empl. 1958 [thousands]	Company type	Industry
142	E. Merck AG	1668	94.1	5.9	FB	Manufacturing
72	Aktien-Gesellschaft der Dillinger Hüttenwerke	1685	227.5	6.3	FS	Manufacturing
96	Buderus'sche Eisenwerke	1731	156.5	11.3	FB	Manufacturing
36	Franz Haniel & Cie. GmbH	1756	482.1	5.8	FB	Commerce
8	Gutehoffnungshütte Aktienverein	1758	1,386.6	71.8	FB	Manufacturing
91	Stahl- u. Walzwerke Rasselstein-Andernach AG	1760 / 1951	185.1	5.6	FB	Manufacturing
117	Christian Dierig AG	1805	128.6	2.7	FB	Manufacturing
87	Neunkircher Eisenwerk AG	1806	191.7	9.4	FB	Manufacturing
67	Steinkohlenwerke Mathias Stinnes AG	1808	252.6	24.4	PC	Mining & quarrying
132	Henschel-Werke GmbH	1810	102.3	8.0	FB	Manufacturing
4	Fried. Krupp, Essen	1811	1,703.1	105.2	FB	Manufacturing
57	Felten & Guilleaume Carlswerk AG	1820	308.3	21.7	FS	Manufacturing
105	Stahlwerke Bochum AG	1820 / 1947	141.6	5.0	PC	Manufacturing
143	Didier-Werke AG	1834	90.0	7.2	PC	Mining & quarrying
181	C. Bertelsmann Verlag	1835	69.0	3.5	FB	Information & communication

(continued)

[49] The ranks in this sub-chapter also relate to the position based on revenue, e.g., *E. Merck AG* is the 142nd largest enterprise of 1958.

Table 5.12 (continued)

#	Company name 1958	Founding year	Rev. 1958 [mEUR]	Empl. 1958 [thousands]	Company type	Industry
51	Eschweiler Bergwerks-Verein	1838	349.2	23.9	FS	Mining & quarrying
82	Kieler Howaldtswerke AG	1838	204.5	13.1	SOE	Manufacturing
125	Howaldtswerke Hamburg AG	1838	109.4	8.6	SOE	Manufacturing
149	Günther Wagner (Pelikan Werke & Verpackungswerke)	1838	86.9	6.0	FB	Manufacturing
229	Wuppertaler Stadtwerke AG	1838	47.2	4.8	SOE	Energy & water
116	Andreae-Noris Zahn AG	1841	131.9	0.0	PC	Commerce
46	Deutsche Gold- und Silber-Scheideanstalt vormals Roessler (Degussa)	1843	373.8	10.3	PC	Manufacturing
69	Stahlwerke Südwestfalen AG	1845 / 1951	245.9	10.0	PC	Manufacturing
84	Carl Zeiss	1846	199.4	24.8	FD	Manufacturing
3	Siemens AG	1847	1,706.2	179.0	FB	Manufacturing

Source: Author's own table.

Table 5.13 The 25 Oldest Enterprises of 2018

#	Company name 2018	Founding year	Rev. 2018 [mEUR]	Empl. 2018 [thousands]	Company type	Industry
46	Merck KGaA	1668	14,836.0	51.7	FB	Manufacturing
120	Franz Haniel & Cie. GmbH	1756	4,683.0	18.8	FB	Commerce
169	Wieland-Werke AG	1820	3,376.0	6.9	FB	Manufacturing
90	Globus Holding GmbH & Co. KG	1828	6,666.0	44.9	FB	Commerce
32	McKesson Europe AG	1835	21,090.0	34.3	FS	Commerce
41	Bertelsmann SE & Co. KGaA	1835	17,673.0	117.0	FD	Information & communication
87	B. Braun Melsungen AG	1839	6,908.1	63.8	FB	Manufacturing
119	Alliance Healthcare Deutschland AG	1841	4,733.0	3.7	FS	Commerce
162	Wilh. Werhahn KG	1841	3,537.0	10.2	FB	Commerce
101	Carl Zeiss AG	1846	5,817.0	29.3	FD	Manufacturing
5	Siemens AG	1847	83,044.0	379.0	PC	Manufacturing
60	Hapag-Lloyd AG	1847	11,515.0	12.8	MCE	Transportation & storage
153	L. Possehl & Co. mbH	1847	3,764.0	13.4	FD	Manufacturing
187	Städtische Werke Nürnberg GmbH	1847	2,985.0	4.6	SOE	Energy & water
69	Freudenberg & Co. KG	1849	9,455.0	49.1	FB	Manufacturing
234	Heidelberger Druckmaschinen AG	1850	2,490.0	11.9	PC	Manufacturing

(continued)

Table 5.13 (continued)

#	Company name 2018	Founding year	Rev. 2018 [mEUR]	Empl. 2018 [thousands]	Company type	Industry
35	Heraeus Holding GmbH	1851	20,295.1	13.9	FB	Commerce
70	Salzgitter AG	1858	9,278.0	25.4	PC	Manufacturing
39	Opel Automobile GmbH	1862	18,715.8	30.4	FS	Manufacturing
17	Bayer AG	1863 / 1951	39,586.0	117.0	PC	Manufacturing
9	BASF SE	1865 / 1952	62,675.0	122.4	PC	Manufacturing
123	Eberspächer Gruppe GmbH & Co. KG	1865	4,610.0	9.9	FB	Manufacturing
63	Aurubis AG	1866	10,424.0	6.7	PC	Manufacturing
79	Tengelmann Warenhandelsgesellschaft KG	1867	7,457.0	58.8	FB	Commerce
131	Voith GmbH & Co. KGaA	1867	4,209.0	19.5	FB	Manufacturing

Source: Author's own table.

Neunkircher Eisenwerk AG (1806) and *Günther Wagner Verwaltungs-Gesellschaft mbH* (1838)[50] are also part of these family firms. Public companies including *Didier-Werke AG* (1834), *Andreae-Noris Zahn AG* (1841) and *Deutsche Gold- und Silber- Scheideanstalt vormals Roessler AG (Degussa)* (1843) follow with six entities (24.0%) which is close to the share in the overall sample. Foreign subsidiaries and state-owned enterprises contribute with three entities each to the 25 oldest enterprises of 1958. The former company type includes *Aktien-Gesellschaft der Dillinger Hüttenwerke* (1685), *Felten & Guilleaume Carlswerk AG* (1820)[51] as well as *Eschweiler Bergwerks-Verein* (1838) and the latter type includes *Kieler Howaldtswerke AG* (1838), *Howaldtswerke Hamburg AG* (1838)[52] and *Wuppertaler Stadtwerke AG* (1838)[53]. With *Carl Zeiss* (1846) one enterprise (4.0%) in the sub-sample is also owned by a foundation. Most of these oldest companies operate in the manufacturing industry. Their share of 72.0% (18 entities) even exceeds the share of the overall sample with 58.0%. In addition, three enterprises (12.0%) are active in mining and quarrying, two (8.0%) in commerce and one each (4.0%) in energy and water as well as information and communication. 13 (52.0%) of the described companies are non-listed compared to twelve (48.0%) listed ones. This ratio is more balanced than the one of the overall sample.

[50] The company is the holding of *Günther Wagner Pelikan-Werke* and *Verpackungswerke* in Hanover. It is exclusively owned by the Wagner and Beindorff family. *Pelikan* is the famous brand of fountain pens and office supplies.

[51] Like other enterprises, *Felten & Guilleaume Carlswerk AG* is the holding or central entity of *Felten & Guilleaume Group*. This group of companies also includes, e.g., *Felten & Guilleaume Carlswerk Eisen u. Stahl AG* and all their subsidiaries.

[52] Both *Howaldtswerke* have the same origin but were split in two separate and independent entities in 1953 (see Ostersehlte (2004) for a corporate publication).

[53] Like several other public utilities, the foundation of *Wuppertaler Stadtwerke AG* goes back to the initial gas supply of a city, in this case of Elberfeld. See Section 4.1 for a more detailed description.

Besides *Merck KGaA* (1668) as the oldest enterprise in the 2018 sub-sample the second oldest company *Franz Haniel & Cie. GmbH* (1756) is already part of the 1958 sub-sample as well.[54] Overall, six companies appear on both lists. These companies survive over the observation period of 60 years, are one of the 250 largest enterprises in both years and are already part of the 25 largest enterprises in 1958.[55] The *youngest* of the 2018 sub-sample is the family-owned business *Voith GmbH & Co. KGaA* founded in 1867. Overall, eleven (44.0%) of the 25 oldest enterprises of 2018 are family firms representing the largest company type including *Globus Holding GmbH & Co. KG* (1828), *Eberspächer Gruppe GmbH & Co. KG* (1865) and *Tengelmann Warenhandelsgesellschaft KG* (1867). In comparison to 1958, the number of family firms declines by one company. The number of public companies remains stable with six (24.0%) again slightly above the overall average of 18.8%. Companies like *Bayer AG* (1863), *BASF SE* (1865) and *Aurubis AG* (1866) are among this company type. Besides *Carl Zeiss* two additional foundation-owned enterprises are among the oldest companies of 2018 with *Bertelsmann SE & Co. KGaA* (1835) and *L. Possehl & Co. mbH* (1847) which have revenues of EUR 17.7bn and EUR 3.8bn, respectively. With *McKesson Europe AG* (1835), *Alliance Healthcare Deutschland AG* (1841) and *Opel Automobile GmbH* (1862) three foreign subsidiaries are also part of the sub-sample.[56] This sub-sample is completed by *Städtische Werke Nürnberg GmbH* (1847) as state-owned enterprise and *Hapag-Lloyd AG* (1847) as multiple companies-owned enterprise.[57] Eight (32.0%) of the 25 oldest enterprises of 2018

---

[54] See also the ranking "Germany's 50 oldest family businesses" introduced in Section 1.1 (see Stiftung Familienunternehmen (2021a, 2021b)).

[55] In addition to the two already mentioned ones, *Bertelsmann SE & Co. KGaA* (1835), *Alliance Healthcare Deutschland AG* (founded in 1841 and named *Andreae-Noris Zahn AG* in 1958), *Carl Zeiss AG* (1846) and *Siemens AG* (1847) are among the reappearing companies. Further, their reappearance is not equivalent to the continuity of their majority ownership structure which is investigated in Chapter 6.

[56] *McKesson Europe AG* is the German branch of US-based *McKesson Corp.* (founded in New York City in 1833). The origins of the German entity go back to *Drogerie- und Farbwarenhandlung Gehe & Co.* which were owned by the Haniel family after World War II.

[57] In 2018, listed *Hapag-Lloyd AG* is owned by *CSAV Germany Container Holding GmbH* (25.8%), a subsidiary of the Chilean shipping company *CSAV, S.A.* which merged its container business with *Hapag-Lloyd* in 2014, *Kühne Holding AG* and *Kühne Maritime GmbH* (25.0%), *Qatar Holding Germany GmbH* (14.5%), *HGV Hamburger Gesellschaft für Vermögens- und Beteiligungsmanagement mbH* (13.9%), the investment management company of the Hanseatic City of Hamburg, and the Public Investment Fund of the Kingdom of Saudi Arabia (10.2%). The remaining shares are in free float (10.6%).

are listed while 17 (68.0%) are non-listed. Compared to the ratio of the overall sample of 250 companies with 28.8% to 71.2% the sub-sample ratio is quite similar. Furthermore, it is noteworthy that only one of the eleven family businesses is listed which is *Merck KGaA*. Again, the majority of companies operates in manufacturing with 15 entities (60.0%). Commerce follows with seven enterprises (28.0%). The remaining three companies are distributed equally among energy and water, information and communication as well as transportation and storage with one entity (4.0%) each. The companies are *Städtische Werke Nürnberg GmbH*, *Bertelsmann SE & Co. KGaA* and *Hapag-Lloyd AG*.

The high share of manufacturing enterprises as part of the oldest enterprises of 1958 remains on a high level in 2018. Furthermore, the share of family businesses among the 25 oldest enterprises of 1958 and 2018 is above the average of the entire sample with 250 companies. This company type can become large and old—especially in manufacturing—in comparison to other types. Nevertheless, the names also show that the oldest enterprises are not necessarily the largest ones.

In comparison, the youngest company of the 250 largest enterprises of 1958 is *Saarbergwerke AG* with the age of only one year (see Table 5.14). This company was just founded in 1957 by the Federal Republic of Germany which owned the majority at that time and the state of Saarland. The foundation was part of the Saar Treaty of 1956 between Germany and France to organize the coal mines in the area which became part of the Federal Republic. The mines themselves were built decades and some even centuries before the founding of *Saarbergwerke*.[58] Such company foundations which have a vast amount of assets right from the start are individual cases and mainly supported by political decisions. A similar case is the foundation of *Ruhrkohle AG* in 1968 which consolidated several coal mining corporations mainly in the Ruhr area. Similar but still very different are the foundations of some of the youngest enterprises of the 2018 dataset (see Table 5.15). Also, *Ceconomy AG* is only one year old in 2018. The public company was founded in 2017 through the carve-out of the consumer electronics shops (mainly *Media Markt* and *Saturn*) from *Metro AG*. Similar reorganizations were executed by *E.ON SE* and *Bayer AG* with their carve-outs of *Uniper SE*, which was *E.ON's* business unit of conventional power generation from coal and gas, and *Covestro AG*, *Bayer's* former materials science unit. These companies were founded in 2016 and 2015 making them the second and third youngest

[58] See Bünte (1972) and Saarbergwerke AG (1982) for the history of the company and some of the mines. A note regarding critical source work: Both publications are edited by the company itself.

Table 5.14 The 25 Youngest Enterprises of 1958

#	Company name 1958	Founding year	Rev. 1958 [mEUR]	Empl. 1958 [thousands]	Company type	Industry
39	Saarbergwerke AG	1957	434.6	63.0	SOE	Mining & quarrying
15	Handelsunion AG	1954	1,022.6	6.1	FB	Commerce
236	Rheinisch-Westfälische Kalkwerke AG	1953	45.2	2.7	PC	Mining & quarrying
212	VÖEST GmbH	1953	51.4	0.0	FS	Commerce
197	Hamborner Bergbau AG	1953	60.0	9.8	FB	Mining & quarrying
121	Friedrich Thyssen Bergbau AG	1953	116.3	9.9	FB	Mining & quarrying
56	Hüttenwerke Siegerland AG	1952	311.9	9.8	PC	Manufacturing
227	Heinrich Bergbau AG	1951	47.6	6.0	PC	Mining & quarrying
157	Mitteldeutsche Mineralöl-Handelsgesellschaft mbH (Caltex)	1951	78.2	0.1	MCE	Commerce
75	Willy H. Schlieker KG	1951	217.3	5.7	FB	Manufacturing
78	Getreide-Import-Gesellschaft mbH	1950	209.9	0.1	MCE	Commerce
70	Neckermann Versand KG	1950	230.1	6.8	FB	Commerce
216	Werner Otto Versandhandel	1949	51.1	1.0	FB	Commerce
213	TOUROPA oHG	1948	51.1	0.7	FB	Service activities
217	Th. Weisser KG	1947	51.1	0.0	FB	Manufacturing

(continued)

Table 5.14 (continued)

#	Company name 1958	Founding year	Rev. 1958 [mEUR]	Empl. 1958 [thousands]	Company type	Industry
159	FERN-SVG-NORD Strassenfernverkehr-Genossenschaft Hamburg und Schleswig Holstein eGmbH	1947	76.7	0.1	COOP	Transportation & storage
92	Grundig-Radio-Werke GmbH	1947	183.0	17.0	FB	Manufacturing
42	Hüttenwerk Oberhausen AG (HOAG)	1947	392.2	14.5	FB	Manufacturing
115	Axel Springer Verlag GmbH	1946	132.0	0.0	FB	Information & communication
188	Stadtwerke Bremen AG	1941	62.4	2.9	SOE	Energy & water
124	Phrix-Werke AG	1941	112.0	7.6	PC	Manufacturing
60	Chemische Werke Hüls AG	1938	295.5	11.4	MCE	Manufacturing
7	Volkswagenwerk GmbH	1937	1,390.2	47.9	SOE	Manufacturing
44	Helmut Horten GmbH	1936	380.9	18.1	FB	Commerce
231	Süddeutsche Zellwolle AG	1935	46.8	2.2	MCE	Manufacturing

Source: Author's own table.

Table 5.15 The 25 Youngest Enterprises of 2018

#	Company name 2018	Founding year	Rev. 2018 [mEUR]	Empl. 2018 [thousands]	Company type	Industry
30	Ceconomy AG	2017	21,418.0	61.8	PC	Commerce
7	Uniper SE	2016	78,176.0	11.8	PC	Energy & water
47	Covestro AG	2015	14,616.0	17.3	PC	Manufacturing
179	AbbVie Deutschland GmbH & Co. KG	2013	3,172.0	2.8	FS	Manufacturing
192	Auto1 Group GmbH	2012	2,900.0	4.0	MCE	Commerce
228	Comparex AG	2011	2,533.0	2.4	FS	Information & communication
199	Dt. Gesellschaft für Intern. Zusammenarbeit GmbH	2011	2,849.0	21.0	SOE	Public administration & defense
108	INEOS Styrolution Holding GmbH	2011	5,367.0	3.4	FFB	Manufacturing
49	Amprion GmbH	2009	13,784.0	1.4	MCE	Energy & water
107	Zalando SE	2008	5,388.0	15.6	PC	Commerce
45	Evonik Industries AG	2007	15,024.0	36.0	FD	Manufacturing
38	TenneT TSO GmbH	2007	19,014.0	1.8	FS	Energy & water
76	Kion Group AG	2006	7,996.0	33.1	PC	Manufacturing
235	Unitymedia GmbH	2005	2,477.0	2.8	FS	Information & communication
183	Novelis Deutschland GmbH	2005	3,151.0	2.3	FFB	Manufacturing

(continued)

Table 5.15 (continued)

#	Company name 2018	Founding year	Rev. 2018 [mEUR]	Empl. 2018 [thousands]	Company type	Industry
93	Agravis Raiffeisen AG	2004	6,578.0	6.5	COOP	Commerce
82	Lanxess AG	2004	7,197.0	15.4	PC	Manufacturing
172	Umicore AG & Co. KG	2003	3,300.0	1.7	FS	Manufacturing
148	Orlen Deutschland GmbH	2003	3,841.0	0.2	FS	Commerce
248	Hydro Aluminium Rolled Products GmbH	2002	2,360.0	3.6	FS	Manufacturing
66	50Hertz Transmission GmbH	2002	10,273.0	1.0	FS	Energy & water
236	Aton GmbH	2001	2,462.0	18.7	FB	Mining & quarrying
55	Vattenfall GmbH	2001	12,793.0	6.6	FS	Energy & water
158	Arrow Central Europe GmbH	2000	3,601.0	1.1	FS	Commerce
54	Airbus Operations GmbH	2000	13,256.0	17.5	FS	Manufacturing

Source: Author's own table.

enterprise in the list of the 250 largest enterprises of 2018. All three carved-out entities became public companies after their parent companies took them public and sold the majority of shares. *AbbVie Deutschland GmbH & Co. KG* the fourth youngest enterprise on the 2018 list is a foreign subsidiary of *AbbVie Inc.* (USA) and was established after the split from *Abbott Laboratories* (USA) in 2013.[59] In contrast, *Auto1 Group GmbH* was established in 2012 from scratch and achieved

[59] Parts of the operations in Germany can be traced back to *Knoll AG* which was founded in 1886 and acquired by *BASF* in 1975 (see Teltz (1980)).

a massive growth within only six years to become one of the 250 largest enterprises in Germany. Its business model is also different from the ones of most of the other companies in the ranking. *Auto1* is an online platform to sell used cars in Europe. It has no production facilities like most of the established industrial companies in the datasets. Coming back to the 25 youngest enterprises of 1958, twelve (48.0%) entities are family-owned making this company type the most frequent one. This group includes *Neckermann Versand KG* (1950), *Werner Otto Versandhandel* (1949), *TOUROPA oHG* (1948), *Grundig-Radio-Werke GmbH* (1947) and *Helmut Horten GmbH* (1936). The founders of these companies established large enterprises within a short period of time, and they are referred to as successful entrepreneurs of the postwar period.[60] The remaining family businesses also include newly founded companies due to the deconcentration of the mining and steel industry like *Hamborner Bergbau AG* which is majority owned by the families of Julius and Hans Thyssen as well as *Hüttenwerk Oberhausen AG (HOAG)* whose owners are the Jacobi, Haniel and Huyssen families, descendants of the founders of *Gutehoffnungshütte*. Public companies and multiple company-owned enterprises are the second largest groups of company types among the 25 youngest enterprises with four entities (16.0%) each. The former type includes *Rheinisch-Westfälische Kalkwerke AG* (1953) and *Phrix-Werke AG* (1941). *Mitteldeutsche Mineralöl-Handelsgesellschaft mbH (Caltex)* (1951) and *Süddeutsche Zellwolle AG* (1935) are part of the latter group.[61] State-owned enterprises follow with three entities (12.0%). Furthermore, in the sub-sample there is one foreign subsidiary *VÖEST GmbH* (1953), which is the German branch of the Austrian state-owned steel group of the same name. In this sub-sample of the 25 youngest enterprises of 1958, only nine (36.0%) operate in the manufacturing industry although this industry still represents the largest group. But in comparison to the overall sample which has a manufacturing share of 58.0% the percentage is quite low. Seven companies (28.0%) are in commerce which is nearly twice the share of the entire sample (14.4%). The third largest company type is mining and

[60] See the German term "*Nachkriegsunternehmer*" in, among others, Büschemann (2014) and Eglau (1982) as well as the critical reflections of their entrepreneurial activities, e.g., about Josef Neckermann (see Pierenkemper (1996)).

[61] *Mitteldeutsche Mineralöl-Handelsgesellschaft mbH* which operate gas stations and distribute gasoline products from *Caltex* (*California Texas Corp.*) a joint venture of the US oil companies *Texaco* and *Standard Oil of California* is owned via the investment vehicle *Caltex-Tank-Kraft Mineralöl GmbH* by *California Texas Corp.* (50.0%), *Braunkohle-Benzin AG* (25.0%) and *Union Rheinische Braunkohlen-Kraftstoff AG* (25.0%). The owners of *Süddeutsche Zellwolle AG* are *Bayerische Vereinsbank* as well as several spinning and weaving mills.

quarrying with five companies (20.0%) which is also a higher share than of the sample with 250 companies (12.0%). One company each operates in the energy and water, information and communication, transportation and storage as well as in service activities. From the 25 enterprises seven (28.0%) are already listed compared to 18 non-listed ones (72.0%).

The 25 youngest enterprises of 2018 consist of eleven foreign subsidiaries (44.0%) including *TenneT TSO GmbH* (2007), *Umicore AG & Co. KG* (2003) and *Arrow Central Europe GmbH* (2000) as well as six public companies (24.0%) including *Covestro AG* (2015), *Zalando SE* (2008) and *Kion Group AG* (2006). In addition, two companies each (8.0%) are multiple companies-owned enterprises, *Auto1 Group GmbH* (2012) and *Amprion GmbH* (2009), as well as foreign family businesses which are *INEOS Styrolution Holding GmbH* (2011) and *Novelis Deutschland GmbH* (2005). Family firms as well as foundations, state-owned enterprises and cooperatives appear only once (4.0%).[62] The share of family firms decreases considerably compared to 1958 with 48.0%. In contrast, the high number of foreign subsidiaries supports the assumption of the attractiveness of the German economy for foreign enterprises. Furthermore, ten of the 25 youngest (40.0%) enterprises operate in manufacturing. Commerce and energy and water follow with six (24.0%) and five (20.0%) entities. The remaining five companies are distributed among information and communication with two entities (8.0%), mining and quarrying as well as public administration and defense with one entity (4.0%) each. *Comparex AG* and *Unitymedia GmbH* belong to the former industry while Aton GmbH and *Deutsche Gesellschaft für Internationale Zusammenarbeit GmbH* belong to the latter two.

In 1958, a proportionally large share of the youngest enterprises operates in commerce. A reason might be that the business model is not capital intensive. The same does not hold for 2018. Here, commerce is on a similar level compared to its overall share. But the industries are more diversified compared to 1958. Furthermore, lots of family businesses (especially in the first-generation representing founders who build their enterprises to one of the largest in 1958 within a short period of time) are among the youngest in 1958. This does not hold for 2018, either. Foreign subsidiaries dominate the sub-sample and only one family business is also part of the youngest entities.

The comparison of the lists shows that some of the companies are established and appear, e.g., as one of the oldest in 1958 as well as in 2018. Others have become one of the largest enterprises in Germany only within some years.

---

[62] The companies are *Aton GmbH* (2001), *Evonik Industries AG* (2007), *Dt. Gesellschaft für Intern. Zusammenarbeit GmbH* (2011) and *Agravis Raiffeisen AG* (2004).

The diversity is high which might also result in diverse developments which are further investigated.

5.8 Family-Owned Enterprises: Gaining Importance Among the Largest Enterprises

After providing an overview of the entire samples the following sub-chapters focus on family-owned enterprises which are included in the 1958 and 2018 datasets. Similar to the entire overview this analysis should form the basis for investigating the developments of the enterprises over 60 years. The characteristics from sub-chapters 5.1 to 5.6 are used to analyze the family businesses in more detail.

Family Business Size Ranges and Modeled Growth Rates

The number of family-owned enterprises remains stable with 87 companies in both years which represent 34.8% of the 250 largest enterprises in 1958 and 2018. Their total revenues of EUR 18.8bn [DM 36.8bn] in 1958 and EUR 891.5bn in 2018 represent a CAGR of 6.6% (see Table 5.16). This rate is similar to the overall growth rate of all 250 enterprises as well as to the CAGR of the average family business in the samples whose revenue grows from EUR 216 m to EUR 10.3bn.[63] In 1958, *Siemens AG* with revenues of EUR 1.7bn [DM 3.3bn] is the largest family business in Germany and the third largest overall. The Siemens family has the majority of voting rights of the listed *AG* at that time.[64] On the other end of the ranking, *Norddeutsche Zucker-Raffinerie AG* on position 247 with revenues of EUR 42.0 m [DM 82.1 m] is the smallest family business in the 1958 dataset. The company is majority-owned by Wolfgang Boettger (75%), a sugar

[63] Because the number of family businesses in 1958 and 2018 remains stable the CAGR of the total revenue and of the average company is similar. Looking at public companies as a reference, their revenue CAGR from 1958 to 2018 is 7.4% based on the average public company. Here, the average CAGR is not similar to the total CAGR (which is 11.2%) because the number of public companies decreases from 56 to 47. The highest average revenue CAGR is seen for foundations with 8.3% while foreign subsidiaries have the lowest CAGR with 5.1% (see Table 63 of the appendix in the electronic supplementary material for the overview of the average company types and their revenue CAGRs). Further, the average family business is smaller than the average enterprise which has revenues of EUR 271 m [DM 529 m] in 1958 and EUR 12.3bn in 2018.

[64] See Section 3.7.3 more details of the Siemens family and their ownership share including multiple voting rights.

wholesaler, while the remaining stake is with *Hildesheimer Speditions- u. Lagerhaus GmbH* (25%).[65] Comparing the revenue figures *Siemens AG* has 40.7 times the revenue of *Norddeutsche Zucker-Raffinerie AG* or, vice versa, the smallest family business has 2.5% of the revenue of the largest one. These numbers are closer to each other than the ones of the entire sample with a multiple of 85.9 or 1.2%. Similar to the average, the median family business[66] is also smaller than the median enterprise with EUR 76.7 m compared to EUR 107.6 m. The slightly lower standard deviation of EUR 352 m [DM 688 m] also confirms that the family business sub-sample is more homogeneous, but the variance is still large between the entities. This indicates that family businesses are distributed across the entire sample with a slight tendency towards the second half of the ranking. To contrast the numbers with a few company names, the 20th, 40th, 60th and 80th largest family businesses of 1958 are mentioned. These are *Feldmühle Papier- und Zellstoffwerke AG* (#80 with EUR 207.6 m [DM 406.0 m] in revenues) majority owned by the Flick and Stinnes families, *Spiesshofer & Braun oHG (Triumph)* (#144 with EUR 89.5 m [DM 175.0 m]) fully owned by the Spiesshofer and Braun families, *Capito & Klein AG* (#193 with EUR 61.4 m [DM120.0 m]) whose majority is with Irmgard Eilenstein and Arnold von Bohlen und Halbach[67] as well as *Wilhelm Karmann GmbH* (#233 with EUR 46.5 m [DM 91.0 m]) fully owned by the Karmann family.

In 2018, the largest family business is also the largest enterprise overall with listed *Volkswagen AG* whose majority of voting rights is with the Porsche and Piëch families. Also, the smallest family business is similar to the smallest enterprise overall in the sample with *Dussmann Stiftung & Co. KGaA* on position 250 owned by the Dussmann family. Therefore, the range and multiples do not change compared to the overall sample. Nevertheless, the value of the average and median family business is again slightly lower than the values of the entire dataset with EUR 10.3bn and EUR 3.9bn compared to EUR 12.3bn and EUR

---

[65] Although the owners of *Hildesheimer Speditions- u. Lagerhaus GmbH* cannot be identified the majority of the smallest family business of 1958 is verified with Wolfgang Boettger.

[66] The median is determined by the 44th largest family business which is *J. A. Schmalbach AG*. The company is majority owned by the Schmalbach family (~71.0%) while US-based *Continental Can Company, Inc.* owns around 20.0%. Later on, the American company will acquire a larger stake and the family loses their majority.

[67] Both are members of the Krupp family. Irmgard Eilenstein is Alfried Krupp von Bohlen und Halbach's sister and Arnold von Bohlen und Halbach is his nephew, son of his brother Claus von Bohlen und Halbach. The majority of *Capito & Klein AG* was transferred in 1953 from Alfried von Bohlen und Halbach to fulfill the requirements of the reorganization of the German steel industry.

4.6bn.[68] Furthermore, the standard deviation of EUR 27.5bn is higher than in the overall sample. While the largest and smallest enterprise remain the same in the family business sub-sample compared to the overall sample the number of companies declines and they are on average smaller (see the revenue of the average family business). Therefore, the standard deviation goes up. Overall, family businesses are on average smaller than the other company types combined. In addition, the 20th, 40th, 60th and 80th largest family enterprises of the 2018 ranking are named to provide more insights on a company level. The enterprises are *Remondis SE & Co. KG* (#77 with EUR 7.9bn) fully owned by the Rethmann family via two investment companies, *Oldendorff Carriers GmbH & Co. KG* (#130 with EUR 4.2bn) fully owned by Henning Oldendorff in second generation, listed *Sixt SE* (#189 with EUR 2.9bn) in which the Sixt family holds 61.6% as well as *Viessmann Werke GmbH & Co. KG* (#233 with EUR 2.5bn) fully owned by the Viessmann family in fourth generation.

From an employee perspective, family enterprises employ around 982,600 people in 1958 which corresponds to a share of 25.7% of the overall sample. This share increases to 33.2% in 2018 with around 3.3 million employees. Only public companies employ more people in both years with shares of 26.8% and 34.6% as well as state-owned enterprises in 1958 with 34.2%. Because the number of family firms remains stable their average size in terms of employees increases. Therefore, family businesses but also public companies become an even more important employer over the observation period of 60 years.[69]

The numbers show that the very top of the largest family businesses is exceptional, generating a multiple of the average revenue of all family businesses even within the group of the 87 largest ones. Furthermore, family businesses do not lose importance in 2018 compared to 1958, rather the opposite. In the more recent year, family businesses represent the largest and the smallest of the 250 enterprises. In addition, in both years they are the largest company type in the overall sample based on the number of entities resulting in a share of 34.8%. This result is challenged by historian Hartmut Kaelble who states in his analysis that "[…] even in the 1960's every sixth large-scale German enterprise was controled by a business family […]"[70] which corresponds to a share of 16.7%. Kaelble's share is much smaller, less than half of the share in this thesis' datasets. Even

---

[68] *Claas KGaA mbH* is the 44th largest family business of 2018 and therefore the median company. The enterprise is still owned by the Claas family who founded the company in 1913.

[69] As a reminder, the number of public companies decreases from 56 in 1958 to 47 in 2018. Nevertheless, they increase their employee and revenue shares over time.

[70] Kaelble (1982, p. 52) and Section 2.2.2.2. as well as Klein and Blondel (2002) who

the share of family businesses within the 25 largest enterprises of 1958 is higher with 28.0%. Therefore, this historical view needs to be revised.

In addition, the family businesses' revenue contribution to the used sample and therefore also to the German economy is substantial. Furthermore, on average they grow like the average of the entire sample population with 6.6% over a period of 60 years. This means that they are a reliable backbone of the economy in 1958 as well as in 2018.

Table 5.16 Family-Owned Enterprise Size Ranges & Modeled Growth Rates 1958 & 2018

87 family-owned businesses	**1958**		**2018**	**1958–2018**
	Revenue [mEUR]	**Revenue** [mDM]	**Revenue** [mEUR]	**CAGR**
Total	18,826	36,821	891,454	*6.6%*
Largest	1,706	3,337	235,849	*8.6%*
Smallest	42	82	2,341	*6.9%*
Range	1,664	3,255	233,508	–
Range (multiple)	*40.7*	*40.7*	*100.7*	–
Average	216	423	10,247	*6.6%*
Median	77	150	3,889	*6.8%*
Standard deviation	352	688	27,488	–
20th largest	208	406	7,900	*6.3%*
40th largest	89	175	4,234	*6.6%*
60th largest	61	120	2,930	*6.7%*
80th largest	47	91	2,500	*6.9%*

Source: Author's own table.

Legal Forms and Listings

As an additional analysis to get a more comprehensive understanding of family businesses, Table 5.17 provides a detailed view of their legal forms distinguished in non-listed and listed entities. As highlighted above, the sole proprietorship is a uniqueness of family firms in 1958 even within the largest enterprises of the

state that more than 50% of the 250 largest listed enterprises in Germany are *patrimonial companies*.

sample like *Fried. Krupp, Essen.* Of course, due to the nature of this legal form all of these four entities are non-listed and can only be categorized as family firms because the owner is a natural person. Similar cases are the *oHG* and *KG* which are also partnerships and require natural persons as owners as well.

All of the 26 listed family firms in 1958 use the legal form of an *AG.* In 2018, only six (46.2%), less than half of the 13 listed family firms, operate as *AG.* Only *Merck* uses the *KGaA* (7.7%) on the stock exchange and three companies (23.1%), *Henkel AG & Co. KGaA, Hornbach Holding AG & Co. KGaA* and *Hella GmbH & Co. KGaA* have chosen the *KGaA* with a legal entity, or more precisely here with a corporation, as general partner (*Co. KGaA*); the latter one in combination with a *GmbH* and the first two with an *AG.* Additional three listed family businesses (23.1%) operate as *SEs* in 2018. In comparison, the 56 public companies of 1958 also only operate as *AGs*, whereas of the 47 public companies of 2018 36 (76.6%) operate as *AGs* and eleven (23.4%) as *SEs.* Therefore, comparing listed family firms and public companies the chosen legal forms are similar except for the various forms of the *KGaA* which are only used by family firms. Similar to the decline in the number of public companies from 1958 to 2018 within the 250 largest enterprises is the decline in listed family firms. Although the overall number of family-owned businesses in the two datasets remains stable with 87 the number of listed family firms drops in half from 26 to 13. Accordingly, the number of non-listed family firms increases by 13 entities over the six decades from 61 to a total of 74.

Overall, also family businesses use the newly created (*SE*) or approved (the *KGaA* with a legal entity as general partner) legal forms in 2018. Of course, some legal forms are only applicable to family businesses because a natural person is required which results in unlimited liability. Furthermore, listed family firms are lose importance within the 250 largest companies in 2018 compared to 1958. The private, non-listed enterprise is the most common choice of the entrepreneurial families.

Table 5.17 Distribution of Legal Forms of Family-Owned Businesses 1958 & 2018

Legal form	**Family-owned businesses** [number of enterprises]											
	Total				**Non-listed**				**Listed**			
	1958		**2018**		**1958**		**2018**		**1958**		**2018**	
AG	42	*48.3%*	12	*13.8%*	16	*26.2%*	6	*8.1%*	26	*100.0%*	6	*46.2%*
GmbH	24	*27.6%*	10	*11.5%*	24	*39.3%*	10	*13.5%*	–	–	–	–
KGaA	2	*2.3%*	1	*1.1%*	2	*3.3%*	–	–	–	–	1	*7.7%*
Co. KGaA	–	–	10	*11.5%*	–	–	7	*9.5%*	–	–	3	*23.1%*
SE	–	–	7	*8.0%*	–	–	4	*5.4%*	–	–	3	*23.1%*
Sole proprietorship	4	*4.6%*	–	–	4	*6.6%*	–	–	–	–	–	–
oHG	4	*4.6%*	–	–	4	*6.6%*	–	–	–	–	–	–
KG	11	*12.6%*	12	*13.8%*	11	*18.0%*	12	*16.2%*	–	–	–	–
Co. KG	–	–	35	*40.2%*	–	–	35	*47.3%*	–	–	–	–
Total	**87**	***100.0%***	**87**	***100.0%***	**61**	***100.0%***	**74**	***100.0%***	**26**	***100.0%***	**13**	***100.0%***

Source: Author's own table.

Industries

From an industry perspective the distribution of family-owned companies differs in some areas compared to the overall distribution of all 250 enterprises especially in 1958 (see Table 5.17).[71] What is not particularly surprising us that of the 87 largest family businesses of 1958 and 2018 none operate in accommodation and food, in financial and insurance activities. in public administration and defense as well as in real estate.[72] These four categories are already small in the overall sample. Furthermore, the energy and water industry is dominated by state-owned enterprises in 1958. Family businesses are not present in this category except in 2018 with *Remondis SE & Co. KG* (1.1%) which is active in recycling and water. An additional small industry category of the datasets are human health and social work activities in which the family company *Asklepios Kliniken GmbH & Co. KGaA* owned by Bernard große Broermann is one of overall two enterprises in 2018. In construction, one family business appears in each of the two datasets with *Ed. Züblin AG* in 1958 and *Goldbeck GmbH* in 2018. The former is majority owned by Ludwig Lenz and other senior executives while the latter is majority owned by the Goldbeck family. The family firms in information and communication are exclusively publishing houses. In 1958, these two (2.3%) are *Axel Springer Verlag GmbH* and *C. Bertelsmann Verlag* both exclusively owned by Axel Springer and Reinhard Mohn, respectively. In 2018, the three publishers (3.4%) are *Axel Springer SE* whose majority remains with the Springer family, *Hubert Burda Media Holding KG* in the hands of the Burda family and *Heinrich Bauer Verlag KG* in which Yvonne Bauer owns around 85.0%.[73] In service activities the number of family businesses increases from one to three. While *TOUROPA oHG* as tourism company is the only one in the overall sample of 1958 as well, *FTI Touristik GmbH*, *Sixt SE* and *Dussmann Stiftung & Co. KGaA* are three service providers of in total seven in the 2018 dataset. Four (4.6%) of

---

[71] In the further course, family businesses are more often compared with public companies because both company types are not dependent on foreign parent companies or states.

[72] Overall, the share of large companies with more than 250 employees in accommodation and food service activities is very small with only 0.09%. 91.8% of the firms have fewer than 10 employees. Although, the share of family businesses might be very high in this industry they are too small to be present in the dataset of this thesis. The same applies to real estate (see German Federal Statistical Office (2019)). Public administration and defense entities are in general in the hands of state-owned companies. Because firms in financial and insurance activities have been excluded of this thesis except for *Deutsche Börse AG* in 2018 it is no surprise that family businesses are not active in this industry either.

[73] The majority of *Bertelsmann* has been transferred to the three foundations *Bertelsmann Stiftung*, *Reinhard Mohn Stiftung* and *BVG-Stiftung*. Therefore, the company is categorized as foundation-owned enterprise in 2018. The Mohn family still owns a share of around 19.1%.

the 87 largest family businesses operate in the transportation and storage industry in 2018 compared to none in 1958. These are *Dachser Group SE & Co. KG*, *Rhenus SE & Co. KG*, *Oldendorff Carriers GmbH & Co. KG* and *Hellmann Worldwide Logistics SE & Co. KG*.[74] The last industry category which experiences an increase over the 60 years and the largest increase in absolute numbers, as well, is commerce. With 14 additional family businesses the number grows more than double from twelve (13.8%) to 26 (29.9%). For example, DKV *MOBILITY SERVICES HOLDING GmbH + Co. KG* majority owned by the Fischer family, *Helm AG* owned by Dieter and Stephan Schnabel as well as *Cronimet Holding GmbH* owned by the Pilarsky family operate in commerce in 2018. The traded products are diverse and include food, metals, shoes, petroleum, computers and much more. This industry classification experiences an increase not only within family businesses but also overall from 36 entities (14.4%) in 1958 to 65 (26.0%) in 2018. Public companies in commerce, on the other hand, only see a small increase from three of 56 (5.4%) to five of 47 enterprises (10.6%).[75] Opposite developments are observed for the industries manufacturing as well as for mining and quarrying. The latter disappears almost completely from six family businesses to one which is *Aton GmbH*, a holding company of a diverse portfolio of companies including mining as the biggest investment.[76] The largest industry of family-owned enterprises in 1958 and 2018 is manufacturing similar to the overall distribution. But with 75.7% (65 / 87 family firms) of the sub-sample the share of manufacturing companies in 1958 exceeds the share of the entire sample of 58.0% (145 / 250 enterprises). Nearly three out of four companies operate in this industry. But this share decreases substantially in 2018 by 18 entities to 54.0% which is closer to the overall share of 46.8%. Even public companies have a slightly higher share in manufacturing with 55.3% (26 / 47 public companies) in 2018 although their share also declines from 62.5% (35 / 56 public companies) in 1958. Adding the listing attribute to the industry view there are no listed family-owned enterprises in 1958 which operate in construction, information and communication or in service activities. These in total four companies are non-listed. In commerce, on the other hand, one out of twelve companies (8.3%) is

[74] As an interesting side note, all four companies already existed in 1958 but none made it to the list of the largest 250 enterprises because their revenues are too small.

[75] The mentioned industry numbers for public companies can be found in Table 64 of the appendix in the electronic supplementary material. This company type has the largest increase in the information and communication industry from zero to six entities.

[76] See Footnote 36 for more details regarding *Aton GmbH*. In comparison, the number of public companies which operate in mining and quarrying decreases from twelve of 56 (21.4%) to one of 47 enterprises (2.1%).

listed while in manufacturing the share is higher with 33.8% (22 / 65 family businesses). In mining and quarrying half of the six family firms are listed which are *Hamborner Bergbau AG*, *Dyckerhoff Portland-Zementwerke AG* majority owned by the Dyckerhoff family and *Rheinpreussen AG für Bergbau und Chemie* majority owned by the Haniel family. In 2018, 13 of the 87 family businesses (14.9%) are listed and are spread over four industries. *Fuchs Petrolub SE* and *Hornbach Holding AG & Co. KGaA*, both majority-owned by the respective families, are the two listed companies in commerce (7.7%). In information and communication as well as in service activities one family firm each (33.3%) is listed which are *Axel Springer SE* and *Sixt SE*. The highest number of listed family-owned enterprises can be found in manufacturing with nine entities (19.1%) including *Jungheinrich AG* whose ordinary shares are all held by the Jungheinrich family, *Krones AG* which is majority owned by the Kroneder family (51.58%) and *Hella GmbH & Co. KGaA* owned by around 59 members of the Hueck and Röpke family.[77]

Again, commerce is a crucial industry for family businesses in 2018. Its importance increases especially compared to the classical industries of manufacturing as well as mining and quarrying of which the latter nearly completely disappears in Germany. From a listing perspective there is a considerable number of listed family businesses in manufacturing. In other industries only individual cases are observed. Overall, the relevance of listed family firms independent of the industry decreases from 1958 to 2018.

From a revenue and employee perspective the drop of family businesses in manufacturing and their rise in commerce is even clearer (see Table 5.18). With 80.4% of revenues and 89.5% of employees of all 87 family businesses, manufacturing enterprises are the key industry in 1958 for this company type. These shares are even higher than the share of the number of family firms in this labor-intensive industry with 74.7%. The revenue and employee shares decline to 55.3% and 55.8% in 2018 similar to the share of the 47 family-owned manufacturers (54.0%). The labor intensity drops as well. The revenue and employee shares are also below the values of the public companies in manufacturing which are 59.9% and 56.8%.[78] Additionally, in commerce the opposite development can be observed. The revenue and employee shares of family businesses rise from 14.9% and very low 4.7%, respectively, to 38.9% and 34.9%. This means that they achieve higher values than the share of the number of companies in

[77] *Hella* was acquired by the listed French automotive supplier *Faurecia SE* in 2021. The Hueck and Röpke families sold their shares. The acquisition is not part of the analysis of this thesis because it happened after the observation period which ends in 2018.

[78] The revenue and employee distribution of public companies is available in Table 65 of the appendix in the electronic supplementary material.

Table 5.18 Industry Distribution of Family-Owned Enterprises of 1958 & 2018

Industry	**Family-owned businesses** [number of enterprises]					
	1958		**2018**		**Change**	
Accommodation & food service activities	–	–	–	–	–	–
Commerce	12	*13.8%*	26	*29.9%*	14	*16.1pp*
Construction	1	*1.1%*	1	*1.1%*	0	*0.0pp*
Energy & water	–	–	1	*1.1%*	1	*1.1pp*
Financial & insurance activities	–	–	–	–	–	–
Human health & social work activities	–	–	1	*1.1%*	1	*1.1pp*
Information & communication	2	*2.3%*	3	*3.4%*	1	*1.1pp*
Manufacturing	65	*74.7%*	47	*54.0%*	−18	*−20.7pp*
Mining & quarrying	6	*6.9%*	1	*1.1%*	−5	*−5.7pp*
Public administration & defense	–	–	–	–	–	–
Real estate	–	–	–	–	–	–
Service activities	1	*1.1%*	3	*3.4%*	2	*2.3pp*
Transportation & storage	–	–	4	*4.6%*	4	*4.6pp*
Total	**87**	***100.0%***	**87**	***100.0%***	**–**	**–**

Source: Author's own table.

2018 of 29.9% (26 / 87 family businesses), starting from 13.8% (12 / 87 family businesses) in 1958. In comparison, the revenue share of public companies in commerce decreases from 8.2% to 7.3% and their employee share increases from 5.1% to 7.2%, respectively. As mentioned earlier the share of public companies in this industry increases from 5.4% (3 / 56 public companies) to 10.6% (5 / 47 public companies). The productivity in commerce does not seem to be suitable for a listed company. In accordance with the decreasing number of family-owned mining and quarrying companies their revenue and employee shares decrease as well, from 3.1% to 0.3% and from 4.8% to 0.6%.[79] The industries construction, information and communication as well as service activities remain relatively stable or increase their revenue or employee shares in accordance with the changing number of family businesses which is a low one-digit number.[80] The industries in which no family firms operate in 1958 but in 2018 like energy and water, human health and social work activities as well as transportation and storage can logically increase their revenue and employee shares in 2018 but all remain in a low one-digit range.

Family businesses have increased their footprint in a broader variety of industries over the last 60 years. This results in a loss of importance of the manufacturing industry whose revenue and employee shares decreases considerably. Nevertheless, looking at the absolute values also the manufacturers increased the number of employees from around 879,100 to around 1,839,900 which corresponds to more than a doubling. The number of employees in commerce of 2018 is even more than 25 times the number of 1958. This again shows the increased importance of the largest enterprises in Germany—be they family-owned firms or other company types.

Age

Staying with the industries but looking at the age, the observations from Section 5.5 and Table 5.5 can be further elaborated. Overall, family businesses are older in 2018 with 105.2 years compared to 1958 with 78.9 years. Additionally, on average listed family businesses are also older (1958: 87.4 years / 2018: 116.8) than non-listed ones (1958: 75.2 years / 2018: 103.1).[81] Digging a little bit deeper into the numbers it can be shown that in 1958 the oldest family firms on average operate in manufacturing with 87.6 years while the youngest industry is service activities with only 10.0 years. But this industry only consists of one

---

[79] Even higher decreases can be observed for public companies and their revenue and employee shares from 27.5% to 0.4% and from 30.8% to 0.4%. This is also in accordance with the decreasing number of public companies in mining and quarrying.

[80] Larger changes in the construction as well as information and communication industries can be observed for public companies. While the number of construction companies drops from four (7.1%) to one (2.1%) their revenue and employee shares also decline from 2.2% in 1958 to 0.4% in 2018 and from 3.6% to 1.0%, respectively. The number of information and communication companies increases from zero to six (6 / 47 public companies or 12.8%) and the revenue and employee shares are 10.3% and 10.0%, respectively, in 2018.

[81] It should be noted that the number of listed family enterprises is 26 compared to 61 non-listed ones in 1958 (29.9%) and 13 compared to 74 in 2018 (14.9%) which is in both cases below the average of the overall sample with 250 companies of which 100 (40.0%) in 1958 and 72 (28.8%) in 2018 are listed.

Table 5.19 Revenue & Employee Distribution per Industry Category of Family-Owned Enterprises of 1958 & 2018

Industry	**Family-owned businesses**							
	Revenue [bnEUR]				**Employees** [thousands]			
	1958		**2018**		**1958**		**2018**	
Accommodation & food service activities	–	–	–	–	–	–	–	–
Commerce	2.8	*14.9%*	347.2	*38.9%*	45.9	*4.7%*	1,153.0	*34.9%*
Construction	0.1	*0.3%*	2.7	*0.3%*	6.5	*0.7%*	6.0	*0.2%*
Energy & water	–	–	7.9	*0.9%*	–	–	36.0	*1.1%*
Financial & insurance activities	–	–	–	–	–	–	–	–
Human health & social work activities	–	–	3.4	*0.4%*	–	–	47.0	*1.4%*
Information & communication	0.2	*1.1%*	8.2	*0.9%*	3.5	*0.4%*	39.6	*1.2%*
Manufacturing	15.1	*80.4%*	493.3	*55.3%*	879.1	*89.5%*	1,839.9	*55.8%*
Mining & quarrying	0.6	*3.1%*	2.5	*0.3%*	46.9	*4.8%*	18.7	*0.6%*
Public administration & defense	–	–	–	–	–	–	–	–
Real estate	–	–	–	–	–	–	–	–
Service activities	0.1	*0.3%*	8.9	*1.0%*	0.7	*0.1%*	83.6	*2.5%*
Transportation & storage	–	–	17.4	*2.0%*	–	–	76.3	*2.3%*
Total	**18.8**	***100.0%***	**891.5**	***100.0%***	**982.6**	***100.0%***	**3,300.0**	***100.0%***

Source: Author's own table.

company which is *TOUROPA oHG.* The second youngest industry is mining and quarrying with 50.3 years (six family businesses) while the second oldest industry, on the other hand, with 67.5 years is information and communication which consists only of the two publishers, *C. Bertelsmann Verlag* and *Axel Springer Verlag GmbH.* The former company was founded in 1835, the latter one in 1946.

Nevertheless, *Axel Springer* is the larger family business on position 115 (EUR 132 m [DM 258 m]) compared to *Bertelsmann* on position 181 (EUR 69 m [DM 135 m]). Commerce and construction have average ages of 55.2 years and 60.0 years. Considering the listing, commerce has the lowest average age with four years because only *Handelsunion AG*, founded in 1954, is a listed firm in this industry within family businesses. Listed manufacturers, on the other hand, are on average 94.5 years followed by mining and quarrying companies with 63.0 years as the last industry with a listed family firm. Among the non-listed companies manufactures are also the oldest industry type. Overall, it can be concluded that single family businesses influence the average age substantially because some are very old or very young. In combination with the small numbers of enterprises when more categories are applied like listing and industry within family firms the averages are defined by single companies (like *TOUROPA oHG* or *Handelsunion AG*). Therefore, the average age of family firms should be compared with other company types, then the informative value is high. The focus on industries and listings within family firms should only be used to highlight single cases.

Furthermore, the 2018 sample confirms prior research by Fernandez Moya et al. who investigate the 100 largest German and Spanish family firms in 2005. The majority of the German enterprises—54 companies—were founded in 1913 or earlier.[82] A similar observation is made for the 2018 sample in which 42 of the 87 family firms were founded before 1914. These observations show the importance of older companies or more specifically of older family firms which become one of the largest enterprises in the German economy with more than 100 years of age.

Family Generation

In relation to the company age the family generation of the owners in 1958 and 2018 is also captured for all family-owned enterprises (see Table 5.20).[83] In 1958, the average generation of a family business is 2.6 which means that on average a company has already experienced more than two successions since its foundation. The median, on the other hand, is three which corresponds to already three successions. Companies in the third generation are also the largest group of family firms with 32 entities (36.8%) followed by the first generation with 24 entities (27.6%). Second generation family firms are in total 18 (20.7%). There

[82] See Fernandez Moya et al. (2020, p. 232).

[83] For the majority of family businesses, the family generation can be identified using primary or secondary sources. In some cases, the average length of a generation which is 30 years is used to estimate the generation.

are even three enterprises (3.4%) in fourth, five (5.7%) in fifth and four (4.6%) in sixth generation. An exception, again, is *E. Merck AG* which is already in the ninth family generation as a single case (1.1%). Examples of a first-generation family business in 1958 are *Th. Weisser KG* fully owned by Theodor Weisser and *Grundig-Radio-Werke GmbH* fully owned as well, by Max Grundig. In these cases, the companies are owned by their founders. But this is not the case for all first-generation companies. *Buderus'sche Eisenwerke AG* was already founded in 1731 but is majority owned by Friedrich Flick since 1956 via several of his controlled companies. Because Friedrich Flick is first family generation *Buderus* is categorized in the same way. Before Flick's involvement the company's ownership was in free float. If a business family acquires an enterprise the company becomes part of the family generation.

In 2018, the average generation of family enterprises is 3.3, again with a median of three. The third generation also remains the largest group with 29 companies (33.3%) which already experienced two successions. Furthermore, the second and fourth generations follow as the second largest groups of family generations with 16 (18.4%) enterprises each. 13 family businesses (14.9%) are in the fifth generation. The second largest group in 1958, the first generation-owned family enterprises, falls to fifth place 60 years later with ten entities (11.5%). This group includes companies like *Müller Holding Ltd. & Co. KG* majority owned by *Erwin Franz Müller*, *FTI Touristik GmbH* majority owned by the founder Dietmar Gunz and his family as well as *Cronimet Holding GmbH* owned by the Pilarsky family. *B. Braun Melsungen AG* owned by the Braun family is the only company which already exists in sixth generation. *Franz Haniel & Cie. GmbH* fully owned by the Haniel family and again *Merck KGaA* majority owned by the Merck family are already in later generations, the former in the eighth and the latter in the 13th generation. From a generation perspective, the family enterprises in 2018 have become more mature and experienced more successions compared to 1958. On the other hand, less young, i.e., first generation, family businesses are among the 250 largest enterprises of 2018. This suggests that becoming one of the 250 largest enterprises in 2018 becomes more difficult within the first generation because the size of the already existing companies is too large to catch up.

Table 5.20 Distribution of Family Generations 1958 & 2018

Family generation	**Family-owned businesses** [number of enterprises]			
	1958		**2018**	
1st	24	*27.6%*	10	*11.5%*
2nd	18	*20.7%*	16	*18.4%*
3rd	32	*36.8%*	29	*33.3%*
4th	3	*3.4%*	16	*18.4%*
5th	5	*5.7%*	13	*14.9%*
6th	4	*4.6%*	1	*1.1%*
7th	–	–	–	–
8th	–	–	1	*1.1%*
9th	1	*1.1%*	–	–
10th	–	–	–	–
11th	–	–	–	–
12th	–	–	–	–
13th	–	–	1	*1.1%*
Total	**87**	***100.0%***	**87**	***100.0%***

Source: Author's own table.

Critical Remarks on Family-owned Enterprises

As a critical reflection of the used company type definitions based on ownership it is necessary to highlight enterprises which are on the edge of one definition and included in the used datasets of this thesis.[84]. In 1958, *Wacker Chemie GmbH* is categorized as a multiple companies-owned enterprise because both owners, the Wacker family and *Farbwerke Hoechst AG*, hold a 50% stake. None of them has the majority. How important a majority is can be seen in the move of the family to acquire one additional percent in 2001 after years of negotiations with *Aventis* (the successor company of *Hoechst AG,* today *Sanofi*). With 51% in the hands of the family the company is categorized as family business and the family can enforce its majority in corporate decisions. In 2018, *Wacker Chemie AG* is listed and the family owns an even higher stake with more than 60.0%. In the 2018 dataset, *BMW AG* and *Continental AG* need to be highlighted. The listed car

[84] See Section 2.2.2.3 for the advantages and disadvantages of the different family business definitions.

manufacturer is often part of family business rankings[85] because Stefan Quandt and his sister Susanne Klatten together own around 46.7% of the voting rights. Nevertheless, based on this thesis' definitions *BMW AG* is a public company because the majority is in free float. A similar case is *Continental AG* with a free float of around 54.0% in 2018 while the remaining 46.0% are ultimately owned by Maria-Elisabeth Schaeffler-Thumann and her son Georg F. W. Schaeffler via their investment holding *IHO Verwaltungs GmbH*. The Schaeffler family is also majority owner of *Schaeffler AG* which started a take-over of *Continental AG* in 2008. Due to the financial crisis that occurred shortly thereafter the take-over attempt has led to a high level of debt at *Schaeffler* and their achieved majority ownership had to be reduced. Overall, the number of enterprises which is on the edge of one company type definition is limited. Nevertheless, it is considered when further analyzing the enterprises' developments.

As an additional note, most of the studied family businesses have the family name included in the company's name like *Sixt SE* and *Miele & Cie. KG*. This is the case for the largest family-owned enterprises of 1958 but also of 2018 (of which some are the same).

Foreign Family-owned Enterprises and Foundations

Besides the family businesses which are owned by German families, foreign family-owned as well as some of the foundation-owned enterprises show similar ownership structures. While, as the name already suggests, the former are owned by families which are based outside of Germany, the latter mainly originate from German family businesses while the foundations themselves have no owners or shareholders.[86] An example is *Robert Bosch GmbH*. In 1958, the enterprise is categorized as family business while in 2018 it is a foundation-owned company, owned by *Robert Bosch Stiftung*.[87] The developments of these two company types

[85] See, among others, the FAZ ranking of the largest family businesses of 2018 in Germany (see Giersberg and F.A.Z.-Archiv (2019)).

[86] See Fleschutz (2009) for an overview of the foundation as a successor solution for family businesses.

[87] In 1958, *Robert Bosch GmbH* was already in a transition after the death of Robert Bosch in 1942. Based on his will a permanent solution was sought for the company. This process results in the majority ownership transfer to *Gemeinnützige Vermögensverwaltung Bosch GmbH* which is later renamed in Robert Bosch Stiftung. The voting rights are transferred to *Robert Bosch Industrietreuhand KG*. The family still has a share of around 7.4% which is reorganized in 2020 / 2021. The ownership is mainly transferred to foundations related to the company and the family while the voting rights remain with the family (see Robert Bosch Stiftung (2020) as well as Bähr and Erker (2013) for the history of the company and the foundation).

are further investigated in Section 6.1.7. But looking at these types only from a statistical perspective the datasets from 1958 and 2018 show the following numbers. While foreign family businesses account for 3.2% (8 / 250) in 1958 the share increases to 7.2% (18 / 250) in 2018. Additional ten companies are owned by a foreign family. In 1958 this company type includes *Klöckner-Werke AG* which is majority owned by *Internationale Industriele Belegging Maatschappij "Amsterdam" N. V.* (>50.0%) a Dutch family foundation in the hands of the Klöckner and Henle family, *Stahl- und Röhrenwerke Reisholz GmbH* which is also majority owned by a family foundation but this time the Kaszony family foundation in Switzerland (63.1%) as well as the Dutch *Bank voor Handel en Scheepvaart N.V.* (36.89%) both are part of the *Thyssen-Bornemisza Group* (a branch of the Thyssen family) and *Steinkohlenbergwerk Friedrich Heinrich AG* which is owned by the French de Wendel family and their corporate group. In 2018, foreign family-owned enterprises are, among others, *Liebherr-EMtec GmbH* ultimately owned by the Liebherr family via their Suisse holding *Liebherr-International S.A.*, *INEOS Styrolution Holding GmbH* majority owned by the British businessman James Arthur Ratcliff, as well as *Sonepar Deutschland GmbH* which is owned by the French Coisne and Lambert families. Companies like *Liebherr* but also *Bauhaus AG*, *Rehaus AG & Co.* as well as *Unternehmensgruppe Theo Müller S.e.c.s.* were founded in Germany but their owners decided to move to other countries, in some cases to optimize their tax burden.

Additionally, in 1958 there are two foundation-owned enterprises, *Carl Zeiss* and *Zahnradfabrik Friedrichshafen AG*, while in 2018 twelve firms belong to this company type. These include *Evonik Industries AG*, *Mahle GmbH* and *Körber AG*. While the former is owned by the *RAG-Stiftung* which was initiated based on a political consensus to phase out the subsidized coal production in Germany the latter ones are owned by foundations which were set up by the founders Hermann and Ernst Mahle as well as Kurt A. Körber, respectively. *Mahle* and *Körber* start as family businesses but become foundation-owned enterprises over time.

Based on their similarities the three company types family-owned, foreign family-owned and foundation-owned enterprises are used side by side in the tables and figures. Adding the numbers of the three types together their share of the 250 largest enterprises of 1958 and 2018 increases from 38.8% (97 / 250) to 46.8% (117 / 250).[88] Therefore, the relevance of family ownership increases over the 60 years.

[88] In 1958, family businesses account for 34.8% (87/250), foreign family businesses for 3.2% (8/250) and foundations for 0.8% (2/250). In 2018, the shares are 34.8% (87/250) for family businesses again, 7.2% (18/250) for foreign family businesses and 4.8% (12/250) for foundations.

Summary

Overall, family ownership was and remains an important part of the enterprise structure in Germany. The diversity of this company type is high and can even be seen within the 87 largest family firms of 1958 and of 2018. The broad range of the revenue size and the number of employees shows that family firms have been and still are essential to the German economy independent of size. Over the past 60 years, commerce has been a growth industry in general but especially for family businesses and with the exception of public companies. In addition, more large family businesses appear in other industries than in manufacturing which is dominant in 1958. The distribution in 2018 is more diverse than in 1958 although manufacturing remains the largest industry of family firms. Structural change might be a driver for this development. The decline of entire industries in Germany like mining and quarrying is also affecting family-owned companies. Furthermore, there is an overall decline in stock exchange listings and the already relatively low share of listed family firms in 1958 follows this trend until 2018 with an even lower share. Also, the chosen legal forms are more diverse in 2018 than in 1958. Especially the *KG* with a limited liability corporation as general partner becomes the most popular form. Families limit their liability based on these legal forms. From an age perspective, family businesses are old compared to most other large enterprises. Only public companies are older on average which supports Chandler's concept of the development of corporations. The relationship between family-owned enterprises and public companies is further investigated in the following chapters.

5.9 Reappearers and New Joiners: Nearly a Quarter Remains Among the 250 Largest Enterprises

After starting the comparisons of the 1958 and 2018 datasets on a company type level some of the previous sub-chapter already provide insights on an enterprise level. The companies that stand out in particular are the ones which appear on both lists of 1958 and 2018 like *VolkswagenAG* as one of the 25 largest and *Merck KGaA* as the oldest enterprise of both datasets. But how many of the 250 largest enterprises of 1958 made it to the list of the 250 largest enterprises of 2018? In answering this question, a first approximation to the long-term development of enterprises and their survival is provided.

Overall, there is a massive change and movement between 1958 and 2018. 62 (24.8%) of the 250 largest enterprises of 1958 reappear as one of the 250 largest companies of 2018. In the following, they are called *Reappearers* and their share is the *Reappearance Rate*. On the other hand, 188 (75.2%) of the 250 largest companies of 2018 are enterprises which are not part of the 1958 ranking. They are called *New Joiners* and their share is the *New Joiner Rate*. The new joiner rate also means that 188 (75.2%) firms of the 1958 list do not make it to the 2018 list (see Figure 5.4). Nevertheless, it is noteworthy to mention that the rate of 24.8% does not correspond to the overall survival rate of the largest enterprises of 1958. The rate only reflects the number of companies which reappear on the list of the 250 largest enterprises of 2018. The survival and downfall rates are further investigated in Section 6.1.1. This is only a first approximation. Moreover, the reappearance rate does not provide information whether a company has experienced a crucial change which includes the change of the majority ownership and hence of their company type. These developments are also investigated in the next chapter. Therefore, the reappearance rate shows that the 62 companies survive as one of the eight defined company types over 60 years and grow at such a high rate that they do not drop out of the list of the 250 largest enterprises.

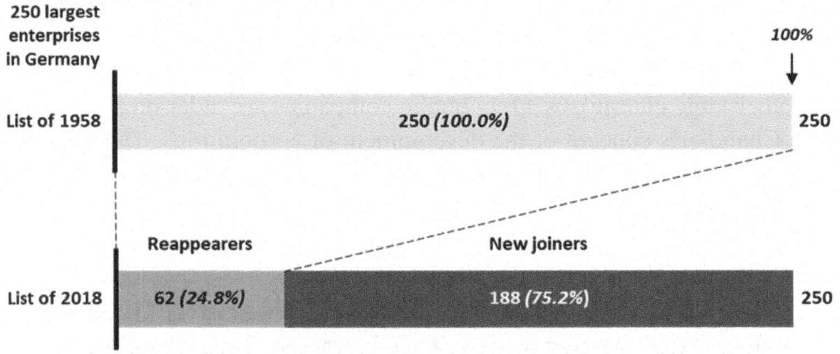

Figure 5.4 Enterprise Reappearers & New Joiners 1958 & 2018. (Source: Author's own figure)

As a reference for the reappearance rate, Hannah provides a similar comparison in his work "Marshall's "Trees" and the Global "Forest"—Were "Giant Redwoods" Different?". The business historian investigates the world's 100 largest industrial enterprises of 1912 by equity market capitalization and their long-term development until 1995.[89] Based on his selection criterion all his enterprises are listed. He provides no further specification of the ownership structure. In his sample, 19.0% or in total 19 of the companies from the 1912 top 100 list

[89] See Section 3.1 for an overview of Hannah's study.

reappear on the 1995 top 100 list which is 5.8% less than the outcome of the reappearers in this thesis.[90] Looking only at the 14 German companies included in Hannah's sample of 1912 their reappearance rate in the top 100 of 1995 is higher with 28.6% (in total four out of 14 firms). When considering only the 100 listed companies of this thesis' 1958 sample (which is more than seven times of Hannah's German sample) their reappearance rate is 22.0%. 22 of the 100 listed enterprises of 1958 reappear on the 2018 list of the largest enterprises. Looking only at the 14 largest listed enterprises which is the similar number of German enterprises in Hannah's sample five (35.7%) of them reappear on the 2018 list. Overall, the comparison shows mixed results depending on the sample size. A large sample is basically preferred. Nevertheless, the observed reappearance rate of the overall sample in this thesis is higher than Hannah's international overall rate. Considering only the German enterprises included in Hannah's study his calculated rate is higher, but the sample is small with only 14 companies. Including only listed companies the reappearance rate decreases slightly in this thesis. In comparison, looking only at the 14 largest listed enterprises that reappear the rate goes up. Overall, the rates are not too far away from each other when considering Hannah's small German sample. Based on the larger datasets of this thesis Hannah's rates can be refined.

To get a better understanding of the reappearing companies all enterprises which appear on both lists are presented in Table 5.21. In addition, the list with all 188 new joiners is available in in Table 68 of the appendix in the electronic supplementary material. The overview is sorted according to the rank of the company in 1958 which can be found in the first column. The second column provides the company's rank in 2018. Similarly, the company's name in 1958 and 2018 are covered in columns three and four. The industry column provides the classification of both years. Only one industry is shown if the classification in 1958 and 2018 is the same. Two industries are included in the column if the classification has changed between both years, e.g., Manufacturing / Commerce for *Esso AG* while the first industry refers to the year 1958 and the second to 2018. The revenues as well as the company types are also provided for both years.

A second table summarizes the two categories of company type and industry from the reappearers (Table 5.22). Both attributes refer to the year 1958 which is the starting point of the study. Family businesses in that year are the largest company type of reappearers with 21 (33.9%) of the 62 entities. This type is followed by public companies with 13 entities (21.0%) and state-owned enterprises

[90] See Hannah (1999) and page 259 for the "Summary Measures of Long-Run Performance of the Hundred Largest Firms of 1912 by 1995".

Table 5.21 Reappearing Companies of 1958 in the List of the 250 Largest Enterprises of 2018

Rank		Company name		Founding year	Revenue [mEUR]		Company type		Industry
1958	2018	1958	2018		1958	2018	1958	2018	
1	15	Deutsche Bundesbahn	Deutsche Bahn AG	1920	3,493	44,065	SOE	SOE	Transportation & storage
2	10	Deutsche Bundespost	Deutsche Post AG	1868	2,294	61,550	SOE	PC	Transportation & storage
3	5	Siemens AG	Siemens AG	1847	1,706	83,044	FB	PC	Manufacturing
5	2	Daimler-Benz AG	Daimler AG	1883	1,611	167,362	FB	PC	Manufacturing
7	1	Volkswagenwerk GmbH	Volkswagen AG	1937	1,390	235,849	SOE	FB	Manufacturing
13	39	Adam Opel AG	Opel Automobile GmbH	1862	1,074	18,716	FS	FS	Manufacturing
14	17	Farbenfabriken Bayer AG	Bayer AG	1863 / 1951	1,028	39,586	PC	PC	Manufacturing
17	9	BASF Badische Anilin- & Soda-Fabrik AG	BASF SE	1865 / 1952	987	62,675	PC	PC	Manufacturing
18	67	Esso AG	ExxonMobil Central Europe Holding GmbH	1890	975	9,700	FS	FS	Manufacturing / Commerce
20	16	August Thyssen-Hütte AG	thyssenkrupp AG	1891 / 1953	908	42,745	FB	PC	Manufacturing
21	70	Salzgitter-Konzern	Salzgitter AG	1858	889	9,278	SOE	PC	Mining & quarrying / Manufacturing
23	34	Deutsche Shell AG	Shell Deutschland Oil GmbH	1902	781	20,390	FS	FS	Manufacturing
25	52	Rheinisch-Westfälisches Elektrizitätswerk AG	RWE AG	1898	752	13,388	SOE	PC	Energy & water
30	216	Kaufhof AG	GALERIA Kaufhof GmbH	1879	677	2,600	PC	FFB	Commerce
31	117	Metallgesellschaft AG	GEA Group AG	1881	665	4,828	PC	PC	Manufacturing

(continued)

Table 5.21 (continued)

Rank		Company name		Founding year	Revenue [mEUR]		Company type		Industry
1958	2018	1958	2018		1958	2018	1958	2018	
32	12	Edeka eGmbH	Edeka Zentrale AG & Co. KG	1907	648	53,600	COOP	COOP	Commerce
34	6	Robert Bosch GmbH	Robert Bosch GmbH	1886	511	78,465	FB	FD	Manufacturing
35	44	Bayerische Warenvermittlung landwirtschaftlicher Genossenschaften AG (BayWa)	BayWa AG	1923	507	16,626	COOP	COOP	Commerce
36	120	Franz Haniel & Cie. GmbH	Franz Haniel & Cie. GmbH	1756	482	4,683	FB	FB	Commerce
37	23	BP Benzin und Petroleum AG	BP Europa SE	1904	468	29,280	FS	FS	Manufacturing
41	31	Ford-Werke AG	Ford-Werke GmbH	1925	399	21,093	FFB	FFB	Manufacturing
47	184	Brown, Boveri & Cie. AG	ABB AG	1891	368	3,135	FS	FS	Manufacturing
49	14	Continental Gummiwerke AG	Continental AG	1871	352	44,404	PC	PC	Manufacturing
61	229	Röchling'sche Eisen- und Stahlwerke GmbH	Saarstahl AG	1873	285	2,528	FB	FD	Manufacturing
63	36	Henkel & Cie. GmbH	Henkel AG & Co. KGaA	1876	272	19,899	FB	FB	Manufacturing
66	37	Preußische Bergwerks- und Hütten AG (Preussag)	TUI AG	1923	260	19,524	SOE	PC	Mining & quarrying / Service activities
81	86	Süddeutsche Zucker-AG	Südzucker AG	1926	205	6,983	PC	COOP	Manufacturing
84	101	Carl Zeiss	Carl Zeiss AG	1846	199	5,817	FD	FD	Manufacturing

(continued)

Table 5.21 (continued)

Rank		Company name		Founding year	Revenue [mEUR]		Company type		Industry
1958	2018	1958	2018		1958	2018	1958	2018	
85	13	Rewe Zentrale Deutscher Lebensmittel-Großhandels-Genossenschaften eGmbH	REWE-ZENTRALFINANZ eG	1927	195	53,378	COOP	COOP	Manufacturing / Commerce
86	137	Salzdetfurth AG	K + S AG	1889	194	4,039	PC	PC	Mining & quarrying
89	63	Norddeutsche Affinerie AG	Aurubis AG	1866	190	10,424	MCE	PC	Manufacturing
99	69	Carl Freudenberg KGaA	Freudenberg & Co. KG	1849	153	9,455	FB	FB	Manufacturing
101	33	Energie-Versorgung Schwaben AG	EnBW Energie Baden-Württemberg AG	1909	146	20,618	SOE	SOE	Energy & water
102	116	Wacker-Chemie GmbH	Wacker Chemie AG	1914	143	4,979	MCE	FB	Manufacturing
104	212	Deutsche FIAT-Gruppe	FCA Germany AG	1922	143	2,677	FFB	FS	Manufacturing / Commerce
108	60	Hamburg-Amerikanische Packetfahrt-Actien-Gesellschaft	Hapag-Lloyd AG	1847	139	11,515	PC	MCE	Transportation & storage
111	147	Internationale Büromaschinen GmbH	IBM Deutschland GmbH	1910	135	3,851	FS	FS	Manufacturing / Information & communication

(continued)

Table 5.21 (continued)

Rank		Company name		Founding year	Revenue [mEUR]		Company type		Industry
1958	2018	1958	2018		1958	2018	1958	2018	
112	40	Portland-Zementwerke Heidelberg AG	HeidelbergCement AG	1873	134	18,075	PC	PC	Mining & quarrying / Manufacturing
113	27	Hochtief AG für Hoch- und Tiefbauten vorm. Gebr. Helfmann	HOCHTIEF AG	1873	133	23,882	PC	FS	Construction
114	73	Stadtwerke Müchen	Stadtwerke München GmbH	1899	133	8,335	SOE	SOE	Energy & water
115	177	Axel Springer Verlag GmbH	Axel Springer SE	1946	132	3,181	FB	FB	Information & communication
116	119	Andreae-Noris Zahn AG	Alliance Healthcare Deutschland AG	1841	132	4,733	PC	FS	Commerce
126	92	Knorr-Bremse AG	Knorr-Bremse AG	1905	106	6,616	FB	FB	Manufacturing
133	18	Zahnradfabrik Friedrichshafen AG	ZF Friedrichshafen AG	1915	102	36,929	FD	FD	Manufacturing
134	4	Bayerische Motoren Werke AG	Bayerische Motoren Werke AG	1916	100	97,480	PC	PC	Manufacturing
136	131	J. M. Voith GmbH	Voith GmbH & Co. KGaA	1867	99	4,209	FB	FB	Manufacturing
140	134	Osram GmbH	Osram Licht AG	1919	96	4,115	MCE	PC	Manufacturing
142	46	E. Merck AG	Merck KGaA	1668	94	14,836	FB	FB	Manufacturing

(continued)

Table 5.21 (continued)

Rank		Company name		Founding year	Revenue [mEUR]		Company type		Industry
1958	2018	1958	2018		1958	2018	1958	2018	
150	20	Deutsche Lufthansa AG	Deutsche Lufthansa AG	1926 / 1953	87	35,844	SOE	PC	Transportation & storage
154	136	Miele & Cie. KG	Miele & Cie. KG	1899	81	4,100	FB	FB	Manufacturing
171	99	Heinrich Lanz AG	John Deere GmbH & Co. KG	1925	74	6,032	FS	FS	Manufacturing
176	187	Städtische Werke Nürnberg	Städtische Werke Nürnberg GmbH	1847	72	2,985	SOE	SOE	Energy & water
181	41	C. Bertelsmann Verlag	Bertelsmann SE & Co. KGaA	1835	69	17,673	FB	FD	Information & communication
189	143	Gebr. Claas Maschinenfabrik GmbH	Claas KGaA mbH	1913	62	3,889	FB	FB	Manufacturing
195	127	Ed. Züblin AG	Ed. Züblin AG	1898	61	4,402	FB	FFB	Construction
206	133	Grün & Bilfinger AG Bauunternehmung	Bilfinger SE	1880	56	4,153	PC	PC	Construction
215	35	W. C. Heraeus GmbH	Heraeus Holding GmbH	1851	51	20,295	FB	FB	Manufacturing / Commerce
216	50	Werner Otto Versandhandel	Otto GmbH & Co. KG	1949	51	13,653	FB	FB	Commerce
217	53	Th. Weisser KG	Marquard & Bahls AG	1947	51	13,286	FB	FFB	Manufacturing / Commerce
219	83	Dr. August Oetker	Dr. August Oetker KG	1891	51	7,140	FB	FB	Manufacturing
235	11	Albrecht KG Lebensmittel-Filialbetrieb	Aldi Süd	1913	46	59,000	FB	FB	Commerce
239	102	Energieversorgung Weser-Ems AG	EWE AG	1930	45	5,704	SOE	SOE	Energy & water

Source: Author's own table.

Table 5.22 Industries & Company Types of Reappearers in 2018

Industry	**Type of company 1958** [number of enterprises]									
	FB	**FFB**	**FD**	**MCE**	**PC**	**COOP**	**SOE**	**FS**	**Total**	**Total** [%]
Accommodation & food service activities	–	–	–	–	–	–	–	–	**–**	**–**
Commerce	3	–	–	–	2	2	–	–	**7**	***11.3%***
Construction	1	–	–	–	2	–	–	–	**3**	***4.8%***
Energy & water	–	–	–	–	–	–	5	–	**5**	***8.1%***
Financial & insurance activities	–	–	–	–	–	–	–	–	**–**	**–**
Human health & social work activities	–	–	–	–	–	–	–	–	**–**	**–**
Information & communication	2	–	–	–	–	–	–	–	**2**	***3.2%***
Manufacturing	15	2	2	3	6	1	1	7	**37**	***59.7%***
Mining & quarrying	–	–	–	–	2	–	2	–	**4**	***6.5%***
Public administration & defense	–	–	–	–	–	–	–	–	**–**	**–**
Real estate	–	–	–	–	–	–	–	–	**–**	**–**
Service activities	–	–	–	–	–	–	–	–	**–**	**–**
Transportation & storage	–	–	–	–	1	–	3	–	**4**	***6.5%***
Total	**21**	**2**	**2**	**3**	**13**	**3**	**11**	**7**	**62**	***100.0%***
Total [%]	***33.9%***	***3.2%***	***3.2%***	***4.8%***	***21.0%***	***4.8%***	***17.7%***	***11.3%***	***100.0%***	**–**

Source: Author's own table.

with eleven (17.7%). This order as well as the rates are close to the distribution of company types in the overall sample of the 250 largest enterprises of 1958 (see Figure 5.1). While the seven foreign subsidiaries (11.3%) exceed their overall share all other company types have slightly lower reappearance rates.[91] The company types with a larger sample size tend to have similar reappearance shares.

From an industry perspective, the majority of reappearers operate in manufacturing in 1958 with 37 (59.7%) of the 62 entities which is close to the company type rate of 58.0% in the overall sample of the 250 largest enterprises of 1958. At a distance follows the second industry commerce with seven companies (11.3%) and the third energy and water with five (8.1%). Both show slightly lower rates than their overall company share which is 14.4% and 9.2%. Again, the category mining and quarrying has a low number with only four reappearers (6.5%). This rate is much lower than the share of this company type in the overall sample with 11.6%. None of the reappearers operate in real estate and service activities. In 1958, three enterprises are associated with these two industries. On the other hand, transportation and storage, information and communication as well as construction show higher reappearance rates compared to their share in the overall sample.[92] Especially the only two information and communication companies from the overall sample, the publishers *Axel Springer Verlag GmbH* and *C. Bertelsmann Verlag*, are among the reappearers in 2018.

As a last category the listing of the reappearers is analyzed. Of the 62 reappearers 22 (35.5%) are listed in 1958 while 40 (64.5%) are non-listed. The share of listed reappearers exceeds the share of listed companies in the datasets of 1958 which is 28.8%.

Currently, the view only considers the company type, industry and listing of 1958. However, until 2018 the companies develop and change—in some cases dramatically. For example, looking at the reappearers' listings in 2018 the status looks different to the one previously described. Now, of the 62 reappearers 29 (46.8%) are listed and not only 22 entities (35.5%); the number which is based on their 1958 status. Enterprises change their listing status during the 60 years and the numbers indicate that there is an increase in listings among the reappearers which might be a reason why they are still among the 250 largest companies in

[91] These are foreign family businesses and foundations with two entities (3.2%) each as well as multiple companies-owned enterprises and cooperatives with three entities (4.8%) each.

[92] The rates are 4.8% (3 / 62) for construction, 3.2% (2 / 62) for information and communication and 6.5% (4 / 62) for transportation and storage.

2018. Therefore, as a next step the developments of the 250 largest enterprises of 1958 including their crucial changes are investigated including the reappearers.

To further investigate these reappearers but also the enterprises which still exist outside of the 250 largest enterprises of 2018 as well as the companies which do not survive, the entities' developments from 1958 to 2018 are studied first by comparing their status in 1958 and 2018 in more detail. Chapter 6 will provide this analysis.

5.10 Summary: Despite Massive Industrial Changes Several Enterprises Remain One of the 250 Largest Enterprises over 60 Years

The previous descriptive findings of the identified conditions for a company's continuity and development are summarized into initial propositions in the following which are then further investigated and analyzed in the long-term in the next two chapters. These additional analyses should lead to profound development propositions helping researchers and practitioners to better understand the conditions and the long-term development of family and non-family enterprises.

Overall, massive changes and movements can be observed between the lists of the 250 largest enterprises of 1958 and 2018. On average, the 250 largest enterprises of 1958 and 2018 grow by 6.6% annually in terms of revenue which is higher than the growth of the German GDP in the same timeframe. They further increase their number of employees more than two and a half times over 60 years making them an important part of the German and the global economy. In this context, the largest companies continue to gain in importance relative to the smaller enterprises in the datasets. With 89.0 years in 2018 the enterprises are much older than in 1958 when they are 70.0 years old on average. Listed companies exceed non-listed ones in both years in terms of age suggesting that a listing is a next development phase of a company. Even listed family businesses exceed non-listed family firms in age. Nevertheless, the datasets show that after 60 years there are fewer listed and public companies among the 250 largest enterprises. This suggests that this type of company has a lower probability of survival. On the other hand, the existing public companies in 2018 become larger, increasing their revenue and employee share despite a decreasing number of entities. From an industry perspective manufacturing remains the most important area. Although the industry distribution is more diverse in 2018 manufacturing represents the most companies in both years. Moreover, commerce proves to be a growth area especially for family-owned enterprises. The two rankings of 1958 and 2018 show that several companies remain in the list of the 250 largest enterprises over 60 years. Nevertheless, not all attributes of these companies remain the same. Some of the ownership structures and thus the company types change as well as some listing statuses and even industry classifications. Also, family firms despite their long-term orientation develop into public companies, get listed or even disappear from the list of the 250 largest enterprises.

Taken all the observations in the previous sub-chapters together some companies survive over the observation period of 60 years while others do not. Therefore, the next chapter describes the developments and crucial changes of the different company types as well as of single companies.

6 Long-term Analysis I: The 250 Largest Enterprises of 1958

In the first long-term analysis the developments of the 250 largest enterprises of 1958 until 2018 are investigated. As a first approximation, the previous chapter provides an overview of the reappearers. But they do not reflect all companies which survive over the observation period of 60 years. Nor does the previous analysis take the downfallen companies into account. Therefore, the following questions arise: How many of the enterprises from the 1958 dataset survive until 2018? What is the survival and downfall rate of the different company types? Furthermore, which ownership discontinuities and crucial changes do the surviving companies experience? These questions are approached in the following on a company type but also on an enterprise level to understand the movements within the 250 largest enterprises. The previously introduced conditions like age and industry which are expected to have an impact on the company's long-term development are used to structure the analyses.

Due to the same applied company type definitions as well as the multi-dimensional conceptualization of survival the tracking of the development of each company is based on a uniform understanding. This ensures that the development of a single company can be compared to other enterprises' developments. Additionally, similar developments can be aggregated to identify patterns which occurred over the last six decades.

Supplementary Information The online version contains supplementary material available at https://doi.org/10.1007/978-3-658-42375-9_6.

M. Lantelme, *The Continuity and Discontinuity of the 250 Largest Enterprises in Germany*, Familienunternehmen und KMU,
https://doi.org/10.1007/978-3-658-42375-9_6

6.1 Overview of the Enterprises' Developments from 1958 to 2018

First, the enterprises' survival and downfall rates are calculated based on the companies' 1958 and 2018 status. The results are further investigated in terms of listing, age and company size. Second, the discontinuities of ownership are analyzed which represent the changes from one company type to another one over the past 60 years. Similarly, industry changes are identified to understand if enterprises survive by switching industries. Third, the growth rates of the surviving enterprises are calculated and compared to understand how much growth is required to enable a long-term development. Fourth, family firms are investigated in more detail to see whether their long-term development is unique. Lastly, the reappearers and additional survivors are studied to understand their differences in the long-term.

6.1.1 Survival and Downfall: Failure is the Normal

"Our current knowledge of survivors dominates our impression of the typical experience, and their triumphs are lionized, while the history of the failures is forgotten or considered untypical."[1] To overcome this perception not only the survivors but also the failed enterprises are investigated in the following. Based on the multi-dimensional conceptualization of survival in this thesis an enterprise can experience a downfall either due to the discontinuity of the operations or the solvency dimension. Furthermore, the combination of the ownership and operations dimension can also lead to a downfall. Using this approach 109 companies of the 250 largest enterprises of 1958 survive as one of the eight defined company types in 2018. This also means that the majority of 141 enterprises does not survive. They experience their downfall. These numbers result in a total survival rate of 43.6% and a total failure rate of 56.4% (see Table 6.1 and the row and columns "Total"). Overall, more than every second company of the 250 largest ones vanishes within 60 years. This shows the high risk of running a business—even among the largest ones.[2]

[1] Hannah (1999, p. 255).

[2] The total failure rate corresponds to a CAGR of −1.4% which is equal to 3.4 enterprises which fail every year on average.

Taking a closer look at the downfalls they can be divided into the two groups of subsidiary companies and narrow downfalls depending on the level of integration. Within the 60 years, eleven (4.4%) of the enterprises become a subsidiary of another German company which is the majority owner. These include, among others, *BV-Aral AG* as part of *BP Europe SE* in 2018, *Wintershall AG* which is a 100% subsidiary of *BASF SE* and *Oelwerke Julius Schindler GmbH* a company of *Hansen & Rosenthal GmbH & Co. KG.*[3] The remaining 130 enterprises (52.0%) which fail can be categorized as a narrow downfall including *Helmut Horten AG, Phoenix Gummiwerke AG* and *Hans Glas GmbH Isaria-Maschinenfabrik*. Overall, only a limited number of companies remain a subsidiary. The majority fails or gets integrated after an acquisition.

The overall survival rate of the 250 largest enterprises of 1958 is 43.6% in comparison to the reappearance rate of 24.8% from Section 5.9. This means that not only the 62 reappearers survive from 1958 to 2018 but also additional 47 enterprises. But these 47 companies do not achieve a sufficient growth rate over the six decades to remain one of the 250 largest enterprises in Germany 60 years later. They drop out of the ranking. These 47 companies are referred to as "additional survivors" in the following. The reappearers and the additional survivors are further analyzed in the upcoming sub-chapters to better understand what distinguishes their developments to remain one of the 250 largest enterprises or not. These developments are then summarized in Section 6.1.8.

The companies are further investigated in terms of their listing status as a key characteristic to prepare additional comparisons. From the 150 non-listed enterprises 67 (44.7%) survive until 2018 while 83 companies (55.3%) experience a downfall which can be split into seven subsidiary companies (4.7%) and 75 narrow downfalls (50.7%). Of the 100 listed enterprises of 1958 42 (42.0%) survive and 58 (58.0%) fail. Here, the split between subsidiary companies and narrow downfalls is four (4.0%) to 54 (54.0%). Overall, the non-listed enterprises of 1958 have a 2.7% higher survival rate than the listed companies.

As a reference to the analyzed survival and failure rates, Hannah reports in his study of the world's 100 largest enterprises of 1912 the survival of 52 companies (52.0%) until 1995. 48 of the enterprises (48.0%) experience their

---

[3] The subsidiary names refer to 1958. In 2018, their names are *Aral AG, Wintershall Holding GmbH* and *HR Ölwerke Schindler GmbH*.

downfall.[4] Looking only at the 14 German companies in his sample the survival rate increases to 57.1%. Eight enterprises reappear as independent in 1995.[5] These overall survival rates which include not only German companies are higher than the overall rate in this thesis' datasets. Looking only at the listed enterprises of the 1958 dataset the survival rate is even lower with 42.0%. Limiting the scope to the 14 largest listed enterprises the survival rate further declines to 35.7% which is similar to the share of the reappearers with five out of 14.[6] Hannah's survival rate of 52.0% from 1912 to 1995 is higher than the rate calculated in this thesis independent which company scope is used. The comparison with the 14 largest listed enterprises of 1958 has the highest discrepancy of 21.4% although it considers the same number of German companies Hannah includes in his sample. Considering the different observation periods the end of the 20th and the beginning of the 21st century might be a more dangerous time for enterprises.[7]

Table 6.1 Survival & Listing of the 250 Largest Enterprises of 1958 to 2018

Listing	**1958** [number of enterprises]	**2018** [number of enterprises]					
		Survivors			**Downfalls**		
		Non-listed	**Listed**	**Total**	**Subsidiary company**	**Downfall** (narrow)	**Total**
Non-listed	**150**	55	12	**67**	7	76	**83**
	60.0%	*36.7%*	*8.0%*	***44.7%***	*4.7%*	*50.7%*	***55.3%***
Listed	**100**	18	24	**42**	4	54	**58**
	40.0%	*18.0%*	*24.0%*	***42.0%***	*4.0%*	*54.0%*	***58.0%***
Total	**250**	**73**	**36**	**109**	**11**	**130**	**141**
	100.0%	***29.2%***	***14.4%***	***43.6%***	***4.4%***	***52.0%***	***56.4%***

Source: Author's own table.

[4] See Hannah (1999, 259). He defines survival as "any independent survival" similar to the broader definition of a downfall in this thesis.

[5] See Hannah (1999, p. 263). In his sample, only British enterprises have a higher survival rate with 60.0% (9/15 companies). From the 54 US companies only 26 survive (48.2%) until 1995.

[6] See Section 5.9.

[7] The eight out of 14 companies (57.1%) which survive in Hannah's sample from 1912 to 1995 are *BASF, Bayer*, *Gewerkschaft Deutscher Kaiser* (*Thyssen*), *Gutehoffnungshütte* (*Maschinenfabrik Augsburg-Nürnberg*), *Hoechst*, *Krupp*, *Mannesmann*, and *Siemens* (see Hannah (1999, pp. 278–281)).

After looking at the overall survival and downfall rates as well as the listing status the focus moves to the ownership structures and the related company types as another basic condition for a company's development. Their operations and solvency continuities are further analyzed (see Table 6.2).

The company type with the astonishing survival rate of 100% are the foundation-owned enterprises. Both of the two companies, *Carl Zeiss* and *Zahnradfabrik Friedrichshafen AG*, survive over the observation period of 60 years which supports the basic idea that a foundation is intended for perpetuity and cannot usually be dissolved.[8] Foreign subsidiaries show the second highest survival rate with 54.5%. Their majority of twelve companies survives while ten (45.5%) fail, of which one becomes a subsidiary company, *Oelwerke Julius Schindler*

Table 6.2 Survival of the 250 Largest Enterprises of 1958 to 2018 per Company Type

Type of company	**1958** [number of enterprises]	**2018** [number of enterprises]			
		Survivors	**Downfalls**		
		Total	**Subsidiary companies**	**Downfalls** (narrow)	**Total**
Family-owned business	**87**	**39**	4	44	**48**
	34.8%	***44.8%***	*4.6%*	*50.6%*	***55.2%***
Foreign family-owned business	**8**	**2**	1	5	**6**
	3.2%	***25.0%***	*12.5%*	*62.5%*	***75.0%***
Foundation-owned enterprise	**2**	**2**	–	–	**–**
	0.8%	***100.0%***	–	–	**–**
Multiple companies-owned enterprise	**20**	**5**	2	13	**15**
	8.0%	***25.0%***	*10.0%*	*65.0%*	***75.0%***
Public company	**56**	**23**	2	31	**33**
	22.4%	***41.1%***	*3.6%*	*55.4%*	***58.9%***
Cooperative	**16**	**5**	–	11	**11**

(continued)

[8] See Fleschutz (2009, p. 369) and Richter (2019) as well as Werner et al. (2019, pp. 30–31) for the fundamentals of the German *Stiftungsrecht* including a foundation's objectives.

Table 6.2 (continued)

Type of company	1958 [number of enterprises]	2018 [number of enterprises]			
		Survivors	Downfalls		
		Total	Subsidiary companies	Downfalls (narrow)	Total
	6.4%	*31.3%*	–	*68.8%*	***68.8%***
State-owned enterprise	**39**	**21**	1	17	**18**
	15.6%	*53.8%*	*2.6%*	*43.6%*	***46.2%***
Foreign subsidiary	**22**	**12**	1	9	**10**
	8.8%	*54.5%*	*4.5%*	*40.9%*	***45.5%***
Total	**250**	**109**	**11**	**130**	**141**
	100.0%	***43.6%***	***4.4%***	***52.0%***	***56.4%***

Source: Author's own table.

GmbH as part of *Hansen & Rosenthal GmbH & Co. KG.* State-owned enterprises follow with the third highest survival rate of 53.8%. While 21 of the 39 companies still exist in 2018, 18 (46.2%) do not. Again, just one (2.6%) of the downfalls is a subsidiary company with *Stadtwerke Bremen AG* which is called *swb AG* in 2018 and is part of *EWE AG.* The remaining 17 entities are narrow downfalls (43.6%). The 87 family-owned enterprises of 1958 have a survival rate of 44.8% until 2018, resulting in 39 survivors and 48 downfalls (55.2%). Of the latter ones four (4.6%) become a subsidiary company.[9] On fifth place in terms of survival rate is the company type of public enterprises with 41.1%. 23 public companies from 1958 survive until 2018, 33 entities (58.9%) vanish. *Deutsche Gold- und Silber- Scheideanstalt vormals Roessler AG (Degussa)* fully owned by *Evonik Industries AG* and *Wintershall AG* a 100% subsidiary of *BASF SE* are the two subsidiary companies (3.6%) next to the 31 narrow downfalls (55.4%) in 2018. The survival rate of the public companies is slightly below the rate of the family businesses and of the overall rate. Cooperatives, multiple companies-owned enterprises, and foreign family businesses have the lowest survival rates of all company types at 31.3% and twice at 25.0%. While five (31.3%) of the 16 cooperatives survive eleven (68.8%) fail. The majority of the downfalls are

[9] Family businesses which become a subsidiary company in 2018 are *Salamander AG* owned by *ara AG, Stahl- u. Walzwerke Rasselstein-Andernach AG* as part of *thyssenkrupp AG, G. M. Pfaff AG Nähmaschinenfabrik* is a 100% subsidiary of *Dürkopp Adler AG* which is ultimately owned by Chinese *Shang Gong Group Co., Ltd.* and *Blohm & Voss AG* owned by *Lürssen Maritime Beteiligungen GmbH & Co. KG.*

consumer and purchasing cooperatives in food retail like *Konsumgenossenscahft Essen eGmbH* or *Kaufring Gemeinschaftseinkauf eGmbH*. Due to the high concentration in this industry over the last decades such cooperatives have become obsolete. *Aldi Süd*, for example, is bigger than the largest cooperative *Edeka Zentrale AG & Co. KG* in 2018. Therefore, it has a huge purchasing power and does not require a purchasing cooperative. Five (25.0%) of 20 multiple companies-owned enterprises and two (25.0%) of eight foreign family firms survive which results in the same survival rate. From the former company type two (10.0%) of the in total 15 downfalls (75.0%) are subsidiary companies.[10]

Overall, the survival rates of the different company types show that all ownership structures are affected by downfalls with failure rates between 45.5% and up to 75.0%. Only foundation-owned enterprises are an exception here—although the sample is quite small. Both companies survive the observation period of 60 years and even centuries. In 2018, *Carl Zeiss AG* is 172 years old and *ZF Friedrichshafen AG* 103 years. Foreign subsidiaries as well as state-owned enterprises still have a survival rate of more than 50.0%. For all other company types more than every second enterprise fails including family firms with a survival rate of 44.8%. Moreover, foreign family businesses have the even lowest survival rate with on average only 25.0%. It can be stated that all company types are affected by downfalls in this sample—except foundations.

From an industry perspective the categories with a small number of enterprises show extreme values (see Table 6.3). Information and communication as well as transportation and storage have a 100.0% survival rate while real estate and service activities have a 100.0% failure rate. Among the survivors are again the two publishers *Axel Springer Verlag GmbH* and *C. Bertelsmann Verlag* as well as the transport companies *Deutsche* Bundesbahn, *Hamburg-Amerikanische Packetfahrt-Actien*-Gesellschaft and the Bremerhaven-based *Fischereihafen-Betriebsgesellschaft mbH*. In 1958, five of the seven transportation and storage companies are state-owned. Because this company type has the third highest survival rate it is not surprising that the transport firms also have a high rate. On the other hand, the real estate company *Deutsche Gesellschaft für öffentliche Arbeiten AG* (*Öffa*) is also state-owned in 1958 but failed. The reason was that the *Bundesrechnungshof* as a supreme federal authority found the funding procedures to be unconstitutional in 1969 and the company

[10] The multiple companies-owned enterprises in 1958 which become subsidiaries are *BV-Aral AG* owned by *BP Europe SE* and *Getreide-Import-Gesellschaft mbH* a subsidiary of *Landwirtschaftliche Rentenbank* in 2018.

was closed several years later.[11] The other real estate company, *"Neue Heimat" Gemeinnützige Wohnungs- und Siedlungsgesellschaft mbH*, is categorized as cooperative because it is owned by the *German Trade Union Confederation* [*Deutscher Gewerkschaftsbund (DGB)*].[12] This enterprise was consolidated due to high debts and illegal activities of the board of directors. In service activities, *TOUROPA oHG* owned by, among others, Carl Degener, ceased its activities after a merger of the founding members of *Touristik Union International* (later *TUI AG*) of which *TOUROPA* was one. The last industry with a small number of enterprises but not such an extreme survival rate is construction. Three out of five enterprises survive from 1958 to 2018 which corresponds to a survival rate of 60.0%. The survivors are *Hochtief AG für Hoch- und Tiefbauten vorm. Gebr. Helfmann, Ed. Züblin AG* and *Grün & Bilfinger AG Bauunternehmung*. The first and the last one are public companies while *Ed. Züblin AG* is a family business. On the other hand, the downfalls are *Philipp Holzmann AG* and *Beton- und Monierbau AG*, both public companies in 1958 that go into insolvency, the latter one in 1979 and the former one in 2002. Nevertheless, due to the small sample size these four industry figures are not particularly meaningful and the detailed analysis of the single cases provides a profound explanation for the high survival rates. Energy and water hast the highest survival rate for an industry with more than 20 enterprises in 1958. 52.2% of the 23 companies survive. Among the twelve survivors are *Rheinisch-Westfälisches Elektrizitätswerk AG*, *Stadtwerke Frankfurt* and *Pfalzwerke* AG. The rate is similar to the survival rate of state-owned enterprises with 53.8%. As already highlighted earlier, one reason is that 22 of the 23 energy and water companies are state-owned. However, this also implies that the majority of downfalls are state-owned, as well. This is the case for ten out of eleven including *Stadtwerke Bremen* becoming a subsidiary company. Several of the downfalls are part of mergers and acquisitions leading to a consolidation of the industry including *Vereinigte Elektrizitätswerke Westfalen AG* which merges with *RWE* in 2000, *Bayernwerk AG Bayerische Landeselektrizitätsversorgung* which gets acquired by *VIAG AG* (later *E.ON AG* after the merger with *VEBA AG* and since 2012 *E.ON SE*) in 1994 and *Hamburger Gaswerke GmbH* which gets acquired by *E.ON AG* in 2001. The largest industry, manufacturing, has a survival rate of 42.1%. More than half of the enterprises fail within the observation period of 60 years which corresponds to 84 companies including four subsidiaries. 61 firms survive. In mining and quarrying 18 out of the 29 enterprises experience a downfall

---

[11] See Bucher (1996, p. 70) and Deutscher Bundestag (1969).

[12] Although this organization is not particularly a cooperative the structure is similar with millions of members in the affiliated unions.

including *Hoesch AG, Metallhüttenwerke Lübeck GmbH* and *Bayerische Berg-, Hütten- und Salzwerke AG* which leads to a survival rate of 37.9%. The foundation of *Ruhrkohle AG* and the resolved consolidation of German hard coal industry has a significant share in the high downfall rate. Six companies of the sample including *Bergwerksgesellschaft Hibernia AG, Friedrich Thyssen Bergbau AG* and *Steinkohlenbergwerk Heinrich Robert AG* are part of this consolidation process. A similarly low survival rate can be observed in the commerce industry of 36.1%. 23 of the 36 enterprises (63.9%) fail and only 13 survive. Among them are the large supermarket chains and wholesalers like *Edeka eGmbH* and *Albrecht KG Lebensmittel-Filialbetrieb* while downfalls also include several supermarkets and wholesalers like *Heinrich Hill AG* and *Gedelfi GmbH*. The high downfall rate of multiple companies-owned enterprises and cooperatives can also be seen within commerce. Multiple companies-owned enterprises and cooperatives are responsible for 15 of the 23 failed companies. A consolidation of the industry cannot be confirmed based on the sample because the enterprises trade with various products, e.g., food, metal, nitrogen, shoes etc., and therefore belong to different sub-industries. The acquisition of *Gedelfi GmbH* by *Edeka eG* in 1993 is the only transaction between companies included in the commerce sample.

Overall, the consolidation of industries as well as the structural change of the economy can lead to high downfall rates, like in the mining and quarrying industry or to a high merger and acquisition volume among the companies in the sample like in the energy and water industry which was dominated by state-owned enterprises in 1958. In addition, entire legal forms, like cooperatives, which mainly operated as purchasing and consumer cooperatives have become obsolete due to the changing industry structure with a high concentration. The low survival rate in commerce—despite being an industry profiting from the structural change—suggests that there is a tough competition in general in this industry and a high number of new companies entering the market with, for example, new business models. Therefore, industry appears to be a major threat to a company's survival in the long-term.

Table 6.3 Industry Survival of the 250 Largest Enterprises of 1958 to 2018

Industry	**1958** [number of enterprises]	**2018** [number of enterprises]			
		Survivors	**Downfalls**		
		Total	**Subsidiary companies**	**Downfalls** (narrow)	**Total**
Commerce	**36**	**13**	2	21	**23**
	14.4%	***36.1%***	*5.6%*	*58.3%*	***63.9%***
Construction	**5**	**3**	–	2	**2**
	2.0%	***60.0%***	–	*40.0%*	***40.0%***
Energy & water	**23**	**12**	1	10	**11**
	9.2%	***52.2%***	*4.3%*	*43.5%*	***47.8%***
Information & communication	**2**	**2**	–	–	**–**
	0.8%	***100.0%***	–	–	**–**
Manufacturing	**145**	**61**	6	78	**84**
	58.0%	***42.1%***	*4.1%*	*53.8%*	***57.9%***
Mining & quarrying	**29**	**11**	2	16	**18**
	11.6%	***37.9%***	*6.9%*	*55.2%*	***62.1%***
Real estate	**2**	**–**	–	2	**2**
	0.8%	**–**	–	*100.0%*	***100.0%***
Service activities	**1**	**–**	–	1	**1**
	0.4%	**–**	–	*100.0%*	***100.0%***
Transportation & storage	**7**	**7**	–	–	**–**
	2.8%	***100.0%***	–	–	**–**
Total	**250**	**109**	**11**	**130**	**141**
	100.0%	***43.6%***	***4.4%***	***52.0%***	***56.4%***

Source: Author's own table.

6.1.2 Age: Get Old to Become Older

Because age is seen as a characteristic which has an impact on the survival of a company the founding decades and the average age of the 109 surviving and 141 failed companies are analyzed.

Comparing the founding decades two observations stand out (Figure 6.1). First, ten of the twelve companies founded in the 1950 s do not exist anymore in 2018. Second, there are just as many surviving as failed enterprises founded before the 1870 s with 34 entities each. The higher share of failed companies was founded in the 1870 s and later. This implies that the surviving companies are the older ones which can be confirmed by the average age of the two groups in 1958. On average, the 109 surviving enterprises are 73.2 years old compared to the failed enterprises which are 67.3 years old in 1958. Overall, the average age is 70.0 years. Therefore, older companies tend to have a higher chance of survival than younger ones. Looking at the different company types no major deviations can be identified. The differences between survivors and downfalls in the groups of family businesses as well as public companies are in line with the overall average age differences. The ten young and failed companies founded in the 1950 s include two enterprises which are established as part of the deconcentration of the German mining and steel industry which are *Hüttenwerke Siegerland AG* and *Friedrich Thyssen Bergbau AG*. The former is bought by *Dortmund Hörder Hüttenunion AG* in 1960 and gets integrated. The latter one becomes part of *Ruhrkohle AG* in the late 1960 s. *Saarbergwerke AG* and *Rheinisch-Westfälische Kalkwerke AG* are two additional companies in mining and quarrying like *Friedrich Thyssen Bergbau AG*. *Saarbergwerke AG* fails after *Ruhrkohle AG* buys it in 1998 and discontinues the operations years later. Additionally, *Hoesch* takes over the majority of *Rheinisch-Westfälische Kalkwerke AG* after its acquisition of *Dortmund Hörder Hüttenunion AG* which was also a shareholder. The lime works are then resold several times and finally integrated. All of the five companies in commerce get finally consolidated or integrated into other enterprises including *Handelsunion AG* in *Thyssen* and *Neckarmann Versand KG* which finally still exists only as a brand of *Otto Versand* after several sales. Overall, these ten companies fail because of acquisitions and consolidations in their industries. Some of these acquisitions are favored by prior deconcentration processes.

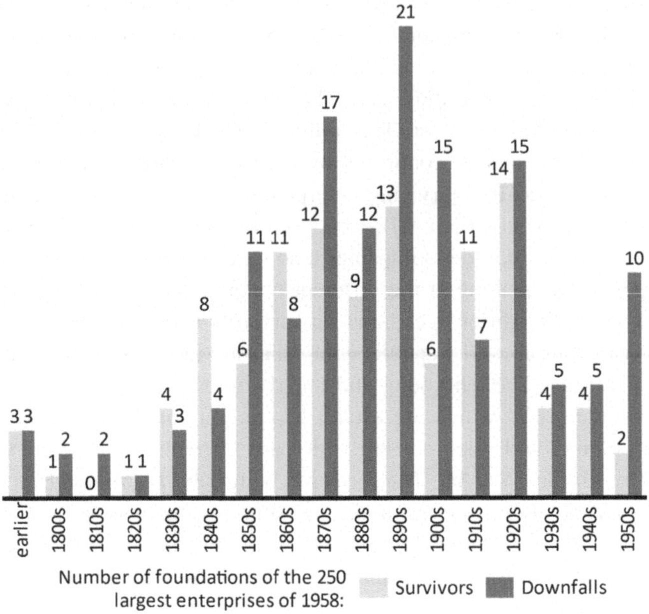

Figure 6.1 Foundation Decade Distribution of the Survivors & Downfalls of the Largest Enterprises of 1958. (Source: Author's own figure)

Looking at the year 2018, the average age of the sample with the 250 largest enterprises is 89.0 years as shown in Section 5.5. The 109 companies of the 1958 dataset which survive until 2018 have an average age in this year of 133.2 years (see Table 6.4) which is—logically—60 years more than their average age in 1958 as highlighted above. This high average age is remarkable, spanning more than four generations.

From a company type perspective, public companies and family businesses are the oldest ones with 141.5 and 140.8 years on average. They are followed by foundation-owned enterprises, foreign subsidiaries and state-owned enterprises with 137.5, 137.1 and 125.7 years, respectively. Only foreign family-owned businesses and cooperatives have an average age below 100 years with 94.5 and 98.2. Multiple companies-owned enterprises are just above with 105.4 years. Here, too, it can be seen that family businesses and public companies can become very old and are the oldest company types of all.

In the following, for the first time the survivors are further analyzed differentiating between the 62 companies which remain one of the 250 largest enterprises in 2018 and the 47 companies which drop out of the ranking. Due to this distinction, the former group includes the larger enterprises in 2018 compared to the latter group. The average age of the reappearers is slightly below the average age of the additional survivors with 130.7 years compared to 136.3 years. This also implies that the survival is not necessarily linked to the size because the additional survivors which are smaller in 2018 are not younger than the reappearers.

In two cases, the different company types[13] show a discrepancy of more than one generation between the reappearers and the additional survivors which are foreign family-owned enterprises and foundation-owned enterprises.

Table 6.4 Average Age per Company Type of the Survivors of 1958 in 2018

#	Type of company in 2018	Survivors		
		Average age in 2018 [years]		
		Reappearers (62 companies)	**Additional survivors** (47 companies)	**Total** (109 companies)
1	Family-owned business	142.4	153.7	**146.6**
2	Foreign family-owned business	105.8	141.7	**127.3**
3	Foundation-owned enterprise	147.0	191.0	**163.5**
4	Multiple companies-owned enterprise	171.0	–	**171.0**
5	Public company	133.7	124.3	**132.4**
6	Cooperative	97.3	97.0	**97.2**
7	State-owned enterprise	117.0	131.8	**126.5**
8	Foreign subsidiary	126.0	123.3	**124.4**
	Total	**130.7**	**136.3**	**133.2**

Source: Author's own table.

[13] The company types reflect the enterprises' status as of 2018.

Taking a closer look at the company types in 1958 and 2018 it can be shown that family businesses in 1958 which remain in a family until 2018 have the highest average age of all survivors with 148.7 years (see Table 6.5).[14] If a public company remains a public company it has the second highest average age with 140.0 years followed by foundations with 137.5 years. Overall, this implies that older family businesses in 1958 are more likely to survive than younger ones.

Table 6.5 Average Age of the Survivors in 2018 per Company Type in 1958 & 2018

Type of company	**Survivors**									
	1958	**Average age in 2018** [years]								
		FB	**FFB**	**FD**	**MCE**	**PC**	**COOP**	**SOE**	**FS**	**Total**
Family-owned business	**39**	148.7	136.8	140.0	–	130.4	–	–	115.0	**140.8**
Foreign family-owned business	**2**	–	93.0	–	–	–	–	–	96.0	**94.5**
Foundation-owned enterprise	**2**	–	–	137.5	–	–	–	–	–	**137.5**
Multiple companies-owned enterprise	**5**	104.0	83.0	–	–	125.5	–	–	89.0	**105.4**
Public company	**23**	198.0	138.0	–	171.0	140.0	92.0	–	139.8	**141.5**
Cooperative	**5**	–	–	–	–	–	98.2	–	–	**98.2**
State-owned enterprise	**21**	81.0	–	–	–	123.4	–	126.5	171.0	**125.7**
Foreign subsidiary	**12**	162.0	–	333.0	–	–	–	–	115.0	**137.1**
Total	**–**	**146.6**	**127.3**	**163.5**	**171.0**	**132.4**	**97.2**	**126.5**	**124.4**	**133.2**
2018	**109**	**24**	**10**	**8**	**1**	**21**	**6**	**14**	**25**	**–**

Source: Author's own table.

6.1.3 Size: Liability of Relative Smallness

Referring to the liability of smallness size might have an impact on the survival and the long-term development of companies. As shown in Section 5.1 the average company of the 1958 sample has revenues of EUR 270.6 m [DM 529.3 m]. The 109 surviving enterprises have an average revenue of EUR 318.8 m [DM

[14] For an explanation of the table see Section 6.1.4

623.5 m] in 1958 compared to the 141 failed enterprises with EUR 233.4 m [DM 456.6 m]. The survivors are on average already larger than the downfalls in 1958.[15] Looking at the ranks of the survivors, 55 of the first half of the 250 largest enterprises of 1958 survive resulting in a survival rate of 44.0%. Of the second 125 companies 54 firms survive which corresponds to a survival rate of 43.2%. Both rates are close to each other. Nevertheless, the surviving entities are on average the larger ones. Analyzing only the 62 reappearers 42 of them (67.7%) are already among the 125 largest enterprises while the remaining 20 entities (32.3%) are in the second half of the ranking. In addition, the average revenue of the 62 reappearers is EUR 447.4 m [DM 875.1 m] which is 1.4 times the average of all 109 survivors. From the 47 additional survivors only 13 companies (27.7%) are in the first half of the ranking while the majority of 34 entities (72.3%) is on a position between 126 and 250. The average revenue of the 47 companies is EUR 149.1 m [DM 291.6 m] and therefore even smaller than the average revenue of the 141 failed enterprises. Overall, larger enterprises from the sample of the 250 largest companies of 1958 remain with a higher probability in the ranking of 2018. Furthermore, size matters in respect to the long-term continuity although a few companies also survive despite being small.

In 2018, the average company size of the 250 largest enterprises of this year is EUR 12.3bn (see Section 5.1). The 109 survivors from 1958 have an average size of EUR 15.8bn in 2018 (see Table 6.6). But there is again a large difference between the 62 reappearers and the 47 additional survivors. The former ones have on average revenues of EUR 26.8bn and the latter ones of EUR 0.9bn. These figures show that the companies develop very differently over 60 years. Large discrepancies can also be identified between the different company types. While foreign family-owned businesses, foreign subsidiaries and state-owned enterprises have a single-digit average revenue with EUR 4.5bn, EUR 5.7bn and EUR 6.5bn public companies as the largest company type on average in 2018 and cooperatives are many times larger with average revenues of EUR 34.6bn and EUR 22.0bn.

[15] Also, the median is larger for the survivors with EUR 128.6 m [DM 251.5 m] in revenues compared to EUR 104.8 m [DM 205.0 m]. The median companies are *Christian Dierig AG* [#117] for the former and *Kali-Chemie AG* [#128] for the latter group.

Table 6.6 Average Revenue per Company Type of the Survivors of 1958 in 2018

#	Type of company 2018	Survivors		
		Average revenue in 2018 [bnEUR]		
		Reappearers	Additional survivors	Total
		(62 companies)	(47 companies)	(109 companies)
1	Family-owned business	27.5	0.7	**17.4**
2	Foreign family-owned business	10.3	0.6	**4.5**
3	Foundation-owned enterprise	28.3	1.7	**18.3**
4	Multiple companies-owned enterprise	11.5	–	**11.5**
5	Public company	40.1	1.1	**34.6**
6	Cooperative	32.6	0.7	**22**
7	State-owned enterprise	16.3	1.1	**6.5**
8	Foreign subsidiary	12.2	1.06	**5.7**
	Total	**26.8**	**0.9**	**15.8**

Source: Author's own table.

Overall, the 109 surviving companies of the 250 largest enterprises of 1958 are on average larger than the failing ones. Additionally, the 62 reappearing enterprises on the list of the 250 largest companies of 2018 are once again larger than the 47 additional survivors. Therefore, the larger the enterprise the greater the probability to survive. Size is important even among the 250 largest companies—therefore this phenomenon is called the *liability of relative smallness*.

6.1.4 Ownership Continuity and Discontinuity: Continuity as an Exception

After providing an overview of the overall and company type-specific survival and failure rates as well as their ages and sizes the focus shifts towards the surviving companies. The following analyses investigate the continuities and discontinuities of the enterprises' ownership structures which are expected to have a major impact on the long-term development of the companies and therefore represent a crucial change. As a reminder, an ownership discontinuity is per se not a downfall. Besides an ownership discontinuity a downfall would also require the discontinuity of operations which means the integration as a subsidiary company or into the acquiring organization. After only an ownership discontinuity the company continues its operations under a new owner without integration. The rate how many enterprises of a certain company type survive and keep their specific company type is called the *ownership continuity rate*.[16] Overall, the ownership continuity rate shows that keeping the same ownership structure is an exception over a period of six decades.

Table 6.7 provides the survival and downfall rates of the various company types again but it also includes the ownership continuities (see the diagonally fields for the ownership continuity rate) and discontinuities of the survivors and therefore the developments of their ownership structures are provided. Many of these changes occur between 1958 and 2018. This means that a company can survive until 2018 but has a different owner 60 years after 1958. The enterprise might experience a discontinuity of the ownership dimension. The group of foundations, on the other hand, is an exception. They do not experience such ownership discontinuities. Similar to their survival rate of 100% the two foundation-owned enterprises in 1958, *Carl Zeiss* and *Zahnradfabrik Friedrichshafen AG*, remain foundation-owned in 2018. Their ownership dimension is continuous. The intention of a permanent ownership structure which is one of the motivations related to foundations is reflected in this number. The other extreme can be observed in the group of multiple companies-owned enterprises. Of the five surviving firms none remains a multiple companies-owned enterprise in 2018. Their ownership dimension discontinues and therefore their company types change. The two companies *Norddeutsche Affinerie AG* and *Osram GmbH* become public companies under the names *Aurubis AG* and *Osram Licht AG* in 2018. Moreover, *Wacker Chemie GmbH* operates as a family business in 2018, which is majority owned by the Wacker family after acquiring additional shares from *Hoechst AG* (*Sanofi*) in 2001. *Eternit AG* turns into a foreign subsidiary owned by Belgian *ETEX N.V.* and *Süddeutsche Zellwolle AG* becomes a foreign family business ultimately owned

[16] The ownership continuity rate refers to the total enterprise number of a specific company type in 1958. Therefore, not only surviving enterprises are considered in 2018 but also downfalls which have a negative effect on the rate.

by the *Barbarossa Privatstiftung.*[17] As highlighted earlier, multiple companies-owned enterprises are much more difficult to run and establish due to stricter competition policies. This is reflected in this company type's ownership continuity rate of 0%. The company type of foreign family businesses in 1958 also experiences an ownership discontinuity in one of the two surviving enterprises which are both car manufacturers which results in the second lowest continuity rate. In 1958, *FIAT Automobil AG* is a subsidiary of Italian *FIAT S.p.A.* which is majority owned by the Agnelli family. But the family loses their majority in the 1990 s and in 2018 the listed parent company, now under the name *FCA Italy S.p.A.*, has no majority owner.[18] Therefore, the foreign family business becomes a foreign subsidiary. On the other hand, *Ford-Werke AG* the second foreign family business in 1958 which survives until 2018 remains as this company type because the Ford family still has the majority of voting rights in 2018. Therefore, including their downfalls (75.0%) foreign family businesses have an ownership continuity rate of 12.5%. It is not possible to use the rate as a general explanation due to the small number of cases.

In the following the ownership continuity rates of family-owned enterprises and public companies are compared to better understand their differences. They have the second and third lowest rates of all company types. With 16.1% public companies have the lower continuity rate compared to family businesses with 23.0% (their survival rates are much closer together with 41.1% and 44.8%). Of the 23 surviving public companies nine remain a public company including *Farbenfabriken Bayer AG, BASF Badische Anilin- & Soda-Fabrik AG* and *Salzdetfurth AG.*[19] On the other hand, 20 of the 39 surviving family enterprises keep the status of a family business in 2018 and remain in the hands of a family located in Germany. *Carl Freudenberg KGaA, J. M. Voith GmbH* and *Theodor Wuppermann GmbH, Walzwerk und Faconschmiede* are part of the continuous

---

17 The names of the latter three companies in 2018 are *Wacker Chemie AG, Eternit GmbH* and *Kelheim Fibres GmbH*.

18 In 2018, the German company is called *FCA Germany AG* after *FIAT* acquires US-based *Chrysler*. The German subsidiary is owned by Italian *FCA Italy S.p.A.* (~99.0%) and Swiss *FCA Switzerland S.A.* (~1.0%). Further, the largest shareholder of the Italian parent is Dutch *Exor N.V.* with around 29.0% of issued common shares. Ultimately, *Exor* is controlled by the Agnelli and Nasi families which are descendants of Giovanni Agnelli, the founder of *FIAT*. Due to a loyalty voting mechanism, *Exor's* voting power is around 42.1%. Overall, the owner's family which has the majority in 1958 is still present in the company in 2018 but does not have the majority of voting rights anymore.

19 Their enterprise names in 2018 are *Bayer AG, BASF SE* and *K + S AG*.

Table 6.7 Ownership Continuity & Discontinuity of the 250 Largest Enterprises of 1958 to 2018

Type of company	**1958**	**2018** [number of enterprises]											
		Survivors									**Downfalls**		
		FB	**FFB**	**FD**	**MCE**	**PC**	**COOP**	**SOE**	**FS**	**Total**	**Subsidiary company**	**Downfall** (narrow)	**Total**
Family-owned business	**87**	20	6	5	–	5	–	–	3	**39**	4	44	**48**
	34.8%	*23.0%*	*6.9%*	*5.7%*	–	*5.7%*	–	–	*3.4%*	***44.8%***	*4.6%*	*50.6%*	***55.2%***
Foreign family-owned business	**8**	–	1	–	–	–	–	–	1	**2**	1	5	**6**
	3.2%	–	*12.5%*	–	–	–	–	–	*12.5%*	***25.0%***	*12.5%*	*62.5%*	***75.0%***
Foundation-owned enterprise	**2**	–	–	2	–	–	–	–	–	**2**	–	–	**–**
	0.8%	–	–	*100.0%*	–	–	–	–	–	***100.0%***	–	–	**–**
Multiple companies-owned enterprise	**20**	1	1	–	–	2	–	–	1	**5**	2	13	**15**
	8.0%	*5.0%*	*5.0%*	–	–	*10.0%*	–	–	*5.0%*	***25.0%***	*10.0%*	*65.0%*	***75.0%***
Public company	**56**	1	2	–	1	9	1	–	9	**23**	2	31	**33**
	22.4%	*1.8%*	*3.6%*	–	*1.8%*	*16.1%*	*1.8%*	–	*16.1%*	***41.1%***	*3.6%*	*55.4%*	***58.9%***
Cooperative	**16**	–	–	–	–	–	5	–	–	**5**	–	11	**11**
	6.4%	–	–	–	–	–	*31.3%*	–	–	***31.3%***	–	*68.8%*	***68.8%***
State-owned enterprise	**39**	1	–	–	–	5	–	14	1	**21**	1	17	**18**
	15.6%	*2.6%*	–	–	–	*12.8%*	–	*35.9%*	*2.6%*	***53.8%***	*2.6%*	*43.6%*	***46.2%***
Foreign subsidiary	**22**	1	–	1	–	–	–	–	10	**12**	1	9	**10**
	8.8%	*4.5%*	–	*4.5%*	–	–	–	–	*45.5%*	***54.5%***	*4.5%*	*40.9%*	***45.5%***
Total	**250**	**24**	**10**	**8**	**1**	**21**	**6**	**14**	**25**	**109**	**11**	**130**	**141**
	100.0%	***9.6%***	***4.0%***	***3.2%***	***0.4%***	***8.4%***	***2.4%***	***5.6%***	***10.0%***	***43.6%***	***4.4%***	***52.0%***	***56.4%***

Source: Author's own table.

family firms.[20] Over 60 years, family-owned enterprises show a higher rate of remaining in the hands of a family than public companies remain in free float. In addition, six (6.9%) of the 39 surviving family businesses are owned by foreign families in 2018. Therefore, they also remain in the hands of a family, in some cases even in the same family despite a move to another country. Including them in the ownership continuity rate the number increases to 29.9%. Examples are *Dyckerhoff Portland-Zementwerke AG*, *WMF Württembergische Metallwarenfabrik* and *Th. Weisser KG*. Five additional family businesses (5.7%) from 1958 become a foundation-owned enterprise in 2018 including *Robert Bosch GmbH*, *Klein, Schanzlin & Becker AG* and *Friedrich Baur GmbH*. Some of them still have connections with the owner's family of 1958.[21] Furthermore, three family-owned businesses (3.4%) change to foreign subsidiaries while five (5.7%) become a public company including *Siemens AG* and *AG der Gerresheimer Glashüttenwerke*. Looking at the surviving public companies of 1958 and the reversal of the last described development one entity (1.8%), *Stahlwerke Bochum AG*, becomes a family-owned enterprise in 2018 after a management buyout in 2004 with the support of a financial investor whose shares are then acquired by the management team in 2007.[22] Additionally, the two department store chains, *Rudolph Karstadt AG* and *Kaufhof AG*, both listed in 1958 are foreign family-owned in 2018 ultimately by the Austrian *Benko Familienstiftung*. With *Süddeutsche Zucker-AG* one public company becomes majority-owned by a cooperation, *Süddeutsche Zuckerrübenverwertungs-Genossenschaft (SZVG)* an organization of beet growers in southern Germany, within the 60 years. One additional public company (1.8%) discontinues its ownership dimension and changes to a multiple companies-owned enterprise in 2018 with *Hamburg-Amerikanische Packetfahrt-Actien-Gesellschaft / Hapag-Lloyd AG*. A similar share as the ownership continuity rate is the change to foreign subsidiaries (16.1%). The ownership majority of nine public companies in 1958 changes to foreign enterprises in 2018 including *Deutsche Erdöl-AG* majority-owned by *Luxembourg LetterOne Holdings S.A.*, *Didier-Werke AG* as part of Dutch *RHI Magnesita N.V.* and *Rosenthal-Porzellan AG* a foreign subsidiary of Italian *Arcturus S.R.L.* None of the public companies turn into a foundation-owned enterprise or a state-owned enterprise.

[20] *Freudenberg & Co. KG*, *Voith GmbH & Co. KGaA* and *Wuppermann AG* are the company names in 2018.

[21] See Section 6.1.7 for a detailed analysis of the ownership continuities and discontinuities of family-owned enterprises.

[22] In 1990, *Stahlwerke Bochum AG* becomes already part of *Thyssen* in the course of their acquisition of *Otto Wolff*. Both companies own 48.5% in Stahlwerke Bochum at that time.

Similar to the foundation-owned enterprises all of the five surviving cooperatives remain this company type in 2018. However, because additional eleven entities (68.8%) fail the ownership continuity rate is 31.3% and not 100% as in the case of the foundations.[23] Enterprises which are owned by the state in 1958 have the third highest ownership continuity rate with 35.9%. Despite all privatization efforts over the last decades, 14 entities remain state owned while seven experience an ownership discontinuity. One entity each (2.6%) becomes a family business, *Volkswagen AG*, and a foreign subsidiary, *Berliner Gaswerke (Gasag)* dominated by Swedish *Vattenfall* (based on a consortium agreement with French *Engie*). The remaining five state-owned enterprises (12.8%) from 1958 turn into public companies until 2018. The companies are *Deutsche Bundespost*, *Salzgitter-Konzern*, *Rheinisch-Westfälisches Elektrizitätswerk AG*, *Preußische Bergwerks- und Hütten AG (Preussag)* and *Deutsche Lufthansa AG*.[24] The majority of their shares are in free float. With an ownership continuity rate of 45.5% the company type of foreign subsidiaries has the second highest share similar to its survival rate. Ten of the twelve surviving enterprises remain foreign subsidiaries. These include *Deutsche Unilever AG* as part of the British-Dutch consumer goods company *Unilever*, *SKF Kugellagerfabriken GmbH* owned by Swedish manufacturing company *AB SKF* and *Internationale Büromaschinen GmbH* as part of the US-based technology company *International Business Machines Corporation* (*IBM*). One foreign subsidiary each becomes a family-owned enterprise with *Harpener Bergbau AG* owned by the family of Albrecht Knauf in 2018 and a foundation-owned enterprise with *Aktien-Gesellschaft der Dillinger Hüttenwerke* ultimately owned by *Montan-Stiftung-Saar*.

Overall, with 61 companies (56.0%) the majority of the 109 surviving enterprises remains the company type in 2018 which they started as in 1958. This also shows that only 24.4% of all 250 enterprises remain the same company type over the observation period. Around three out of four companies experience an ownership discontinuity or a downfall. Furthermore, 48 companies (44.0% of the 109 surviving enterprises / 19.2% of the entire sample of 250 enterprises) belong to a different company type in 2018 compared to 1958. Looking at the 48 ownership discontinuities 15 have turned into foreign subsidiaries which is

---

[23] The surviving cooperatives are *Edeka eGmbH*, *Bayerische Warenvermittlung landwirtschaftlicher Genossenschaften AG (BayWa)*, *Rewe Zentrale Deutscher Lebensmittel-Großhandels-Genossenschaften eGmbH*, *Raiffeisen-Warenzentrale Hessenland GmbH* and *FERN-SVG-NORD Strassenfernverkehr-Genossenschaft Hamburg und Schleswig Holstein eGmbH*.

[24] In 2018, their company names are *Deutsche Post AG*, *Salzgitter AG*, *RWE AG*, *TUI AG* and *Deutsche Lufthansa AG* which remains as in 1958.

the largest group followed by public companies with twelve entities and foreign family businesses with nine additional firms. Foundation-owned enterprises add additional six enterprises and family-owned ones additional four. Multiple companies-owned enterprises and cooperatives add one entity each. These numbers lead to the assumption that over the last 60 years ownership discontinuities occur predominantly due to acquisitions of foreign companies and families as well as to the sale of shares to become a public company. In contrast, foundations stabilize the ownership continuity also in the long-term.

After analyzing the survival rates of non-listed and listed enterprises the developments of the companies' listing statuses are investigated (coming back to Table 6.1). Because the listing can change within the observation period not only the 1958 listing status but also the 2018 listing status are now included in the analysis.[25] Of the 67 surviving enterprises (44.7%) which are non-listed in 1958 55 (36.7%) are non-listed in 2018 as well and twelve (8.0%) are listed in the meantime.[26] Vice versa, of the 42 surviving enterprises (42.0%) which are listed in 1958 24 (24.0%) remain listed in 2018 and 18 (18.0%) are non-listed 60 years later. Although the survival rates of enterprises which are non-listed and listed in 1958 are close to each other with 44.7% and 42.0% the survivors of the latter group change their listing status in 42.9% of the cases (18 / 42) while the survivors of the initially non-listed firms change their status only in 17.9% of the cases (12 / 67). This results in lower survival rates for enterprises which are listed in both years of 24.0% and for companies which are non-listed in both years to 36.7%. Listing seems to be no long-term solution if only 24.0% of enterprises remain listed over 60 years.

In summary, ownership continuity is an exception over the observation period of 60 years. Only around one out of four enterprises keeps its structure. All other companies change their ownership structure or fail. Based on the sample it can be concluded that foundations improve the conditions for ownership continuity. Family firms also show higher continuity rates compared to public companies with a majority in free float which are more likely to change their structure, e.g.,

---

[25] The eleven subsidiary companies as part of the downfalls are all non-listed in 2018. This means that the four listed enterprises in 1958 which become subsidiaries in 2018 change their listing status. These subsidiaries are *Salzgitter Klöckner-Werke GmbH* (part of *Salzgitter AG*), *Evonic Degussa GmbH* (*Evonik Industries AG*), *Wintershall Holding GmbH* (*BASF SE*) and *Salamander GmbH* (*ara AG*).

[26] The percentages in the development analyses refer to the share of all enterprises that have the specific characteristic in 1958 including the downfalls.

via acquisitions. Especially foreign enterprises acquire German companies over the last 60 years. They represent the largest group of the surviving companies of 1958 with 25 entities.

6.1.5 Industry: A Company's Destiny

When looking at the overview of the reappearers (Table 5.21) not only company types change between 1958 and 2018 but also some of the industry classification. This is also the case for some of the 47 additional survivors which do not appear on the list of the 250 largest enterprises of 2018. But changes do not occur as often as they do in the case of ownership structures analyzed in the previous sub-chapter. 92 of the 109 survivors (84.4%) keep their industry classification from 1958 to 2018 while 17 enterprises (15.6%) change it (see Table 6.8). These 17 companies have only two different industry classifications in 1958 which are manufacturing as well as mining and quarrying with eight and nine entities which change industries. The survivors in all other industries do not change their classifications. These industries only gain additional firms in 2018. Overall, these numbers show that the majority of enterprises survives over decades by remaining in their initial key industry. However, the remaining 18 companies change their industry classification between 1958 and 2018 and survive, as well. Therefore, they are investigated in more detail. Looking at the eight manufacturers which change their industry, seven of them shift their focus to commerce. Because the companies stick to their initial products, they just move to another step in the value chain. For example, *Th. Weisser KG* mainly refines petroleum in 1958 but in 2018 under the name *Marquard & Bahls AG* their revenue majority comes from mineral oil trading which is the same product but another step. Similarly, *FIAT Automobil AG* with its subsidiary *NSU Automobil-AG* produces cars in 1958. 60 years later the German subsidiary of *FCA* (*Fiat Chrysler Automobiles*) does not produce cars anymore. It is a pure trading company which does not have a single plant in Germany. *Internationale Büromaschinen GmbH* also started as a manufacturer with their own plants in Germany but closed all of them in the meantime. In 2018, *IBM Deutschland GmbH* is categorized as an information and communication company and hence the only manufacturer which doe not change to commerce. Of the initial eleven mining and quarrying companies nine change their industry which again shows the consolidation of the industry over the last decades. Six entities change to manufacturing, two to real estate and one to service activities. Among the manufactures are *Heinrich Bergbau AG* called *Littelfuse GmbH* in 2018 which produces fuses and sensors, *Didier-Werke AG* which manufactures refractory products as part of Dutch *RHI Magnesita N.V.* and *Salzgitter AG* whose focus is on steal. The two real estate companies in 2018 are *HAMBORNER REIT AG* and *Harpen AG* initially called *Hamborner Bergbau AG* and *Harpener Bergbau AG* in 2018. The mining operations of both companies are acquired by *Ruhrkohle AG* in the late 1960 s. Afterwards, *Harpen* manages its existing real estate portfolio and *Hamborner* acts as asset management company for the Thyssen family. Several portfolio and ownership changes later both companies are purely in real estate and asset management in 2018. The last company which changes their industry from mining and quarrying is *Preußische Bergwerks- und Hütten AG* (*Preussag*). In 2018, the company operates in the tourism sector and therefore in the services industry. The last described change which is based on several more or less successful strategic moves within the 60 years can be classified as an actual change of an industry. Today's business has nothing to do with the company's products of 1958. This is also the case for *Littelfuse GmbH*. However, all other 15 companies move either within the value chain of a product or focus on one particular area in which they were already active like the real estate of the mining companies. In the case of the real estate companies, they have changed their portfolio considerably over the decades but built it on existing assets.

Overall, there are just single cases of major industry changes. Nevertheless, these cases exist and can be successful. Yet it is not normal to change the industry within the observation period of 60 years. It needs to be considered that the used industry classification is on a high level. Without a detailed analysis of the companies' product portfolios the assumption is that the enterprises are adapting their products and services over the years. Several areas of their businesses might be successful others are less successful. However, radical changes are rare. Therefore, the structural changes of the German economy between 1958 and 2018 are based on the downfall of enterprises and not on the existing companies' change of industries.

Table 6.8 Industry Development of the Survivors from 1958 to 2018

Industry	**Survivors** [number of enterprises]						
	1958		**2018**				
			Remain		**Change Δ**	**Total**	
Accommodation & food service activities	–	–	–	–	–	**–**	**–**
Commerce	13	*11.9%*	13	*100.0%*	*+ 7*	**20**	***18.3%***
Construction	3	*2.8%*	3	*100.0%*	–	**3**	***2.8%***
Energy & water	12	*11.0%*	12	*100.0%*	–	**12**	***11.0%***
Financial & insurance activities	–	–	–	–	–	**–**	**–**
Human health & social work activities	–	–	–	–	–	**–**	**–**
Information & communication	2	*1.8%*	2	*100.0%*	*+ 1*	**3**	***2.8%***
Manufacturing	61	*56.0%*	53	*86.9%*	*−2*	**59**	***54.1%***
Mining & quarrying	11	*10.1%*	2	*18.2%*	*−9*	**2**	***1.8%***
Public administration & defense	–	–	–	–	–	**–**	**–**
Real estate	–	–	–	–	*+ 2*	**2**	***1.8%***
Service activities	–	–	–	–	*+ 1*	**1**	***0.9%***
Transportation & storage	7	*6.4%*	7	*100.0%*	–	**7**	***6.4%***
Total	**109**	***100.0%***	**92**	***84.4%***	**–**	**109**	***100.0%***

Source: Author's own table.

Two cases of enterprises in the sample which change their major focus but do not exist anymore or cancel this transformation are *Mannesmann AG* and *Daimler-Benz AG*. In 1990, *Mannesmann* whose roots lie in the production of steel pipes back in the late 19th century starts to invest in a new telecommunications business area. Within ten years they become one of the largest mobile operators in Germany and in several other European countries. Due to their success in changing from a manufacturing towards an information and communication company *Mannesmann* becomes an acquisition target of British *Vodafone AirTouch plc.* which in the end takes over the established German company and splits it.[27] Due to *Mannesmann's* successful transformation they are taken over

[27] See Section 3.7.1.3 for more details of *Mannesmann AG*.

which is only possible because they are listed. Today, *Mannesmann* does not exist as an independent company anymore.

In the 1980 s and 1990 s, *Daimler* with its origins as car manufacturer is on the way to become a technology conglomerate based on the experiences of the oil crises. The objective is to become more independent of the fluctuations in the automotive sector, therefore *Daimler* acquires, among others, *Messerschmitt-Bölkow-Blohm*, *MTU München*, *Dornier* and struggling *AEG*. This leads to a holding structure with several subsidiaries including *Deutsche Aerospace AG* (*DASA*) which bundles the aerospace activities. Because the diversification is not as successful as expected *Daimler* refocuses on its core in the mid-1990 s. Another huge acquisition of / merger with US-based *Chrysler Corp.* follows in 1998 to become one of the largest car manufacturers in the world. But already in 2007 *Daimler* sells its majority in *Chrysler*. Since then, *Daimler* focuses on passenger cars (including *Mercedes-Benz* and *smart*) as well trucks (including *Mercedes-Benz* and *Freightliner Trucks*). Despite several attempts to change the industry or diversify the activities *Daimler* is back to manufacturing passenger cars as well as trucks. Of course, over the last decades the portfolio within the car and truck business changes but it remains the same industry.

6.1.6 Growth, Stagnation and Decline: The Broad Range to Survive

Although the 109 enterprises survive from 1958 to 2018, their development differs from each other and not only in terms of ownership and industry continuity. Their achieved growth over the six decades and therefore their size varies, as well. This also leads to the differentiation between reappearers and additional survivors. In reference to the liability of smallness and the previously described liability of relative smallness, size is an important attribute of a company in order to survive or fail. Therefore, the enterprises growth rates from 1958 to 2018 are analyzed to better understand which rates and size need to be achieved for a continuing company (see Table 6.9).

On average, all 109 survivors achieve a compound annual growth rate of their revenues of 5.2% between 1958 and 2018. This corresponds to a doubling of their size every 13.7 years within the timeframe of six decades. Nevertheless, the growth rate is below the CAGR of 5.7% of the German GDP in the same period which represents the development of all enterprises based on the produced final goods and services.[28] As highlighted, this average measure includes companies that do well and those that do poorly. Similarly, the survivors of this thesis' sample include enterprises which develop well but also which develop less well. Distinguishing between the reappearing companies which are part of both lists of the 250 largest enterprises of 1958 and of 2018 as well as the additional survivors which are only part of the 1958 ranking but also survive until 2018 the difference becomes obvious. The 62 reappearers have a revenue CAGR of 7.1% which is above the GDP growth rate and the 47 additional survivors of only 2.8% which is far below the GDP rate.[29] Hence the reappearers grow two and a half times as much as the additional survivors. Due to the exponential development the size differences can be extreme after 60 years. Looking at the different company types of 1958 every group of reappearers grows faster than the corresponding group of the additional survivors. This is logical because the latter category does not appear in the list of the 250 largest enterprises of 2018. Their growth of the past six decades is not sufficient to reappear on the ranking. The average growth of the reappearers is even higher than the modeled growth rate of 6.6% which describes the required growth of the average company of 1958 to become the average company of 2018. Therefore, the reappearers outperform the average which often results in better rankings. 38 of the reappearers (61.3%) can improve their ranking with *Albrecht KG Lebensmittel-Filialbetrieb* as the strongest climber from position 235 to position eleven (+224) and with *Daimler-Benz AG* which has the smallest improvement by three positions from rank five to two (but there are not many larger companies ahead at all). To achieve such a leap *Aldi Süd* has an average growth rate of 12.7% between 1958 and 2018 which is also the highest rate in the entire sample. *Daimler AG* still grows with 8.0% annually to become the second largest enterprise in 2018. On the other hand, 24 of the reappearers (28.7%) slip in their ranking, some more sharply like *Kaufhof AG* from position 30 to 216 (−186), others less sharply like *Siemens AG* from position three to five (−2). *GALERIA Kaufhof GmbH* achieves a CAGR of 2.3% which is far below average and GDP. *Siemens AG* grows by 6.7% annually which is only slightly below the reappearers' average but still higher than the growth of the GDP. Furthermore, 48 of the 62 reappearers (77.4%) are among the 125 largest enterprises of 2018 which is an even higher number than in 1958 when 42 entities (67.7%) of the reappearers are in the first half of the ranking. The remaining 14 reappearers (22.6%) are in the second half of the 2018 ranking

[28] For the overview of the GDP see Section 4.1.

[29] A CAGR of 7.1% corresponds to a doubling of revenues in slightly more than every ten years and 2.8% to a doubling only every 25 years.

which means that if a company reappears on the 2018 list it is part of the larger entities even within the 250 largest companies.

It stands out that enterprises with a high share of exports like *Daimler AG* (8.0%), *Siemens AG* (6.7%) as well as *Bayerische Motoren Werke AG* (12.0%) achieve superior growth rates between 1958 and 2018. On the other hand, companies with a national focus like *GALERIA Kaufhof GmbH* (2.3%), *Karstadt Warenhaus GmbH* (1.8%) and *Unilever Deutschland GmbH* (0.5%) achieve below-average growth rates. Lower rates can also be found at companies with a regional focus like *Fischereihafen-Betriebsgesellschaft mbH* and *Straßenverkehrsgenossenschaft Hamburg eG.* This leads to the assumption that to achieve above-average rates over the last 60 years it requires a business focus on other countries than Germany. A second way to achieve such high growth rates can be exemplified by *Aldi Süd* which has a CAGR of 12.7%. In the meantime, *Aldi Süd* is also present in countries outside of Germany but its focus is the German market similar to *Aldi Nord* which has a CAGR of 10.9%. These companies have changed the business model of grocery stores and implemented a new way for customers to shop groceries. This business model innovation in the German market led to two-digit growth rates between 1958 and 2018.

Investigating the different company types as of 1958 including the reappearers and the additional survivors, foundation-owned enterprises show the highest growth rate with 8.0%. Both entities are among the reappearers which means that no additional survivor reduces their average. Similarly, the two foreign family-owned enterprises are also only reappearers and have the second highest growth rate with 5.9%. Family firms and cooperatives follow with 5.7% and 5.4%. Both types and all remaining ones include additional survivors whose growth rate decreases their total rate. Public companies and state-owned enterprises have the same CAGR of 4.7%. The five multiple companies-owned enterprises and the twelve foreign subsidiaries grow only by 4.5% and 3.8%, respectively.

In reference to the continuity and discontinuity of ownership in Section 6.1.4 the revenue CAGR of all 109 survivors is calculated taking into account if the enterprises remain or change their company types (see Table 6.10). In contrast to Table 6.9 the type of company in 2018 is also considered.

First, the enterprises which continue with their ownership structure and therefore with their company type are analyzed (the diagonal fields).[30] Again, foundations show the highest CAGR with 8.0%. These are *Carl Zeiss* and *Zahnradfabrik Friedrichshafen AG.* The former company's revenues grow from EUR 199.4 m [DM 390.0 m] in 1958 to EUR 5.8bn in 2018 which corresponds to a

[30] For the number of enterprises of each continuing company type see Table 6.7.

Table 6.9 Revenue CAGR of Reappearers & Additional Survivors from 1958 to 2018 per Company Type in 1958

#	Type of company	Survivors			
		1958	**2018** [revenue CAGR (%) 1958–2018]		
			Reappearers	**Additional survivors**	**Total**
1	Family-owned business	**39**	*7.7%*	*3.3%*	***5.7%***
2	Foreign family-owned business	**2**	*5.9%*	–	***5.9%***
3	Foundation-owned enterprise	**2**	*8.0%*	–	***8.0%***
4	Multiple companies-owned enterprise	**5**	*6.5%*	*1.5%*	***4.5%***
5	Public company	**23**	*6.9%*	*1.4%*	***4.7%***
6	Cooperative	**5**	*7.8%*	*1.7%*	***5.4%***
7	State-owned enterprise	**21**	*6.9%*	*4.2%*	***4.7%***
8	Foreign subsidiary	**12**	*5.5%*	*1.4%*	***3.8%***
	Total	**–**	***7.1%***	***2.8%***	***5.2%***
	2018	**109**	**62**	**47**	**–**

Source: Author's own table.

CAGR of 5.8%. *ZF Friedrichshafen AG*, on the other hand, performs a CAGR of 10.3% from EUR 102.3 m [DM 200.0] to EUR 36.9bn. Based on these revenues the average growth rate is 8.0% and both companies remain among the 250 largest enterprises in 2018. The nine public companies and the one foreign family firm, *Ford Werke GmbH*, which continue as their company type have the second highest growth rates with 6.8% each. For example, with the mentioned rate *Ford* grows from EUR 399.3 m [DM 781.0 m] in 1958 to EUR 21.1bn in 2018. As public companies, for example, *Bayerische Motoren Werke AG* which has the second highest growth rate of all 109 survivors with 12.2%, grows from EUR 99.7 m [DM 195.9 m] to EUR 97.5bn within 60 years while *Deutz AG* only grows with a CAGR of 2.7% from already EUR 351.8 m [DM 688.0 m] in 1958 to EUR 1.8bn in 2018. *Deutz AG* is not part of the 250 largest enterprises of 2018 anymore. 20 of the 39 family businesses from 1958 continue as family businesses in 2018 and they grow on average by 6.2%. As earlier mentioned, *Aldi Süd* is the fastest growing company with 12.7% and belongs to the continuous family firms. Additionally, *Claas KGaA mbH* and *Carl Spaeter GmbH* are also part of this group with growth rates of 7.1% and 2.6%, respectively. The first company with a negative growth rate over 60 years also appears in the group of the continuous family businesses. It is *Dierig Holding AG* with revenues of EUR 128.6 m [DM 251.5 m] in 1958 which declines on average by 1.3% annually to revenues of EUR 60 m in 2018.[31]

The ten foreign subsidiaries have the lowest growth rate with 4.5%. But the spread is high. *Unilever Deutschland GmbH* grows only by 0.5% while *John Deere GmbH & Co. KG* has a growth rate of 7.6%. Depending on the parent company's strategy thc subsidiaries can fulfill various purposes, i.e., first, the subsidiary can mainly act as a sales office for Germany and therefore has a limited market area, second, the subsidiary has also production facilities which are used to fulfill the demand for Germany or third, the production facilities are also used to produce products which are exported. In the cases of the first and second strategy the growth opportunities are much more limited due to a smaller market compared to an export orientation. Therefore, the growth rate is expected to be smaller if the focus is on the German market only.[32] *John Deere* exports its vehicles globally and is an example of the third strategy. Although *Unilever* manufactures certain products in Germany and exports them the focus is on the German market. The same applies to *Philips GmbH*. The three oil companies *ExxonMobil Central Europe Holding GmbH*, *Shell Deutschland Oil GmbH* and *BP Europa SE* have production (and research) facilities in Germany and export the products to a larger extent. It seems possible that the export orientation has an impact on the past growth of the mentioned foreign subsidiaries.

All five surviving cooperatives remain cooperatives in 2018 and achieve a growth rate of 5.4% on average. They include the two supermarket operators and wholesalers *Edeka Zentrale AG & Co. KG* and *REWE-ZENTRALFINANZ eG* which show the highest growth rates of this company type with 7.6% and 9.8%, respectively. *BayWa AG* and *Raiffeisen Waren GmbH* follow with 6.0% and 4.8% while *Straßenverkehrsgenossenschaft Hamburg eG* declines by −1.5%. The first two are wholesalers of, among others, grain, seeds and animal feeds while the latter is a service provider for the transport and logistics industry limited to

[31] See Section 6.1.7 for a more detailed analysis of family firms.

[32] As highlighted earlier in the chapter the national focus can also be a strategy for German enterprises, e.g., *GALERIA Kaufhof GmbH* with a low growth rate or *Aldi Süd* which was able to achieve a high market share.

the Hamburg area. In the meantime, *BayWa* has also international operations in energy and building materials while *Raiffeisen* has shifted its focus from the state of Hesse to Germany with a few activities in Denmark.

The 14 of the 21 state-owned enterprises which remain state-owned in 2018 have a CAGR of 5.2% which is slightly lower than the GDP growth. *EnBW Energie Baden-Württemberg AG* and *EWE AG* have the highest rates with 8.6% and 8.4% followed by the two public utilities *Stadtwerke München GmbH* and *Stadtwerke Frankfurt am Main Holding GmbH* with 7.1% and 6.4%. Both do not only operate in the cities which own them. They also have operations outside of Germany like wind parks in Belgium and Norway or the stake in *Fraport AG* which operates airports around the world. *Deutsche Bahn AG* remains the largest state-owned enterprise but declines from position one to 15 within the six decades with a growth rate of 4.3%.

For multiple companies-owned enterprises no average growth rate can be calculated because none of these enterprises from 1958 remain this company type until 2018.

Table 6.10 Average Revenue CAGR (1958–2018) of the Survivors of 1958 per Company Type in 1958 & 2018

Type of company	**Survivors**									
	1958	**2018** [revenue CAGR (%) 1958–2018]								
		FB	**FFB**	**FD**	**MCE**	**PC**	**COOP**	**SOE**	**FS**	**Total**
Family-owned business	**39**	*6.2%*	*4.6%*	*6.5%*	–	*5.3%*	–	–	*3.6%*	***5.7%***
Foreign family-owned business	**2**	–	*6.8%*	–	–	–	–	–	*5.0%*	***5.9%***
Foundation-owned enterprise	**2**	–	–	*8.0%*	–	–	–	–	–	***8.0%***
Multiple companies-owned enterprise	**5**	*6.1%*	*2.2%*	–	–	*6.7%*	–	–	*0.8%*	***4.5%***
Public company	**23**	*−2.4%*	*2.0%*	–	*7.6%*	*6.8%*	*6.1%*	–	*3.3%*	***4.7%***
Cooperative	**5**	–	–	–	–	–	*5.4%*	–	–	***5.4%***
State-owned enterprise	**21**	*8.9%*	–	–	–	*6.5%*	–	*5.2%*	*4.7%*	***5.7%***
Foreign subsidiary	**12**	*−3.3%*	–	*3.9%*	–	–	–	–	*4.5%*	***3.8%***
Total	**–**	***5.6%***	***4.0%***	***6.6%***	***7.6%***	***6.4%***	***5.5%***	***5.2%***	***3.8%***	***5.2%***
2018	**109**	**24**	**10**	**8**	**1**	**21**	**6**	**14**	**25**	**–**

Source: Author's own table.

The growth rates with regard to the listing of the 109 survivors are similar for enterprises which remain non-listed or listed over the six decades with 5.4% and 5.8%, respectively (see Table 6.11).[33] Therefore, listed companies grow 0.4% faster on average. But both rates are close to the average GDP rate. Enterprises which are delisted between 1958 and 2018 grow only by 2.5% including *Stahlwerke Bochum GmbH* with −2.4%, *WMF Group GmbH* with 4.2% and *Alliance Healthcare Deutschland AG* with 6.1%. On the other hand, companies which go public during that period grow by 7.2% on average including Salzgitter AG with 4.0%, *Henkel AG & Co. KGaA* with 7.4% and *Deutsche Lufthansa AG* with 10.6%. This relatively high average growth rate reflects the often-highlighted intention of an IPO and the related told equity story of accelerated growth.

Table 6.11 Revenue CAGR of Survivors from 1958 to 2018 per Listing Status in 1958 & 2018

Listing	**Survivors**			
	1958	**2018** [revenue CAGR (%) 1958–2018]		
		Non-listed	**Listed**	**Total**
Non-listed	**67**	*5.4%*	*7.2%*	***5.7%***
Listed	**42**	*2.5%*	*5.8%*	***4.4%***
Total	–	***4.7%***	***6.3%***	***5.2%***
2018	**109**	**73**	**36**	–

Source: Author's own table.

Overall, the data provides evidence that a company's export orientation has a positive impact on the growth rates from 1958 to 2018 independent if the enterprise is founded in Germany or if it is a foreign subsidiary. A national or regional focus lowers the long-term growth rates unless an innovative business model allows to capture a large share of the limited market. The average revenue growth rate of the sample with the 109 survivors (5.2%) is below the average of the GDP rate between 1958 and 2018 (5.7%). Both, GDP and the sample, include companies which perform well and poorly. The company rates vary widely from two-digit growth rates to negative ones which supports a growing spread between the largest and smaller enterprises in 2018. To further investigate the required growth rates to remain one of the largest enterprises in 2018 the 25 fastest and

[33] See Table 6.1 for the number of entities. 55 entities (50.5%) remain non-listed while 24 entities (22.0%) remain listed.

slowest growing enterprises are presented. This also helps to understand which companies are behind the presented average figures.

6.1.6.1 The 25 Fastest Growing Enterprises

Of the 25 fastest growing companies of the 1958 sample five confirm that two-digit average growth rates can be achieved even over a period of 60 years (see Table 6.12). Growing by 12.7% annually *Aldi Süd* has the highest CAGR in the sample and has doubled its business every 5.8 years—more than ten times in the observation period. This growth as well as the high rates of *REWE-ZENTRALFINANZ eG* (9.8%) on position six of the 25 fastest growing companies and *Edeka Zentrale AG & Co. KG* (7.6%) on position 21 support the earlier mentioned high concentration in food retail. There are only a few big players left. In general, commerce is an industry in which high growth rates could be achieved between 1958 and 2018—including *Heraeus Holding GmbH* and *Otto GmbH & Co. KG* outside of food retail. Extraordinary growth can also be identified in the automotive industry led by *Bayerische Motoren Werke AG* (12.2%) and the suppliers *ZF Friedrichshafen AG* (10.3%) as well as *Robert Bosch GmbH* (8.8%). *Volkswagen AG* as the only company changing from a state-owned enterprise to a family-owned business achieves a CAGR of 8.9% to become the largest enterprise in 2018.

Overall, two-digit growth rates are feasible even over a period of 60 years but they remain exceptions. Such rates are often linked to the rise or change of industries like automotive within manufacturing or to food retail within commerce.

6.1.6.2 The 25 Slowest Growing Enterprises

Besides extraordinary growth rates the dataset also shows that companies can survive with a low one-digit or even negative growth rate over six decades (see Table 6.13). In the latter case, the size of the company—based on revenue—is smaller in 2018 compared to 1958. *Harpen AG* as a former mining and quarrying company changed to real estate and decreased annually on average by 3.3% which is the highest negative rate in the sample. *Dierig Holding AG* remains in the hands of the Dierig family but the company experiences a decline of on average 1.3% annually. The company mainly operated in textile and has a large revenue share in real estate in 2018. The list of the 25 slowest growing enterprises contains a disproportionate number of companies which are a foreign subsidiary (9) or a foreign family-business (6) in 2018. Of these 15 companies only *Philips GmbH* and *Unilever Deutschland GmbH* were a foreign subsidiary in 1958. The remaining 13 enterprises experienced ownership discontinuities and have been

Table 6.12 The 25 Fastest Growing Enterprises of 1958 [1958–2018]

#[34]	Company name 2018	Founding year	Rev. 1958 [mEUR]	Rev. 2018 [mEUR]	CAGR '58-'18	Company type[35]	Industry
11	Aldi Süd[36]	1913	46	59,000	12.7%	FB	Commerce
4	Bayerische Motoren Werke AG	1916	100	97,480	12.2%	PC	Manufacturing
20	Deutsche Lufthansa AG	1926 / 1953	87	35,844	10.6%	PC	Transportation & storage
35	Heraeus Holding GmbH	1851	51	20,295	10.5%	FB	Commerce
18	ZF Friedrichshafen AG	1915	102	36,929	10.3%	FD	Manufacturing
13	REWE-ZENTRALFINANZ eG	1927	195	53,378	9.8%	COOP	Commerce
50	Otto GmbH & Co. KG	1949	51	13,653	9.8%	FB	Commerce
53	Marquard & Bahls AG	1947	51	13,286	9.7%	FFB	Commerce
41	Bertelsmann SE & Co. KGaA	1835	69	17,673	9.7%	FD	Information & communication
27	HOCHTIEF AG	1873	133	23,882	9.0%	FS	Construction
1	Volkswagen AG	1937	1,390	235,849	8.9%	FB	Manufacturing

(continued)

34 The rank, the name as well as the company type and industry reflect the 2018 status.

35 The explanations of the company type abbreviations can be found in Table 60 of the appendix in the electronic supplementary material.

36 *Aldi Süd* is defined as the successor company of *Albrecht KG Lebensmittel-Filialbetrieb*. Therefore, *Aldi Nord* does not appear on the list. If the 1958 numbers of *Albrecht KG Lebensmittel-Filialbetrieb* are used to calculate the revenue CAGR for *Aldi Nord* the company achieves a growth rate of 10.9%.

Table 6.12 (continued)

#	Company name 2018	Founding year	Rev. 1958 [mEUR]	Rev. 2018 [mEUR]	CAGR '58-'18	Company type	Industry
46	Merck KGaA	1668	94	14,836	8.8%	FB	Manufacturing
6	Robert Bosch GmbH	1886	511	78,465	8.8%	FD	Manufacturing
33	EnBW Energie Baden-Württemberg AG	1909	146	20,618	8.6%	SOE	Energy & water
83	Dr. August Oetker KG	1891	51	7,140	8.6%	FB	Manufacturing
40	HeidelbergCement AG	1873	134	18,075	8.5%	PC	Manufacturing
102	EWE AG	1930	45	5,704	8.4%	SOE	Energy & water
14	Continental AG	1871	352	44,404	8.4%	PC	Manufacturing
2	Daimler AG	1883	1,611	167,362	8.0%	PC	Manufacturing
60	Hapag-Lloyd AG	1847	139	11,515	7.6%	MCE	Transportation & storage
12	Edeka Zentrale AG & Co. KG	1907	648	53,600	7.6%	COOP	Commerce
99	John Deere GmbH & Co. KG	1925	74	6,032	7.6%	FS	Manufacturing
37	TUI AG	1923	260	19,524	7.5%	PC	Service activities
133	Bilfinger SE	1880	56	4,153	7.4%	PC	Construction
36	Henkel AG & Co. KGaA	1876	272	19,899	7.4%	FB	Manufacturing

Source: Author's own table.

acquired by foreign companies. The causal relationship between the acquisition and the low growth rate cannot be identified based on the available data. It can be assumed that the 13 companies have become an acquisition target of a foreign enterprise because of their poor performance and with the objective to improve the situation.

GEA Group AG and *Galeria Kaufhof AG* remain among the 250 largest enterprises in 2018 although they have one of the lowest growth rates of the sample. Due to their sizes in 1958 (EUR 665 m / EUR 677 m), they achieve EUR 4.8bn and EUR 2.6bn in revenue in 2018 with a CAGR of 3.4% and 2.3%. *DEA Deutsche Erdoel AG* and *Busch-Jaeger Elektro GmbH* have similar growth rates (3.3% / 3.1%) but drop out of the ranking due to their smaller sizes in 1958 (EUR 268 m / EUR 76 m).

Overall, companies can survive despite negative or small growth rates but then they often experience ownership discontinuities, for example, being acquired by foreign companies. A high initial size helps to remain one of the largest enterprises but also bears the risk of being acquired like *Kaufhof AG*.

6.1.7 Family-Owned Enterprises: Applied Long-Term Orientation

In the following the family business specific results of the previous sub-chapters are consolidated as well as additional in-depth analyses regarding family firms are performed to further approach the research question. Overall, large German family firms show a much higher survival and ownership continuity rate than research often refers to. Furthermore, the surviving family enterprises become the oldest company type in 2018 which supports the attributed long-term orientation. Extending the view and considering foreign family firms and family foundations it can be confirmed that family-owned enterprises have a more pronounced long-term orientation. However, the differences in the development of family firms—growth and decline—are huge.

Survival and Family Ownership Continuity

The 87 family-owned enterprises of 1958 have a survival rate of 44.8% (39 / 87) which is slightly higher than the overall survival rate of 43.6% (109 / 250). 55.2% of the family firms experience a downfall between 1958 and 2018. These results are compared to the often-cited study by John Ward who identifies a survival rate of only 20.0% in his sample of 200 US-based family-owned manufacturers

Table 6.13 The 25 Slowest Growing Enterprises of 1958 [1958–2018]

#[37]	Company name 2018	Founding year	Rev. 1958 [mEUR]	Rev. 2018 [mEUR]	CAGR '58-'18	Company type[38]	Industry
117	GEA Group AG	1881	665	4,828	3.4%	PC	Manufacturing
–	DEA Deutsche Erdoel AG	1899	268	1,892	3.3%	FS	Mining & quarrying
–	Busch-Jaeger Elektro GmbH	1879	76	476	3.1%	FS	Manufacturing
–	RÜTGERS Germany GmbH	1849	89	543	3.1%	FS	Manufacturing
–	Deutz AG	1864	352	1,779	2.7%	PC	Manufacturing
–	Carl Spaeter GmbH	1875	307	1,418	2.6%	FB	Commerce
216	GALERIA Kaufhof GmbH	1879	677	2,600	2.3%	FFB	Commerce
–	Varta AG	1887	71	272	2.3%	FFB	Manufacturing
–	Kelheim Fibres GmbH	1935	47	169	2.2%	FFB	Manufacturing
–	Dyckerhoff GmbH	1864	99	352	2.1%	FFB	Manufacturing
–	Philips GmbH	1926	380	1,248	2.0%	FS	Manufacturing
–	Karstadt Warenhaus GmbH	1881	735	2,088	1.8%	FFB	Commerce
–	Didier-Werke AG	1834	90	243	1.7%	FS	Manufacturing
–	Pelikan Group GmbH	1838	87	227	1.6%	FFB	Manufacturing

(continued)

[37] The rank, the name as well as the company type and industry reflect the 2018 status. If no rank is provided the company is not part of the 250 largest enterprises of 2018.

[38] The explanations of the company type abbreviations can be found in Table 60 of the appendix in the electronic supplementary material.

Table 6.13 (continued)

#	Company name 2018	Founding year	Rev. 1958 [mEUR]	Rev. 2018 [mEUR]	CAGR '58-'18	Company type	Industry
–	WV Energie AG	1904	104	197	1.1%	SOE	Commerce
–	Eternit GmbH	1929	83	131	0.8%	FS	Manufacturing
–	HAMBORNER REIT AG	1953	60	83	0.5%	PC	Real Estate
–	Unilever Deutschland GmbH	1930	1,079	1,489	0.5%	FS	Commerce
–	Rosenthal GmbH	1879	54	75	0.5%	FS	Manufacturing
–	Fischereihafen-Betriebsgesellschaft mbH	1896	58	28	−1.2%	SOE	Transportation & storage
–	Dierig Holding AG	1805	129	60	−1.3%	FB	Manufacturing
–	Straßenverkehrsgenossen-schaft Hamburg eG	1947	77	32	−1.5%	COOP	Transportation & storage
–	Gerflor DLW GmbH	1899	99	34	−1.8%	FS	Manufacturing
–	Stahlwerke Bochum GmbH	1820 / 1947	142	34	−2.4%	FB	Manufacturing
–	Harpen AG	1856	216	28	−3.3%	FB	Real Estate

Source: Author's own table.

between 1924 and 1984.[39] The findings of this dissertation show a much higher survival rate with 44.8% for large German enterprises compared to Ward's 20.0%. Moreover, Ward finds a 13.0% ownership continuity rate in his sample including growing, stagnating, and declining companies. In comparison, 23.0% (20) of the 87 family firms in this thesis remain in the hands of the family independent of their performance. Again, the rate is much higher than Ward calculates for the US family firms. The results show that the survival and ownership continuity rates need to be adopted for large German family businesses compared to Ward.[40]

On the other hand, 19 of the 87 family businesses of 1958 (21.8%) experience ownership discontinuities until 2018. Six family firms (6.9%) become foreign family businesses of which only one remains in the hand of the same family—*Marquard & Bahls AG*—and the other five change ownership.[41] Five family firms (5.8%) of 1958 become foundation-owned enterprises of which four are related to the family.[42] Only *Saarstahl* is owned by a foundation which was not initiated by the owner family.

Overall, German family enterprises have higher survival and ownership continuation rates than public companies in the same sample and the often-cited rates by Ward have. Foundations are a way to perpetuate the ownership of a company whereas the move of the family abroad remains an exception.

Family businesses change to different company types but there are also different company types which become a family enterprise. This is the case for four companies of the 250 largest enterprises of 1958—*Volkswagenwerk GmbH*, *Wacker-Chemie GmbH*, *Stahlwerke Bochum AG* and *Harpener Bergbau AG*. *Volkswagen* is a very special case because it changes from a state-owned enterprise to a family-owned business. It is even more fascinating that descendants of the engineer who developed the initial *Volkswagen*, Ferdinand Porsche, are now the majority-owner of the company which was founded by the state to produce this car—the Porsche and Piëch family. In the case of *Wacker*, the Wacker family becomes majority owner in 2001 after decades of owning a 50% share. Both examples show a shared history with the company. This is not applicable to *Stahlwerke Bochum* and *Harpener Bergbau*. In these cases, a management team and an external investor acquire the majorities. Overall, the development from

---

[39] See Ward (2011, p. 2) as well as Section 2.2.2.2.

[40] See Table 6.2 and Table 6.7 in Section 6.1.1 and Section 6.1.4, respectively.

[41] The six foreign family-owned are *Marquard & Bahls AG*, *Ed. Züblin AG*, *WMF Group GmbH*, *Varta AG*, *Dyckerhoff GmbH* and *Pelikan Group GmbH*.

[42] The five foundation-owned enterprises are *Bertelsmann SE & Co. KGaA*, *Robert Bosch GmbH*, *KSB SE & Co. KGaA*, *BAUR Versand GmbH & Co. KG* and *Saarstahl AG*.

a non-family business to a family business is an exception in the cases of the largest enterprises in Germany. The trend is rather in the opposite direction.

Ownership Continuity Exceptions

Although an enterprise has the status of a family business in 1958 and 2018 based on the applied framework to track ownership changes, the company can experience one or multiple ownership discontinuities between both years. Therefore, all the 20 family businesses of 1958 which remain family-owned in 2018 are investigated if an ownership discontinuity happens. In 19 cases the owner family remains the same as for *Carl Spaeter GmbH*, *Voith GmbH & Co. KGaA* and *Bahlsen GmbH & Co. KG.* Only in the case of *Knorr-Bremse AG* does the ownership change from one family to another. In 1958, Joachim Vielmetter owns the majority of the manufacturing company. In 2018, Heinz Hermann Thiele is the majority owner and there is no family connection between the two. Thiele, who is part of the management board at that time, acquires the majority in 1985 / 1986 from Jens-Diether von Bandemer who is a member of the Vielmetter family in fourth generation after quarrels within the family and a lack of strategic orientation of the company.[43] The family business remains a family-owned enterprise, now in first generation again, and becomes quite successful over the last decades. On the other hand, a family business can remain majority owned by the same family but change its company type to a foreign family enterprise because the family moves abroad. Checking the six cases of family firms of 1958 which have become a foreign family business in 2018 *Th. Weisser KG / Marquard & Bahls AG* is the only entity which experiences such a company type change but in the hands of the same family. The Weisser family now in third generation owns 100% of the company in 2018 but is based in Switzerland in the meantime.

Age

Family-owned enterprises become the oldest company type with 148.7 years in 2018 when looking at all enterprise types and their continuous entities over the observation period of 60 years.[44] This development supports the long-term orientation of family firms. Nevertheless, surviving public companies which also do not change their company type between 1958 and 2018 achieve an average age of 140.0 years. This, on the other hand, shows that public companies can also operate in the long-term. However, their ownership continuity rate is much lower than the one of family firms. Only nine of the 56 public companies (16.1%)

---

[43] See, among others, Bößenecker (1985).

[44] See Table 6.5 in Section 6.1.2.

remain a public company over 60 years—compared to 23.0% of family firms which remain a family business (20 / 87). Nine public companies (16.1%) also become a foreign subsidiary which means that the public companies are acquired. Overall, taking into consideration the average age and the ownership continuity the attributed long-term orientation of family firms is supported.

Growth, Stagnation and Decline

The 1958 family businesses show an above-average growth with 5.7% compared to the average of 5.2% between 1958 and 2018.[45] Their growth rate is similar to the GDP CAGR in the same period.[46] Family firms which do not experience an ownership continuity have a higher growth rate of 6.2%. However, this rate is below the growth rate of continuous public companies (6.8%) as well as of foundations (8.0%) and foreign family firms (6.8%). But there are huge differences in the development of the continuous family businesses. 13 of the 20 continuous family businesses (65.0%) are reappearers which means that they are one of the 250 largest enterprises in 1958 as well as in 2018. These companies have a growth rate of 7.8% which is the second highest rate after foundations and similar to that of cooperatives. This sub-sample also includes *Aldi Süd* with the highest CAGR of the entire sample of 12.7%. Public companies show a lower rate of 7.3% among the reappearers.[47] The remaining seven family firms (35.0%) which are additional survivors and do not appear in the 2018 ranking have on average a growth rate of 3.2% including *Dierig Holding AG* with a negative rate of –1.3%.[48] In the highlighted cases the developments are linked to the industries the companies operate in—food retail in commerce and textile in manufacturing. Therefore, family-owned enterprises show a broad range of developments including growth as well as decline over the observation period of 60 years. Their growth rate is above-average looking at the reappearers but at the same time there are several firms which remain in the hands of a family despite a declining or stagnating development—the additional survivors.

Foreign Family-owned Businesses

A closer look is taken to foreign family-owned businesses due to certain similarities. Foreign family businesses have the lowest survival rate of all company

---

45 See Table 6.10 in Section 6.1.6.

46 See Figure 4.1 in Section 4.1.

47 See Table 6.21 in Section 6.1.8.

48 See Table 6.22 in Section 6.1.8.

types with only 25.0% from 1958 to 2018. Six of the eight enterprises fail. Analyzing these companies in more detail several patterns appear. Two of the firms, *Steinkohlenbergwerk Friedrich Heinrich AG* and *Steinkohlenbergwerk Heinrich Robert AG*, operate in mining and quarrying. Furthermore, both are ultimately owned by the French de Wendel family in 1958. Due to the consolidation and political decisions in Germany regarding the national hard coal production the two companies are acquired by or sold to *Ruhrkohle AG* in the late 1960 s and early 1970 s. Two additional foreign family businesses are owned by the Thyssen-Bornemisza family which are *Stahl- und Röhrenwerke Reisholz GmbH* and *Bremer Vulkan Schiffbau und Maschinenfabrik AG*—both in the manufacturing industry. 50.0% of the former company gets acquired by *Thyssen* in the 1960 s and later the company is sold to *Mannesmann*. The full integration follows. Shares of the latter company of the Thyssen-Bornemisza family are sold in the 1980 s which results in the loss of the family's majority. In 1996, *Bremer Vulkan Schiffbau und Maschinenfabrik AG* enters insolvency. The ownership of the Thyssen-Bornemisza family is mainly based on the kinship to the Thyssen family and the results of the disentanglement of *Vereinigte Stahlwerke AG*. Therefore, the shareholdings are more of an investment rather than an entrepreneurial activity.

Family Generations

The discontinued and failed family firms are also investigated regarding in which generation the companies stop being family-owned in reference to Ward's analysis and regarding the family generation in which a family business fails (see Table 6.14).[49] As shown in Section 5.8, most of the family firms in the 1958 dataset are in the third generation—32 entities (see Table 5.20). Similarly, most of the family firms also fail in the third generation—21 entities out of in total 67 discontinuing family-owned enterprises.[50] The second highest downfalls are in the first generation with 15 (22.4%) followed by the second generation with 12 (17.9%). This means that 48 of the 67 discontinued companies (71.6%) do not last through the third generation.

---

[49] See Section 2.2.2.2 for an overview of Ward.

[50] 67 is the result of the 87 family firms of 1958 minus the 20 continuous family-owned businesses which remain in the hands of the family. There are only two exceptions: The analysis includes *Knorr-Bremse* which is a family business in 1958 and 2018 but the family owner changes, and it excludes *Th. Weisser KG* because it remains in the hands of the same family although the company type changes from a family-owned company to a foreign family business.

Table 6.14 Family Generation Distribution of Discontinued Family-Owned Businesses of 1958

Family generation	**Discontinued family-owned businesses** [number of enterprises]	
	1958	
1st	15	*22.4%*
2nd	12	*17.9%*
3rd	21	*31.3%*
4th	8	*11.9%*
5th	6	*9.0%*
6th	3	*4.5%*
7th	2	*3.0%*
Total	**67**	***100.0%***

Source: Author's own table.

Of the 20 surviving family firms seven (35.0%) are not yet through the third generation while 13 (65.0%) are in the fourth or an older generation.[51] This means that 13 family firms have already proven to survive the third generation. This represents 14.9% of the 87 initial family-owned companies and additional 8.1%—seven entities—are still working on the long-term objective to survive the third generation. Overall, it can be stated that in 2018 48 of the 87 family firms (55.2%) of 1958 have not survived the third generation. In the best case, this number remains as it is but most likely it will increase because some of the seven companies in their first three generations still need to survive. In addition, 19 enterprises also failed in a later generation. Although the number of discontinuing companies decreases—also due to the smaller number in the sample—the risk remains.

Listing Status

In a next step, the listing statuses of 1958 and 2018 are considered again. They are applied to the ownership changes of family-owned enterprises (see Table 6.15). Overall, 61 (70.1%) of the 87 family businesses of 1958 are non-listed compared to 26 listed ones (29.9%). Of the former group 28 companies (45.9%) survive while 33 (54.1%) fail. The downfalls can be further split into three subsidiary

[51] The seven companies are *Knorr-Bremse AG, Axel Springer SE, Otto GmbH & Co. KG, Grillo Handel Holding GmbH, Aldi Süd, Claas KGaA mbH* and *Bahlsen GmbH & Co. KG.*

companies (4.9%) and 30 narrow downfalls (49.2%). Of the latter group, the listed family firms in 1958, eleven enterprises (42.3%) survive and 15 (57.7%) experience a downfall of which only one (3.8%) becomes a subsidiary company. Although the survival rates of non-listed and listed family-owned enterprises are close to each other with 45.9% and 42.3% only one (3.8%) out of 26 listed family businesses survives as a listed family business over 60 years. The company is *Christian Dierig AG* which is called *Dierig Holding AG* in 2018. None of the listed family firms becomes a non-listed family firm. The remaining ten family-owned enterprises (38.5%) experience an ownership change to become another company type. Of the 28 survivors which are non-listed in 1958 19 (31.1%) remain a family business while nine (14.8%%) change their company type. Interestingly, four non-listed firms (6.6%) become listed in 2018. Their names are *Henkel AG & Co.* KGaA, *Axel Springer SE*, *Knorr-Bremse AG* and *Merck KGaA* in 2018.[52]

The numbers show that listed family firms either fail or discontinue as family-owned over the observation period of 60 years. Only one of the 26 family businesses, *Dierig Holding AG*, remains listed and continuous as a family firm. However, as mentioned in the previous sub-chapter *Dierig* has a negative growth rate of −1.3% leading from revenues of EUR 128.6 m [DM 251.5 m] in 1958 to EUR 60 m in 2018.[53]

[52] *Knorr Bremse AG* is a special case among the four listed family businesses in 2018 because the company experienced an ownership change in 1985 from the Vielmetter and von Bademer family to Hermann Thiele but remains a family-owned enterprise.

[53] See Stotmeister (in press) for a detailed analysis of the development of family firms after their IPOs. Her results also confirm that families divest their shares of the family business after going public.

Table 6.15 Listing Development of the 87 Largest Family-Owned Enterprises of 1958 to 2018

Listing of family-owned enterprises	**1958**	**2018**							
		Survivors					**Downfalls**		
		Family-owned enterprises		**Other company types**		**Total**			
		Non-listed	**Listed**	**Non-listed**	**Listed**		**Subsidiary companies**	**Downfalls** (narrow)	**Total**
Non-listed	**61**	15	4	9	–	**28**	3	30	**33**
	70.1%	*24.6%*	*6.6%*	*14.8%*	–	***45.9%***	*4.9%*	*49.2%*	***54.1%***
Listed	**26**	–	1	3	7	**11**	1	14	**15**
	29.9%	–	*3.8%*	*11.5%*	*26.9%*	***42.3%***	*3.8%*	*53.8%*	***57.7%***
Total	**87**	**15**	**5**	**12**	**7**	**39**	**4**	**44**	**48**
	100.0%	***17.2%***	***5.7%***	***13.8%***	***8.0%***	***44.8%***	***4.6%***	***50.6%***	***55.2%***

Source: Author's own table.

6.1.8 Reappearers and Additional Survivors: The Big Difference in Development

In Sections 5.9 and 6.1.1 the reappearers and additional survivors are introduced. From the 250 largest enterprises of 1958 109 (43.6%) survive. These survivors can be divided into 62 reappearers (24.8%) which are also part of the list of the 250 largest enterprises of 2018 and 47 additional survivors (18.8%) which survive the observation period of 60 years, but which are not part of the 2018 list anymore (see Figure 6.2). They are too small. In the following, the characteristic developments of both groups are investigated.

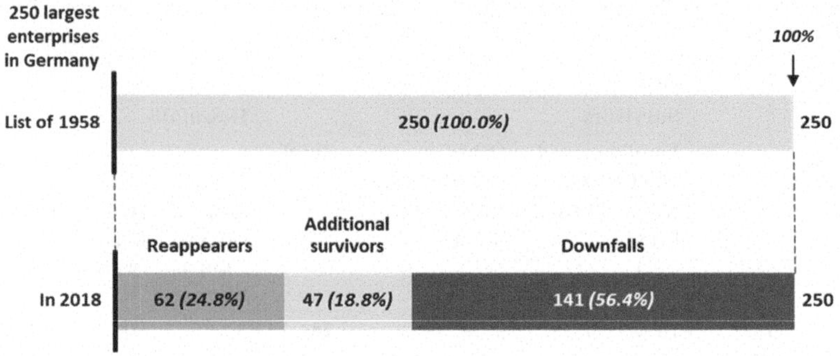

Figure 6.2 Reappearers, Additional Survivors & Downfalls of 1958 in 2018. (Source: Author's own figure)

Company Type

39 of the 62 reappearers remain the same company type over 60 years. It stands out that most changes happen towards public companies which represent the largest type in 2018. Ten enterprises in total become free float-owned—three family firms, two multiple companies-owned enterprises and five state-owned companies (see Table 6.16). This development supports Chandler's description of the evolution towards public companies. On the other hand, five public companies develop into a different company type. Two are acquired to become a foreign subsidiary. With two out of two and seven out of seven foundations and foreign subsidiaries experience no ownership discontinuity. These developments support the ideas of a foundation and show the strength of foreign companies for the German market. They remain among the largest enterprises over a period of 60 years.

Among the additional survivors which drop out of the 250 largest enterprises in 2018 it stands out that nine out of ten state-owned companies remain in the hands of the state or municipality despite lower or even negative growth rates (see Table 6.17). This can be seen as a commitment of the state to run the business independent of growth. A contrary development can be seen among public companies. Only one out of ten companies remains public while seven are acquired by a foreign entity. Public companies with low or negative growth rates experience ownership discontinuities. With seven out of 18 family firms also show a low ownership continuity rate. Again, with low growth rates the ownership discontinuity is higher.

Table 6.16 Ownership Continuity & Discontinuity of the Reappearers of 1958 to 2018

Type of company	Reappearers								
	1958	2018 [number of enterprises]							
		FB	FFB	FD	MCE	PC	COOP	SOE	FS
Family-owned business	21	*13*	*2*	*3*	–	*3*	–	–	–
Foreign family-owned business	2	–	*1*	–	–	–	–	–	*1*
Foundation-owned enterprise	2	–	–	*2*	–	–	–	–	–
Multiple companies-owned enterprise	3	*1*	–	–	–	*2*	–	–	–
Public company	13	–	*1*	–	*1*	*8*	*1*	–	*2*
Cooperative	3	–	–	–	–	–	*3*	–	–
State-owned enterprise	11	*1*	–	–	–	*5*	–	*5*	–
Foreign subsidiary	7	–	–	–	–	–	–	–	*7*
2018	**62**	**15**	**4**	**5**	**1**	**18**	**4**	**5**	**10**

Source: Author's own table.

Table 6.17 Ownership Continuity & Discontinuity of the Additional Survivors of 1958 to 2018

Type of company	Additional survivors								
	1958	2018 [number of enterprises]							
		FB	FFB	FD	MCE	PC	COOP	SOE	FS
Family-owned business	18	*7*	*4*	*2*	–	*2*	–	–	*3*
Foreign family-owned business	–	–	–	–	–	–	–	–	–
Foundation-owned enterprise	–	–	–	–	–	–	–	–	–
Multiple companies-owned enterprise	2	–	*1*	–	–	–	–	–	*1*
Public company	10	*1*	*1*	–	–	*1*	–	–	*7*
Cooperative	2	–	–	–	–	–	*2*	–	–
State-owned enterprise	10	–	–	–	–	–	–	*9*	*1*
Foreign subsidiary	5	*1*	–	*1*	–	–	–	–	*3*
2018	**47**	**9**	**6**	**3**	**–**	**3**	**2**	**9**	**15**

Source: Author's own table.

Overall, 22 of the 47 additional survivors remain the same company type in 2018 compared to 1958. It can be stated that a lower or negative growth rate is more often linked to ownership discontinuities than higher growth rates which keep the companies among the 250 largest enterprises between 1958 and 2018.

Age

Considering the age as a characteristic for survival there is only a small difference between the average age of the reappearers (130.7 years) and the additional survivors (136.3 years). Additional survivors tend to be slightly older than reappearers which can also be seen looking at the company types in 2018 (see Table 6.18). The largest difference is found for foundation-owned enterprises with 44.0 years. This can be explained by the small sample of only three foundations within the additional survivors including the old enterprise *Aktien-Gesellschaft der Dillinger Hüttenwerke* which was founded in 1685 and was the first German

Table 6.18 Average Age in 2018 of the Reappearers & Additional Survivors from 1958

#	Type of company in 2018	Survivors		
		Average age in 2018 [years]		
		Reappearers (62 companies)	**Additional survivors** (47 companies)	**Total** (109 companies)
1	Family-owned business	142.4	153.7	**146.6**
2	Foreign family-owned business	105.8	141.7	**127.3**
3	Foundation-owned enterprise	147.0	191.0	**163.5**
4	Multiple companies-owned enterprise	171.0	–	**171.0**
5	Public company	133.7	124.3	**132.4**
6	Cooperative	97.3	97.0	**97.2**
7	State-owned enterprise	117.0	131.8	**126.5**
8	Foreign subsidiary	126.0	123.3	**124.4**
	Total	**130.7**	**136.3**	**133.2**

Source: Author's own table.

company in 1809 to issue shares.[54] Overall, it can be stated that a company can also become old without becoming one of the largest enterprises 60 years later. This is also supported by the ranking "Germany's 50 oldest family businesses" introduced in Section 1.1. None of the 15 oldest family-owned enterprises is part of the 250 largest enterprises of 1958.[55]

Size

The key differentiator between the reappearers and the additional survivors is their size in 2018. As shown in Table 6.6 in Section 6.1.3, the 62 reappearers are on average nearly 30 times the size of the 47 additional survivors—EUR 26.8bn compared to EUR 0.9bn.[56] However, already in 1958, the average sizes of the companies show significant differences (see Table 6.19 and Table 6.20). All company types among the reappearers show a higher revenue on average in 1958 compared to the additional survivors. For example, the 21 family businesses in 1958 which reappear on the list of the 250 largest enterprises of 2018 have an average revenue of EUR 327.7 m compared to the 18 additional survivors with an average revenue of EUR 108.6 m. This applies to all other company types as well. The 2018 reappearers have three times the average revenue of the additional survivors already in 1958—EUR 447.4 m compared to EUR 149.1 m. The reappearers are already large in 1958 compared to the additional survivors. Overall, it can be stated that a higher initial revenue is supportive of the achievable size in the long-term.

[54] For the early development including the issue of shares see, for example, the commemorative publication for the 250th anniversary of *Dillinger Hütte* by Ham (1935).

[55] For the ranking see Stiftung Familienunternehmen (2021a, 2021b).

[56] For an overview of the average revenue size in 2018 based on the company types in 1958 and 2018 see Table 63 of the appendix in the electronic supplementary material.

Table 6.19 Average Revenue (1958) of the Reappearers of 1958 per Company Type in 1958 & 2018

Type of company	Reappearers									
	1958	2018 [average revenue mEUR in 1958]								
		FB	FFB	FD	MCE	PC	COOP	SOE	FS	Total
Family-owned business	**21**	129.2	56.2	288.5	–	1,408.3	–	–	–	**327.7**
Foreign family-owned business	**2**	–	399.3	–	–	–	–	–	142.7	**271.0**
Foundation-owned enterprise	**2**	–	–	150.8	–	–	–	–	–	**150.8**
Multiple companies-owned enterprise	**3**	143.2	–	–	–	142.9	–	–	–	**143.0**
Public company	**13**	–	677.0	–	139.1	439.3	204.5	–	132.4	**369.2**
Cooperative	**3**	–	–	–	–	–	450.1	–	–	**450.1**
State-owned enterprise	**11**	1,390.2	–	–	–	856.1	–	777.8	–	**869.1**
Foreign subsidiary	**7**	–	–	–	–	–	–	–	553.4	**553.4**
Total	**–**	**214.2**	**297.2**	**233.5**	**139.1**	**683.7**	**388.7**	**777.8**	**428.2**	**447.4**
2018	**62**	**15**	**4**	**5**	**1**	**18**	**4**	**5**	**10**	**–**

Source: Author's own table.

Table 6.20 Average Revenue (1958) of the Additional Survivors of 1958 per Company Type in 1958 & 2018

Type of company	**Additional survivors**									
	1958	**2018** [average revenue mEUR in 1958]								
		FB	**FFB**	**FD**	**MCE**	**PC**	**COOP**	**SOE**	**FS**	**Total**
Family-owned business	**18**	115.5	79.5	62.4	–	82.4	–	–	179.8	**108.6**
Foreign family-owned business	**–**	–	–	–	–	–	–	–	–	**–**
Foundation-owned enterprise	**–**	–	–	–	–	–	–	–	–	**–**
Multiple companies-owned enterprise	**2**	–	46.8	–	–	–	–	–	83.3	**65.1**
Public company	**10**	141.6	734.7	–	–	351.8	–	–	121.2	**207.7**
Cooperative	**2**	–	–	–	–	–	79.8	–	–	**79.8**
State-owned enterprise	**10**	–	–	–	–	–	–	58.9	74.1	**60.5**
Foreign subsidiary	**5**	215.8	–	227.5	–	–	–	–	545.9	**416.2**
Total	**–**	**129.6**	**183.3**	**117.4**	**–**	**172.2**	**79.8**	**58.9**	**212.2**	**149.1**
2018	**47**	**9**	**6**	**3**	**–**	**3**	**2**	**9**	**15**	**–**

Source: Author's own table.

Growth

To reappear on the list of the 250 largest enterprises of 2018 the 62 companies have an average growth rate of 7.1% over 60 years. In comparison, the 47 additional survivors grow with a CAGR of 2.8%. In total, the 109 survivors have an average growth rate of 5.2% which is below the GDP rate for the same period.[57]

Within the group of reappearers specific family businesses show extraordinary growth rates. Continuous family-owned businesses achieve the second highest growth rate of 7.8% similar to that of cooperatives. Only continuous foundation-owned companies have a higher rate with 8.0% (see Table 6.21). *Volkswagen AG* as the only company which changes from a state-owned company to a family firm is responsible for an 8.9% growth rate. The two family businesses which become a foreign family firm achieve 8.5% on average. These are the highest *average* rates of all company types. Enterprises which become public companies

[57] See Table 6.9 in Section 6.1.6.

do achieve only average or below-average growth rates between 7.1% and 6.5%. They are also below the CAGR of continuous public companies with 7.3%.

The rates drop sharply looking at the additional reappearers (see Table 6.22). These companies survive over 60 years but are not among the 250 largest enterprises of 2018. Among the continuous companies state-owned companies achieve the highest rate with 4.2% followed by family firms with 3.2%. Continuous public companies achieve only a rate of 2.7%. Enterprises which become a family-owned business in the observation period even have negative CAGRs.

Overall, the rates show that the largest enterprises of 1958 grow on average by 7.1% to remain among the largest companies in 2018. This rate is slightly higher than the modeled CAGR from Section 5.1 of 6.6% (average company). It is closer to the rate of 7.3% to remain the largest company. This shows that the reappearers improve their position on average. On the other hand, companies can also survive with low one-digit or even negative growth rates.

Table 6.21 Average Revenue CAGR (1958–2018) of the Reappearers of 1958 per Company Type in 1958 & 2018

Type of company	**Reappearers**									
	1958	**2018** [revenue CAGR (%) 1958–2018]								
		FB	**FFB**	**FD**	**MCE**	**PC**	**COOP**	**SOE**	**FS**	**Total**
Family-owned business	**21**	*7.8%*	*8.5%*	*7.4%*	–	*7.1%*	–	–	–	***7.7%***
Foreign family-wned business	**2**	–	*6.8%*	–	–	–	–	–	*5.0%*	***5.9%***
Foundation-owned enterprise	**2**	–	–	*8.0%*	–	–	–	–	–	***8.0%***
Multiple companies-owned enterprise	**3**	*6.1%*	–	–	–	*6.7%*	–	–	–	***6.5%***
Public company	**13**	–	*2.3%*	–	*7.6%*	*7.3%*	*6.1%*	–	*7.6%*	***6.9%***
Cooperative	**3**	–	–	–	–	–	*7.8%*	–	–	***7.8%***
State-owned enterprise	**11**	*8.9%*	–	–	–	*6.5%*	–	*7.0%*	–	***6.9%***
Foreign subsidiary	**7**	–	–	–	–	–	–	–	*5.5%*	***5.5%***
Total	**–**	***7.8%***	***6.5%***	***7.6%***	***7.6%***	***7.0%***	***7.4%***	***7.0%***	***5.9%***	***7.1%***
2018	**62**	**15**	**4**	**5**	**1**	**18**	**4**	**5**	**10**	**–**

Source: Author's own table.

Table 6.22 Average Revenue CAGR (1958–2018) of the Additional Survivors of 1958 per Company Type in 1958 & 2018

Type of company	**Additional survivors**									
	1958	**2018** [revenue CAGR (%) 1958–2018]								
		FB	**FFB**	**FD**	**MCE**	**PC**	**COOP**	**SOE**	**FS**	**Total**
Family-owned business	**18**	*3.2%*	*2.6%*	*5.2%*	–	*2.5%*	–	–	*3.6%*	***3.3%***
Foreign family-owned business	–	–	–	–	–	–	–	–	–	–
Foundation-owned enterprise	–	–	–	–	–	–	–	–	–	–
Multiple companies-owned enterprise	**2**	–	*2.2%*	–	–	–	–	–	*0.8%*	***1.5%***
Public company	**10**	*−2.4%*	*1.8%*	–	–	*2.7%*	–	–	*1.8%*	***1.4%***
Cooperative	**2**	–	–	–	–	–	*1.7%*	–	–	***1.7%***
State-owned enterprise	**10**	–	–	–	–	–	–	*4.2%*	*4.7%*	***4.2%***
Foreign subsidiary	**5**	*−3.3%*	–	*3.9%*	–	–	–	–	*2.2%*	***1.4%***
Total	–	***1.9%***	***2.4%***	***4.8%***	–	***2.6%***	***1.7%***	***4.2%***	***2.4%***	***2.8%***
2018	**47**	**9**	**6**	**3**	–	**3**	**2**	**9**	**15**	–

Source: Author's own table.

Listing

The listing in 1958 of the 109 survivors is distributed similarly to the entire sample of the 250 largest enterprises (see Table 6.23). Non-listed companies account for 61.5% compared to 60.0% and listed companies account for 38.5% compared to 40.0%.[58] In 2018, the percentage of the listed survivors also decreases similar to the overall trend to 33.0% (37 / 109). In the 2018 dataset, the ratio is 28.8% (72 / 250). Nevertheless, within the reappearers the share of listed enterprises increases. Twelve non-listed companies go public and only five listed enterprises become private. Therefore, the share of listed firms within the reappearers is 46.8% (29 / 62). On the other hand, none non-listed company of the additional survivors goes public. They all remain non-listed. Furthermore, 13 of the 20 listed additional survivors in 1958 become private in 2018. 40 (85.1%) of all 47

[58] See Section 5.4 for more details on the listing status of the datasets.

additional survivors are non-listed. Overall, this analysis shows that if a company remains one of the 250 largest enterprises in 2018 it is more likely a listed company compared to the status of the observation period in 1958.

Table 6.23 Listing of the Reappearers & Additional Survivors of 1958 to 2018

Listing	**1958** [number of enterprises]	**2018** [number of enterprises]					
		Reappearers			**Additional survivors**		
		Non-listed	**Listed**	**Total**	**Non-listed**	**Listed**	**Total**
Non-listed	**67**	28	12	**40**	27	–	**27**
	61.5%	*41.8%*	*17.9%*	***59.7%***	*40.3%*	–	***40.3%***
Listed	**42**	5	17	**22**	13	7	**20**
	38.5%	*11.9%*	*40.5%*	***52.4%***	*31.0%*	*16.7%*	***47.6%***
Total	**109**	**33**	**29**	**62**	**40**	**7**	**47**
	100.0%	***30.3%***	***26.6%***	***56.9%***	***36.7%***	***6.4%***	***43.1%***

Source: Author's own table.

6.2 Patterns of the Enterprises' Developments to 2018

The previous long-term analysis of the 250 largest enterprises of 1958 provides patterns of the movements in the sample until 2018 including surviving and failed companies. It further provides detailed insights into the surviving enterprises and their characteristics—distinguishing between companies which remain one of the 250 largest enterprises even after 60 years and those which do not achieve such a size.

Overall, all company types are affected by downfalls over the observation period of 60 years except foundation-owned companies. Although the sample only consists of two cases, they show ownership continuity as well as high growth rates. Their objective to perpetuate the ownership and ensure the survival can be supported by the historical data of this dissertation. In addition, family-owned enterprises show a superior performance compared to the survival and failure rates Ward calculates in his study. Instead of a downfall rate of 80.0% only 55.2% of the 87 family enterprises between 1958 and 2018 fail. Furthermore, 23.0% of the family firms remain in the hands of the same family compared to Ward's rate of 13.0%. These numbers do not disprove Ward. They extend the knowledge about large German family-owned businesses to better understand their development as well as to further future research. In comparison to the other company types, their survival rate of 44.8% is only slightly above the sample's average of 43.9%. However, their ownership continuity rate of 23.0% is slightly below the average of 24.4%. Therefore, in comparison with all company types family firms perform close to the average—including state-owned companies as well as foreign entities. In comparison with public companies only, which is the most common comparison in research, family-owned businesses show a superior performance because public companies have a survival rate of 41.1% and an ownership continuity rate of 16.1%. Therefore, family-owned businesses show a relatively stable ownership structure over 60 years which is in favor of their attributed long-term orientation. However, the observed development of listed family companies is contrary to this characteristic. Only one of the 26 listed family firms of 1958 survive as a listed family company until 2018. None becomes a non-listed family firm. In general, history shows that a listing of a family business leads to the loss of the family majority. The observation of listed companies across all company types also shows that only 24.0% of them survive and remain listed after six decades. Additional 18.0% become private and 58.0% fail. A listing carries a higher risk of a downfall looking at the entire sample. On the other hand, within the group of the reappearers the number of companies which develop from a non-listed to a listed company is higher than the number of listed companies which become private. Therefore, it is more likely to remain one of the 250 largest enterprises and become a listed company than to remain one of the 250 largest enterprises and become private. The listing carries more risk but it is also linked to the higher growth rates to remain one of the largest enterprises decades later.

A higher risk of a downfall is also applicable to smallness—more precisely to the relative smallness within the 250 largest enterprises. Companies which have a higher revenue in 1958 are more likely to survive until 2018. The *liability of relative smallness* means that although all companies are one of the 250 largest the smaller ones are more likely to fail in the long-term. Size protects from the downfall. In this case, age does not play a significant role. The similar average age of the reappearers and the additional survivors shows that a company can also survive and become old without remaining one of the largest enterprises.

Furthermore, a key driver of the long-term development of enterprises is the industry a company operates in. It has a major impact on the survival of companies. Nearly no industry changes of enterprises are observed but several enterprises have failed because they have operated in an industry which declined. This also shows that the structural changes of the German economy between 1958 and 2018 are based on the downfall of enterprises as well as on the rise of new ones and not on the existing companies' change of industries. Furthermore, over the last 60 years companies in a thriving industry had the chance to grow above average by either a strong focus on exports (like the German automotive manufacturers) or by business model innovations which allowed them to capture a major share of the German market (like *Aldi Süd* and *Aldi Nord*). In exceptional cases, these developments have led to double-digit growth rates. Nevertheless, on average, a growth rate of 5.2% can be observed for all 109 survivors which is even below the GDP CAGR of 5.7%. This average includes the growth of the 47 additional survivors which do not remain within the 250 largest enterprises in 2018. Analyzed alone, these 47 companies have an annual growth rate of only 2.8%. On the other hand, the 62 reappearers show an annual growth rate of 7.1% which is required to remain within the 250 largest enterprises in Germany after 60 years. This rate is a quarter higher than the CAGR of the GDP. Such higher growth rates are also associated with fewer ownership discontinuities. Overall, despite the destiny of the downfall which is the average development of an enterprise the historical developments show that certain characteristics and patterns can postpone it indefinitely.

In a second analysis the development of the 250 largest enterprises of 2018 back to 1958 is studied.

Long-term Analysis II: The 250 Largest Enterprises of 2018

7

In the second long-term analysis the developments of the 250 largest enterprises of 2018 back to 1958 are investigated. The 2018 dataset consists of the 62 reappearers (24.8%) analyzed in the previous chapter as well as of the 188 new joiners (75.2%) as highlighted in Section 5.9. The focus is on the second group with references to the reappearers where necessary. Failed companies are not part of this analysis because all enterprises exist at the end of the observation period—in 2018. Nevertheless, some companies do not yet exist at the beginning of the observation period—in 1958. Therefore, the following questions arise: How many of the enterprises from the 2018 dataset already exist in 1958? Which companies are the new joiners and where do they come from? Which ownership discontinuities and crucial changes do the companies experience in the observation period? How fast are the new joiners growing to become one of the largest enterprises? Similar to the previous analysis the questions are approached on a company type but also on an enterprise level to understand the movements within the 250 largest enterprises and their long-term developments.

7.1 Overview of the Enterprises' Developments back to 1958

First, the rate of enterprises which already exist in 1958 is investigated. The characteristics of these companies like listing, age and company size are further studied. Second, the continuities and discontinuities of ownership are analyzed over the last 60 years. Third, the growth rates of the new joiners are calculated to understand how much growth is required to become one of the largest enterprises without belonging to this group in 1958. Fourth, family firms are again

M. Lantelme, *The Continuity and Discontinuity of the 250 Largest Enterprises in Germany*, Familienunternehmen und KMU,
https://doi.org/10.1007/978-3-658-42375-9_7

investigated in more detail for a better in-depth understand of their long-term development.

In the following sub-chapters, several comparisons are made between the reappearers and the new joiners to understand how enterprises which are not part of the 250 largest companies of 1958 become ranked in the 2018 list.

7.1.1 New Joiners & Reappearers: Two Worlds Collide

In Section 5.9 the distribution of new joiners and reappearers is mentioned briefly. Compared to 1958, 188 new companies (75.2%) join the list of the 250 largest enterprises of 2018. 62 (24.8%) companies remain the same. Furthermore, 80 of the 250 companies (32.0%) as well as of the 188 companies (42.6%) were founded after 1958 (see Figure 7.1).[1] They are younger than 60 years. Therefore, they cannot be tracked back to the starting year of the observation period. The remaining 170 enterprises (68.0%) are older than 60 years. They already exist before 1958 and include all reappearers as well because the reappearers are all founded before 1958. This also means that 108 companies of the new joiners (57.4%) already exist in 1958 but are smaller than the 250 largest enterprises at that time. These companies require a higher growth rate than the reappearers and the modeled growth rate to become one the largest firms in 2018 which will be further analyzed in Section 7.1.5.[2] But where do the new joiners come from?

The new joiners which are founded before 1958 are studied in more detail and compared to the reappearers (see Table 7.1). The listing status of all 170 enterprises which are founded before 1958 shows that 143 (84.1%) are non-listed and 27 (15.9%) are listed in 1958. The share of non-listed firms is much higher than the share of the 250 largest enterprises of 1958 (60.0%) as well as of 2018 (71.2%). This is especially the case for the 108 new joiners of which 103 (95.4%) are non-listed. These companies are small in 1958—otherwise they would be part of the 250 largest enterprises of 1958 already—and a listing is not a suitable solution at that time. Over the last 60 years this share declines to 76.9% (83 / 108) which is closer to the overall 2018 sample but still above the share of the reappearers of 53.2% (33 / 62). 22 non-listed firms become listed and only two listed firms become private. In the course of becoming one of the 250

[1] *Fritz Dräxlmaier GmbH & Co. KG* is the only company founded in 1958 under the name *Lisa Dräxlmaier Kabelkonfektion.*

[2] See Section 5.1 for the modeled growth rate of the two samples and Section 6.1.8 for the historical growth rate of the reappearers.

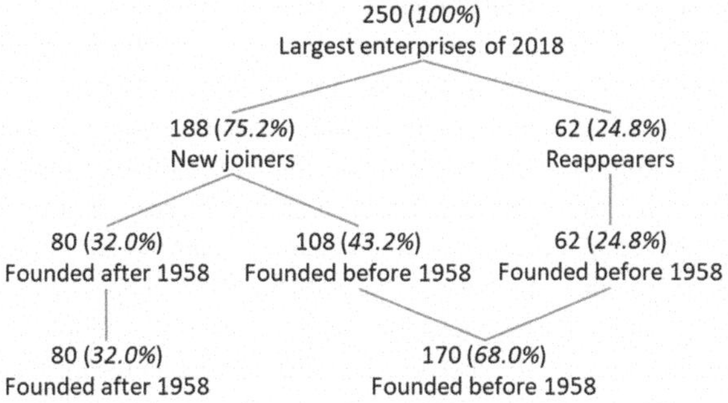

Figure 7.1 Distribution of New Joiners & Reappearers based on Year of Foundation. (Source: Author's own figure)

largest enterprises the small companies tend to go public. The long-term trend of the reappearers is also supported by the new joiners. Furthermore, the share of non-listed enterprises of the new joiners founded after 1958 is 77.5% (62 / 80). These companies are younger and also support the trend that a company goes public with age as highlighted above. This also shows that the capital market does not gain in importance for the funding of new enterprises over the last 60 years.

Table 7.1 Listing of the 170 Enterprises Founded before 1958 of 1958 to 2018. (Source: Author's own table)

Listing	**1958** [number of enterprises]	**2018** [number of enterprises]					
		Reappearers			**New joiners** (founded before 1958)		
		Non-listed	**Listed**	**Total**	**Non-listed**	**Listed**	**Total**
Non-listed	**143**	28	12	**40**	81	22	**103**
	84.1%	*19.6%*	*8.4%*	***28.0%***	*56.6%*	*15.4%*	***72.0%***
Listed	**27**	5	17	**22**	2	3	**5**
	15.9%	*18.5%*	*63.0%*	***81.5%***	*7.4%*	*11.1%*	***18.5%***
Total	**170**	**33**	**29**	**62**	**83**	**25**	**108**
	100%	***19.4%***	***17.1%***	***36.5%***	***48.8%***	***14.7%***	***63.5%***

Cooperatives and family firms show the highest share of companies which are already founded in 1958 with 90.0% and 85.1% (see Table 7.2). The high share of family firms supports their attributed long-term orientation. On the other hand, multiple companies-owned enterprises and foreign subsidiaries have the lowest share. 71.4% and 60.0% of their entities are founded between 1958 and 2018. This supports the earlier statement that both company types do not start from scratch to build a company but they can use the assets of their parent companies to become one of the largest enterprises in a shorter period of time. Foundation-owned companies, cooperatives and state-owned enterprises also have a lower share of companies which are not yet founded in 1958. This is also in line with their objectives to either perpetuate a business or serve the people.

Overall, new joiners to the list of the 250 largest enterprises of 2018 can either be old and become large after being small in 1958 or be young and be

Table 7.2 Foundations of the 250 Largest Enterprises of 2018 back to 1958 per Company Type. (Source: Author's own table)

Type of company	**2018**	**1958** [number of enterprises]	
		Not yet founded	**Already founded**
Family-owned business	**87**	13	74
	34.8%	*14.9%*	*85.1%*
Foreign family-owned business	**18**	6	12
	7.2%	*33.3%*	*66.7%*
Foundation-owned enterprise	**12**	3	9
	4.8%	*25.0%*	*75.0%*
Multiple companies-owned enterprise	**7**	5	2
	2.8%	*71.4%*	*28.6%*
Public company	**47**	16	31
	18.8%	*34.0%*	*66.0%*
Cooperative	**10**	1	9
	4.0%	*10.0%*	*90.0%*
State-owned enterprise	**14**	3	11
	5.6%	*21.4%*	*78.6%*
Foreign subsidiary	**55**	33	22
	22.0%	*60.0%*	*40.0%*
Subsidiary company	–	–	–
	–	–	–
Total	**250**	**80**	**170**
	100.0%	***32.0%***	***68.0%***

founded during the observation period and have higher growth rates. Family firms, cooperatives, foundations and state-owned enterprises tend to follow the first way and foreign subsidiaries as well as multiple companies-owned enterprises follow the second way. Furthermore, companies tend to go public in their development to become large.

7.1.2 Age: The Two Exceptions of an Average Age of a Hundred Years

The new joiners have an impact on the average age as well and show a big difference compared to the reappearers. The 188 new joiners to the 2018 list have an average age of 75.3 years. They are 55.4 years younger than the 62 reappearers with 130.7 years as shown in Table 6.18 in Section 6.1.8. The younger age of the new joiners supports the previous finding that failed enterprises and new companies are the drivers of the structural change and not existing companies which change their industry focus.

Furthermore, the average age of the company types with a high share of enterprises which are founded between 1959 and 2018 (e.g., foreign subsidiaries and public companies) decreases significantly in comparison to their average age without the newly founded enterprises (see Table 7.3). For example, continuous public companies are on average 134.1 years old. The 2018 public companies which are founded after 1958 have an average age of only 22.7 years. This leads to a total average age of public companies of 89.3 years. In summary, they can become very old and large but on the other hand they can also become large in a short period of time taking into account Table 7.2 and the high share of companies which are not yet founded in 1958. Foreign subsidiaries show a similar decrease from 114.3 years to 67 years. Continuous public companies are overall the second oldest company type behind continuous foundations with 148.7 years. Continuous family businesses follow on third position with 117.2 years. Taking into account all 1958 company types and the firms founded after 1958 the average age of family firms is the second highest with 105.2 years. Only foundations are on average a little bit older—106.8 years. These numbers support the long-term orientation of family businesses as well as of foundations. Both company types are exceptionally old.

Table 7.3 Average Age of the 250 Largest Enterprises in 2018 per Company Type in 1958 & 2018. (Source: Author's own table)

Type of company	**2018**	**1958** [average age]										
		FB	**FFB**	**FD**	**MCE**	**PC**	**COOP**	**SOE**	**FS**	**SC**	**Not yet founded**	**Total**
Family-owned business	87	117.2	–	–	104.0	–	–	81.0	–	106.0	41.3	**105.2**
Foreign family-owned business	18	98.1	107.0	–	–	117.0	–	–	–	–	32.7	**79.4**
Foundation-owned enterprise	12	122.7	–	148.7	–	–	–	–	–	–	33.0	**106.8**
Multiple companies-owned enterprise	7	108.0	–	–	–	171.0	–	–	–	–	34.4	**64.4**
Public company	47	116.0	–	–	125.5	134.1	–	115.1	–	131.3	22.7	**89.3**
Cooperative	10	–	–	–	–	92.0	90.5	–	–	–	14.0	**83.0**
State-owned enterprise	14	–	–	–	81.0	–	–	110.4	–	–	17.7	**88.4**
Foreign subsidiary	55	108.7	104.0	–	65.0	156.7	–	–	114.3	183.0	32.2	**67.0**
Total	–	**115.5**	**105.5**	**148.7**	**100.2**	**135.9**	**90.5**	**110.6**	**114.3**	**135.7**	**31.2**	**89.0**
2018	**250**	**98**	**4**	**3**	**5**	**16**	**8**	**18**	**12**	**6**	**80**	**–**

7.1.3 Size: The Extraordinary Case of the Reappearers

Like age, the 188 new joiners of the 250 largest enterprises of 2018 are on average also smaller than the reappearers. The new joiners have an average size of EUR 7.5bn in 2018 compared to EUR 26.8bn of the 62 reappearers. Excluding the 80 new joiners which are founded after 1958 the average size of the remaining (and older) 108 new joiners even decreases to EUR 6.7bn. The average size of the 80 younger new joiners is EUR 8.5bn. Despite their higher age the older new joiners are smaller than the younger new joiners. The distance to the reappearers is in both cases huge. The reappearers are a very special type of enterprises which achieves high growth rates to become one of the largest enterprises in Germany but also to continue this pace and remain one of the largest enterprises even six decades later.

7.1.4 Ownership Continuity and Discontinuity: Family Firms' Long-Term Orientation

Similar to the ownership continuity and discontinuity analysis of the largest enterprises of 1958 in Section 6.1.4 the following analysis identifies the company type changes of the 250 largest enterprises of 2018 between 1958 and 2018. It focuses on the 170 enterprises which are founded in 1958 or earlier (which include the reappearers) because the investigated ownership continuity refers to the entire observation period of 60 years (see Table 7.4).

In total, 115 (67.6%) of the 170 enterprises keep their company type between 1958 and 2018. 55 (32.4%) change it. A remarkable observation are family-owned businesses. 74 (85.1%) of the 87 family firms in 2018 are already founded in 1958. Of the 74 family firms extraordinary 71 companies (95.9%) are already family-owned 60 years earlier. This represents the highest share among all company types. Only state-owned enterprises and cooperatives have approximately similar rates with 90.0% and 88.9% on second and third position. Only three enterprises change from another company type to a family firm. These are *Volkswagen AG, Rhenus SE & Co. KG* and *Wacker Chemie AG.* In the latter case, the Wacker family already owns 50.0% of the company in 1958. Rhenus is acquired by the Rethmann family in 1998 and the Porsche and Piëch families take over the majority of *Volkswagen* in 2009. All other family-owned businesses in 2018 are owned by families six decades earlier. This consistency also supports the attributed long-term orientation of family firms. On the other hand, foreign family firms have the smallest continuity rate with 16.7%. Taking a closer look at the underlying companies it becomes obvious that in most cases the same families remain the owners of the companies, but the company type changes because the families move abroad. This is the case, for example, for *Marquard & Bahls AG*, *Liebherr-EMtec GmbH*, *Unternehmensgruppe Theo Müller S.e.c.s.* as well as *Rehau AG & Co.* Considering these moves the ownership continuity rate of foreign family businesses is much higher. Public companies have the second lowest ownership continuity rate with 29.0%. Over the last 60 years family businesses are the company type with the highest number of entities which change to a public company with nine followed by state-owned enterprises with seven. The former family firms are, for example, *Siemens AG*, *Adidas AG*, *Klöckner & Co. SE*, *Dürr AG* and *Hugo Boss AG*. The former state-owned companies are privatized, and their share majority is in free float in 2018. These companies are, for example, *Deutsche Post AG*, *Deutsche Lufthansa AG* and *RWE AG*. The only company type which becomes a foundation are family-owned businesses. The six cases are *Robert Bosch GmbH*, *Fresenius SE & Co. KGaA*, *Bertelsmann SE & Co. KGaA*, *Mahle GmbH*, *Körber AG* and *Saarstahl AG*.

Overall, family firms show a high continuity over the last 60 years which supports their attributed long-term orientation. The development of public companies mirrors the privatization trend as well as the raised tendency of listed family firms. The family loses the majority in the mid- to long-term after the IPO.

Table 7.4 Ownership Continuity & Discontinuity of the 250 Largest Enterprises of 2018 back to 1958. (Source: Author's own table)

Type of company	**2018**	**1958**		**1958** [number of enterprises]									
		Not yet founded	**Already founded**	**FB**	**FFB**	**FD**	**MCE**	**PC**	**COOP**	**SOE**	**FS**	**SC**	**Total**
Family-owned business	**87**	13	74	71	–	–	1	–	–	1	–	1	**74**
	34.8%	*14.9%*	*85.1%*	*95.9%*	–	–	*1.4%*	-	–	*1.4%*	–	*1.4%*	***43.5%***
Foreign family-owned business	**18**	6	12	8	2	–	–	2	–	–	–	–	**12**
	7.2%	*33.3%*	*66.7%*	*66.7%*	*16.7%*	–	–	*16.7%*	–	–	–	–	***7.1%***
Foundation-owned enterprise	**12**	3	9	6	–	–	–	–	–	–	–	–	**9**
	4.8%	*25.0%*	*75.0%*	*66.7%*	–	–	–	–	–	–	–	–	***5.3%***
Multiple companies-owned enterprise	**7**	5	2	1	–	–	–	1	–	–	–	–	**2**
	2.8%	*71.4%*	*28.6%*	*50.0%*	–	–	–	*50.0%*	–	–	–	–	***1.2%***
Public company	**47**	16	31	9	–	–	2	9	–	7	–	4	**31**
	18.8%	*34.0%*	*66.0%*	*29.0%*	–	–	*6.5%*	*29.0%*	-	*22.6%*	–	*12.9%*	***18.2%***
Cooperative	**10**	1	9	–	–	–	–	1	8	–	–	–	**9**
	4.0%	*10.0%*	*90.0%*	–	–	–	–	*11.1%*	*88.9%*	–	–	–	***5.3%***
State-owned enterprise	**14**	3	11	–	–	–	1	–	–	10	–	–	**11**
	5.6%	*21.4%*	*78.6%*	–	–	–	*9.1%*	–	–	*90.9%*	–	–	***6.5%***
Foreign subsidiary	**55**	33	22	3	2	–	1	3	–	–	12	1	**22**
	22.0%	*60.0%*	*40.0%*	*13.6%*	*9.1%*	–	*4.5%*	*13.6%*	–	–	*54.5%*	*4.5%*	***12.9%***

(continued)

Table 7.4 (continued)

Type of company	2018	1958		1958 [number of enterprises]									
		Not yet founded	Already founded	FB	FFB	FD	MCE	PC	COOP	SOE	FS	SC	Total
Subsidiary company	–	–	–	–	–	–	–	–	–	–	–	–	–
	–	–	–	–	–	–	–	–	–	–	–	–	–
Total	**250**	**80**	**170**	**98**	**4**	**3**	**5**	**16**	**8**	**18**	**12**	**6**	**170**
	100.0%	*32.0%*	*68.0%*	*57.6%*	*2.4%*	*1.8%*	*2.9%*	*9.4%*	*4.7%*	*10.6%*	*7.1%*	*3.5%*	*100.0%*

7.1.5 Growth: Accelerated to Become One of the Largest Enterprises of 2018

The previous findings show that the new joiners independent of their year of foundation are required to have growth rates which outperform the rates of the reappearers to achieve a place within the 250 largest enterprises in 2018. Therefore, the 1958 revenue data of the new joiners is gathered to analyze their growth. The chosen approach focuses on the 108 new joiners which are founded before 1959.

After extensive historical research, the 1958 revenue data of 27 new joiners founded before 1959 is identified.[3] These enterprises show an accelerated CAGR of 11.0% between 1958 and 2018. This is nearly twice the rate of the GDP. Moreover, with a CAGR of 11.0% the revenue doubles every 6.6 years. During the observation period from 1958 to 2018 a company with such a growth rate would double its revenue around nine times. 16 of the 27 companies show on average a two-digit growth rate over 60 years. The fastest growing company in this sub-sample is the foundation-owned enterprise *Fresenius SE & Co. KGaA* (2018 revenues of EUR 33.5bn) with 18.9% followed by the foreign subsidiary *McKesson Europe AG* (EUR 21.1bn) with 15.7% and the family-owned business *Globus Holding GmbH & Co. KG* (EUR 6.7bn) with 13.6%.[4] On the lower end of the sub-sample are the family company *BENTELER International AG* (EUR 8.1bn) with a growth rate of 9.3% as well as the foreign subsidiaries *3M Deutschland GmbH* (EUR 2.4bn) with 8.8% and *Basell Polyolefine GmbH* (4.2bn) with 8.2%.[5]

As shown in Section 6.1.8, the 62 reappearers have an average growth rate of 7.1%. The difference of 3.9% leads to the appearance of the new joiners in 2018 without being part of the group of the 250 largest enterprises in 1958. The 27 enterprises show that two-digit growth is feasible over six decades and is quite

[3] Unfortunately, research efforts have reached a limit for this analysis. Despite extensive research including requests sent to the living companies 1958 revenue data is only available for 27 of the 108 new joiners founded before 1959. For the remaining 81 companies these data could not be identified.

[4] In 1958, the names of these three companies are *Dr. Eduard Fresenius KG Chemisch pharmazeutische Industrie* (a family-owned business with revenues of EUR 1.0 m), *Gehe & Co. AG* (a subsidiary company of *Chemische Fabrik von Heyden AG* with revenues of EUR 3.3 m) and *Franz Bruch GmbH* (a family-owned business with revenues of EUR 3.1 m).

[5] In 1958, the names of these three companies are *Benteler-Werke AG* (a family-owned business with revenues of EUR 39.1 m), *Minnesota Mining & Manufacturing Company mbH* (a foreign subsidiary with revenues of EUR 15.3 m) and *Rheinische Olefinwerke GmbH* (a multiple companies-owned enterprise with revenues of EUR 35.8 m).

common within the new joiners. In comparison to the 62 reappearers of which only five had two-digit growth rates the new joiners start from a much smaller size. The reappearers are more mature. This shows that the growth rates decline with increasing size within the largest enterprises in Germany.

Although no revenue data besides the 2018 one has been gathered for the new joiners which are founded after 1958 several observations can be made. These companies have to grow with even higher rates than the previously calculated 11.0% to become one of the 250 largest enterprises of 2018. Nevertheless, this only applies if they start from scratch. As shown in Section 3.7.2.3 several of the youngest companies are carve-outs from enterprises which already start in their first year with billions in revenue (e.g., like *Covestro AG*, *Uniper SE* and *Ceconomy AG*). They already exist as a business unit before the official year of foundation. Other cases include foreign subsidiaries which are founded with the support of the parent company. They can also become large in a short period (e.g., *INEOS Styrolution Holding GmbH* and *AbbVie Deutschland GmbH & Co. KG*)—sometimes also by acquiring additional existing operations in Germany. Exceptions to the described examples are the two companies *Zalando SE* and *Auto1 Group GmbH* founded in 2008 and 2012, respectively, which start with an innovative or new business model.[6] They are able to grow from zero revenue to EUR 5.4bn and EUR 2.9bn in ten and six years—with the large support of investors who provide money at the beginning when the companies make hundreds of millions in losses. Nevertheless, these developments are exceptions within the 250 largest enterprises of 2018 in Germany.

7.1.6 Family-Owned Enterprises: Pass the Long-Term Orientation

Family-owned businesses remain the largest company type within the 250 largest enterprises of 2018 with 87 entities. As shown in Section 7.1.2, they have an exceptional average age with more than 100 years which supports their attributed long-term orientation. On the other hand, 74 of the 87 firms are already founded before 1958. There are only 13 family firms which are founded after 1958 and become one of the largest enterprises of 2018. This is the second smallest share of all company types. Although family-owned businesses show a relatively stable development in the long-term the data show that family firms find it difficult to become one of the 250 largest enterprises in Germany within less than 60 years.

[6] See also Section 5.7.2 for a brief description of *Auto1 Group GmbH*.

Ownership Continuity and Discontinuity

71 of the 74 (95.9%) family-owned businesses in 2018 which are already founded before 1959 are already a family firm in 1958. But are they owned by the same family? Similar to the analysis of the continuous family businesses of 1958 and their ownership continuities and discontinuities the same is done for the 2018 ranking. Although a company has the status of a family business in both years one or multiple ownership discontinuities can occur. In the 1958 dataset this is the case for *Knorr-Bremse AG.*[7] Because the company is a reappearer it is also included in the 2018 dataset. However, with *Wieland-Werke AG* there is a second enterprise in the 2018 ranking which remains a family business but has a different owner family compared to 1958. The Wieland family sells shares starting in the 1970s. One of the new shareholders is Eberhard Schleicher (of *SCHWENK Zement KG*) with around 25.0% in 2001. He takes over the majority in the following years and is still the majority owner in 2018. Besides these two companies all other 69 continuous family businesses remain in the hands of the same family in 2018 as in 1958. This includes enterprises like *Gebr. Heinemann SE & Co. KG*, *Webasto SE* and *Wilhelm Hoyer GmbH & Co. KG*. Excluding the two cases of *Knorr-Bremse* and *Wieland-Werke* 93.2% of the family-owned businesses remain continuous which is still the highest value.

Listing Status

In 2018, 13 (14.9%) of the 87 family businesses are listed which is below the average of 28.8% of the entire sample. None of these 13 listed companies is already listed in 1958. Furthermore, none of the 71 continuous family firms is listed in 1958 at all. There is no example of a family firm being listed for 60 years.[8]

As the analysis in Section 6.1.7 shows there is no family business which remains majority-owned by the family and listed over 60 years. In most cases the family divests their shares in the mid- to long-term. The 2018 sample and the analysis in Table 7.5 support these findings because none of the 2018 listed

[7] See Section 6.1.7 for the ownership discontinuity of *Knorr-Bremse AG*.

[8] The eleven continuous family firms which are listed in 2018 but not in 1958 are *Henkel AG & Co. KGaA*, *Merck KGaA*, *Schaeffler AG*, *Hella GmbH & Co. KGaA*, *Knorr-Bremse AG*, *Hornbach Holding AG & Co. KGaA*, *Krones AG*, *Jungheinrich AG*, *Axel Springer SE*, *Sixt SE*, as well as *Fuchs Petrolub SE*. The additional two listed family firms in 2018 which are a different company type and non-listed in 1958 are *Volkswagen AG* and *Wacker Chemie AG*. It is noteworthy that *Hella GmbH & Co. KGaA* as one of the continuous family firms and listed in 2018 is sold in 2021 by the owner family.

family firms is already listed in 1958.[9] If there is no example of a family firm which remains listed during the observation period what does this imply for the future development of the eleven listed family businesses in 2018? Based on the historical observations it can be expected that the majority of the 13 listed family firms of 2018 will not remain in the hands of the family over the next decades. This proposition is also supported by the 1958 company types of the 2018 public companies as shown in Table 7.4 in Section 7.1.4. Nine of the 31 public companies in 2018 which are already founded in 1958 are family-owned business 60 years earlier. Family firms are the largest company type to develop into public companies in the sample—even before state-owned enterprises of which seven become public companies.

Table 7.5 Listing Development of the 87 Largest Family-Owned Enterprises of 2018 back to 1958. (Source: Author's own table)

Listing of family-owned enterprises	**2018**	**1958** [number of enterprises]					
		Family-owned enterprise		**Other company type**		**Total**	**Not yet founded**
		Non-listed	**Listed**	**Non-listed**	**Listed**		
Non-listed	**74**	60	–	1	–	**61**	**13**
	85.1%	*81.1%*	–	*1.4%*	–	***82.4%***	***17.6%***
Listed	**13**	11	–	2	–	**13**	–
	14.9%	*84.6%*	–	*15.4%*	–	***100.0%***	–
Total	**87**	**71**	–	**3**	–	**74**	**13**
	100.0%	***81.8%***	–	***3.4%***	–	***85.1%***	***14.9%***

Overall, the developments of the largest family-owned businesses of 2018 back to 1958 show their long-term orientation and a stable ownership structure. They remain the largest company type in the sample and therefore contribute to a large extent to the economy. Listing is a risk for families to lose their majority ownership and the company's independence.

[9] See Stotmeister (in press) for the detailed analysis of family firms' IPOs which also support the findings of this thesis.

7.2 Patterns of the Enterprises' Developments to 2018

The second long-term analysis studies the developments of the 250 largest enterprises of 2018 back to 1958. It provides patterns of the companies' movements including the new joiners as well as their ownership continuities and discontinuities. In addition, growth patterns are identified showing how the companies become one of largest enterprises.

Overall, the majority of the largest enterprises of 2018 are founded before 1959 and the average age of 89.0 years shows a survival of around three generations. Hence, the basis for the largest enterprises have already been laid early. Especially family firms show an exceptionally high rate of long-term developments beyond 100 years similar to that of foundations. Nevertheless, this successful long-term orientation also has a downside. Only a few family firms become large in less than 60 years compared to other company types including public companies and foreign subsidiaries. These companies require high double-digit growth rates to become one of the largest enterprises or they do not start from scratch like the high number of carve-outs and the foreign parent companies show. On the other hand, new joiners founded before 1958 also show growth rates of up to 18.9% over 60 years—also family firm reach two-digit growth rates.

The development of listed companies implies that the capital market does not gain in importance for the funding of new enterprises which become large over the last 60 years. On the other hand, listings are a risk for family firms to lose their independence and the family's majority ownership. There is no historical evidence in the 2018 dataset of a family-owned business which remains listed over 60 years. Furthermore, the movements of the company types show that lots of family firms become public companies in the observation period. The families lose their majority ownership.

8 Propositions for the Future Development of Enterprises

Following Alexander Gerst's quotation from the beginning "[...] that the future is more important than the past [...]" the historical analyses can help to better understand the long-term developments of German family as well as non-family enterprises to prepare for the future. The overarching development patterns are provided in the next sub-chapter based on which propositions as well as practical implications are derived.

8.1 Overarching Patterns: Downfall is the Average Long-Term Development

Founding and running a business is risky. There is hardly any company type or industry which is not affected by drastic economic or business changes in the observation period between 1958 and 2018. The long-term analyses show that everyone is affected—some by more favorable conditions others by less favorable conditions and some companies survive these changes while others fail. In total, 56.4% of the 250 largest enterprises of 1958 do not survive over the next 60 years. They are sold, insolvent, merged or dissolved. The remaining 43.6% survive but their developments are very different. On average, these surviving companies have a lower growth rate than the GDP with 5.7%—some companies grow, some stagnate and still others even decline. On the other hand, most of the surviving enterprises remain one of the 250 largest companies also in 2018. On average, the larger a company in 1958 the more likely it survives until 2018. This development postulates the *liability of relative smallness.* The smaller companies of the 250 largest enterprises of 1958 fail more often.

Despite all the changes, family-owned businesses represent most of the companies within the 250 largest enterprises in Germany in 1958 as well as in 2018

M. Lantelme, *The Continuity and Discontinuity of the 250 Largest Enterprises in Germany*, Familienunternehmen und KMU,
https://doi.org/10.1007/978-3-658-42375-9_8

with 34.8%—by far. Although the share of family firms in the German economy is higher with around 90% the majority of these companies has only up to ten employees. Taking into account the development of foreign family firms as well as foundations which are linked to families, owner families become more important over 60 years. In comparison to public companies, family-owned businesses show a slightly higher survival rate over 60 years—44.8% compared to 41.1%. More important from the perspective of the owner family is the ownership continuity rate. For family-owned businesses the rate is 23.0% which is also higher than the one of public companies with 16.1%. Family firms show a relatively stable development within the different company types. Contributing to family business theory, the previous historical analyses support the attributed characteristic of long-term orientation. Family companies, especially in comparison to public companies, show a superior survival and ownership continuity rate over two generations. Furthermore, families keep their enterprise longer and more often. It is sold or acquired less often. Even if the company is declining it remains in the ownership of the family for generations. Therefore, the theoretical understanding of family firms with their long-term orientation is supported by the analyzed historical and long-term data. Additionally, the analyses also show that the most long-term oriented company type are foundation-owned enterprises. The 1958 sample is small with only two cases, but both keep their ownership structure and survive. Additionally, they remain within the 250 largest enterprises in 2018 and can improve their positions. They are growing proportionately faster. Furthermore, foundations can be seen as a next development stage of family firms. All of the foundations included in the 2018 dataset are family-owned businesses 60 years earlier except three which are foundation-owned already in 1958. In the observation period the family firms become foundations to perpetuate their ownership structure and their operations.

Overall, the two long-term analyses show that there are three ways to become one of the largest enterprises over the observation period of 60 years—under the condition that the company survives: 1) If the company is already part of the largest enterprises in 1958 it needs to achieve a minimum growth rate between 6.6% and 7.1%; 2) if the company is in the upper part of the ranking even a stagnating revenue can keep it in the ranking, 3) if the company is not within the 250 largest enterprises of 1958 it requires average growth of 11.0%.[1] Such high growth rates are either possible based on innovative business models (e.g., *Aldi* and a consolidated market in food retail) or the entering of new markets (e.g., like *SAP* in the information and communication industry). Therefore, growth is

[1] For the detailed explanations see Sections 5.1, 6.1.8 and 7.1.5.

also linked to industries. Summarizing the findings from the various industry analyses it can be shown that the industry a company operates in is a major risk—most likely the biggest one for large enterprises. The dramatic changes between the economic sectors in 1958 and 2018 show an aggregated picture of this development. Moreover, the number of companies in the different applied industry categories changes substantially. In 1958, 29 of the 250 largest enterprises operate in mining and quarrying. This number drops by 93.1% to only two companies in 2018. Eleven of the 29 enterprises of 1958 survive until 2018 which represents the second lowest survival rate among all industries and only two companies continue to operate in mining and quarrying.[2] Although the decline of the mining and quarrying industry in Germany is a special case because it is politically intended and state-subsidized it shows the importance of the industry for the long-term development of enterprises. On the other hand, the importance of services including commerce increases substantially similar to information and communication over the last 60 years. Commerce represents the second largest industry among the 250 largest enterprises of 2018 compared to the third smallest industry in 1958. As a company in one of these industries the prospects over the last 60 years have been much more promising than, for example, in mining and quarrying. In addition, there is only one exceptional case of a company which successfully changes its industry in the observation period. All other enterprises remain in the same industry (or in an adjacent industry) as 60 years earlier. Furthermore, several companies which initiated a (successful) industry change are acquired and lose their independence. Therefore, the industry a company operates in needs to be chosen wisely because it is unlikely to change it even in the long-term.

The high rate of companies remaining in the same industry also shows that the changes of the German economy over the last 60 years, especially the uprise of the services sector, are not driven by the surviving enterprises. The structural change is driven by the failing companies and by the new foundations in other industries which ultimately replace the failed enterprises within the 250 largest companies. It is a renewal by *death.*

Within all these changes, the importance of the German capital market decreases within the 250 largest enterprises between 1958 and 2018. In total, the rate of companies which are listed at the end of the observation period compared to its beginning declines from 40.0% to 28.8%. Nevertheless, enterprises

[2] These are *K + S AG* (*Salzdetfurth AG*) and *DEA Deutsche Erdoel AG* (*Deutsche Erdöl-AG*). Furthermore, nine companies also show that enterprises can adapt their business model to change their major industry. Nevertheless, only three of them remain one of the 250 largest enterprises of 2018.

which remain one of the 250 largest companies are more likely to become listed in the observation period compared to the rate in the overall sample. Therefore, extraordinary growth is often associated with a listing of the company. On the other hand, listed companies are also more likely to fail compared to non-listed ones. It appears that a listing can enable higher growth, but this comes with a higher risk. Especially for family-owned businesses a listing has a downside. The family loses its ownership majority- in the mid- to long-term. All 26 families from the 1958 sample owning a listed enterprise have lost their company either by downfall or by divestiture of their majority stake in the listed firm until 2018—except for one: the Dierig family whose company declined over the last 60 years remains the majority owner of the listed enterprise. The other 25 enterprises do not remain family-owned and listed in 2018. Additionally, based on the second long-term analysis none of the listed family firms of 2018 is already listed in 1958. They go public during the observation period. These cases are important for family owners because the historical observations show that there is no large family business which has been able to remain in the hands of the family after it went public and also remain large. Furthermore, the observations show that in 2018 there is no listed family businesses which has been listed for at least two generations. Therefore, an IPO needs to be chosen wisely because history teaches that the IPO leads to the divestment and discontinuity of the family's majority ownership in the mid- to long-term.[3] This proposition can be further tested. In the 2018 dataset, 13 family-owned businesses are listed including *Henkel AG & Co. KGaA*, *Merck KGaA* and *Jungheinrich AG*. If the proposition proves true none of the families remain the majority owner over the next couple of decades.[4] Furthermore, another typical development of the largest enterprises of 1958 is the acquisition by a foreign company. The largest group of the surviving enterprises of 1958 are foreign subsidiaries—followed by family-owned businesses. Again, listing is a key characteristic of the acquired companies. Most of them are public companies in 1958. This again shows the additional risk of being listed.

Despite all the growth histories and the long-term orientation of family firms, shareholders, managers, employees and families should always keep in mind that a downfall is the average development of a company in the long-term.

---

[3] See Stotmeister (in press) for a more detailed analysis of the IPOs of family firms.

[4] *Hella GmbH & Co. KGaA* as one of the listed family-owned companies in 2018 was already acquired in 2021. The owner families sold their shares.

8.2 Practical Implications: Choose Wisely

Based on the overarching patterns and some single case observations practical implications can be derived which should support shareholders, managers, employees and families in their decisions. These implications follow the third research objective of this dissertation. Some of them are specifically related to family-owned businesses, other apply to any business that is to exist in the long-term.

Growth: An achievable and long-term growth rate to remain among the largest enterprises is between 6.6% and 7.1%. Low two-digit growth rates which are historically proven can lead to an improvement of the ranking. Growth rates below the average of the GDP or even negative rates do not necessarily lead to a downfall of the company. Therefore, growth strategies should be planned for the long-term. A year-over-year rate does not tell where the company will be after the next decade.

Survival: Doing business is risky. More than half of the 250 largest enterprises fail within two generations. This also shows that the downfall is the average development of every company in the long-term. Therefore, the focus should be on avoiding the downfalls to enable the survival and, in some cases, also growth.

Industry: For a large enterprise, the industry in which it operates is the key risk. Therefore, it needs to be chosen wisely from the beginning. Products or markets which can hardly be replaced or changed can favor the company's long-term development (e.g., food). Furthermore, in history, there are only few enterprises which change their industry and remain independent. Diversifying and establishing a new business in a different successful industry could lead to the acquisition of the company. A stable ownership structure can counteract this risk.

Foreign subsidiaries: Over the last 60 years, the majority of new companies within the 250 largest enterprises in Germany are foreign subsidiaries. They are established in Germany with the support of the parent company which often has large financial as well as non-financial resources. They are large from their foundation and can become a major competitor on the German and adjacent markets for established companies. Therefore, a new market player can be a major competitor from day one. Another threat for existing companies is to be acquired by a foreign entity. The historical data show that the majority of surviving enterprises of 1958 are foreign subsidiaries.

Listing: A listing is often linked to above-average growth (however, the causality is not defined). At the same time, listed companies are more likely to fail in the long-term. Therefore, a listing involves a higher risk and a higher growth potential. For family-owned businesses, a listing leads to the loss of the majority ownership of the family. In the past 60 years there is only one example within the 250 largest enterprises of 1958 which survives as a listed family firm until 2018—*Dierig Holding AG.* Although the company survives its revenue declines. Furthermore, most public companies of 2018 are family-owned in 1958. Over the observation period, the families also lose their majority. On the other hand, if the family intends to divest its company an IPO can also be a tool to do so in the mid- to long-term.

Voting rights: Although a family loses the ownership majority of a listed enterprise it can safeguard its influence to a certain degree by issuing preferential stocks. These stocks can all be in free float but the family keeps the majority of voting rights based on common stocks. By issuing preferential stocks the company (/ family) receives funding and the family participates to a lesser extent in the financial success of the company. The owner family needs to consider if they want to keep control of the company although they do not entirely benefit from its success or if they want to waive voting rights in order to benefit more from the company's success.

Wealth: Several examples of discontinued family enterprises show that families have protected their wealth by separating their company into an operating and a management firm (e.g., *Zündapp-Werke GmbH*). Then, in the case of an insolvency or the sale of the business the discontinuity is only applicable to the operating entity while the management firm including the real estate assets was continued. This can protect a share of the family's wealth.

3rd generation: The Law of Three Generations is often quoted in research but often without data to support it. Unfortunately, the historical data collected in this dissertation show that the majority of family-owned businesses fails in the third generation—in most cases the family members sell their shares. There is a little bias in the data because at the same time the majority of enterprises is already in the third generation. Therefore, family firms can become one of the largest enterprises within three generations, but this also increases the risk of failure. Independent if the third generation itself or the surrounding factors lead to a high rate of downfalls in the third generation, family-owned businesses should take special arrangements to overcome this period.

Conclusion 9

After highlighting the overarching development patterns as well as the practical implications this chapter provides the consolidated results to the research questions and outlines potential future research based on the findings. The chapter concludes with an overall summary of this dissertation.

9.1 Results on the Research Question

In the following, the research questions from Section 3.6 are answered based on the quantitative and long-term analyses as well the identified overarching patterns.

MRQ: How did the 250 largest enterprises of Germany develop between 1958 and 2018?

The objective of this dissertation has been the explanation of the long-term development of German enterprises including downfalls. A history-informed research approach is chosen to meet the attributed characteristic of family-owned businesses of a long-term orientation.

Overall, a broad variety of different developments is observed for the 250 largest enterprises of 1958. Nevertheless, with 56.4% the majority of them experiences a downfall until 2018. However, within the surviving enterprises the majority keeps it ownership structure and does not experience an ownership discontinuity.

The overall development of the enterprises is further strongly linked to the development of industries. The industry in which a company operates is its destiny over the entire observation period. Accordingly, if industries diminish enterprises will do the same. On the other hand, new enterprises rise with the development of new industries. Nevertheless, it can be shown that the structural change of the German economy is driven by failing and new companies and not by the surviving enterprises.

M. Lantelme, *The Continuity and Discontinuity of the 250 Largest Enterprises in Germany*, Familienunternehmen und KMU,
https://doi.org/10.1007/978-3-658-42375-9_9

Furthermore, the role of the capital market declines in the observation period. The number of listed as well as of public companies decreases between 1958 and 2018. On the other hand, the average size of public companies increases significantly in the observation period. On average, it is the largest company type of the entire sample. In addition, listed enterprises are often acquired by foreign companies which shows the increased risk for an ownership discontinuity. Furthermore, listed firms also have a higher downfall rate. However, a listing is often linked to higher growth rates. Enterprises of 1958 which survive and remain one of the 250 largest enterprises of 2018 have a higher share of listed companies compared to the entire sample. A listing increases an enterprise's risk to fail but it also provides above-average growth opportunities.

In addition, the distribution of the 250 largest enterprises changes drastically between 1958 and 2018. The only constant are family-owned businesses. All other company types lose or gain shares. An exceptional increase is seen by foreign subsidiaries. More and more foreign entities build large enterprises on the German market or acquire established German enterprises.

The average age of the companies rises despite all these changes. Listed companies are on average older than non-listed enterprises although public companies are much younger than listed family or multiple companies-owned firms. Continuous family-owned businesses achieve the highest age of all enterprises.

SRQ1: Which of the enterprises survive or fail between 1958 and 2018 and what underlying patterns can be identified?

Foundations, foreign subsidiaries and state-owned enterprises have the highest survival rates of all company types. They confirm the objective and capabilities of their shareholder structures. In the case of foundations, these are the perpetuation of the ownership and operations. In the case of foreign subsidiaries and state-owned enterprises they are the large financial and non-financial resources.

Comparing family-owned businesses and public companies, the former company type shows a superior survival rate. Furthermore, listed companies have a slightly higher downfall rate than non-listed companies which shows an increased risk. It can be concluded that companies are acquired and foundations stabilize the ownership structure.

Within the 250 largest enterprises size plays an important role. Smaller enterprises are more likely to fail in the observation period which establishes the *liability of relative smallness*. Furthermore, the survival or failure is linked to the industry as highlighted above. It is a destiny like the mining and quarrying industry as a declining example with a high rate of failures and the information and communications industry as a growing example with several new joiners in 2018. Furthermore, the industry is also connected to certain legal forms like cooperatives in food retail. With the concentration of the market the majority of these forms disappears.

For family firms, the 3rd generation seems to represent a risk for the survival of the company with the highest number of downfalls in this generation. Nevertheless, Ward's survival rate for family-owned businesses needs to be adjusted for the case of large German family-owned enterprises from 20.0% to 44.8% which is a major increase.

SRQ2: How do the enterprises' ownership structures change between 1958 and 2018 and which characteristic pattern can be identified?

If a company survives the observation period it can still change its ownership structure in the same time. For family-owned business this would mean the loss of the ownership majority. However, the majority of the ownership structures of the surviving enterprises of 1958 does not change over 60 years. Again, foundations, foreign subsidiaries and state-owned companies show the highest rates. Family-owned business again have a higher ownership continuity rate than public companies. Nearly every fourth family firm survives and remains in the hands of the same family over 60 years.

The same applies to the 250 largest enterprises of 2018. Most of the companies which are already founded before 1959 remain in their ownership structure of 1958. Especially family firms have an exceptional high rate of 95.9%. Nevertheless, the public companies of 2018 show that a large share is family-owned in 1958. If family businesses become listed they turn into public companies in the mid- to long-term and the family loses its majority. There is only one example of a listed family-owned company which remains listed and in the hands of the same family over two generations. This is not the case for the majority of family firms which go public.

Another pattern of family-owned businesses is their development into foundations. The majority of the foundation-owned companies of 2018 is family-owned 60 years earlier. Although family businesses change into different company types in the observation period it is an exception that a non-family business becomes a family business. Single cases are, for example, *Volkswagen AG*. Again, Ward's ownership continuity rate of family businesses needs to be adjusted for the case of large German family-owned enterprises from 13.0% to 23.0% which is again a major adjustment.

A different kind of ownership change can be seen especially by listed family companies which issue preferential stocks (e.g., *Schaeffler* and *Henkel*). To keep the majority of voting rights but allow additional funding the families sell preferential shares which do not have a voting right. This also means that the family benefits less from the financial success of the company.

In addition, in 2018 the largest company type of the 109 surviving companies of the 1958 enterprises are foreign subsidiaries with 25 entities. 15 companies have changed to this company type in the observation period of 60 years—especially public companies become foreign subsidiaries with nine entities. This shows that a very common development of German (public) enterprises is the acquisition by a foreign company.

SRQ3: How do the enterprises grow, stagnate or decline between 1958 and 2018 and which characteristic pattern can be identified?
The average CAGR of the GDP between 1958 and 2018 is 5.7%. The surviving entities of the 250 largest enterprises of 1958 have a CAGR of 5.2%. On average they grow less than the GDP. However, the differences between the individual rates are high. Companies survive even with on average negative or stagnating growth rates over 60 years. Family businesses often remain a family business although the company is stagnating or declining. Their number within the additional survivors is high with seven entities which is only exceeded by state-owned companies with nine entities.

On the other hand, to remain one of the 250 largest enterprises between 1958 and 2018 a growth rate between 6.6% and 7.1% is required. This corridor allows a sustainable development in comparison to the other companies. Nevertheless, two-digit growth rates are also feasible—for foundations, family firms as well as for public companies. Two-digit growth rates of small firms over 60 years can lead to a place within the 250 largest enterprises (e.g., *Fresenius*).

Overall, public companies can achieve on average the largest size although they do not have the highest survival rate. Being a public company can lead to above average growth compared to other company types. Additionally, continuous public companies have a higher CAGR between 1958 and 2018 with 6.8% compared to continuous family-owned businesses with 6.2%. In addition, the historical data show that extraordinary growth can be based on new business models (e.g., discounter) or on new industries (e.g., commerce, information & communication).

9.2 Future Research

The answers to the research questions provide several insights on the long-term development of German enterprises. At the same time, new questions come up and others are not yet answered. Therefore, this chapter proposes avenues for future research to better understand the development of family and non-family companies including their decline and downfall.

First, the institutional conditions for enterprises in Germany have changed drastically over the last decades as seen in Chapter 4. Due to their strong focus on international markets (‘*Export World Champion*’) as well the expansion of the EU which has gained further competences in various areas the development of German enterprises does not stop at national borders. Future research should build on existing national findings and broaden its scope by including the global challenges of the enterprises in comparison with companies from other countries in a historical context. However, the national characteristics should not be abandoned in the process. They are still crucial variables in the explanation of the development.

Second, the thesis provides insights into family and non-family firms from a business perspective. This is reflected by measuring the continuity and discontinuity of a company’s majority ownership. The required data for the long-term analysis of 250 enterprises over 60 years can be collected using predominantly secondary sources as well as some primary sources like company publications. As a next step, the family perspective should become the research focus. Based on a detailed analysis of a small number of owner families over a long study period—like the 60 years used in this thesis—the processes in the family which have an impact on the family firm could be further analyzed. This could help to better understand the heterogeneity in the development of family firms observed in this study.[1] Such analysis might require access to additional primary sources including the possibility to interview owners and managers which can only be implemented with a smaller number of companies compared to the sample in this thesis due to the required effort and time. For discontinued companies such an approach becomes even more difficult. Nevertheless, in-depth analyses from a family perspective could provide additional insights into a firm’s development as well as into the underlying family processes. These process analyses should also take into account the development of the term “family” over time as well as family businesses as one type of entrepreneurial activity within a specific group.[2]

Third, based on the long-term analyses individual cases are identified which appear important to provide more in-depth knowledge of specific developments. *Dierig Holding AG* is such a case. It is the only continuous listed family-owned business over 60 years. The family keeps the ownership majority although (or because) the company size decreases between 1958 and 2018. At the end of the

---

[1] See Rovelli et al. (2021) for their future research agenda including the topic of heterogeneity.

[2] See the initial view by Stamm (2016) as well as the broader concept of “entrepreneurial groups” in Stamm, Discua Cruz, and Cailluet (2019).

observation period the company is in the seventh generation. At the beginning of the observation period *Dierig* operates exclusively in textile. In 2018, this business unit remains the largest revenue contributor, but it is declining for years. At the same time, the revenue of the real estate business unit is increasing.[3] A second interesting case is *Globus Holding GmbH & Co. KG*. The continuous family business achieves an above-average revenue CAGR of 13.6% between 1958 and 2018 and is in the fifth generation.[4] It operates in commerce. Therefore, it benefits from the structural change or is a driver of it, respectively. These single cases can further improve the understanding of growth and decline drivers. In the quantitative analyses of this dissertation only the drivers' outcomes are visible.

Lastly, and as an overarching research avenue, there is the increased use of historical methods in business and economics. They can capture especially long-term developments more holistically and provide the context of the developments to better understand the underlying decisions. Family business research would benefit from these methods in particular because of their long-term research object. Furthermore, the historical context could enrich case studies as well as qualitative research and the observation period of quantitative research could be increased. Based on the results of this dissertation and the use of historical methods the identified overarching patterns including the propositions can be tested in follow-up studies every ten years. Then, for example, the listing proposition of family firms could be further investigated and maybe there will be another listed family firm besides *Dierig* which remains majority-owned by the family for more than two generations.

9.3 Concluding Summary

Family businesses are seen as long-term oriented not only in research but also by consumers and employees. Despite this often repeated characteristic (also in scientific theory) family business research as well as historical sciences have not systematically studied the long-term development of family and non-family enterprises. Therefore, this dissertation combines both research areas to provide insights how enterprises in Germany develop over two generations.

The created datasets to investigate the developments include the 250 largest enterprises of 1958 and 2018 as well as their ownership, operations and solvency continuities and discontinuities in between. The ranking of the 250 largest

[3] See Dierig Holding AG (2019).

[4] See Bruch (1995) for an autobiographical publication of the early years.

enterprises of 1958 provides the most comprehensive historical overview of this period—to the author's knowledge. This unique ranking preserves historical corporate data which can be used for further research as well. This data preservation has also been the second research objective of this dissertation. Besides a comprehensive description of the statuses of the largest enterprises in Germany in 1958 and 2018 as well as their developments over 60 years this thesis provides overarching patterns and propositions of these developments as well as implications for action.

The survival of an enterprise is an exception in the long-term—independent of the ownership structure. Over six decades more than half of the companies in the sample fails and less than a quarter keeps its ownership structure. These developments include, next to family firms, companies which are founded for long-term purposes like state-owned enterprises and foundations. Despite the high risk of a downfall family-owned businesses show a relatively stable and long-term development especially in comparison to public companies. History tells that owner families should avoid a listing and should choose the industry of their company wisely. Furthermore, an average growth rate of 6.7% to 7.1% over decades provides a guideline to remain one of the largest enterprises. If the company is not yet one of the largest enterprises two-digit growth rates are required. Although growth is favorable there are also (family) firms which survive with lower growth rates. Nevertheless, size is also a protection from a downfall which requires growth.

Overall, this doctoral thesis proposes new findings towards a more comprehensive view on the long-term development of family and non-family enterprises. The author trusts that each owner can gain valuable insight through learning from history—first from the history of his or her own company but even more from the history of the relevant peer group which are described and analyzed in this thesis. If the readers discover something new, something beyond their horizon—then this is a good day.

References

Abelshauser, W. (1984). *Der Ruhrkohlenbergbau seit 1945: Wiederaufbau, Krise, Anpassung. Bergbau und Bergarbeit*. Munich: C.H. Beck.

Abrams, L. (2006). *Bismarck and the German Empire, 1871–1918* (2nd ed.). *Lancaster Pamphlets*. New York: Routledge.

Aldrich, H. E., & Auster, E. R. (1986). Even Dwarfs Started Small: Liabilities of Age and Size and Their Strategic Implications. *Research in Organizational Behavior*, *8*, 165–198.

Allais, M. (1988). Richtig ist die Empirie. *WirtschaftsWoche*. (45), 119–124.

Almus, M., & Nerlinger, E. A. (1999). Growth of New Technology-Based Firms: Which Factors Matter? *Small Business Economics*, *13*(2), 141–154.

Amato, S., Basco, R., & Lattanzi, N. (2021). Contextualizing employment outcomes in family business research: current findings and future research avenues. *Management Review Quarterly*.

Anderson, R. C., & Reeb, D. M. (2003). Founding-Family Ownership and Firm Performance: Evidence from the S&P 500. *The Journal of Finance*, *58*(3), 1301–1328.

Argyres, N. S., Massis, A. de, Foss, N. J., Frattini, F., Jones, G., & Silverman, B. S. (2020). History-informed strategy research: The promise of history and historical research methods in advancing strategy scholarship. *Strategic Management Journal*, *41*(3), 343–368.

Aronoff, C. (1999). Family Business Survival: Understanding the Statistics "Only 30%". *The Family Business Advisor*, *8*(7), 1 & 7.

Ashkenas, R. N., & Manville, B. (2019). *Harvard Business Review Leader's Handbook: Make an Impact, Inspire Your Organization, and Get to the Next Level. The Harvard Business Review Handbooks Series*. Boston: Harvard Business Review Press.

Astrachan, J. H., & Binz Astrachan, C. (2021). Whatever Happened to Relevance? In T. A. Rüsen (Ed.), *Theorie und Praxis der Unternehmerfamilie und des Familienunternehmens—Theory and Practice of Business Families and Family Businesses: Festschrift für Arist von Schlippe—Commemorative Publication for Arist von Schlippe* (pp. 21–29). Göttingen: Vandenhoeck & Ruprecht.

M. Lantelme, *The Continuity and Discontinuity of the 250 Largest Enterprises in Germany*, Familienunternehmen und KMU,
https://doi.org/10.1007/978-3-658-42375-9

Astrachan, J. H., Klein, S. B., & Smyrnios, K. X. (2002). The F-PEC Scale of Family Influence: A Proposal for Solving the Family Business Definition Problem. *Family Business Review, 15*(1), 45–58.

Astrachan, J. H., & Shanker, M. C. (2003). Family Businesses' Contribution to the U.S. Economy: A Closer Look. *Family Business Review, 16*(3), 211–219.

August Thyssen-Hütte AG (1959). *Bericht über das Geschäftsjahr 1957/1958*. Duisburg-Hamborn.

Bähr, J. (2015). *Thyssen in der Adenauerzeit: Konzernbildung und Familienkapitalismus. Familie—Unternehmen—Öffentlichkeit: Thyssen im 20. Jahrhundert: Vol. 5*. Paderborn: Ferdinand Schöningh.

Bähr, J. (2016). *Werner von Siemens 1816–1892: Eine Biographie*. Munich: C.H. Beck.

Bähr, J., Banken, R., & Flemming, T. (Eds.) (2019). *Die MAN: Eine deutsche Industriegeschichte* (4th ed.). Munich: C.H. Beck.

Bähr, J., & Erker, P. (2013). *Bosch: Geschichte eines Weltunternehmens*. Munich: C.H. Beck.

Bähr, J., & Erker, P. (2017). *NetzWerke: Die Geschichte der Stadtwerke München*. Munich: Piper.

Bayer, W., & Habersack, M. (Eds.) (2007). *Aktienrecht im Wandel: Entwicklung des Aktienrechts* (Vol. 1). Tübingen: Mohr Siebeck.

Beckhard, R., & Dyer, W. G., Jr. [W. G.] (1983a). Managing Change in the Family Firm—Issues and Strategies. *Sloan Management Review, 24*(3), 59–65.

Beckhard, R., & Dyer, W. G., Jr. [W. G.] (1983b). Managing Continuity in the Family-Owned Business. *Organizational Dynamics, 12*(1), 5–12.

Berger, R. (2015). Unternehmen und Beratung im Wandel der Zeit. In T. Deelmann & D. M. Ockel (Eds.), *Handbuch der Unternehmensberatung: Organisationen führen und entwickeln* (0100). Berlin: Erich Schmidt.

Berghoff, H. (2016a). Familienunternehmen. Stärken und Schwächen einer besonderen Unternehmensverfassung. In M. Spitz, N. Roth, K. Bosecker, & A. Kambartel (Eds.), *Phänomen Familienunternehmen: Vol. 2. Phänomen Familienunternehmen: Überblicke* (pp. 15–23). Mettingen: Draiflessen Collection.

Berghoff, H. (2016b). *Moderne Unternehmensgeschichte: Eine themen- und theorieorientierte Einführung* (2nd ed.). Berlin/Boston: De Gruyter Oldenbourg.

Berghoff, H., & Köhler, I. (2019). *Family Businesses in Germany and the United States since Industrialisation: A Long-Term Historical Study*. Munich: Stiftung Familienunternehmen.

Bird, B., Welsch, H., Astrachan, J. H., & Pistrui, D. (2002). Family Business Research: The Evolution of an Academic Field. *Family Business Review, 15*(4), 337–350.

Block, J. H. (2009). *Long-term Orientation of Family Firms: An Investigation of R&D Investments, Downsizing Practices, and Executive Pay. Innovation und Entrepreneurship*. Wiesbaden: Gabler.

Block, J. H., Jarchow, S., Kammerlander, N., Hosseini, F., & Achleitner, A.-K. (2020). Performance of foundation-owned firms in Germany: The role of foundation purpose, stock market listing, and family involvement. *Journal of Family Business Strategy, 11*(4), 100356.

Block, J. H., May, P., Betzer, A., & Au, D. von (Eds.) (2020). *Die Familienstiftung: Ein Instrument zur Zukunftssicherung von Familienunternehmen*. Wiesbaden: Springer Gabler.

Boerse.de Finanzportal AG (2021). Größte Unternehmen in Deutschland. Retrieved from https://www.boerse.de/wissen/groesste-unternehmen-deutschland

Bößenecker, H. (1980, March 14). Kein Siemens bei Siemens: Vom nächsten Jahr an wird der Aufsichtsrat des größten deutschen Elektro-Konzerns nicht mehr von einem Mitglied der Gründer familie geführt. Hat sie abgedankt? *DIE ZEIT*.

Bößenecker, H. (1985, December 27). Der Aufsteiger folgt dem Aussteiger. *DIE ZEIT*.

Brockstedt, J. (1984). Family Enterprise and the Rise of Large-Scale Enterprises in Germany [1871–1914]—Ownership and Mangement. In A. Ōkōchi & S. Yasuoka (Eds.), *International Conference on Business History. Family Business in the Era of Industrial Growth: Its Ownership and Management* (10th ed., pp. 237–267). Tokyo: University of Tokyo Press.

Brose Fahrzeugteile GmbH & Co. KG (2019). Disappointing fiscal year 2018 for Brose. Retrieved from https://www.brose.com/de-en/press/2019/disappointing-fiscal-year-2018-for-brose.pdf

Brose Fahrzeugteile SE & Co. KG (2021). Die Gründerjahre: 1908–1968. Retrieved from https://www.brose.com/de-de/unternehmen/historie/1908-1968/

Brown, J. H. (2018). Establishment Survivorship in U.S. Manufacturing, 1987–1992. *Review of Industrial Organization, 53*(2), 347–366.

Bruch, F. J. (1995). *Die Geschichte der Firma Franz Bruch St. Wendel*. St. Wendel.

Brüderl, J., & Schüssler, R. (1990). Organizational Mortality: The Liabilities of Newness and Adolescence. *Administrative Science Quarterly, 35*(3), 530.

Bucher, A. (1996). *Privatisierung von Bundesfernstrassen. Schriften zum öffentlichen Recht: Band 703*. Berlin: Duncker & Humblot.

Bundeskartellamt (2008, May 30). *Fusionsverfahren EDEKA Zentrale AG & Co. KG & Tengelmann Warenhandelsgesellschaft KG*. Bonn. Retrieved from https://www.bundeskartellamt.de/SharedDocs/Entscheidung/DE/Entscheidungen/Fusionskontrolle/2008/B2-333-07.pdf?__blob=publicationFile&v=3

Bundeskartellamt (2018). *60 Jahre: Bundeskartellamt 1958–2018*. Bonn.

Bundesministerium der Finanzen (2017). *Veräußerung/Verwertung von Bundesunternehmen: Unmittelbare Beteiligungsunternehmen des Bundes* (No. VIII A 4). Berlin. Retrieved from https://www.bundesfinanzministerium.de/Content/DE/Standardartikel/Themen/Bundesvermoegen/Privatisierungs_und_Beteiligungspolitik/Privatisierungspolitik/privatisierungspolitik-anlage-2-uebersicht-privatisierungen-des-bundes.pdf?__blob=publicationFile&v=4

Bundesministerium der Finanzen (2021). Übersichten zur finanzwirtschaftlichen Entwicklung: Tabelle: Entwicklung der Staatsquote. Retrieved from https://www.bundesfinanzministerium.de/Monatsberichte/2017/05/Inhalte/Kapitel-6-Statistiken/6-1-12-entwicklung-der-staatsquote.html

Bundesministerium für wirtschaftlichen Besitz des Bundes (1959). *Der Bund als Unternehmer: Bericht über die Entwicklung des vom Bundesministerium für wirtschaftlichen Besitz des Bundes verwalteten industriellen Bundesvermögens in der Zeit vom 1. April 1958 bis 31. März 1959*. Bad Godesberg.

Bünte, H. (1972). *Der Saarberg-Konzern*. Saarbrücken.

Bureau van Dijk (2021). dafne: Germany. Retrieved from https://www.bvdinfo.com/en-us/our-products/data/national/dafne

Büschemann, K.-H. (2014, June 18). Der Nierentisch im Buchgeschäft. *Süddeutsche Zeitung*, p. 17.

Calder, G. H. (1953). *Some management problems of the small family controlled manufacturing business. Doctoral Dissertation.* Indiana: Indiana University.

Casson, M. (2000). *Enterprise and Leadership: Studies on Firms, Markets, and Networks.* Cheltenham: Edward Elgar.

Center for Family Business at the University of St.Gallen (2021). The Global Family Business Index methodology. Retrieved from https://familybusinessindex.com/#impressum

Chandler, A. D. (1962). *Strategy and Structure: Chapters in the History of the Industrial Enterprise.* Cambridge: MIT Press.

Chandler, A. D. (1977). *The Visible Hand: The Managerial Revolution in American Business.* Cambridge: Belknap Press.

Chandler, A. D. (1990). *Scale and scope: The dynamics of industrial capitalism.* Cambridge: Belknap Press.

Chandler, J. A., Zachary, M. A., Brigham, K. H., & Payne, G. T. (2016). Long-Term Orientation: Reviewing the Past and Identifying Future Opportunities for Family Business Research. In F. Kellermanns & F. Hoy (Eds.), *The Routledge Companion to Family Business* (pp. 70–89). New York: Routledge.

Chrisman, J. J., Chua, J. H., Pearson, A. W., & Barnett, T. (2012). Family Involvement, Family Influence, and Family–Centered Non–Economic Goals in Small Firms. *Entrepreneurship Theory and Practice, 36*(2), 267–293.

Chrisman, J. J., Chua, J. H., & Sharma, P. (2005). Trends and Directions in the Development of a Strategic Management Theory of the Family Firm. *Entrepreneurship Theory and Practice, 29*(5), 555–575.

Christensen, C. R. (1953). *Management succession in small and growing enterprises.* Boston: Harvard University.

Chua, J. H., Chrisman, J. J., & Sharma, P. (1999). Defining the Family Business by Behavior. *Entrepreneurship Theory and Practice, 23*(4), 19–39.

Church, R. (1993). The Family Firm in Industrial Capitalism: International Perspectives on Hypotheses and History. *Business History, 35*(4), 17–43.

CNN (2021). 1958 Full list: A database of 50 years of FORTUNE's list of America's largest corporations. Retrieved from https://money.cnn.com/magazines/fortune/fortune500_archive/full/1958/

Colli, A. (2003). *The History of Family Business, 1850–2000. New Studies in Economic and Social History.* Cambridge: Cambridge University Press.

Colli, A. (2013). Risk, Uncertainty, and Family Ownership. In P. Fernández Pérez & A. Colli (Eds.), *The Endurance of Family Businesses* (pp. 85–108). Cambridge: Cambridge University Press.

Colli, A., & Fernández Pérez, P. (2020). Chapter 5: Historical methods in family business studies. In A. de Massis & N. Kammerlander (Eds.), *Handbooks of Research Methods in Management. Handbook of Qualitative Research Methods for Family Business* (pp. 98–123). Northampton: Edward Elgar Publishing.

Colli, A., & Larsson, M. (2014). Family business and business history: An example of comparative research. *Business History, 56*(1), 37–53.

Colli, A., & Rose, M. B. (2003). Family Firms in Comparative Perspective. In F. Amatori & G. Jones (Eds.), *Comparative perspectives in business history. Business History around the World* (pp. 339–352). Cambridge: Cambridge University Press.

Collins, J. C. (2001). *Good to Great: Why some companies make the leap -and others don't*. New York: Harper Collins.
Commerzbank AG (1959). *Wer gehört zu wem: Mutter und Tochtergesellschaften von A-Z* (4th ed.). Düsseldorf: Commerzbank AG.
Conrad, A. H., & Meyer, J. R. (1958). The Economics of Slavery in the Ante Bellum South. *Journal of Political Economy*, *66*(2), 95–130.
Covestro AG (2016). *Geschäftsbericht 2015*. Leverkusen.
Covestro AG (2017). *Geschäftsbericht 2016*. Leverkusen.
Covestro AG (2018). *Geschäftsbericht 2017*. Leverkusen.
Covestro AG (2019). *Geschäftsbericht 2018*. Leverkusen.
Covestro AG (2021). Aus Tradition innovativ: Die Geschichte von Covestro. Retrieved from https://www.covestro.com/de/company/history/overview
Cronauge, U., & Pieck, S. (2016). *Kommunale Unternehmen* (6th ed.). Berlin: Erich Schmidt Verlag.
DACHSER Group SE & Co. KG (2019). *Konzernabschluss 2018*. Kempten.
Daimler AG (2019). *Geschäftsbericht 2018*. Stuttgart.
Daimler-Benz AG (1959). *Geschäftsbericht 1958*. Stuttgart.
Daske, S. (2019). *Vorzugsaktien in Deutschland: Historische und rechtliche Grundlagen, ökonomische Analyse, empirische Befunde* (1st ed.). Wiesbaden: Springer Fachmedien Wiesbaden.
Daunfeldt, S.-O., Elert, N., & Johansson, D. (2014). The Economic Contribution of High-Growth Firms: Do Policy Implications Depend on the Choice of Growth Indicator? *Journal of Industry, Competition and Trade*, *14*(3), 337–365.
Deckers, D. (2021). *Der Wein der „Gutehoffnungshütte": 100 Jahre Weingut St. Antony. Schriften zur rheinisch-westfälischen Wirtschaftsgeschichte: Vol. 49*. Cologne: Böhlau Verlag.
Delmar, F. (1997). Measuring Growth: Methodological Considerations and Empirical Results. In R. Donckels & A. Miettinen (Eds.), *Entrepreneurship and SME Research: On its Way to the Next Millennium* (1st ed., pp. 199–216). Aldershot: Ashgate.
Denton, G., Forsyth, M., & MacLennan, M. C. (2017). *Economic Planning and Policies in Britain, France and Germany. Routledge Library Editions: The German Economy: Vol. 3*. Abingdon: Routledge.
Deutsche Bundesbank (2014, October 6). *Irrevocable euro conversion rate: EUR 1 = DEM 1.95583 / Germany / from 1 January 1999*. Frankfurt (Main). Retrieved from https://www.bundesbank.de/statistic-rmi/StatisticDownload?tsId=BBEX3.D.DEM.EUR.BA.AC.000&its_csvFormat=en&its_fileFormat=csv&mode=its
BGBl (Bundesgesetzblatt) 1185.
Deutscher Bundestag (1960). *Bericht über die Deutsche Bundesbahn (DB)* (No. Bundesdrucksache III/1602). Bonn.
Deutscher Bundestag (1969). *Denkschrift des Präsidenten des Bundesrechnungshofes vom 15. Februar 1969* (No. Bundesdrucksache V/4660). Bonn.
Gesetz zur Änderung des Gesetzes betreffend die Erwerbs- und Wirtschaftsgenossenschaften, Bundesgesetzblatt Teil I 1451 (1973).
Diaz-Moriana, V., Clinton, E., Kammerlander, N., Lumpkin, G. T., & Craig, J. B. (2020). Innovation Motives in Family Firms: A Transgenerational View. *Entrepreneurship Theory and Practice*, *44*(2), 256–287.

Dierig, C. G. (1993). *Über uns und etwas mehr*. Augsburg.

Dierig Holding AG (2019). *Jahresabschluss zum Geschäftsjahr vom 01.01.2018 bis zum 31.12.2018*. Augsburg.

LEONINE (Producer). & Dommenget, O. (Director) (2016). *Duell der Brüder—Die Geschichte von Adidas und Puma*.

Donges, J. B. (1986). *The West German economy towards the year 2000: an analysis of structural change* (Kiel Working Paper No. 268). Kiel.

(1958). OeFa, P13/45611958, Dr. August Oetker.

Dr. August Oetker KG (1972). *Geschäftsbericht 1971*. Bielefeld.

Dr. August Oetker KG (2019). *Konzernabschluss 2018*. Bielefeld.

Dunne, P., & Hughes, A. (1994). Age, Size, Growth and Survival: UK Companies in the 1980s. *The Journal of Industrial Economics*, *42*(2), 115.

Edwards, J., & Fischer, K. (1994). *Banks, finance and investments in Germany*. Cambridge: Cambridge University Press.

Eglau, H.-O. (1982, September 3). Ein Wunderknabe weniger: Der Wienerwald-Gründer Friedrich Jahn scheiterte an sich selbst. *DIE ZEIT*.

Ehrhardt, O., & Nowak, E. (2002). Evolution von Aktionärsstrukturen, Kontrolltransfers und Performanceunterschiede bei Börsengängen deutscher Familienunternehmen. In H. Albach & B. Schauenberg (Eds.), *ZfB-Ergänzungshefte: Vol. 2. Unternehmensentwicklung im Wettbewerb* (pp. 25–32). Wiesbaden: Gabler Verlag.

Eichengreen, B. J. (Ed.) (1995). *Europe's Postwar Recovery*. Cambridge: Cambridge University Press.

Elsevier (2022). Journal of Family Business Strategy. Retrieved from https://www.journals.elsevier.com/journal-of-family-business-strategy

Erker, P. (2008). *Das Logistikunternehmen Dachser: Die treibende Kraft der Familie als Erfolgsfaktor im globalen Wettbewerb*. Frankfurt (Main): Campus.

European Statistical Office (2022). Gross domestic product at market prices. Retrieved from https://ec.europa.eu/eurostat/databrowser/view/TEC00001__custom_1177227/bookmark/table?lang=en&bookmarkId=8e5010e8-4789-4728-a917-d6a2c3fcd13a

Fabry, B., & Appel, M. (Eds.) (2011). *Unternehmen der öffentlichen Hand: Handbuch* (2nd ed.). Baden-Baden: Nomos Verlagsgesellschaft.

Fastrich, L. (2017). Einleitung. In A. Baumbach & A. Hueck (Eds.), *Beck'sche Kurz-Kommentare: Vol. 20. Gesetz betreffend die Gesellschaften mit beschränkter Haftung* (21st ed., 1–29). Munich: C.H. Beck.

FAZ (1959, January 6). Zusammenschluß Bochumer Verein—Rheinhausen genehmigt. *Frankfurter Allgemeine Zeitung*, 12.

Fear, J. R. (2005). *Organizing control: August Thyssen and the construction of German corporate management. Harvard Studies in Business History: Vol. 45*. Cambridge, London: Harvard University Press.

Federal Ministry of Justice and for Consumer Protection (2021). Bundesanzeiger. Retrieved from https://www.bundesanzeiger.de/pub/en/start?0

Fehr, M., & F.A.Z.-Archiv (2021, July 7). Die 100 Größten. *Frankfurter Allgemeine Zeitung*, 19–22.

Feldenkirchen, W., & Hilger, S. (2001). *Menschen und Marken: 125 Jahre Henkel 1876–2001*. Düsseldorf.

Fenner, J. N. (2005). Cross-cultural Estimation of the Human Generation Interval for Use in Genetics-based Population Divergence Studies. *American Journal of Physical Anthropology, 128*(2), 415–423.

Fernandez Moya, M., Fernandez-Perez, P., & Lubinski, C. (2020). Standing the test of time: External factors influencing family firm longevity in Germany and Spain during the twentieth century. *Journal of Evolutionary Studies in Business, 5*(1), 221–264.

Fett, T., & Stütz, D. (2017). 20 Jahre Kapitalgesellschaft & Co. KGaA. *Neue Zeitschrift Für Gesellschaftsrecht, 20*(29), 1121–1131.

Fiedler, M. (1999). Die 100 größten Unternehmen in Deutschland—nach der Zahl ihrer Beschäftigten—1907,1938, 1973 und 1995. *Zeitschrift Für Unternehmensgeschichte / Journal of Business History, 44*(1), 32–66.

Fleschutz, K. (2009). *Die Stiftung als Nachfolgeinstrument für Familienunternehmen: Handlungsempfehlungen für die Ausgestaltung und Überführung* (1st ed.). Wiesbaden: Gabler Verlag.

Fogel, R. W. (2003). *The Slavery Debates, 1952–1990: A Retrospective. The Walter Lynwood Fleming lectures in southern history.* Baton Rouge, London: Louisiana State University Press.

Fohlin, C. (2005). The History of Corporate Ownership and Control in Germany. In R. Morck (Ed.), *National Bureau of Economic Research conference report. A History of Corporate Governance around the World: Family Business Groups to Professional Managers* (pp. 223–282). Chicago, London: University of Chicago Press.

Fortune Media IP Ltd. (2020a). Fortune 500. Retrieved from https://fortune.com/fortune500/

Fortune Media IP Ltd. (2020b). Global 500. Retrieved from https://fortune.com/global500/2018/search/?hqcountry=Germany

Frank, H., Kessler, A., Rusch, T., Suess–Reyes, J., & Weismeier–Sammer, D. (2017). Capturing the Familiness of Family Businesses: Development of the Family Influence Familiness Scale (FIFS). *Entrepreneurship Theory and Practice, 41*(5), 709–742.

(1959a). *Blick durch die Wirtschaft. Zeitung für Finanzen, Steuern, Recht und Management.* (1–4). Frankfurt (Main): Frankfurter Allgemeine Zeitung.

Frankfurter Allgemeine Zeitung (1959b). Hat die Schering-Bilanz genug Fenster für den Aktionär? Bedenken der Verwaltung gegen eine zu "gläserne" Rechnungslegung / Keine Klarheit über Paketkäufe. In Frankfurter Allgemeine Zeitung (Ed.), *Blick durch die Wirtschaft: Zeitung für Finanzen, Steuern, Recht und Management* (135 (15.06.1959b), p. 3). Frankfurt (Main): Frankfurter Allgemeine Zeitung.

Frankfurter Allgemeine Zeitung (1962, March 3). Die Siemens-Aktionäre sind zufrieden: Umsätze der Inlandsunternehmen in den ersten vier Monaten 1961/62 um 14 Prozent höher / Nächste Hauptversammlung in Berlin? *Frankfurter Allgemeine Zeitung*, p. 9.

Frankfurter Allgemeine Zeitung (1978, June 24). Osram jetzt voll bei Siemens. *Frankfurter Allgemeine Zeitung*, p. 14.

Fraport AG (2019). *Geschäftsbericht 2018.* Frankfurt (Main).

Fraport AG (2021). Geschichte: Fraport AG. Retrieved from https://www.fra-history.de/#1959-2

Freeman, J., Carroll, G. R., & Hannan, M. T. (1983). The Liability of Newness: Age Dependence in Organizational Death Rates. *American Sociological Review, 48*(5), 692.

Frericks, S. (2019). *Downfall of Large German Listed Companies: A Two-Dimensional Analysis of Failure Factors. BestMasters.* Wiesbaden: Springer Gabler.

Fridenson, P. (2008). Business History and History. In G. Jones & J. Zeitlin (Eds.), *The Oxford Handbook of Business History* (pp. 9–36). Oxford: Oxford University Press.

Fuchs, A., Munninger, N., & Schu, J. (2010). *Chronik: 1685—2010. 325 Jahre Dillinger Hütte: Vol. 1.* Dillingen: AG der Dillinger Hüttenwerke.

Gall, L. (2000). *Krupp: Der Aufstieg eines Industrieimperiums.* Berlin: Siedler.

Gall, L., Feldman, G. D., James, H., Holtfrerich, C.-L., & Buschen, H. E. (1995). *The Deutsche Bank, 1870–1995.* London: Weidenfeld & Nicolson.

Ge, B., Massis, A. de, & Kotlar, J. (2022). Mining the Past: History Scripting Strategies and Competitive Advantage in a Family Business. *Entrepreneurship Theory and Practice, 46*(1), 223–251.

Gedajlovic, E., & Carney, M. (2010). Markets, Hierarchies, and Families: Toward a Transaction Cost Theory of the Family Firm. *Entrepreneurship Theory and Practice, 34*(6), 1145–1171.

German Federal Statistical Office (1958, December 19). *Kurs, Dividende und Rendite der börsennotierten Aktien Ende November 1958* (Statistische Brichte No. Arb.Kr.VII/27/32). Wiesbaden.

German Federal Statistical Office (2008). xlsx.

German Federal Statistical Office (2019). *Statistisches Unternehmensregister: Rechtliche Einheiten nach Wirtschaftsabschnitten und Größenklassen der sozialversicherungspflichtig Beschäftigten im Berichtsjahr 2018.* Bonn.

German Federal Statistical Office (2020a). *Volkswirtschaftliche Gesamtrechnungen: Bruttoinlandsprodukt, Bruttonationaleinkommen, Volkseinkommen.* Lange Reihen ab 1925. Wiesbaden. Retrieved from https://www.destatis.de/DE/Themen/Wirtschaft/Volkswirtschaftliche-Gesamtrechnungen-Inlandsprodukt/Tabellen/inlandsprodukt-volkseinkommen1925-xls.xlsx?__blob=publicationFile

German Federal Statistical Office (2020b). *Volkswirtschaftliche Gesamtrechnungen: Inlandsproduktberechnung.* Lange Reihen ab 1970. Wiesbaden. Retrieved from https://www.destatis.de/DE/Themen/Wirtschaft/Volkswirtschaftliche-Gesamtrechnungen-Inlandsprodukt/Publikationen/Downloads-Inlandsprodukt/inlandsprodukt-lange-reihen-pdf-2180150.pdf?__blob=publicationFile

German Federal Statistical Office (2021a). *Außenhandel: Oktober 2021.* Statistischer Bericht. Wiesbaden. Retrieved from https://www.destatis.de/DE/Themen/Wirtschaft/Aussenhandel/Publikationen/Downloads-Aussenhandel/statistischer-bericht-aussenhandel-2070100211105.xlsx?__blob=publicationFile

German Federal Statistical Office (2021b). *Preise: Verbraucherpreisindizes für Deutschland.* Lange Reihen ab 1948. Wiesbaden. Retrieved from https://www.destatis.de/DE/Themen/Wirtschaft/Preise/Verbraucherpreisindex/Publikationen/Downloads-Verbraucherpreise/verbraucherpreisindex-lange-reihen-pdf-5611103.pdf?__blob=publicationFile&v=5

German Federal Statistical Office (2021c). Registrierte Arbeitslose und Arbeitslosenquote nach Gebietsstand: Konjunkturindikatoren. Retrieved from https://www.destatis.de/DE/Themen/Wirtschaft/Konjunkturindikatoren/Lange-Reihen/Arbeitsmarkt/lrarb003ga.html

German Federal Statistical Office (2022a). Erwerbstätige im Inland nach Wirtschaftssektoren: Konjunkturindikatoren. Retrieved from https://www.destatis.de/DE/Themen/Wirtschaft/Konjunkturindikatoren/Lange-Reihen/Arbeitsmarkt/lrerw13a.html;jsessionid=5E8ABBD6FD436F6F8CB36F82946EC818.live731#fussnote-1-242416

German Federal Statistical Office (2022b). Insolvenzen nach Jahren. Retrieved from https://www.destatis.de/DE/Themen/Branchen-Unternehmen/Unternehmen/Gewerbemeldungen-Insolvenzen/Tabellen/lrins01.html

Gerst, A. (2018, November 25). *Letter to my grandchildren*. International Space Station, Paris. Retrieved from European Space Agency website: https://www.esa.int/ESA_Multimedia/Videos/2018/12/Letter_to_my_grandchildren

Geus, A. de (1997). *The Living Company*. Boston: Harvard Business School Press.

Giersberg, G., & F.A.Z.-Archiv (2019, July 3). Die 100 Größten. *Frankfurter Allgemeine Zeitung*, H1–H8.

Giersch, H., Paqué, K.-H., & Schmieding, H. (1992). *The Fading Miracle: Four Decades of Market Economy in Germany*. Cambridge: Cambridge University Press.

Goldrichs UG (2022). Weingut Staffelter Hof. Retrieved from https://www.goldrichs.com/weingut-staffelter-hof/#

Gómez-Mejía, L. R., Haynes, K. T., Núñez-Nickel, M., Jacobson, K. J. L., & Moyano-Fuentes, J. (2007). Socioemotional Wealth and Business Risks in Family-controlled Firms: Evidence from Spanish Olive Oil Mills. *Administrative Science Quarterly*, *52*(1), 106–137.

Goslich, L. (1984, September 21). Aufgespalten in Eigentümer und Betrieb: Konkurs über Zündapp eröffnet / Noch 6800 Maschinen auf Lager. *Frankfurter Allgemeine Zeitung*, p. 16.

Goslich, L. (1986, April 5). Puma geht an die Börse. *Frankfurter Allgemeine Zeitung*, p. 17.

Goslich, L. (1989, May 19). Die Puma-Übernahme ist perfekt. *Frankfurter Allgemeine Zeitung*, p. 17.

Goto, T. (2006). Longevity of Japanese family firms. In P. Z. Poutziouris, K. X. Smyrnios, & S. B. Klein (Eds.), *Handbook of Research on Family Business* (pp. 517–534). Cheltenham: Edward Elgar.

Goto, T. (2014). Family Business and Its Longevity. *Kindai Management Review*, *2*, 78–96.

Gottschalk, S., Lubczyk, M., Hauer, A., & Keese, D. (2019). *Die volkswirtschaftliche Bedeutung der Familienunternehmen*. Munich.

Götz, H. H. (1975, December 17). Osram lockert die Bindungen zu Philips: Siemens kann die Osram-Anteile von AEG übernehmen / "Auflagen" des Kartellamts. *Frankfurter Allgemeine Zeitung*, p. 11.

Greger, H. (1986). Acht Jahrhunderte Münchener Münzgeschichte. In Bayerisches Hauptmünzamt (Ed.), *Festschrift zur Einweihung des Bayerischen Hauptmünzamtes: 16. Juli 1986: Neubau des Bayerischen Hauptmünzamtes* (pp. 13–38). Munich,

Groote, J. K. de, Conrad, W., & Hack, A. (2020). How can family businesses survive disruptive industry changes? Insights from the traditional mail order industry. *Review of Managerial Science*.

Grottel, B., & Kreher, M. (2020). § 290 Pflicht zur Aufstellung. In W. D. Budde, H. Clemm, U. Störk, M. Deubert, & M. Sarx (Eds.), *Beck'scher Bilanz-Kommentar: Handels- und Steuerbilanz, §§ 238 bis 339, 342 bis 342e HGB* (12th ed., pp. 1591–1613). Munich: C.H. Beck.

Grziwotz, H. (2018). Entwicklung, Erscheinungsformen und wirtschaftliche Bedeutung der GmbH. In H.-J. Priester, D. Mayer, H. Wicke, & E.-M. Bernauer (Eds.), *Münchener Handbuch des Gesellschaftsrechts: Vol. 3. Gesellschaft mit beschränkter Haftung* (5th ed., pp. 1–17). Munich: C.H. Beck.

Gupta, V., Koller, T., & Stumpner, P. (2021). *Reports of corporates' demise have been greatly exaggerated* (Strategy & Corporate Finance Practice). Retrieved from https://www.mckinsey.com/business-functions/strategy-and-corporate-finance/our-insights/reports-of-corporates-demise-have-been-greatly-exaggerated?cid=other-eml-alt-mip-mck&hdpid=57c5765b-1da0-4f1e-96b4-0a3e1882d148&hctky=12882202&hlkid=88d4570d6d9e4755b7a05fddbcf04542

Habbershon, T. G., & Williams, M. L. (1999). A Resource-Based Framework for Assessing the Strategic Advantages of Family Firms. *Family Business Review, 12*(1), 1–25.

Haberlandt, K. (1970). *Das Wachstum der industriellen Unternehmung*. Erlangen-Nuremberg: Luchterhand.

Ham, H. van (1935). *Beiträge zur Geschichte der Aktiengesellschaft der Dillinger Hüttenwerke: 1685–1935*. Saarlautern.

Handelsblatt (2021). Die 500 größten börsennotierten Unternehmen in Europa 2018. Retrieved from https://tool.handelsblatt.com/infografik/top_500/

Hannah, L. (Ed.) (1982). *Eighth International Economic History Congress: Vol. 9. From Family Firm to Professional Management: Structure and Performance of Business Enterprise*. Budapest: Akadémiai Kiadó.

Hannah, L. (1999). Marshall's "Trees" and the Global "Forest": Were "Giant Redwoods" Different? In N. R. Lamoreaux, D. M. G. Raff, & P. Temin (Eds.), *National Bureau of Economic Research conference report. Learning by Doing in Markets, Firms, and Countries* (pp. 253–294). Chicago: University of Chicago Press.

Hegmann, G. (2014, February 27). Siemens-Dynastie mischt weiter im Konzern mit. *Die Welt*. Retrieved from https://www.welt.de/print/die_welt/wirtschaft/article125239432/Siemens-Dynastie-mischt-weiter-im-Konzern-mit.html

HeidelbergCement AG (2013). *Die Geschichte von HeidelbergCement: Der Weg des süddeutschen Unternehmens zum internationalen Konzern*. Heidelberg. Retrieved from https://www.hc-museum.de/system/files_force/assets/document/53/3b/8_hc_140_jahre_web.pdf?download=1

HeidelbergCement AG (2019). *Geschätsbericht 2018*. Heidelberg.

Heiss, F., & Köke, J. (2004). Dynamics in Ownership and Firm Survival: Evidence from Corporate Germany. *European Financial Management, 10*(1), 167–195.

Helmer, W. (1982, October 26). IWKA nicht bei Quandt. *Frankfurter Allgemeine Zeitung*, 16.

Hengstmann, W. (1935). *Die Familiengesellschaft. Doctoral Dissertation*. Halle-Wittenberg: Martin-Luther-Universität.

Henkel AG & Co. KGaA (2018, October 12). *Stimmrechtsmitteilung: Veröffentlichung gemäß § 40 Abs. 1 WpHG* [Press release]. Düsseldorf. Retrieved from https://www.henkel.de/resource/blob/882852/389bb574b9f7adcf11daf3fd3a3f2326/data/2018-10-12-stimmrechtsmitteilung.pdf

Henkel AG & Co. KGaA (2019). *Geschäftsbericht 2018*. Düsseldorf.

Henkel AG & Co. KGaA (2021). Unternehmensgeschichte: Mehr als 140 Jahre Markenerfolg. Retrieved from https://www.henkel.de/unternehmen/meilensteine-und-errungenschaften/geschichte

Henkel KGaA (2006). *Chronik 130 Jahre Henkel*. Düsseldorf.

Hernández-Linares, R., Sarkar, S., & Cobo, M. J. (2018). Inspecting the Achilles heel: A quantitative analysis of 50 years of family business definitions. *Scientometrics, 115*(2), 929–951.

Herr, J. (2007, July 18). PPR hält 62 Prozent von Puma: Unterstützung von Banken für Übernahmeofferte aus Frankreich. *Frankfurter Allgemeine Zeitung*, p. 15.

Herrmann, H.-C. (2012). Das Saarland als Bundesland—trotz Dauerkrise auch eine Geschichte der Erfolge. In H.-C. Herrmann & J. Schmitt (Eds.), *Das Saarland: Geschichte einer Region* (pp. 339–398). St. Ingbert: Röhrig Universitätsverlag.

Institut für Mittelstandsforschung Bonn (2021). Family business definition of the IfM Bonn. Retrieved from https://www.ifm-bonn.org/en/about-us/about-us

International Monetary Fund (2019). World Economic Outlook Database: April 2019. Retrieved from https://www.imf.org/-/media/Files/Publications/WEO/WEO-Database/2019/WEOApr2019all.ashx

International Monetary Fund (2021). Special Data Dissemination Standard Plus: Germany. Retrieved from https://dsbb.imf.org/sddsplus/dqaf-base/country/DEU/category/NAG00

James, H. (2006). *Family Capitalism: Wendels, Haniels, Falcks, and the Continental European Model.* Cambridge, London: Belknap.

James, H. (2012). *Krupp: A History of the Legendary German Firm.* Princeton: Princeton University Press.

Jaskiewicz, P., & Dyer, W. G. [W. Gibb] (2017). Addressing the Elephant in the Room: Disentangling Family Heterogeneity to Advance Family Business Research. *Family Business Review, 30*(2), 111–118.

Johanson, J., & Vahlne, J.-E. (2009). The Uppsala internationalization process model revisited: From liability of foreignness to liability of outsidership. *Journal of International Business Studies, 40*(9), 1411–1431.

John Deere GmbH & Co. KG (2019). *Konzernabschluss zum Geschäftsjahr vom 01.11.2017 bis zum 31.10.2018.* Mannheim.

Joly, H. (1998). *Großunternehmer in Deutschland: Soziologie einer industriellen Elite; 1933–1989. Beiträge zur Universalgeschichte und vergleichenden Gesellschaftsforschung: Vol. 18.* Leipzig: Leipziger Univ.-Verl.

Jones, G., & Rose, M. B. (1993). *Family Capitalism.* London: Frank Cass.

Jordan, S. (2018). *Theorien und Methoden der Geschichtswissenschaft* (4th ed.). Paderborn: UTB.

Josefy, M. A., Harrison, J. S., Sirmon, D. G., & Carnes, C. (2017). Living and Dying: Synthesizing the Literature on Firm Survival and Failure across Stages of Development. *Academy of Management Annals, 11*(2), 770–799.

Jovanovic, B. (1982). Selection and the Evolution of Industry. *Econometrica, 50*(3), 649.

Kaelble, H. (1982). From the Family Enterprise to the Professional Manager: the German Case. In L. Hannah (Ed.), *Eighth International Economic History Congress: Vol. 9. From Family Firm to Professional Management: Structure and Performance of Business Enterprise* (pp. 50–59). Budapest: Akadémiai Kiadó.

Kahneman, D. (2011). *Thinking, fast and slow.* New York: Farrar, Straus and Giroux.

Karstadt Warenhaus GmbH (2019). Galeria Karstadt Kaufhof: Warenhausunternehmen werden verschmolzen: Guido Mager in die Geschäftsführung berufen. Retrieved from https://www.presseportal.de/pm/16971/4432670

Kellermanns, F. W., & Eddleston, K. A. (2006). Corporate Entrepreneurship in Family Firms: A Family Perspective. *Entrepreneurship Theory and Practice, 30*(6), 809–830.

Kellermanns, F. W., Eddleston, K. A., Barnett, T., & Pearson, A. (2008). An Exploratory Study of Family Member Characteristics and Involvement: Effects on Entrepreneurial Behavior in the Family Firm. *Family Business Review, 21*(1), 1–14.

Kets de Vries, M. F. (1993). The Dynamics of Family Controlled Firms: The Good and the Bad News. *Organizational Dynamics, 21*(3), 59–71.

Kieser, A., & Nicolai, A. T. (2005). Success Factor Research: Overcoming the Trade-Off Between Rigor and Relevance? *Journal of Management Inquiry, 14*(3), 275–279.

Kipping, M. (1996). The U.S. Influence on the Evolution of Management Consultancies in Britain, France, and Germany Since 1945. *Business and Economic History, 25*(1), 112–123.

Kipping, M. (1999). American Management Consulting Companies in Western Europe, 1920 to 1990: Products, Reputation, and Relationships. *Business History Review, 73*(2), 190–220.

Kipping, M., & Üsdiken, B. (2008). Business History and Management Studies. In G. Jones & J. Zeitlin (Eds.), *The Oxford Handbook of Business History* (pp. 96–119). Oxford: Oxford University Press.

Klein, S. B., & Blondel, C. (2002). *Ownership Structure of the 250 Largest Listed Companies in Germany* (INSEAD Working Papers No. 2002/123/IIFE). Fontainebleau.

Knipp, T. (2007). *Der Deal: Die Geschichte der grössten Übernahme aller Zeiten* (1st ed.). Hamburg: Murmann.

Knust, C. (1996, November 7). Proventus steigt bei Puma aus. *Frankfurter Allgemeine Zeitung*, p. 23.

Koch, B., & Scharrenbroch, C. (2018, February 16). Die Aldi-Schwestern erhöhen ihre Schlagkraft: In Einkauf und Marketing wollen beide Discountketten enger kooperieren. *Frankfurter Allgemeine Zeitung*, p. 26.

Koch, H. (1965). *75 Jahre Mannesmann: 1890–1965*. Düsseldorf.

Kocka, J. (1969). *Unternehmensverwaltung und Angestelltenschaft am Beispiel Siemens 1847–1914: Zum Verhältnis von Kapitalismus und Bürokratie in der deutschen Industrialisierung. Industrielle Welt: Vol. 11*. Stuttgart: Ernst Klett Verlag.

Kocka, J. (1971). Family and Bureaucracy in German Industrial Management, 1850–1914: Siemens in Comparative Perspective. *Business History Review, 45*(2), 133–156.

Kocka, J. (1980). Großunternehmen und der Aufstieg des Manager-Kapitalismus im späten 19. und frühen 20. Jahrhundert: Deutschland im internationalen Vergleich. In International Committee of Historical Sciences (Ed.), *Rapports: Vol. 2. Section chronologique, XVe Congrès International des Sciences Historiques, Bucarest, 10–17 août 1980* (pp. 599–612). Bucarest: Editura Academiei Republicii Socialiste România.

Kocka, J. (2004). Organisationsstrukturen, historische Entwicklung von. In G. Schreyögg & A. von Werder (Eds.), *Enzyklopädie der Betriebswirtschaftslehre: Vol. 2. Handwörterbuch Unternehmensführung und Organisation* (4th ed., pp. 1060–1068). Stuttgart: Schäffer-Poeschel.

Kocka, J., & Siegrist, H. (1979). Die hundert größten deutschen Industrieunternehmen im späten 19. und frühen 20. Jahrhundert. In N. Horn & J. Kocka (Eds.), *Kritische Studien zur Geschichtswissenschaft: Vol. 40. Recht und Entwicklung der Großunternehmen im 19. und frühen 20. Jahrhundert / Law and the Formation of the Big Enterprises in the 19th and Early 20th Centuries: Wirtschafts-, sozial- und rechtshistorische Untersuchungen zur Industrialisierung in Deutschland, Frankreich, England und den USA / Studies in the History of Industrialization in Germany, France, Great Britain and the United States* (pp. 55–122). Göttingen: Vandenhoeck & Ruprecht.

Köhler, I., & Rossfeld, R. (2012). Bausteine des Misserfolgs: Zur Strukturierung eines Forschungsfeldes. In I. Köhler & R. Rossfeld (Eds.), *Pleitiers und Bankrotteure: Geschichte des ökonomischen Scheiterns vom 18. bis 20. Jahrhundert* (pp. 9–34). Frankfurt (Main): Campus.

Köhn, R. (2013, July 9). Osram gibt ein schwaches Börsendebüt. *Frankfurter Allgemeine Zeitung*, p. 17.

Köhn, R. (2015, September 4). Kuka bekommt einen Joker aus dem Reich der Mitte. *Frankfurter Allgemeine Zeitung*, 21.

Köhn, R. (2016, June 2). Bundesregierung startet Gegenoffensive für Kuka: Wirtschaftsminister Gabriel bestätigt Bemühungen um ein Alternativangebot zu den Chinesen. Kanzlerin Merkel unterstützt ihn. *Frankfurter Allgemeine Zeitung*, 26.

Köhn, R. (2018, April 25). Kering mischt Aktionärsstruktur der Sportmarke Puma durch: Verkaufsdruck von Mitte Mai an möglich. *Frankfurter Allgemeine Zeitung*, p. 25.

Kormann, H. (2011). Vermeidung existenzbedrohender Fehler—Ein Weg zur Reduzierung der Insolvenzgefahr –. In M. Flitsch, A. Hagebusch, T. Oberle, C. Seagon, & W. Schreiber (Eds.), *Festschrift für Jobst Wellensiek zum 80. Geburtstag* (pp. 39–54). München: Beck.

Kormann, H. (2012). Grundfragen des Familienunternehmens. In S. Scherer, M. Blanc, H. Kormann, T. Groth, & R. Wimmer (Eds.), *Familienunternehmen: Erfolgsstrategien zur Unternehmenssicherung* (2nd ed.). Frankfurt (Main): Fachmedien.

Kormann, H. (2017). *Strategy as a challenge*. Working Paper.

Kormann, H., & Suberg, B. (Eds.) (2021). *Topics of Family Business Governance: Insights on Structures, Strategies, and Executives* (1st ed.). Cham: Springer International Publishing.

Kormann, H., & Wimmer, R. (2018). Vom Ursprung der Forschung zu Familienunternehmen: Über die Anfänge und den aktuellen Stand der wissenschaftlichen Auseinandersetzung. *Zeitschrift Für Familienunternehmen Und Stiftungen*. (5), 148–153.

Koselleck, R. (1979). Historia Magistra Vitae. Über die Auflösung des Topos im Horizont neuzeitlich bewegter Geschichte. In R. Koselleck (Ed.), *Theorie. Vergangene Zukunft: Zur Semantik geschichtl. Zeiten* (1st ed., pp. 38–66). Frankfurt am Main: Suhrkamp.

Köster, R. (2020). *Einführung in die Wirtschaftsgeschichte: Theorien, Methoden, Themen. UTB: Vol. 4630*. Paderborn: Ferdinand Schöningh.

Kotlar, J., & Massis, A. de (2013). Goal Setting in Family Firms: Goal Diversity, Social Interactions, and Collective Commitment to Family–Centered Goals. *Entrepreneurship Theory and Practice*, *37*(6), 1263–1288.

Kropff, B. (2007). Reformbestrebungen im Nachkriegsdeutschland und die Aktienrechtsreform von 1965. In W. Bayer & M. Habersack (Eds.), *Aktienrecht im Wandel: Entwicklung des Aktienrechts* (pp. 670–888). Tübingen: Mohr Siebeck.

Kruk, M. (1959a). Die drei Universalfirmen der deutschen Elektroindustrie. In Frankfurter Allgemeine Zeitung (Ed.), *Blick durch die Wirtschaft: Zeitung für Finanzen, Steuern, Recht und Management* (112 (16.05.1959), p. 5). Frankfurt (Main): Frankfurter Allgemeine Zeitung.

Kruk, M. (1959b, November 7). Die Hundert Grössten Unternehmen. *Frankfurter Allgemeine Zeitung*, p. 5.

Kruk, M. (1960, February 5). Siemens erwartet eine Umsatzsteigerung um zehn Prozent: Die Bilanz noch flüssiger als im Vorjahr / Gutes Bezugsrecht an Stelle von Zusatzaktien. *Frankfurter Allgemeine Zeitung*, p. 19.

Kubisch, U. (1986). *Zündapp: Aufstieg und Niedergang. Berliner Beiträge zur Technikgeschichte und Industriekultur: Vol. 6*. Berlin: Nicolai.

Kuchenbaur, D. (2020). *Current status and short-term development of companies operating in the paper producing industry of Germany: The internal factors influencing their downfall risk* (Bachelor thesis). Zeppelin University, Friedrichshafen.

KUKA AG (2019). *Geschäftsbericht 2018*. Augsburg.

KUKA AG (2021). Die KUKA Geschichte. Retrieved from https://www.kuka.com/de-de/%C3%BCber-kuka/geschichte

Kurzlechner, W. (2009). *Fusionen, Kartelle, Skandale: Das Bundeskartellamt als Wettbewerbshüter und Verbraucheranwalt* (1st ed.). München: Redline Verlag.

La Porta, R., Lopez-De-Silanes, F., & Shleifer, A. (1999). Corporate Ownership Around the World. *The Journal of Finance, 54*(2), 471–517.

Lamoreaux, N. R., Raff, D. M. G., & Temin, P. (2008). Economic Theory and Business History. In G. Jones & J. Zeitlin (Eds.), *The Oxford Handbook of Business History* (37–66). Oxford: Oxford University Press.

Lantelme, M. (2017). *The Rise and Downfall of Germany's Largest Family and Non-Family Businesses: A Historical Study and Strategic Analysis from 1971 to 2011*. Wiesbaden: Springer Gabler.

Lantelme, M., Seibold, L. K. C., & Kormann, H. (2021). *German Family Enterprises: A Sourcebook of Structure, Growth, Downfall and Corporate Longevity* (2nd ed.). Cham: Springer International Publishing.

Le Breton-Miller, I., & Miller, D. (2015). Learning Stewardship in Family Firms: For Family, by Family, Across the Life Cycle. *Academy of Management Learning & Education, 14*(3), 386–399.

Le Breton–Miller, I., & Miller, D. (2013). Socioemotional Wealth across the Family Firm Life Cycle: A Commentary on "Family Business Survival and the Role of Boards". *Entrepreneurship Theory and Practice, 37*(6), 1391–1397.

Lepenies, P. (2016). *The Power of a Single Number: A Political History of GDP*. New York: Columbia University Press.

Lieder, J. (2007). Die 1. Aktienrechtsnovelle vom 11. Juni 1870. In W. Bayer & M. Habersack (Eds.), *Aktienrecht im Wandel: Entwicklung des Aktienrechts* (pp. 318–387). Tübingen: Mohr Siebeck.

Linsmayer, L., & Reicherlt, B. (2012). Das autonome Saarland. In H.-C. Herrmann & J. Schmitt (Eds.), *Das Saarland: Geschichte einer Region* (pp. 313–338). St. Ingbert: Röhrig Universitätsverlag.

Littelfuse, Inc. (2019). *2018 Annual Report*. Chicago. Retrieved from https://investor.littelfuse.com/static-files/15757f99-31c0-4886-93ef-c9579c9ad863

Lorandini, C. (2015). Looking beyond the Buddenbrooks syndrome: the Salvadori Firm of Trento, 1660s–1880s. *Business History, 57*(7), 1005–1019.

Lubinski, C. (2010). *Familienunternehmen in Westdeutschland: Corporate Governance und Gesellschafterkultur seit den 1960er Jahren. Schriftenreihe zur Zeitschrift für Unternehmensgeschichte: Band 21*. Munich: C.H. Beck.

Lubinski, C. (2016). Familienlegenden: Zeitlose Geschichten zwischen Vergangenheit und Zukunft. In M. Spitz, N. Roth, K. Bosecker, & A. Kambartel (Eds.), *Phänomen Familienunternehmen: Vol. 2. Phänomen Familienunternehmen: Überblicke* (pp. 43–50). Mettingen: Draiflessen Collection.

Lumpkin, G. T., & Brigham, K. H. (2011). Long–Term Orientation and Intertemporal Choice in Family Firms. *Entrepreneurship Theory and Practice, 35*(6), 1149–1169.

Lupa, M. (2008). *Volkswagen Chronik: Der Weg zum Global Player. Historische Notate: Vol. 7*. Wolfsburg: Volkswagen AG.

Lutz, M. (2013). *Carl von Siemens 1829–1906: Ein Leben zwischen Familie und Weltfirma*. Munich: C.H. Beck.

MacAdams, A. J. (1993). *Germany Divided: From the Wall to Reunification*. Princeton: Princeton University Press.

Malycha, A. (2022). *Vom Hoffnungsträger zum Prügelknaben: Die Treuhandanstalt zwischen wirtschaftlichen Erwartungen und politischen Zwängen 1989–1994* (1st ed.). Berlin: Ch. Links Verlag.

Manager magazin new media GmbH & Co. KG (2005). Merckle bietet für HeidelbergCement: Übernahme. Retrieved from https://www.manager-magazin.de/unternehmen/artikel/a-360168.html

Mann, T. (1901a). *Buddenbrooks: Verfall einer Familie* (Vol. 1). Berlin: Fischer.

Mann, T. (1901b). *Buddenbrooks: Verfall einer Familie* (Vol. 2). Berlin: Fischer.

Massis, A. de, Kotlar, J., Campopiano, G., & Cassia, L. (2013). Dispersion of family ownership and the performance of small-to-medium size private family firms. *Journal of Family Business Strategy, 4*(3), 166–175.

May, P. (2012). *Erfolgsmodell Familienunternehmen: Das Strategie-Buch*. Hamburg: Murmann.

McCraw, T. K. (2008). Alfred Chandler: His Vision and Achievement. *The Business History Review, 82*(2), 207–226.

Miller, D., & Le Breton-Miller, I. (2005). *Managing for the long run: Lessons in competitive advantage from great family businesses*. Boston: Harvard Business School Press.

Mohnen, A. (2020). *Personalmanagement in Familienunternehmen: Recruiting, Arbeitsbedingungen, Weiterbildung*. Munich: Stiftung Familienunternehmen.

Monopolkommission (2020). *Hauptgutachten: Kapitel II: Stand und Entwicklung der Unternehmenskonzentration in Deutschland*. Bonn. Retrieved from https://www.monopolkommission.de/images/HG23/HGXXIII_Kap2_Unternehmenskonzentration.pdf

Morton, J. (1971). *Three Generations in a Family Textile Firm*. London: Routledge & Keagan Paul.

Mühlfriedel, W., Walter, R., & Hellmuth, E. (Eds.) (1996). *Carl Zeiss: Die Geschichte eines Unternehmens, Zeiss 1846–1905* (Vol. 1). Weimar: Böhlau.

Müller, S. (2018). *Aktiengesellschaften des 19. Jahrhunderts. Augsburger Schriften zur Rechtsgeschichte: Vol. 30*. Berlin: LIT.

Müller-Haeseler, W. (1973, January 24). Mehr Maschinenbau bei Mannesmann: Bekanntgabe der Beteiligung an der Demag erwartet. *Frankfurter Allgemeine Zeitung*, p. 18.

Mußler, H. (2015, October 7). Bayer beschert Covestros Aktionären satte Kursgewinne: Börsengang glückt nach Preiszugeständnissen. *Frankfurter Allgemeine Zeitung*, p. 23.

Neubürger, H.-J. (2000). Wertorientierte Unternehmensführung bei Siemens. *Schmalenbachs Zeitschrift Für Betriebswirtschaftliche Forschung, 52*(2), 188–196.

Neumann, I. (1959, July 3). Mannesmann bleibt krisenfest. *DIE ZEIT*.

Nowak, E., Ehrhardt, O., & Weber, F. M. (2006). "Running in the Family": The Evolution of Ownership, Control, and Performance in German Family-Owned Firms, 1903–2003. *Swiss Finance Institute Research Paper No. 06–13*.

O'Boyle, E. H., Pollack, J. M., & Rutherford, M. W. (2012). Exploring the relation between family involvement and firms' financial performance: A meta-analysis of main and moderator effects. *Journal of Business Venturing*, *27*(1), 1–18.

Odrich, P. (1976, February 18). Fusion WTAG-Rhenus perfekt. *Frankfurter Allgemeine Zeitung*, 15.

OECD (2019). *Age of mothers at childbirth and age-specific fertility* (OECD Family Database No. SF2.3). Paris. Retrieved from https://www.oecd.org/els/soc/SF_2_3_Age_mothers_childbirth.pdf

Oetker, A. (1969). *Wachstumssicherung von Familienunternehmen*. Munich: Verlag Moderne Industrie.

Opgenoorth, E., & Schulz, G. (2010). *Einführung in das Studium der Neueren Geschichte: Von den Grundlagen unserer Kultur in der griechischen Antike* (7th ed.). *UTB: Vol. 1553*. Paderborn: Schöningh.

Osram Licht AG (2019). *Geschäftsbericht des OSRAM Licht-Konzerns: Geschäftsjahr 2018*. Munich.

Oster, S. M. (1999). *Modern Competitive Analysis* (3rd ed.). New York: Oxford University Press.

Ostersehlte, C. (2004). *Von Howaldt zu HDW: 165 Jahre Entwicklung von einer Kieler Eisengiesserei zum weltweit operierenden Schiffbau- und Technologiekonzern*. Hamburg: Koehler.

Pahlow, L. (2007). Aktienrecht und Aktiengesellschaft zwischen Revolution und Reichsgründung. Das Allgemeine Deutsche Handelsgesetzbuch von 1861. In W. Bayer & M. Habersack (Eds.), *Aktienrecht im Wandel: Entwicklung des Aktienrechts* (pp. 237–286). Tübingen: Mohr Siebeck.

Paul, H. (2014, December 4). Voith wird neuer Großaktionär von Kuka: Anlagenhersteller erwirbt 25 Prozent und will vom Industrie-4.0-Wissen profitieren. *Frankfurter Allgemeine Zeitung*, 23.

Paulus, C. G. (2015). § 1 InsO und sein Insolvenzmodell. *Neue Zeitschrift Für Insolvenz- Und Sanierungsrecht*, *18*(24), 1001–1006.

Pearson, A. W., Carr, J. C., & Shaw, J. C. (2008). Toward a Theory of Familiness: A Social Capital Perspective. *Entrepreneurship Theory and Practice*, *32*(6), 949–969.

Pieper, T. M. (2007). *Mechanisms to Assure Long-Term Family Business Survival: A Study of the Dynamics of Cohesion in Multigenerational Family Business Families. European University Studies. Series V, Economics and Management: Vol. 3285*. Frankfurt (Main): Peter Lang.

Pieper, T. M. (2010). *Zusammenhalt in Unternehmerfamilien: Eine Voraussetzung zur Sicherung des Überlebens von Familienunternehmen* (2nd ed.). *EQUA-Schriftenreihe: Vol. 4*. Bonn: Unternehmer Medien.

Pieper, T. M. (2021). The Importance of Family Cohesion for Long-term Family Business Survival. In T. A. Rüsen (Ed.), *Theorie und Praxis der Unternehmerfamilie und des Familienunternehmens—Theory and Practice of Business Families and Family Businesses:*

Festschrift für Arist von Schlippe—Commemorative Publication for Arist von Schlippe (157–163). Göttingen: Vandenhoeck & Ruprecht.

Pieper, T. M., Kellermanns, F. W., & Astrachan, J. H. (2021). *Update 2021: Family Businesses' Contribution to the US Economy*. Retrieved from Family Enterprise USA website: https://familyenterpriseusa.com/wp-content/uploads/2021/02/Family-Businesses-Contribution-to-the-US-Economy_v.02202021-FINAL.pdf

Pieper, T. M., & Klein, S. B. (2007). The Bulleye: A Systems Approach to Modeling Family Firms. *Family Business Review*, *20*(4), 301–319.

Pierce, J. L., Kostova, T., & Dirks, K. T. (2001). Toward a Theory of Psychological Ownership in Organizations. *Academy of Management Review*, *26*(2), 298.

Pierenkemper, T. (1996). Josef Neckermann (1912–1992)—Anmerkungen zur Autobiographie. *Economic History Yearbook*, *37*(2).

Plumpe, W. (2014). *Eine Vision, zwei Unternehmen: 125 Jahre Carl-Zeiss-Stiftung*. Munich: Verlag C.H. Beck.

Plumpe, W. (2018). *Unternehmensgeschichte im 19. und 20. Jahrhundert. Enzyklopädie deutscher Geschichte: Vol. 94*. Berlin, Boston: De Gruyter Oldenbourg.

Plumpe, W., & Steiner, A. (2016). Der Mythos von der postindustriellen Welt. In W. Plumpe & A. Steiner (Eds.), *Der Mythos von der postindustriellen Welt: Wirtschaftlicher Strukturwandel in Deutschland 1960–1990* (pp. 7–14). Göttingen: Wallstein Verlag.

Pohl, H. (1991). Die Überlebenschancen von Unternehmensgründungen in der Zeit von 1870 bis 1918. In H. Pohl (Ed.), *Zeitschrift für Unternehmensgeschichte. Beiheft: Vol. 63. Überlebenschanchen von Unternehmensgründungen: Referate und Diskussionsbeiträge der wissenschaftlichen Vortragsveranstaltung der Gesellschaft für Unternehmensgeschichte e.V. und des Instituts für Bankhistorische Forschung am 3. November 1989 in Frankfurt am Main* (pp. 29–47). Stuttgart: Steiner.

Pöllmann, H. (2005). *Dierig, Weber seit 1805*. Heidelberg: Edition Braus im Wachter-Verlag.

Porter, M. E. (1989). From Competitive Advantage to Corporate Strategy. In D. C. Asch & C. Bowman (Eds.), *Readings in Strategic Management* (pp. 234–255). London: Palgrave Macmillan.

Psotta, M. (1991, February 18). Aritmos hält jetzt alle Stammaktien von Puma. *Frankfurter Allgemeine Zeitung*, p. 18.

PUMA SE (2019). *Geschäftsbericht 2018*. Herzogenaurach.

Rantanen, N., & Jussila, I. (2011). F-CPO: A collective psychological ownership approach to capturing realized family influence on business. *Journal of Family Business Strategy*, *2*(3), 139–150.

Rau, S. B. (2010). *Familienunternehmen: Theoretische und empirische Grundlagen* (3rd ed.). *Family Business: Vol. 1*. Lohmar: Josef Eul Verlag.

Rauch, S., & Kletzke, H. (1996). *Zündapp: 60 Jahre Zündapp-Technik*. Lemgo: Johann Kleine Vennekate.

Rhenus SE & Co. KG (2018). *Ein Fluss als Pate: Die Rhenus-Story*. Holzwickede. Retrieved from https://www.rhenus.group/fileadmin/7_Newsroom/Brochures/DE-20-02-02-0418.pdf

Rhenus SE & Co. KG (2021). Über die Rhenus Gruppe: Chronik. Retrieved from https://www.rhenus.group/de/rhenus-group/ueber-uns

Richter, A. (Ed.) (2019). *Stiftungsrecht: Handbuch*. Munich: C.H. Beck.

Ritzer, U. (2010, May 17). Hässliche braune Flecken: Historiker streiten über die Rolle der Brüder Schaeffler im Dritten Reich—offenbar war die Firma stärker verstrickt als bisher bekannt. *Süddeutsche Zeitung*. Retrieved from https://sz.de/1.483170

Robert Bosch Stiftung (2020). Familie regelt Beteiligung an der Robert Bosch GmbH neu. Retrieved from https://www.bosch-stiftung.de/de/presse/2020/12/familie-regelt-beteiligung-der-robert-bosch-gmbh-neu

Roth, K. H. (1996). Zwangsarbeit im Siemens-Konzern (1938–1945): Fakten—Kontroversen—Probleme. In H. Kaienburg (Ed.), *Konzentrationslager und deutsche Wirtschaft 1939–1945* (pp. 149–168). Wiesbaden: VS Verlag für Sozialwissenschaften.

Rovelli, P., Ferasso, M., Massis, A. de, & Kraus, S. (2021). Thirty years of research in family business journals: Status quo and future directions. *Journal of Family Business Strategy*, 100422.

S&P Dow Jones Indices LLC (2021). S&P 500: Overview. Retrieved from https://www.spglobal.com/spdji/en/indices/equity/sp-500/#overview

Saarbergwerke AG (1982). *25 Jahre Saarbergwerke-Aktiengesellschaft: 1957–1982*. Saarbrücken.

Sachse, W. (1991). Familienunternehmen in Wirtschaft und Gesellschaft bis zur Mitte des 20. Jahrhunderts. Ein historischer Überblick. *Zeitschrift Für Unternehmensgeschichte / Journal of Business History*, *36*(1), 9–25.

Sack, D. (2019). *Vom Staat zum Markt: Privatisierung aus politikwissenschaftlicher Perspektive*. Wiesbaden: Springer Fachmedien.

SAGE Publishing (2022). Family Business Review. Retrieved from https://journals.sagepub.com/home/fbr

Sasaki, I., Kotlar, J., Ravasi, D., & Vaara, E. (2020). Dealing with revered past: Historical identity statements and strategic change in Japanese family firms. *Strategic Management Journal*, *41*(3), 590–623.

Schaeffler AG (2015). *Prospectus for the admission of trading*. Herzogenaurach.

Schaeffler AG (2016). *Geschäftsbericht 2015*. Herzogenaurach.

Schaeffler AG (2019). *Geschäftsbericht 2018*. Herzogenaurach.

Schlippe, A. von (2010). Vorwort zur deutschen Ausgabe. In A. Gimeno, G. Baulenas, & J. Coma-Cros (Eds.), *Familienunternehmen führen Komplexität managen: Mentale Modelle und praktische Lösungen* (pp. 9–18). Göttingen: Vandenhoeck & Ruprecht.

Schlippe, A. von, & Frank, H. (2013). The Theory of Social Systems as a Framework for Understanding Family Businesses. *Family Relations*, *62*(3), 384–398.

Schmoller, G. von (1890a). Die geschichtliche Entwicklung der Unternehmung. In G. von Schmoller (Ed.), *Jahrbuch für Gesetzgebung, Verwaltung und Volkswirtschaft im Deutschen Reich* (pp. 735–783). Leipzig: Duncker & Humblot.

Schmoller, G. von (1890b). Die geschichtlie Entwicklung der Unternehmung. In G. von Schmoller (Ed.), *Jahrbuch für Gesetzgebung, Verwaltung und Volkswirtschaft im Deutschen Reich* (pp. 1036–1076). Leipzig: Duncker & Humblot.

Scholtyseck, J. (2011). *Der Aufstieg der Quandts: Eine deutsche Unternehmerdynastie*. Munich: C.H. Beck.

Schubert, W. (1981). Die Abschaffung des Konzessionssystems durch die Aktienrechtsnovelle von 1870. *Zeitschrift Für Unternehmens- Und Gesellschaftsrecht*, *10*(2), 285–317.

Schubert, W., & Hommelhoff, P. (1985). *Hundert Jahre modernes Aktienrecht: Eine Sammlung von Texten und Quellen zur Aktienrechtsreform 1884 mit zwei Einführungen*.

Zeitschrift für Unternehmens- und Gesellschaftsrecht. Sonderheft: Vol. 4. Berlin: De Gruyter.

Seibold, L. K. C. (2017). *Wachstum von Familienunternehmen*. Wiesbaden: Gabler.

Seibold, L. K. C. (2020). *Family Businesses' Growth: Unpacking the Black Box. Familienunternehmen und KMU*. Wiesbaden: Springer Gabler.

Selgert, F. (2018). Börsenzulassungsstellen, Reichsregierung und die (Selbst-)Regulierung der Mehrstimmrechtsaktie, 1919–1937. *Jahrbuch Für Wirtschaftsgeschichte / Economic History Yearbook, 59*(1), 77–103.

Sharma, A., & Kesner, I. F. (1996). Diversifying Entry: Some Ex Ante Explanations for Postentry Survival and Growth. *Academy of Management Journal, 39*(3), 635–677.

Siegrist, H. (1980). Deutsche Großunternehmen vom späten 19. Jahrhundert bis zur Weimarer Republik: Integration, Diversifikation und Organisation bei den hundert größten deutschen Industrieunternehmen (1887–1927) in international vergleichender Perspektive. *Geschichte Und Gesellschaft, 6*(1), 60–102.

Siemens AG (2021a). Aktionärsstruktur und Stimmrechtsmitteilungen. Retrieved from https://new.siemens.com/de/de/unternehmen/investor-relations/aktie-anleihen-rating/aktionaersstruktur-stimmrechtsmitteilungen.html

Siemens AG (2021b). Siemens Historical Institute: Gegenwart meistern und Zukunft gestalten—auf Basis der eigenen Geschichte. Retrieved from https://new.siemens.com/de/de/unternehmen/konzern/geschichte/siemens-historical-institute.html

Simon, H. (2009). *Hidden Champions of the Twenty-First Century: Success Strategies of Unknown World Market Leaders*. New York: Springer.

Sirmon, D. G., & Hitt, M. A. (2003). Managing Resources: Linking Unique Resources, Management, and Wealth Creation in Family Firms. *Entrepreneurship Theory and Practice, 27*(4), 339–358.

Solow, R. M. (1985). Economic History and Economics. *The American Economic Review, 75*(2), 328–331.

Sombart, W. (1929a). *Organisation und Geschichte des Gewerbes. Gewerbewesen: Vol. 1*. Berlin: De Gruyter.

Sombart, W. (1929b). *Das Gewerbe im Zeitalter des Hochkapitalismus. Gewerbewesen: Vol. 2*. Berlin: De Gruyter.

Sonfield, M. C., & Lussier, R. N. (2008). The Influence of Family Business Size on Management Activities, Styles and Characteristics. *New England Journal of Entrepreneurship, 11*(2), 47–56.

Der Spiegel (1984, August 19). Zu spät geschaltet: Den Münchner Zündapp-Werken, Deutschlands letztem Motorrad-Hersteller in Familienbesitz, droht die Schließung. *Der Spiegel*.

Der Spiegel (1995, January 29). Konzern Deutschland. *Der Spiegel*.

Der Spiegel (2009, January 6). Milliardär Merckle begeht Selbstmord. *Der Spiegel*. Retrieved from https://www.spiegel.de/wirtschaft/finanzkrise-milliardaer-merckle-begeht-selbstmord-a-599774.html

Spitz, M., Roth, N., Bosecker, K., & Kambartel, A. (Eds.) (2016). *Phänomen Familienunternehmen: Vol. 1. Phänomen Familienunternehmen: Einblicke*. Mettingen: Draiflessen Collection.

Stadler, C. (2011). *Enduring Success: What We Can Learn from the History of Outstanding Corporations*. Stanford: Stanford Business Books.

Stamm, I. (2016). Unternehmertum als Familienprojekt heute. In M. Spitz, N. Roth, K. Bosecker, & A. Kambartel (Eds.), *Phänomen Familienunternehmen: Vol. 2. Phänomen Familienunternehmen: Überblicke* (pp. 129–136). Mettingen: Draiflessen Collection.

Stamm, I., Discua Cruz, A., & Cailluet, L. (2019). Entrepreneurial Groups: Definition, Forms, and Historic Change. *Historical Social Research / Historische Sozialforschung, 44*(4), 7–41.

Stamm, I., & Lubinski, C. (2011). Crossroads of family business research and firm demography: A critical assessment of family business survival rates. *Journal of Family Business Strategy, 2*(3), 117–127.

Statista GmbH (2021). Beteiligungen des Vermögensverwalters BlackRock am Aktienkapital von im DAX gelisteten Unternehmen. Retrieved from https://de.statista.com/statistik/daten/studie/518085/umfrage/groesste-blackrock-beteiligungen-am-aktienkapital-von-dax-unternehmen/

Steiger, T., Duller, C., & Hiebl, M. R. W. (2015). No Consensus in Sight: An Analysis of Ten Years of Family Business Definitions in Empirical Research Studies. *Journal of Enterprising Culture, 23*(01), 25–62.

Steiner, A. (2016). Abschied von der Industrie? Wirtschaftlicher Strukturwandel in West- und Ostdeutschland seit den 1960er Jahren. In W. Plumpe & A. Steiner (Eds.), *Der Mythos von der postindustriellen Welt: Wirtschaftlicher Strukturwandel in Deutschland 1960–1990* (pp. 15–54). Göttingen: Wallstein Verlag.

Stiftung Familienunternehmen (2021a). Die ältesten Familienunternehmen Deutschlands. Retrieved from https://www.familienunternehmen.de/media/public/pdf/pressebereich/meldungen/2021a/deutschlands-50-aelteste-familienunternehmen_2021-12-13/die-aeltesten-familienunternehmen-deutschlands.pdf

Stiftung Familienunternehmen (2021b). Deutschlands 50 älteste Familienunternehmen: Über Jahrhunderte Krisen überwunden. Retrieved from https://www.familienunternehmen.de/de/pressebereich/meldungen/2021/2021-12-13/deutschlands-50-aelteste-familienunternehmen

Stiglitz, J. E., Sen, A., & Fitoussi, J.-P. (2010). *Mismeasuring Our Lives: Why GDP Doesn't Add Up*. New York: New Press.

Stinchcombe, A. L. (1965). Social Structures and Organizations. In J. March (Ed.), *Handbook of Organizations* (1st ed., pp. 142–193). Chicago: Rand McNally.

Stotmeister, K. (in press). *Going Public—Making or Breaking Family Businesses? A Long-Term Study on Family Involvement and Company Longevity* (Doctoral Thesis). Zeppelin University, Friedrichshafen.

Suddaby, R., Silverman, B. S., Massis, A. de, Jaskiewicz, P., & Micelotta (2020). Call for Papers for the 2023 Family Business Review (FBR) Special Issue on History-informed Family Business Research. *Family Business Review, 33*(3), 331–334.

Tagiuri, R., & Davis, J. (1996). Bivalent Attributes of the Family Firm. *Family Business Review, 9*(2), 199–208.

Taz (1993, February 9). HV der Kritiker. *Taz*, p. 6.

Teltz, H.-P. (1980). Knoll, Albert. In Historische Kommission bei der Bayerischen Akademie der Wissenschaften (Ed.), *Neue Deutsche Biographie* (pp. 207–208). Berlin: Duncker & Humblot.

Theisen, M. R., & Wenz, M. (2005). Hintergründe, historische Entwicklung und Grundkonzeption. In M. R. Theisen & M. Wenz (Eds.), *Der Betrieb. Die europäische Aktiengesellschaft: Recht, Steuern und Betriebswirtschaft der Societas Europaea (SE)* (2nd ed., pp. 13–56). Stuttgart: Schäffer-Poeschel.

Thomsen, S., Poulsen, T., Børsting, C., & Kuhn, J. (2018). Industrial foundations as long-term owners. *Corporate Governance: An International Review, 26*(3), 180–196.

Thyssenkrupp AG (2018). *Geschäftsbericht 2018.* Essen.

Tosh, J. (2015). *The Pursuit of History: Aims, methods and new directions in the study of history* (6th ed.). London: Routledge.

Treue, W. (1966). *Die Feuer verlöschen nie: August Thyssen-Hütte 1890–1926* (Vol. 1). Düsseldorf, Wien: Econ Verlag.

Treue, W. (1969). *Die Feuer verlöschen nie: August Thyssen-Hütte 1926–1966* (Vol. 2). Düsseldorf, Wien: Econ Verlag.

Uhl, B. (1979). Die Hofmarks- und Braurechte des Klosters Weihenstephan: Einige Anmerkungen zur Überlieferung und Fälschung von Urkunden Bischof Ottos I. von Freising. *29. Sammelblatt Des Historischen Vereins Freising*, 9–47.

Urban, T. (2018). Die Krisenfestigkeit der Unternehmerfamilie—Haniel, Stumm und der «doppelte» Strukturwandel. *Zeitschrift Für Unternehmensgeschichte / Journal of Business History, 63*(2), 185–219.

Verkaufsvereinigung für Teererzeugnisse (VfT) AG (1955). *Fünfzig Jahre VfT*. Essen.

Verlag Hoppenstedt & Co. (1958). *Saling Aktienführer: Die Aktienwerte der deutschen Börsen 1959.* Darmstadt.

Verlag Hoppenstedt & Co. (1959a). *Handbuch der Groß-Unternehmen: 1960 Band I A-K* (7th ed., Vol. 1). Darmstadt: Verlag Hoppenstedt & Co.

Verlag Hoppenstedt & Co. (1959b). *Handbuch der Groß-Unternehmen: 1960 Band II L-Z* (7th ed., Vol. 2). Darmstadt: Verlag Hoppenstedt & Co.

Verlag Hoppenstedt & Co. (1959c). *Saling Aktienführer: Die Aktienwerte der deutschen Börsen 1960* (53rd ed.). Darmstadt: Verlag Hoppenstedt & Co.

Villalonga, B., & Amit, R. (2006). How do family ownership, control and management affect firm value? *Journal of Financial Economics, 80*(2), 385–417.

Wagner, D., Block, J. H., Miller, D., Schwens, C., & Xi, G. (2015). A meta-analysis of the financial performance of family firms: Another attempt. *Journal of Family Business Strategy, 6*(1), 3–13.

Walmart Inc. (2019). *2018 Annual Report: Accelerating Innovation.* Bentonville.

Ward, J. L. (2011). *Keeping the Family Business Healthy: How to Plan for Continuing Growth, Profitability, and Family Leadership. A Family Business Publication.* New York: Palgrave Macmillan.

Weber, F.-M. (2005). *Der Einfluss der Postgründer-Generation auf die Performance: Eine empirische Analyse deutscher und österreichischer Familienunternehmen. FGF Entrepreneurship-Research-Monographien: Vol. 50.* Lohmar: Eul.

Weber, M., & Winckelmann, J. (2002). *Wirtschaft und Gesellschaft: Grundriss der verstehenden Soziologie.* Tübingen: Mohr Siebeck.

Wehler, H.-U. (2006). *Von der "Deutschen Doppelrevolution" bis zum Beginn des Ersten Weltkrieges: 1849–1914. Deutsche Gesellschaftsgeschichte: Vol. 3.* Munich: C.H. Beck.

Weidenfeld, W. (2020). Europäische Einigung im historischen Überblick. In W. Weidenfeld, W. Wessels, & F. Tekin (Eds.), *Europa von A bis Z* (15th ed., pp. 11–35). Wiesbaden: Springer VS.

Wennberg, K., Wiklund, J., Hellerstedt, K., & Nordqvist, M. (2011). Implications of intra-family and external ownership transfer of family firms: short-term and long-term performance differences. *Strategic Entrepreneurship Journal*, *5*(4), 352–372.

Werner, O., Saenger, I., Fischer, C., & Andrick, B. (Eds.) (2019). *Die Stiftung: Recht, Steuern, Wirtschaft* (2nd ed.). Baden-Baden: Nomos.

Wessel, H. A. (2008). *Stahl und Technologie: Die Geschichte der Salzgitter AG. 1858–2008*. Salzgitter: Salzgitter AG.

Williams, R. I., Pieper, T. M., Kellermanns, F. W., & Astrachan, J. H. (2018). Family Firm Goals and their Effects on Strategy, Family and Organization Behavior: A Review and Research Agenda. *International Journal of Management Reviews*, *20*, S63–S82.

Wilson, N., Wright, M., & Scholes, L. (2013). Family Business Survival and the Role of Boards. *Entrepreneurship Theory and Practice*, *37*(6), 1369–1389.

Wirth, S. von (2019). Das sind Deutschlands größte Automobilzulieferer: Bosch und Continental sind große Automobilzulieferer. Auch kleine, meist Familienunternehmen, sind erfolgreich. Wir stellen die 15 umsatzstärksten Firmen vor. Retrieved from https://www.handelsblatt.com/unternehmen/handel-konsumgueter/bosch-continental-zf-friedrichshafen-das-sind-deutschlands-groesste-automobilzulieferer/25228788.html?ticket=ST-836008-SBGy63XHYJEFjdyPy9v3-ap4

The World Bank (2021). Listed domestic companies, total. Retrieved from https://data.worldbank.org/indicator/CM.MKT.LDOM.NO?end=2020&start=1975&view=map&year=2018

Woywode, M. (2018). Theoretische Ansätze zur Erklärung der Überlebenswahrscheinlichkeit von Unternehmen. In T. C. Knecht, U. Hommel, & H. Wohlenberg (Eds.), *Handbuch Unternehmensrestrukturierung: Grundlagen—Konzepte—Maßnahmen* (2nd ed., pp. 45–88). Wiesbaden: Springer Fachmedien.

WSW Wuppertaler Stadtwerke GmbH (2021). Historie: Erste Anfänge. Retrieved from https://www.wsw-online.de/unternehmen/ueber-uns/historie/

Xi, J., Kraus, S., Filser, M., & Kellermanns, F. W. (2015). Mapping the Field of Family Business Research: Past Trends and Future Directions. *International Entrepreneurship and Management Journal*, *11*(1), 113–132.

Zeisberger, C., Prahl, M., & White, B. (2017). *Mastering Private Equity: Growth via Venture Capital, Minority Investments & Buyouts* (1st ed.). Hoboken, New Jersey: John Wiley & Sons.

Die Zeit (1960, November 4). Der Leser fragt…: Wer sind die Eigentümer von BV Aral? *DIE ZEIT*.

Zellweger, T. M., Eddleston, K. A., & Kellermanns, F. W. (2010). Exploring the Concept of Familiness: Introducing Family Firm Identity. *Journal of Family Business Strategy*, *1*(1), 54–63.

Zellweger, T. M., Nason, R. S., & Nordqvist, M. (2012). From Longevity of Firms to Transgenerational Entrepreneurship of Families: Introducing Family Entrepreneurial Orientation. *Family Business Review*, *25*(2), 136–155.

Zugehör, R. (2003). *Die Zukunft des rheinischen Kapitalismus. Forschung Soziologie*. Opladen: Leske + Budrich.

Zündapp Vertriebsgesellschaft mbH (2021). Die Zündapp-Story: Vom Zünder zum Zweirad—der Anfang der Geschichte. Retrieved from https://www.zuendapp.com/zp/geschichte/

The manufacturer's authorised representative in the EU is Springer Nature Customer Service Centre GmbH, Europaplatz 3, 69115 Heidelberg, Germany. If you have any concerns regarding our products, please contact ProductSafety@springernature.com

Printed and bound by CPI Group (UK) Ltd, Croydon, CR0 4YY
01/10/2026
02225834-0003